R. Gupta's®

SSC
Staff Selection Commission

Junior Engineer Exam
Civil & Structural

PAPER-II (Conventional)

Previous Years' Papers
(Solved)

2019
EDITION

Ramesh Publishing House, New Delhi

Published by
O.P. Gupta *for* Ramesh Publishing House

Admin. Office
12-H, New Daryaganj Road, Opp. Officers' Mess,
New Delhi-110002 ① 23261567, 23275224, 23275124

E-mail: info@rameshpublishinghouse.com
Website: www.rameshpublishinghouse.com

Showroom
● Balaji Market, Nai Sarak, Delhi-6 ① 23253720, 23282525
● 4457, Nai Sarak, Delhi-6, ① 23918938

Book Code: R-1828

ISBN: 978-93-5012-821-3

HSN Code: 49011010

CONTENTS

YOUR SPACE

SSC-Junior Engineer (Civil & Structural) Exam, 2017*

PAPER-II (Conventional)

1. (*a*) Determine the dissolved oxygen at the end of 2 days for the following data: 15

Characteristics	Stream water	Waste water
Flow (m³/sec)	22	3
DO (mg/litre)	10	0
BOD (mg/litre)	3	190

Assume: Deoxygenation constant

$$K = 0.11 \text{ per day}$$

Reoxygenation constant

$$R = 0.33 \text{ per day}$$

(*b*) A clay stratum has 2.5 m thickness and has initial overburden pressure of 45 kN/m². The clay is over consolidated with a preconsolidation pressure of 65 kN/m². Find the final settlement due to increment of pressure of 55 kN/m² at the middle of clay layer. Use the following data: 15

Initial void ratio = 1.2

Compression index = 0.27

Swelling index = 0.06

(*c*) Discuss the factors affecting duty of water.   15

(*d*) Calculate the safe overtaking sight distance for a design speed of 100 km/hr. Assume maximum overtaking acceleration as 1.92 km/hr/sec.   15

2. (*a*) What are the requirements of a good ballast in railway engineering? Explain how the minimum depth of ballast cushion is estimated.   15

(*b*) Determine the correct bearings of the lines of a closed traverse PQRSTP. The readings are as follows :

Line	Fore bearing	Back bearing
PQ	195°30′	17°0′
QR	73°30′	250°30′
RS	36°15′	214°30′
ST	266°45′	84°45′
TP	234°15′	57°0′

Identify the stations affected by local attraction.   20

(*c*) What are the factors affecting selection of contour interval?   10

(*d*) A trapezoidal dam with a vertical water face is 2.5 m wide at the top and 14 m wide at the base. The height of the dam is 27 m. Find the maximum depth of water so that the dam section is free from tension. Assume unit weight of dam material as 21 kN/m³ and that of water as 9.81 kN/m³.   15

3. (*a*) Describe plate load test as per IS 1888. Discuss the limitations. What are the effects of size of plate on bearing capacity and settlement?   20

(*b*) A classroom is of the size 8.5 m × 3.6 m. Design a simply supported roof slab for this room. The superimposed load is 5 kN/m². Use M 20 grade concrete and HYSD Fe 415 steel. Use limit state method for the design.   25

$100\ A_s/bd$	0.15	0.25	0.50	0.75	1.0
τ_c N/mm²	0.19	0.36	0.49	0.57	0.64

(*c*) Explain the steps for the design of column with helical reinforcement in limit state method.   15

4. (*a*) What are the characteristics of a good quality timber? **10**

(*b*) Derive the condition for the trapezoidal channel of best section. Prove that the hydraulic mean depth for such a channel is one-half the depth of flow. **15**

(*c*) The discharge of a Pelton wheel turbine is 5 m³/sec at a head of 300 m at the nozzle. There are two runners and each runner has two jets. The length of the pipeline is 1900 m. The efficiency of the transmission for the pipe is 90%. Assume friction factor *f* as 0.008. Determine jet diameter, pipe diameter and output of the turbine. The overall efficiency of turbine is 85%. **15**

(*d*) What is workability of concrete? Explain slump test and compacting factor test. Discuss the factors affecting workability. **20**

5. (*a*) A 6 m high vertical wall supports a saturated cohesive soil with horizontal surface. The top 3.5 m of the backfill has bulk density 18 kN/m³ and apparent cohesion of 16 kN/m². The bulk density and apparent cohesion of the bottom 2.5 m is 19.5 kN/m² and 18 kN/m² respectively. What will be total active earth pressure on the wall? Draw the pressure distribution diagram. Assume that tension cracks will develop. Locate the point of application of the resultant pressure. **20**

(*b*) A direct shear test was conducted on a silty sand. At failure the normal and shear stresses were found to be 66 kPa and 40 kPa respectively. Draw Mohr's circle and determine :

(*i*) Angle of shearing resistance

(*ii*) Principal stresses at failure

(*iii*) Locate the pole and find orientation of failure plane. **20**

(*c*) The pump-out test was performed to determine the field permeability of an unconfined aquifer and the following observations were made:

RL of original water table before pumping = 250.5 m

RL of water in the well at constant pumping = 245.6 m

RL of the rock of impervious layer = 220.0 m

RL of water in observation well = 249.8 m

The distance of observation well from tubewell = 48 m

Determine

(*i*) Coefficient of permeability of the aquifer (*k*)

(*ii*) Error in *k* if observations are not taken in the observation well and radius of influence is assumed to be 298 m

(*iii*) Actual radius of influence based on the observations of observation well

(*iv*) Radius of influence using Sichart equation

The diameter of the well is 20 cm and discharge is 250 m³/hr. **20**

6. (*a*) In a roof truss, the member consists of 2 ISA 100 × 75 × 8 mm. The angles are connected to either side of a 10 mm gusset plate and member is subjected to a working pull of 280 kN. Design the welded connection assuming they are made in the workshop. The centre of gravity of the section from the top may be considered as 31 mm. **25**

(*b*) Draw the shear force and bending moment diagram for the beam as shown below : **25**

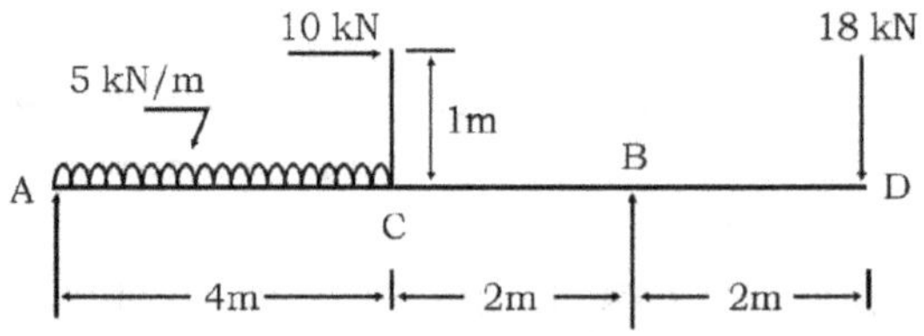

(*c*) Define the following terms :

Scrap value, Salvage value, Sinking fund and Depreciation **(10)**

ANSWERS

1.(a) $(BOD_{mix}) = \dfrac{22 \times 3 + 3 \times 190}{25} = 25.44 \; mg/l$

Assume saturation $D_o = 9.2 \; mg/l$

D_o = initial Deficit = $9.2 - 8.8 = 0.4 \; mg/l$

Deficit at any time t is given by stretcher phelp

Equation :

$$D_t = \dfrac{K_D \times L_o}{K_R - L_D}\left[(10)^{-K_D \cdot t} - (10)^{-K_R \cdot t}\right]$$

$$+ \left[D_0 \times (10)^{-K_R \cdot t}\right]$$

$$= \dfrac{0.11 \times 25.44}{0.33 \times 0.11}\left[(10)^{-0.11 \times 2} - (10)^{-0.33 \times 2}\right]$$

$$+ \left[0.4 \times (10)^{-0.33 \times 2}\right]$$

$$= 12.72 \times 0.38378 + 0.08751$$

$$= 4.969 \; mg/l$$

1.(b) $H = 2.5m$ $\sigma_0 = 45 \; KN/m^2$

$e = 1.2m$ $\sigma_c = 65 \; KN/m^2$

$c_c = 0.27m$ $\Delta\bar\sigma = 55 KN/m^2$

$c_s = 0.06$

$$\Delta H = \dfrac{C_s H}{1+e}\log\left(\dfrac{\bar\sigma_c}{\bar\sigma_c}\right) + \dfrac{C_c}{1+e}\log\left(\dfrac{\bar\sigma_0 + \Delta}{\bar\sigma_c}\right)$$

$$= \dfrac{0.06 \times \left(2.5 \times 10^{+3}\right)}{1+1.2}\log_{10}\left(\dfrac{65}{45}\right)$$

$$+ \dfrac{0.27 \times 2.5 \times 10^{+3}}{1+1.2}\log\left(\dfrac{45+55}{65}\right)$$

$$= 10.89 + 57.40$$

$$\Delta H = 68.29 \; mm$$

1.(c) Factors Affecting Duty of Water

1. **Types of crop:** Duty of water varies from crop to crop. The crops which require large quantity of water have lower duty.

2. **Climate condition:** The climatic condition affecting the duty of water are temperature, wind velocity, humidity and rainfall.

3. **Method of Irrigation:** Duty of water is high for sprinkler and drip irrigation method as compared to surface irrigation.

4. **Types of soil:** In coarse grained soil there will be more percolation hence duty of water will be less.

5. **Quality of irrigation water:** Water containing large amount of salts and alkalies is required in large amount so that salts are leached off. Due to this duty of water is lowered.

Duty of water also depends on

• method of cultivation

• canal condition

• topography of land

• base period of crop

1.(d)

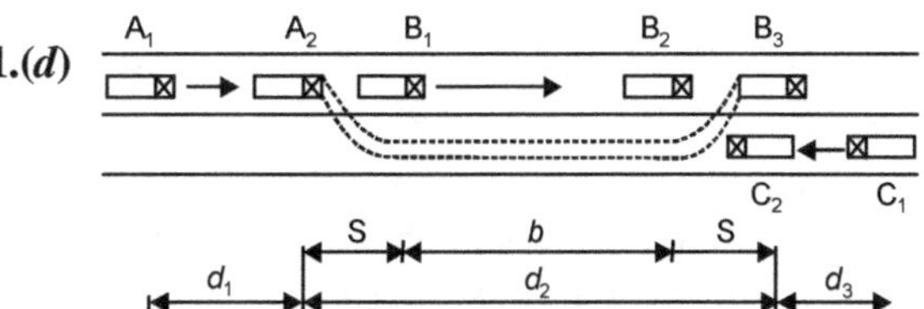

Overtaking sight distance:- (OSD)

one lane two way traffic

OSD = $d_1 + d_2 + d_3$

One lane one way traffic

OSD = $d_1 + d_2$

According to IRC

$$V_b = V - 16 \quad (V - \text{in Km/h})$$

$$V_b = V - 4.5 \quad (V - \text{in m/s})$$

Where V = design speed or speed of over taking vehicle.

$$V = 100 \times \dfrac{5}{18} = 27.778 \; (m/sec)$$

$$V_b = (27.778 - 4.5)$$
$$V_b = 23.278 \text{ m/s}$$

The time taken by overtaking vehicle is 2 sec (According to IRC)

$$d_1 = V_b \times t = 23.278 \times 2$$
$$d_1 = 46.556 \text{ m}$$
$$d_2 = b + 2s$$
$$S = 0.7 \times V_b + 6$$

According to IRC any length of vehicle = 6m

$[S = 0.7 \times 23.278 + 6 = 22.294 \text{ m.}]$

2.(a) Requirement of Good Ballast

1. The ballast should be clean and graded crushed stone aggregate with hard, dense, angular particle structure providing sharp corners and cubical fragments with a minimum of flat and elongated pieces. These qualities will provide for proper drainage of the ballast section.

   The angular property will provide interlocking qualities which will grip the sleeper firmly to prevent movement. Excess flat and elongated particles could restrict proper consolidation of the ballast section.

2. The ballast must have high wear and abrasive qualities to with stand the impact of traffic loads without excessive degradation. Excessive abrasion loss of an aggregate will result in reduction of particle size, failing of the ballast section, reduction of drainage and loss of supporting strength of the ballast section.

3. The ballast particles should have high internal shearing strength to have high stability.

4. The ballast material should possess sufficient unit weight to provide a stable ballast section and in turn provide support and alignment stability to the track structure.

5. The ballast should provide high resistance to temperature changes, chemical attack, exhibit a high electrical resistance and low absorption properties.

6. Ballast material should be free from cementing properties. Deterioration of the ballast particles should not induce cementing together of the degraded particles.

7. The ballast material should have less absorption of water as excessive absorption can result in rapid deterioration during alternate wetting and drying cycles.

8. The Ballast should be cheap and economical.

The depth of ballast can be calculated as

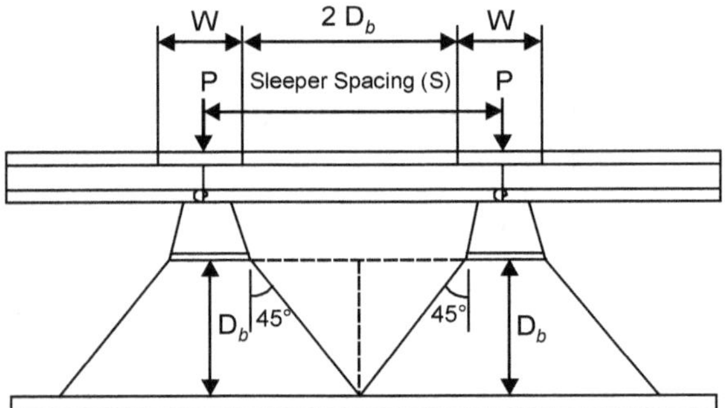

S = sleeper spacing

W = width of sleeper density

D_b = Depth of the ballast

$$D_b = \frac{S - W}{2} = \text{minimum Depth of ballast}$$

For example, with a sleeper density as $(n + 7)$, a sleeper spacing of 65 cm and a width of sleeper of 25 cm the minimum depth of ballast from the above formula works out to be 20 cm, which is minimum depth of ballast generally prescribed on Indian Railways.

2.(*b*)

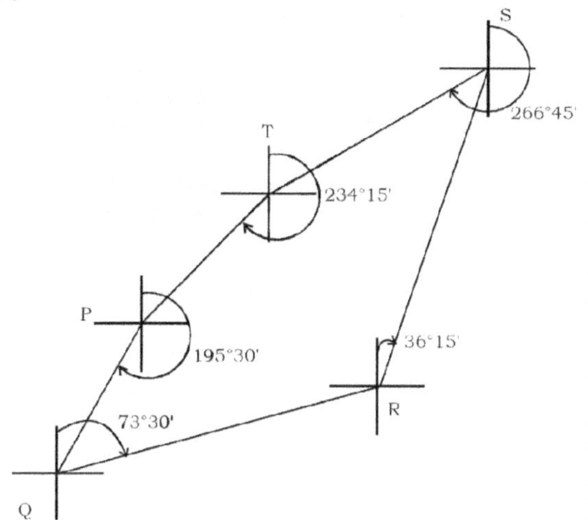

Line	FB	B.B	F.B. – B.B
PQ	195° 30'	12° 0',	178° 30'
QR	73° 30'	250° 30'	–177° 0'
RS	36° 15'	214° 30'	–178° 15'
ST	266° 45'	84° 45'	182° 0'
TP	234° 15'	57° 0'	177° 15'

- To find included angles.

$\angle P = \text{F.B.}_{PQ} - \text{B.B.}_{TP} = 195° \, 30 - 57° \, 0'$
$= 138° \, 30'$

$\angle Q = \text{F.B.}_{QR} - \text{B.B.}_{PQ} = 73° \, 30' - 17° \, 0'$
$= 56° \, 30'$

$\angle R = \text{F.B.}_{RS} - \text{B.B.}_{QR} = 36°15' - 250° \, 30'$
$+ \, 360° = 145° \, 45'$

$\angle S = \text{F.B.}_{ST} - \text{B.B.}_{RS} = 266° \, 45' - 214° \, 30'$
$= 52° \, 15'$

$\angle T = \text{F.B.}_{TP} - \text{B.B.}_{ST} = 234° \, 15' - 84° \, 15'$
$= 150° \, 0'$

Check : $\angle A + \angle B + \angle C + \angle D + \angle E = 543° \, 0'$

& Theoretical sum $= (2n - 4)90$
$= (2 \times 5 - 4)90 = 540°00'$

Error $= 543° \, 0' - 540°00' = + \, 3°$

Correction $= -3°$

Correction in each angle

$$= \frac{-3°}{5} = \frac{-3°}{5} = -0°36'$$

So, Correct included angles are,

$\angle P = 138° \, 30' - 36' = 137° \, 54'$

$\angle Q = 56° \, 30' - 36' = 55° \, 54'$

$\angle R = 145° \, 45' - 36' = 145° \, 09'$

$\angle S = 52° \, 15' - 36' = 51° \, 39'$

$$\angle T = 150° \, 0' - 36' = \frac{149° \, 24'}{540° \, 00'}$$

Since, here no line has the difference of 180°, so, we take that line which has the nearest difference to 180° as line PQ So, for line PQ,

Error $= 178°30' - 180° = - \, 1°30°$

Correction $= + \, 1°30'$

Correction in F.B. of line PQ $= \dfrac{+1°30'}{2} = + \, 45'$

So,

Correct $\text{FB}_{PQ} = 195° \, 30' + 45' = 196° \, 15'$
Correct $\text{BB}_{PQ} = 196°15' - 180° = 16° \, 15'$
Now,

Correct $\text{FB}_{QR} = \text{Correct BB}_{PQ} + \text{Correct} \angle R$
$= 16°15' + 55° \, 54' = 72° \, 09'$

Correct $\text{BB}_{QR} = 72° \, 09' + 180° = 252° \, 09$

Correct $\text{FB}_{RS} = \text{Correct BB}_{QR} + \text{Correct} \angle R$
$= 252° \, 09' + 145° \, 09' - 360$
$= 37° \, 18'$

Correct $\text{BB}_{RS} = 37° \, 18' + 180° = 217° \, 18'$

Correct $\text{FB}_{ST} = \text{Correct BB}_{RS} + \text{Correct} \angle S$
$= 217° \, 18' + 51° \, 39' = 268° \, 57'$

Correct $\text{BB}_{ST} = 268° \, 57' - 180° = 88° \, 57'$
$= 88° \, 57' + 149° \, 24' = 238° \, 21'$

Correct $\text{BB}_{TP} = 238° \, 21' - 180° = 58° \, 21'$

Correct $\text{FB}_{TP} = \text{Correct BB}_{ST} + \text{Correct} \angle T$

Correct $\text{FB}_{PQ} = \text{Correct BB}_{TP} + \text{Correct} \angle P$
$= 58° \, 21' + 137° \, 54'$
$= 196° \, 15'$

2.(*c*) Factors affecting selection of contour interval are

1. Scale of map: If scale of map is large, contour interval is kept small where as if scale of map is small contour interval is kept large.

2. **Topography of land:** For flat ground contour interval is small and for steep slope contour interval is large.

3. **Purpose of map:** Contour interval is taken small but it should not be too small else it will increase the cost of work. Therefore C.I should be taken small when plan is required in detail design.

4. **Cost and time:** C.I should be kept large when time is less and it should be taken large for economical survey.

2.(d)

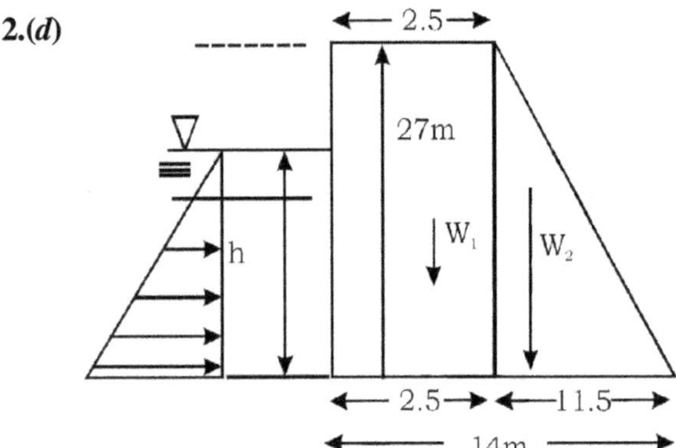

For zero tension.

$$e \leq \frac{B}{6}$$

$$\Rightarrow \quad \frac{B}{6} - \bar{x} \leq \frac{B}{6}$$

$$\Rightarrow \quad \frac{B}{3} \leq \bar{x}$$

$$\Rightarrow \quad \frac{B}{3} \leq \frac{\Sigma m}{\Sigma U}$$

$$\Rightarrow \quad \frac{B}{3} \Sigma U \leq \Sigma m$$

$$\Rightarrow \quad \frac{14}{3}(W - U) \leq \frac{W}{2} \times \frac{2B}{3} \frac{-P \times H}{3} \frac{-U \times 2B}{3}$$

$$+ W_1 \times \left(11.5 + \frac{2.5}{2}\right)$$

$$\Rightarrow \quad \frac{14}{3}\left[21 \times \frac{1}{2} \times (14 + 2.5) \times 27 - \frac{1 \times 9.81 \times 14 \times 27}{2}\right]$$

$$\leq \frac{1}{2} \times 11.5 \times 26 \times 21 \times \frac{2}{3} \times 11.5 - \frac{1}{2} \times r_w$$

$$\times \frac{h^3}{3} - \frac{1}{2} .1 \times 9.81 \times 14 \times 27 \times 2 \times \frac{11.5}{3}$$

$$+ \ 21 \times 2.5 \times 27(12.75)$$

$$\Rightarrow \quad 13177.08 \leq 24995.25 - \frac{1}{6} \times 9.81 \times h^3$$

$$- \ 17304.84 + 18.073$$

$$\frac{9.81}{6} \times h^3 \leq 1258645$$

$$\Rightarrow \quad h = 19.74 \text{ m}$$

3.(a) Plate load test is usually adopted to find out the Settlement and Engineering Properties of Soil such as Shear strength and Safe bearing Capacity. A plate of circular or square in shape is placed in the bottom of the Experiment and load is applied incrementally. The Incremental load should be one fourth of the design load. By this test, settlement of load can be calculated and Load Settlement Curve and Time-Settlement Curve can be drawn.

Limitations of Plate Load Test:
  (*i*) The Depth of Influence is Limited to certain extent
  (*ii*) The determined bearing capacity is only for the soil that is up to 2 times of the diameter of the plate
  (*iii*) Long time consolidation of soil can not be found out
  (*iv*) To do this test, small amount of excavation is carried out and this may cause significant Ground Disturbance.
  (*v*) If ground is disturbed, then the soil properties will be changed and this paves the way for wrong observation
  (*vi*) The effect of Scale is very small

Size of plates affect the settlement and bearing capacity as smaller size plates are used in dense or stiff soil where as larger plates are used in loose or soft soil.

3.(b) Assume $l_{eff} = l = 3.6$ m $= 3600$ mm

$$\frac{l_{eff}}{d} < K_1\, K_2\, K_3\, K_4 \text{ (value)}$$

$$\Rightarrow \quad \frac{3600}{d} < 1 \times 1.25 \times 1 \times 1(20)$$

$$\Rightarrow \qquad d > 144$$

$\Rightarrow$ Provide $d = 150$ mm.

$$D = 150 + 30 = 180 \ (E_{ef} \text{ cover})$$

$\therefore$ Space is simply supported.

$\therefore$ Let support width $= 250$ mm each.

$$l_{eff} = \begin{cases} l_c + d = 3.6 + 0.15 = 3.75 \\ l_c + \dfrac{b_1}{2} + \dfrac{b_2}{2} = 3.6 + \dfrac{0.25}{2} + \dfrac{0.25}{2} = 3.85 \end{cases}$$

$$= 3.75 \text{ m}$$

Assume 1m width and 1m length of slab.

$$\delta L = 0.18 \times 1 \times 1 \times 25 = 4.5 \text{ KN/m}$$

Super imposed load $= 5$ kN/m

Total factored load $= (4.5 + 5.1 \times 1.5)$

$$= 14.25 \text{ KN/m}$$

Maximum Bending moment

$$= \frac{w_u l^2}{8} = \frac{14.25 \times 3.75^2}{8} = 25.05 \text{ KN}-m$$

For Fe 415, $BM_{lim} = 0.138\, f_{ck}\, bd^2$

$$\Rightarrow 25.05 = 0.138 \times 20 \times 1000 \times d^2$$

$$\Rightarrow \qquad d = 95.26 \text{ mm} < 150 \text{ mm}$$

$$A_{st} = \frac{0.5 f_{ck} bd}{f_y} \left[1 - \sqrt{1 - \frac{1 - 4.6 BM_u}{f_{ck} bd^2}} \right]$$

$$= \frac{0.5 \times 20 \times 1000 \times 150}{415}$$

$$\left[1 - \sqrt{1 - \sqrt{\frac{4.6 \times 25.05 \times 10^6}{20 \times 1000 \times 150^2}}} \right]$$

$$= 496.93 \text{ mm}^2$$

$$Ast_{min} = 0.12\% \text{ of } bd$$

$$= 0.12 \times \frac{1}{100} \times 100 \times 180$$

$$= 216 \text{ mm}^2$$

Assuming 12mm bar

$$\text{Spacing} = \frac{1000}{\dfrac{496.93}{\dfrac{\pi}{4} \times (12)^2}} = 227.476 \text{ mm}$$

check for maximum spacing

$$= \min \text{ of } \begin{cases} 3 \times 150 = 300 \text{ mm} \\ 300 \end{cases}$$

$\therefore$ Provide 12 mm main bars (@) 235 mm spacing

Also distribution bars should be provide to present shrinkage maximum spacing for distribution bars:

$$\min \text{ of } \begin{cases} 5d \rightarrow 5 \times 150 \\ 300 \text{ mm} \end{cases} = 300 \text{ mm}$$

Distribution bar 8mm (@) 225mm also

Now, check for shear

$$P_t = \frac{100\, A_{st}}{bd} = \frac{100 \times 496.93}{1000 \times 150} = 0.33\%$$

$$\tau_{c(at\,0.33\%)} = 0.36 + \frac{0.49 - 0.36}{0.50 - 0.25}\,(0.33 - 0.25)$$

$$= 0.40116 \text{ N/mm}^2$$

$$(\tau_{v\,max}) = \frac{\dfrac{w_u \times l}{2}}{bd} = \frac{14.25 \times 3.75 \times 1000}{2 \times 1000 \times 150}$$

$$= 0.178 \text{ N/mm}^2$$

$$\therefore \qquad \tau_v < \tau_c$$

No need to design for shear.

3.(c) Design of circular helical column :

$$\text{Slenderness ratio} = \frac{l_{eff}}{B} < 12$$

Small column else long.

Circular column with helical reinforcement:

(i) Load carrying capacity

LCC of column increases by 5%

$$P = 1.05 \times Cr\,[A_c . \sigma_{cc} + A_{sc} . \sigma_{sc}]$$

Due to helical reinforcement both the strength and ductiliy is increased.

(*ii*) Design of helical reinforcement

If following condition is satisfied the pitch of helical reinforcement can be found.

$$0.36 \frac{f_{ck}}{R_1}\left[\frac{A_g}{A_c} - 1\right] \le \frac{V_h}{V_c} \qquad ....(i)$$

Gross diameter = D_g

Gross area (A_g) = $\frac{\pi}{4} \times D^2$

Core diameter (D_c) measured outside of helical reinforcement

$$D_c = D_g - 2 \times (40)$$
$$= (D_g - 80)$$

Area of core, $\quad A_c = \frac{\pi}{4} \times D_c^2$

Volume of core. (for unit length)

$$V_c = A_c \times 1000 \text{ mm}$$

V_h – volume of helical reinforcement

In some unit length of the column as considered for V_c

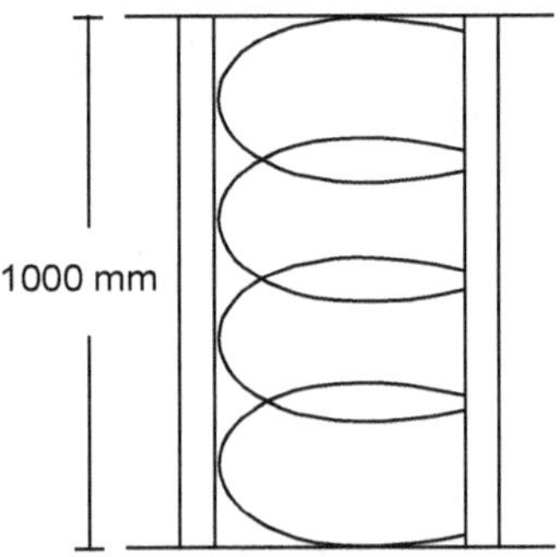

V_h = no. of turns × length in one turns × c/s area of helical reinforcement.

$$= \left(\frac{1000}{P}\right)(\pi.\phi_h)\left(\frac{\pi}{4}.\phi_h^2\right)$$

where,

D_h. diameter

$$D_h = D_c - \phi_h$$

Actual length of helical reinforcement

In one turn

$$= \sqrt{(\pi\phi h)^2 + P^2} \approx \pi D_h$$

∴ Calculate P from $\qquad$ ... (*i*)

As per IS code, the value of '*p*' should be such that

(*i*) $\qquad$ P $\not> $ 75 mm

(*ii*) $\qquad$ P $\not< \dfrac{1}{6} D_c$

(*iii*) $\qquad$ P $\not< $ 25 mm

(*iv*) $\qquad$ P $\not< $ 3 ϕ_h

Some IS code recommendations:

(*i*) Minimum % of steel = 0.8%

(*ii*) Maximum % of steel

$\qquad$ 4 % (if bars are lapped)

$\qquad$ 6 % (if bars are not lapped)

(*iii*) Minimum dia. of bar = 12 mm

(*iv*) Minimum no. of bars

$\qquad$ For rectangular – 4

$\qquad$ For circular – 6

(*v*) Maximum spacing of longitudinal bars = 300 mm

4.(*a*) Following are the characteristics or qualities of a good timber:

(*a*) **Appearance:** A freshly cut surface of timber should have hard and shining appearance.

(*b*) **Colour:** The colour of timber should be dark. Light colour usually indicates timber with low strength.

(*c*) **Smell:** A good timber should have sweet. An unpleasant smell indicates decayed timber.

(*d*) **Defects:** A good timber should be free from serious defects such as knots, flaws, shakes, etc.

(*e*) **Sound:** A good timber should be given out a clear ringing sound when struck. A dull heavy sound, when struck indicates decayed timber.

(*f*) **Structure:** It should be uniform. The fibres should be firmly added. The medullary rays should be hard and compact. The annual rings should be regular and they should be closely located.

(*g*) **Strength:** A good timber should be strong for working as structural member such as joist, beam, rafter, etc. It should be capable of taking loads slowly or suddenly. It should also possess enough strength in direct and transverse directions.

(*h*) **Hardness:** A good timber should be hard *i.e.*, it should offer resistance when it is being penetrated by another body.

(*i*) **Durability:** A good timber should be durable. It should be capable of resisting the action of fungi insects, chemicals, physical agencies and mechanical agencies.

(*j*) **Fire Resistance:** A dense wood offers good resistance to the fire and it requires sufficient heat to cause a flame.

4.(*b*)

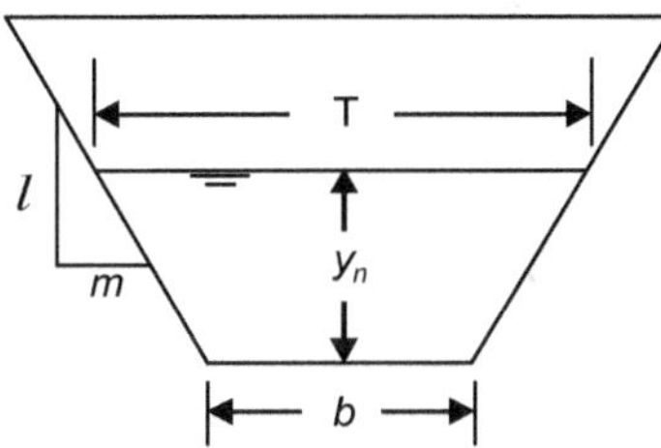

Area, $A = \dfrac{1}{2}(B + B + 2my)y$

$A = \dfrac{1}{2}(2B + 2my)y$

$A = (B + my)y$

Top flow width, $T = B + 2ym$

Perimeter, $P = B + 2y\sqrt{m^2 + 1}$

Substituting, $B = \dfrac{A}{y} - my$

$P = \dfrac{A}{y} - my + 2y\sqrt{m^2 + 1} \,...(i)$

(A & *m* are constant)

For efficient channel the wetted perimeter should be minimum so.

$$= \frac{d\rho}{dy} = 0$$

So differentiation of eq^n θ w.r.t. *y*

$$\frac{d\rho}{dy} = \frac{-A}{y^2} - m + 2\sqrt{1 + m^2}$$

$$0 = \frac{-A}{y^2} - m + 2\sqrt{1 + m^2}$$

$$\frac{A}{y^2} + m = 2\sqrt{1 + m^2}$$

$$\frac{(B + my)y}{y^2} + m = 2\sqrt{1 + m^2}$$

$$B + 2my = 2y\sqrt{1 + m^2}$$

$$\left(\frac{B + 2my}{2}\right) = y\sqrt{1 + m^2}$$

For the most efficient channel the half the top width of trapezoidal section is equal to the one side of triangular section.

Hydraulic Mean Depth (R):

$$R = \frac{\text{Wetted Area}}{\text{Wetted Perimeter}}$$

$$= \frac{By + my^2}{\left(B + 2y\sqrt{1 + m^2}\right)}$$

$$= \frac{y(B + my)}{(B + B + 2my)} = \frac{y(B + my)}{2(B + my)}$$

$$R = \frac{y}{2} \text{ Hence proved.}$$

4.(*c*) Given:
$$Q = 5\text{m}^2/\text{s}$$
$$Hg = 300$$
$$L = 1900$$
$$F = 0.008$$
$$\eta_0 = 85\%$$
$$\eta \text{ pipe} = 90\%$$

(1)
$$\eta \text{ pipe} = 1 - \frac{h_F}{H_g}$$

$$0.9 = \frac{1 - h_F}{300}$$

$$h_f = 30 \text{ m}$$

(2)
$$V_1 = \sqrt{2gH_{net}}$$
$$= \sqrt{2 \times 9.81 \times 270}$$
$$= 92.78 \text{ m/s}$$

(3)
$$\frac{\text{Total discharge (Q)}}{\text{Total No. of jet}} = \text{discharge required}$$
$$\text{per jet } (q)$$

$$\frac{5}{4} = q$$
$$q = 1.25 \text{ m}^3/\text{s}$$
$$q = \frac{\pi}{4} \times d^2 \times V_1$$
$$d = .130 \text{ m}$$

(4) Assume dia. of pipe (D)

$$h_f = \frac{4f\,LV^2}{2gD}$$

V = average velocity in pipe

$$V = \frac{Q}{A} = \frac{Q}{\frac{\pi}{4}D^2}$$

$$h_f = \frac{8f\,LV^2}{\pi^2 gD^5}$$

$$30 = \frac{8 \times .008 \times 150 \times 5^2}{\pi^2 \times 9.81 \times D^5}$$

$$D^5 = 1.046$$
$$D = 1.009 \text{ m}$$

(5)
$$\eta_0 = \frac{\text{output power}}{\rho Q g \, H_{net}}$$

$$0.85 \times \rho QgH_{net} = \text{output power}$$
$$P = 11256.975 \text{ KW}$$

4.(*d*) Workability can be defined as that property of freshly mixed concrete or mortar determines the ease and homogeneity with which it can be mixed, placed, compacted and finished.

The factors affecting the workability of concrete are:

1. **Water Content:** Water content in a given volume of concrete will have significant influences on the workablility. The higher will be the fluidity of concrete, which is one of the important factors affecting workablity.

2. **Mix Proportions:** Aggregate cement ratio is an important factor influencing workablity. The higher the aggregate cement ratio, the leaner is the concrete.

3. **Size of Aggregates:** The bigger the size of aggregate, the less is the surface area and hence less amount of water is required for wetting the surface.

4. **Shape of Aggregates:** The shape of aggregates influences workablitiy in good measure. Angular, elongated or flaky aggregate makes the concrete very harsh when compared to rounded aggregates of cubical shaped aggregates.

5. **Surface Texture:** The influence of surface texture on workability is again due to the fact that the total surface area of rough textured aggregate is more than the surface area of smooth rounded aggregate of same volume. Thus the rough textured aggregate will show poor workablity and smooth or glassy textured aggregate will give better workability.

6. **Grading of Aggregates:** This is one of the factors which will have maximum influence on workbality.

1. **Slump test**

- Slump test does not measure workability of concrete, although it gives a measure of consistency but is very useful in detecting variations in uniformity of mix of given nominal proportions.

- Dimensions of the mould are, bottom diameter = 200 mm, top diameter = 100 mm, and height = 300 mm.

- Mould is filled in with fresh concrete in four layers, each layer of approximately one quarter of the height of the mould and tamped with 25 strokes of the rounded end of the tamping rod (Dia = 16mm and length is 60 mm).

- Strokes are distributed in uniform manner over the cross-section and for the second and subsequent layers should penetrate into the underlying layer.

- After the top layer has been rodded, the concrete is struck off level with a trowel or the tamping rod, such that the mould is exactly filled.

- Mould is removed immediately by raising it slowly and carefully in a vertical direction.

- It allows the concrete to subside and the slump is measured immediately by determining the difference between the height of the mould and that of the highest point of the specimen being tested.

- Slump measured is recorded in terms of millimeters of subsidence of the specimen.

2. Compacting Factor test

- This test is more accurate and sensitive than the slump test especially for it is useful for concrete mixes of medium and low workabilities *i.e.,* compacting factor of 0.9 to 0.8.

- Sample of concrete to be tested is placed gently in the upper hopper, and levelled.

- Trap-door is then opened to allow the concrete to fall into the lower hopper.

- Sticked concrete in the upper hopper at sides is gently pushed into lower one.

- The trap-door of the lower hopper is opened so that the concrete falls in the cylinder.

- Weight of the concrete in the cylinder is then determined to the nearest 10 gm this is known as wt of partially compacted concrete.

- Cylinder is refilled with concrete from the same sample in layers of 50 mm deep. Each layer being heavily rammed or preferably vibrated so as to obtain full compaction.

- The mass of concrete in the cylinder should be measured and it is known as the mass of fully compacted concrete.

- Compacting factor is defined as ratio of the weight of partially compacted concrete to the weight of fully compacted concrete. *i.e.,*

$$\text{C.F} = \frac{\text{mass of partially compacted concrete}}{\text{mass of fully compacted concrete}}$$

5.(a) Soil I

$$p_a = k_a \gamma z - 2c\sqrt{k_a}$$
$$\phi' = 0$$
$$K_{a1} = \frac{1 - \sin\phi'}{1 + \sin\phi'} = 1$$

at point A $z = 0$

$$P_a = 0 - 2 \times 16\sqrt{1} = -32 \text{ kN/m}^2$$

at point B, $p_b = K_a \gamma H - 2c\sqrt{k_a}$

$$H = 3.5 \text{ m}$$
$$= 1 \times 18 \times 3.5 - 2 \times 16\sqrt{1}$$
$$= 31 \text{ kN/m}^2$$

$$Z_0 = \frac{2c}{\gamma\sqrt{k_a}} = \frac{2 \times 16}{18\sqrt{1}} = 1.78 \text{ m}$$

Soil II Overburden

$$q = \gamma h = 18 \times 3.5 = 63 \text{ kN/m}^2$$
$$P_b = K_a(\gamma z + q) - 2c\sqrt{k_a}$$
$$= 1(0 + 63) - 2 \times 18\sqrt{1}$$
$$= 27 \text{ kN/m}^2$$
$$P_c = 1(19.5 \times 2.5 + 63) - 2 \times 18\sqrt{1}$$
$$= 75.75 \text{ kN/m}^2$$

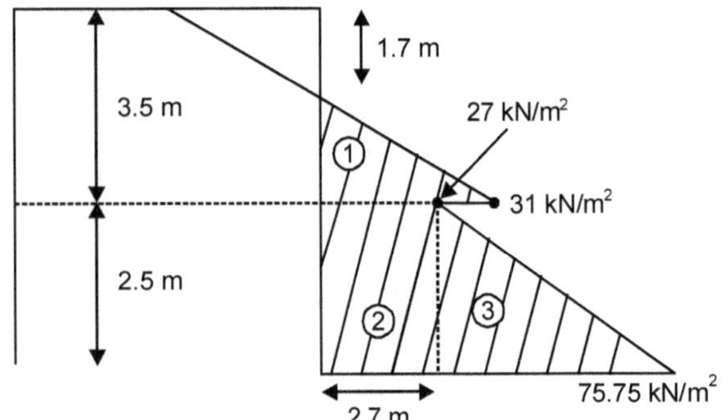

Total active pressure on wall due to soil

$$= \frac{1}{2}(3.5 - 1.78)31 + \left(\frac{27 + 75.75}{2}\right)$$

$$= 26.66 + 128.43$$

$$P_a = 155.09 \text{ kN/m}^2$$

Point of application

$$26.66\left(2.5 + \left(\frac{3.5 - 1.78}{3}\right)\right)$$

$$Z = \frac{+ 27 \times 2.5 \times \dfrac{2.5}{2} + \dfrac{1}{2}(75.75 - 27)2.5}{26.66 + 27 + 2.5 + \dfrac{1}{2}(75.75 - 27)2.5}$$

$$Z = 5.26 \text{ m. from base}$$

5.(b) $\sigma = 66 \text{ kpa}$

$\tau = 40 \text{ kpa}$

(i) $\phi = \tan^{-1}\left(\dfrac{\tau}{\sigma}\right) = \tan^{-1}\left(\dfrac{44}{66}\right)$

$\phi = 31.22°$

(ii) $\sigma = \left(\dfrac{\sigma_1 + \sigma_3}{2}\right) + \left(\dfrac{\sigma_1 + \sigma_3}{2}\right)\cos 2\theta_f$

$\theta_f = 45 + \dfrac{\phi}{2} = 45 + \dfrac{31.22}{2} = 60.61°$

$66 = \left(\dfrac{\sigma_1 + \sigma_3}{2}\right) + \left(\dfrac{\sigma_1 - \sigma_3}{2}\right) + \cos(2 \times 60.61°)$

$66 \times 2 = (\sigma_1 + \sigma_3) + (\sigma_1 - \sigma_3) + (-0.52)$

$\tau = \left(\dfrac{\sigma_1 - \sigma_3}{2}\right)\sin 2\theta_f$

$$40 = \left(\frac{\sigma_1 - \sigma_3}{2}\right)\sin(2 \times 60.61°)$$

$$0.855 \,\sigma_1 = 0.855 \,\sigma_3 = 80$$

$$\boxed{\begin{array}{l} \sigma_1 = 137.11 \text{ kN/m}^2 \\ \hline \sigma_3 = 43.54 \text{ kN/m}^2 \end{array}}$$

(iii)

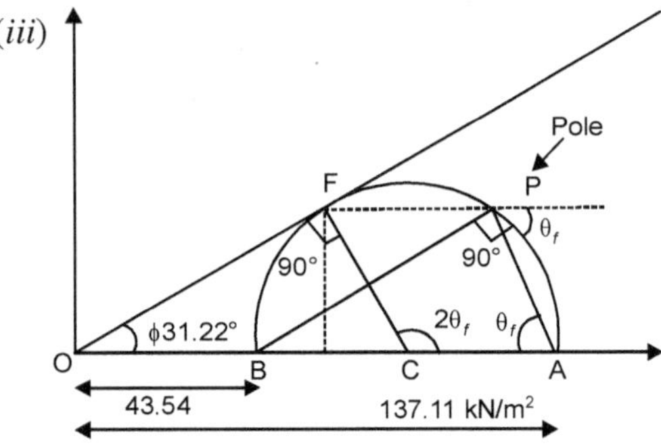

PA = Major principal plane

PB = Minor principal plane

Obliquity of PB = 29.31°

5.(c)

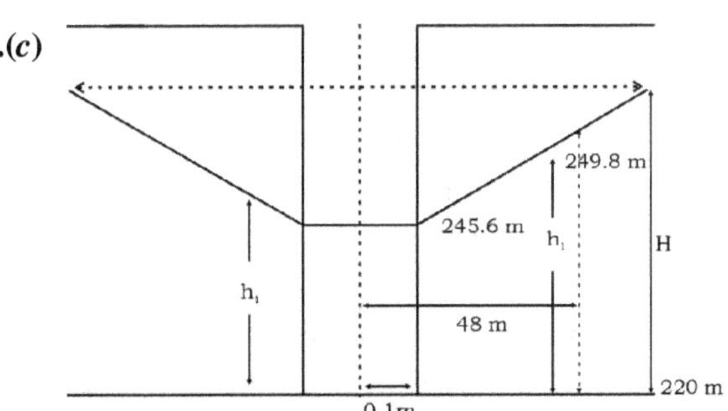

$$H = 30.5 \text{ m}$$

$$q = 250 \text{ m}^3/\text{s}$$

$$= \frac{250}{60 \times 60} = 0.07 \text{ m}^3/\text{s}$$

$$h = 25.6 \text{ m}$$

$$h_1 = 28.6 \text{ m}$$

(i) $$q = \frac{1.36R\left(h_2^2 - h_1^2\right)}{\log 10\left(\dfrac{r_2}{r_1}\right)}$$

13

$$\therefore \qquad 0.07 = \frac{1.36R\left((29.8)^2-(25.6)^2\right)}{\log_{10}\left(\dfrac{48}{0.1}\right)}$$

$$R = 5.93 \times 10^{-4} \text{ cm/s}$$

(*ii*) Error in K is R = 298 m.

    if R = 298 m

$$q = \frac{1.36R\left(H^2-h^2\right)}{\log_{10}\left(\dfrac{R}{r}\right)}$$

$$0.07 = \frac{1.36R\left((30.5)^2-(25.6)^2\right)}{\log_{10}\left(\dfrac{298}{0.1}\right)}$$

$$R = 6.505 \times 10^{-4} \text{ m/s}$$

$$\text{Error} = 6.505 \times 5.93 \times 10^{-4}$$

$$\Delta K = 0.575 \times 10^{-4} \text{ m/s}$$

(*iii*) Actual radius of influence

$$q = \frac{1.36R\left(H^2-h^2\right)}{\log_{10}\left(\dfrac{R}{r}\right)}$$

$$\log_{10}\left(\frac{R_1}{0.1}\right) = \frac{1.36\times 5.93\times 10^{-4}\left((30.5)^2-(25.6)^2\right)}{0.07}$$

$$\log_{10}\left(\frac{R_1}{0.1}\right) = 3.167$$

$$\frac{R}{0.1} = 10^{3.167}$$

$$\frac{R}{0.1} = 1.469.08$$

$$R = 146.90 \text{ m}$$

(*iv*) According to Sichart equation

$$R = 3000\, s\sqrt{R}$$

$$S = \text{Drawdown} = H - h$$

$$R = 3000 \times 4.9\sqrt{5.93\times 10^{-4}}$$

$$R = 357.968 \text{ m}$$

6.(a)

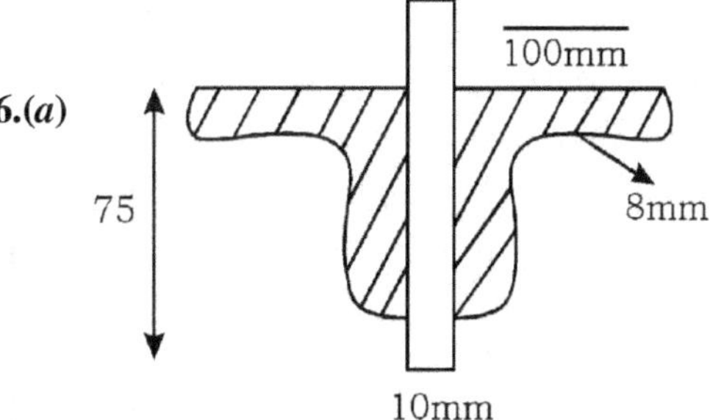

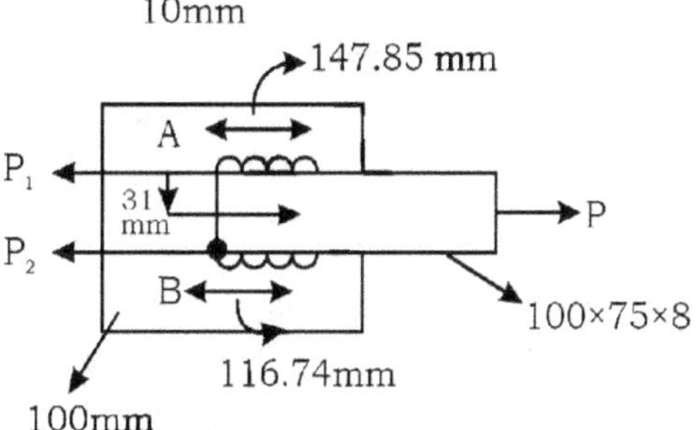

Working load = 280 kN

Design load = 280 × 1.5 = 420 kN

Since angles are connected two side of gusset plate

$$\therefore \text{ Load on each angle} = \frac{420}{2} = 210 \text{ kN}$$

Moment abt. B $\underline{\quad}$

    P × (75 – 31) = P₁ × 75

$\Rightarrow$ 210 × 42 = P1 × 75

$\Rightarrow$ P_1 = 117.6 kN

    P_2 = 210 – 117.6 = 92.4 kN

$$P_1 = K_s l_{eff} \times \frac{fu}{\sqrt{3}\times r_{min}}$$

    (workshop weld r_{mn} = 1.25)

$$\Rightarrow \qquad 117.6 = 0.7 \times Sl_{eff} \times \frac{410}{\sqrt{3}\times 1.25}$$

$$S = ?$$

At A Square Edge. (size of weld)

Minimum size of weld is 3mm $\rightarrow$ Plate thickness (10 mm)

Maximum on size of weld $\rightarrow 8 - 1.5 = 6.5$ mm

At B $\rightarrow$ Rounded Edge. (size of weld)

Minimum size $\rightarrow$ 30 mm

Maximum size $\rightarrow 3/4 \times 8 = 6$ mm

$$P_1 = 117.6$$

$$= 0.7 \times 6 \times l_{eff} \times \frac{410}{1.25 \times \sqrt{3}}$$

$$= l_{eff} = 147.85 \text{ mm}$$

$$P_2 = 92.4$$

$$= 0.7 \times 6 \times l_{eff} \times \frac{410}{1.25 \times \sqrt{3}}$$

$$= l_{eff} = 116.174 \text{ mm}$$

So provide 147.85 mm and 116.174 mm weld length on top and bottom side of angles, and both side.

6.(b)

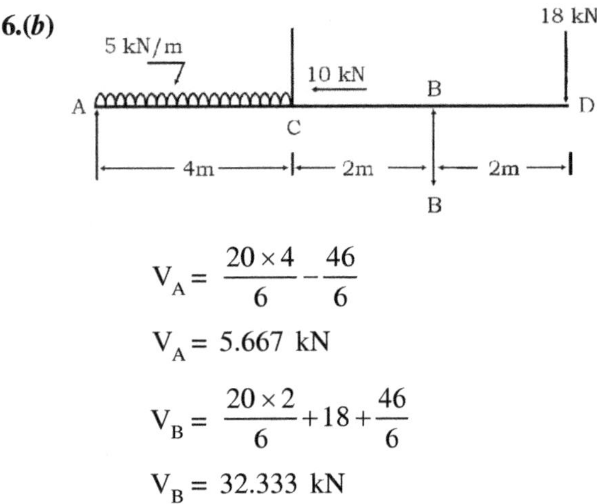

$$V_A = \frac{20 \times 4}{6} - \frac{46}{6}$$

$$V_A = 5.667 \text{ kN}$$

$$V_B = \frac{20 \times 2}{6} + 18 + \frac{46}{6}$$

$$V_B = 32.333 \text{ kN}$$

SFD

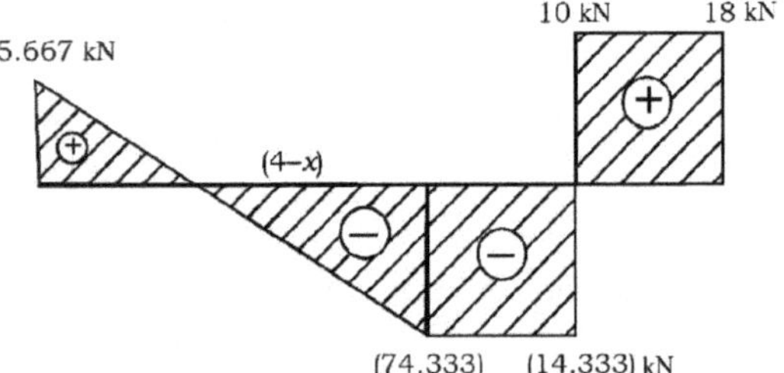

BMD

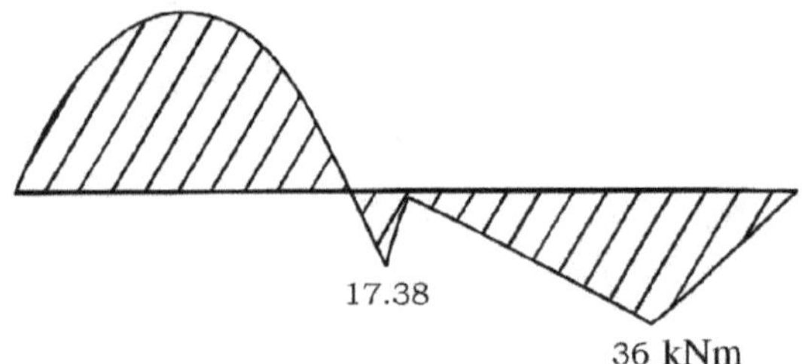

Shear force calculation:

from left side $\begin{bmatrix} \uparrow & \downarrow \\ + & - \end{bmatrix}$

$$V_A = 0$$

$$V_A = 5.667 \ \left[\uparrow\right]$$

$$V_c = 5.667 - 5 \times 4 = -14.33$$

$$= 14.33 \text{ (kN) } \left[\downarrow\right]$$

$$V_B = 14.33 \text{ (kN) } \left[\downarrow\right]$$

$$V_B = -14.3 + 32.333$$

$$V_B = 18 \text{ kN } \left[\uparrow\right]$$

$$V_D = 18 \text{ kN } \left[\uparrow\right]$$

$$V_D = 18 - 18 = 0 \text{ [OK]}$$

Location of zero S. F from support 'A'

$$\frac{5.667}{x} = \frac{14.333}{(4 - x)}$$

$$5.667 \ (4-x) = 14.33 \, x$$

$$x = 1.1334 \text{ m}$$

Bending moment calculation:

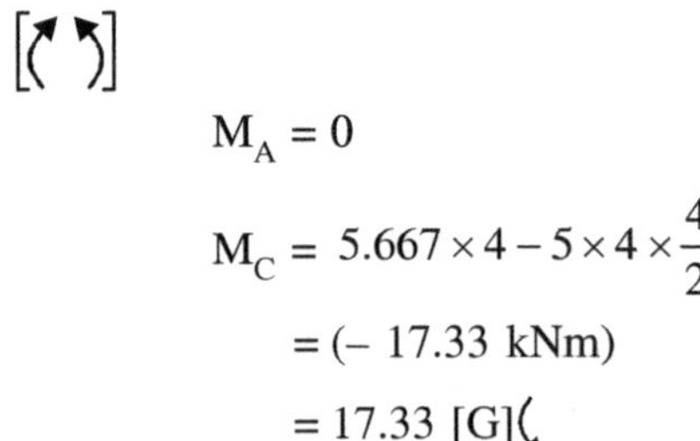

$$M_A = 0$$

$$M_C = 5.667 \times 4 - 5 \times 4 \times \frac{4}{2}$$

$$= (-17.33 \text{ kNm})$$

$$= 17.33 \text{ [G]}$$

$$M_C = -17.33 + 10$$
$$= -7.333 \text{ kN} = 7.333[G] \downarrow$$
$$M_B = 5.667 \times 6 - 5.4 = -3.6$$
$$M_D = 0$$

Note: Maximum bending moment of the location of zero shear force [$x = 1.133$m form left suppost]

$$\text{B. } M_{max} = 5.667 \times 1.133 - 5 \times 1.333$$
$$\times \left(\frac{1.333}{2} \right)$$

$$\text{B.M}_{max} = \oplus 3.2115 \text{ kNm}$$

6.(c) Depreciation is the gradual exhaustion of the usefulness of a property. This may be defined as the decrease or loss in the value of a property due to structural deterioration, life wear and tear, decay and obsolescence.

Scrap value of an asset may be defined as the maximum value that can be fetched by salvaging or selling it after its useful life. It is also known as salvage value, residual value or break-up value.

A sinking fund is an account that is used to deposit and save money to repay a debt or replace a wasting asset in the future. In other words, it's like a savings account that you deposit money in regularly and can only be used for a set purpose.

Salvage value is the estimated value that the owner is paid when the item is sold at the end of its useful life.

———————

| YOUR SPACE |

SSC-Junior Engineer (Civil & Structural) Exam, 2016*

PAPER-II (Conventional)

1. (*a*) A town on the bank of river Ganga discharges 18000 m³/day of treated wastewater into the river. The treated wastewater has a BOD_5 of 20 mg/L and a BOD decay constant of 0.12 day^{-1} at 20°C. The river has a flow rate of 0.43 m³/sec and an ultimate BOD of 5.0 mg/L. The DO of the river is 6.0 mg/L and the DO of the wastewater is 0.4 mg/L. Compute the DO and initial ultimate BOD in the river, immediately after mixing.

(*b*) A sample of normally consolidated clay was subjected to a consolidated undrained triaxial compression test that was carried out until the specimen failed at a deviator stress of 50 kN/m². The pore water pressure at failure was recorded to be 20 kN/m² and confining pressure of 50 kN/m² was used in the test. Determine the consolidated undrained friction angle.

(*c*) Using Lacey's theory, design an irrigation channel carrying 30 m³/sec. Take silt factor as 1.0.

(*d*) Discuss the various causes of disintegration and the major faults occurring in WBM and surface-treated (asphalt roads) in India.

2. (*a*) Differentiate between the following with reference to bituminous construction:

(*i*) Prime coat and Tack coat

(*ii*) Bituminous concrete and Bituminous macadam.

(*b*) A road is to be constructed with a uniform rising gradient of 1 in 100. Determine the staff readings required for setting the tops of the two pegs on the given gradient at 30 metres interval from the last position of the instrument. The RL of the first peg is 384.500 m. A fly levelling was carried out from a BM of RL 387.000 m. The following observations (in m) were recorded.

Backsight 1.625 2.345 2.045 2.955
Foresight 1.315 3.560 2.355

(*c*) What are the errors induced in theodolite survey?

(*d*) A solid shaft transmits 250 kW at 100 r.p.m. If the shear stress is not to exceed 75 N/mm², what should be the diameter of the shaft?

If this shaft is to be replaced by a hollow shaft whose internal diameter shall be 0.6 times the outer diameter, determine the size and percentage saving in weight, maximum stresses being the same.

3. (*a*) Design a circular column with helical reinforcement subjected to a working load of 1500 kN. Diameter of the column is 450 mm. The column has unsupported length of 3.5 m and is effectively held in position at both ends but not restrained against rotation. Use limit state design method. Use M-25 concrete and HYSD Fe-415 steel.

(*b*) Design a constant thickness footing for a reinforced concrete column of 300 mm × 300 mm. The column is carrying an axial working load of 600 kN. The bearing capacity of soil is 200 kN/m². Use M-25 concrete and HYSD Fe-415 bars.

Use limit state design method.

100 (A_{st}/bd)	0.15	0.25	0.50	0.75	1.0
τ_c (N/mm²)	0.19	0.36	0.49	0.57	0.64

(*c*) State and discuss different factors influencing compaction of soil in the field.

4. (*a*) Classify the solid wastes, giving suitable example for each of them. Also explain the different methods of disposal of solid wastes.

    (*b*) Estimate for 1 : 20 model of a spillway (*i*) prototype velocity corresponding to a model velocity of 2 m/sec, (*ii*) prototype discharge per unit width corresponding to a model discharge per unit width of 0.3 m^3/sec/m., (*iii*) pressure head in the prototype corresponding to a model head of 5 cm of mercury at a point, and (*iv*) the energy dissipated per second in the model corresponding to a prototype value of 1.5 kW.

    (*c*) A centrifugal pump having an impeller of 35 cm outside diameter rotates at 1050 r.p.m. The vanes are radial at exit and are 7.0 cm wide. The velocity of radial flow through the impeller is 3 m/sec. The velocity in the suction and delivery pipes are 2.5 m/sec and 1.5 m/sec respectively. Neglecting frictional losses, determine the height through which the pump lifts and the horse-power of the pump.

    (*d*) Name the four important constituents of cement and also state the role of each in achieving its properties.

5. (*a*) A retaining wall with a smooth vertical back is 9 m high and retains a two-layer sand backfill with the following properties :

$0 - 3$ m depth : $c' = 0.0,\ \varphi = 30°,$
$$\gamma = 18\ kN/m^3$$
$3 - 9$ m depth : $c' = 0.0,\ \varphi = 35°,$
$$\gamma = 20\ kN/m^3$$

Show the active earth pressure distribution and determine the total active thrust on the wall. Assume that the water table is well below the base of the wall.

    (*b*) A layer of sand 6.0 m thick lies above a layer of clay soil. The water table is at a depth of 2.0 m below the ground surface. The void ratio of the sand layer is 0.6 and the degree of saturation of the sand layer above the water table is 40%. The void ratio of the clay layer is 0.7. Determine the total stress, neutral stress and effective stress at a point 10 m below the ground surface. Assume specific gravity of the sand and clay soil respectively as 2.65 and 2.7.

    (*c*) What is grit? Why should grit be removed from wastewater? What is the basic principle behind the design of grit chambers? What is the reason to have constant velocity of flow in a grit chamber (conventional horizontal flow) and how is it achieved?

6. (*a*) Design riveted splices for a tie of a steel bridge, 20 cm wide, 20 mm thick, carrying an axial tensile force of 50,000 kg. Use 12 mm thick cover plates and 22 mm dia rivets.

Permissible stresses:

Tension in plates = 1500 kg/cm^2
Shear in rivets = 1000 kg/cm^2
Bearing in rivets = 3000 kg/cm^2
Give a neat sketch of the arrangement.

    (*b*) Draw BMD and SFD for the beam shown below.

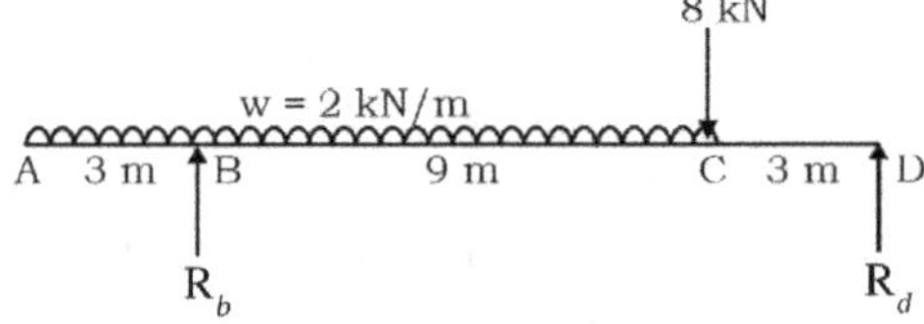

    (*c*) Enumerate the situation in which doubly reinforced concrete beams become necessary. What is the role of compression steel?

ANSWERS

1. (*a*) Discharge of treated wastewater,
$$Q_t = 18000\ m^3/day$$
5 day BOD of treated wastewater,
$$BOD_5 = 20\ mg/l$$

Ultimate BOD of treated wastewater,

$$BOD_t = \frac{BOD_{5t}}{(1-10^{-kt})} = \frac{20}{(1-10^{-0.12\times5})}$$
$$= 26.77\ mg/l$$

DO of treated wastewater,
$$DO_t = 0.4 \text{ mg/l}$$
Discharge of river Ganga,
$$Q_R = 0.43 \text{ m}^3/s$$
$$= 0.43 \times 3600 \times 24^2/\text{day}$$
$$= 37152^2/\text{day}$$
Ultimate BOD of river,
$$BOD_R = 5.0 \text{ mg/l}$$
DO of water,
$$DO_R = 6.0 \text{ mg/l}$$
Ultimate BOD of the mix, BOD_{mix}

$$= \frac{Q_R BOD_R + Q_t BOD_t}{Q_R + Q_t}$$

$$= \frac{37152 \times 5.0 + 18000 \times 26.77}{37152 + 18000}$$

DO of the mix,

$$DO_{mix} = \frac{Q_R DO_R + Q_t DO_t}{Q_R + Q_t}$$

$$= \frac{37152 \times 6.0 + 18000 \times 0.4}{37152 + 18000}$$
$$= 4.17 \text{ mg/l}$$

1.(b)
$$\sigma_3 = 50 \text{ kN/m}^2$$
Deviator stress, $(\Delta\sigma_d)_f = 50 \text{ kN/m}^2$
Pore water pressure at failure $(u_d)_f = 20 \text{ kN/m}^2$
$$\sigma_1 = \sigma_3 + (\Delta\sigma_d)_f$$
$$= 50 + 50 = 100 \text{ kN/m}^2$$
For normally consolidated clay with C = 0

$$\sigma_1 = \sigma_3 \tan^2\left(45° + \frac{\phi}{2}\right)$$

$$100 = 50 \tan^2\left(45° + \frac{\phi}{2}\right)$$

$$\left(\frac{100}{50}\right)^{0.5} = \tan\left(45° + \frac{\phi}{2}\right)$$

$$\tan^{-1}(1.414) = 45° + \frac{\phi}{2}$$

$$54.73 = 45° + \frac{\phi}{2}$$

$$\frac{\phi}{2} = 54.73 - 45$$

$$\frac{\phi}{2} = 9.73$$
$$\phi = 19.46°$$

1.(c) Using the slope equation,

(1) $\quad S = 0.0003\dfrac{f^{5/3}}{Q^{1/6}} = 0.0003 \times \dfrac{1^{5/3}}{30^{1/6}}$

$$= 0.00017 \text{ or } \frac{1}{8528} \text{ or say } \frac{1}{8500}.$$

(2) $\quad P = 4.84 \, Q^{1/2} = 4.84 \times 30^{1/2}$
$$= 26.52 \text{ meters.}$$

(3) $\quad R = 0.4804\dfrac{Q^{1/3}}{f^{1/3}} = 0.4804 \times \dfrac{30^{1/3}}{1^{1/3}}$
$$= 1.5 \text{ meters.}$$

From the properties of a trapezoidal section, assuming side-slopes as 1/2 : 1 (near elliptical shape)

$$R = \frac{A}{P} = \left(\frac{B + \dfrac{d}{2}}{P}\right)d$$

But, $P = B + 2.24 \, d \quad \therefore \quad B = P - 2.24 \, d$

Substituting the values,

$$R = \frac{\left(P - 2.24d + \dfrac{d}{2}\right)d}{P}$$

$$PR - Pd + 1.74 \, d^2 = 0$$

$$d = \frac{P \pm \sqrt{P^2 - 6.96 \, PR}}{3.48}$$

Substituting these values of P and R already obtained, we get

Depth = 1.83 meters

Bed width = P – 2.24 d = 26.52 – 2.24 × 1.83
= 22.42 meters.

So, the final section is 22.42 × 1.83 m with a longitudinal slope of 0.00017.

1.(d) Various Cause of Disintegration of Water Bound Macadam and Surface Treated (Asphalt Roads):
1. Inadequate stability or strength
2. **Loss of** Binding Action
3. Loss of Base Course Materials

4. Inadequate Weaving Course
5. Use of Inferior Materials
6. Lack of Lateral Confinement for the Granular Base Course.

1. **Inadequate Stability or Strength:** Poor Mix proportioning or inadequate thickness are main reasons for the lack of stability or strength of sub-base or base course.

2. **Loss of Binding Action:** Due to internal movements of aggregate in sub-base a base course layers under the stress applications, the component structures of the layer get disturbed. There is also loss of binding action resulting in low stability and poor load transmitting property of the pavement layer.

3. **Loss of Base Course Materials:** The loss of base course materials is only possible when either the base course is not covered with a weaving course or the weaving course has completely worn out. This causes removal of binding material in WBM base and the stones aggregator are left in a loose state.

4. **Inadequate Weaving Course:** Absence of weaving course or inadequate thickness or stability of weaving course expose the base course to the damaging effect of climatic variation mainly due to rains, frost action and the traffic.

5. **Use of Inferior Materials:** Many failures, mainly structural failure are attributed due to use of inferior materials in the passing jobs.

6. **Lack of Lateral Confinement for the Granular Base Course:** Due to lack of lateral confinement of granular base course, deterioration occurs.

Main faults occurring in WBM and surface treated (asphalt) roads:

(1) Alligator cracking
(2) Consolidation of pavement layers
(3) Shear failure
(4) Longitudinal cracking
(5) Frost heaving
(6) Lack of binding to lowers course
(7) Reflection crushing
(8) Formation of waves and corrugation

2.(a) (i) Tack Coat and Prime Coat: A tack coat is a very light application of asphalt, usually asphalt emulsion diluted with water, used to ensure a bond between the surface being paved and the overlying course. It is important that each layer in

Fig. Typical cross section of a conventional flexible pavement (1 in. = 25.4 mm).

an asphalt pavement be bonded to the layer below. Tack coats are also used to bond the asphalt layer to a PCC base or an old asphalt pavement. The three essential requirements of a tack coat are that it must be very thin, it must uniformaly cover the entire surface to be paved, and it must be allowed to break or cure before the HMA is laid.

A prime coat is an application of low-viscosity cutback asphalt to an absorbent surface, such as an untreated granular base on which an asphalt layer will be placed. Its purpose is to bind the granular base to the asphalt layer. The difference between a tack coat and a prime coat is that a tack coat does not require the penetration of asphalt into the underlying layer, whereas a prime coat penetrates into the underlying layer, plugs the voids, and forms a watertight surface. Although the type and quantity of asphalt used are quite different, both are spray applications.

(ii) Bituminous concrete is a type of constru-ction material used for paving roads, driveways, and parking lots. It's made from a blend of stone and other forms of aggregate materials joined together by a binding agent. This binding agent is called "bitumen" and is a by-product of petroleum refining. It has a thick, sticky texture like tar when heated, then forms a dense solid surface once it dries. Bituminous concrete is also widely known as asphalt in many parts of the world.

Despite its name, this material is quite different than standard concrete, and contains no cement. While most cement-based surfaces are white or gray, bituminous concrete is known for its distinctive black appearance. It is often laid right over a gravel base layer to form new roads and parking lots, but may also be poured over existing concrete to repair or smooth out bumps and voids. Once the bituminous concrete has been poured onto the roadway, installers use large paving machines to smooth and compact the surface.

While asphalt paving doesn't offer the same strength as traditional concrete, it's still the most popular material for most paving applications. Bituminous concrete is strong enough to handle years of vehicle traffic, and is relatively easy to repair or refinish. It also provides a smoother and quieter ride than cement surfaces, which helps to reduce noise pollution around highways and other busy roads.

Bituminous Macadam is a pavement constructed by spreading two or more layers of crushed stone on a suitable base and pouring a bituminous binder on each. Macadam is a very old road. Basically, macadam is densely packed rock layered together. They usually bind it together with tar or bitumen. Macadam was used before asphalt.

Bituminous Macadam (BM) shall consist of mineral aggregate and appropriate binder, mixed in a hot mix plant and laid with a mechanized paver. It is an open graded mixture suitable for base course. It is laid in a single course or in a multiple layers on a previously prepared base.

Thickness of the single layer shall be 50 mm to 100 mm.

Since the bituminous macadam is an open-graded mixture there is a potential that it may trap water or moisture vapour within the pavement system. Therefore, providing proper drainage outlet to the BM layer should be considered to prevent moisture-induce damage to the BM and adjacent bituminous layers.

2.(b)

B.S.(m)	F.S.(m)	H.I.(m)	R.L.(m)
1.625		388.625	387.0
2.345	1.315	389.655	387.31
2.045	3.56	388.14	386.095
2.955	2.355	388.74	385.785

H.I. at last position of instrument = 388.74 m

R.L. of first peg = 384.50 m

Staff reading at first peg

$$= 388.74 - 384.5 = 4.24 \text{ m}$$

Therefore,

Staff reading at second peg

$$= 4.24 - 30 \times \frac{1}{100} = 3.94 \text{ m}$$

2.(c) Theodolite Errors:

- The trunnion axis is not perpendicular to the vertical axis.
- The line of sight is not perpendicular to the trunnion axis.
- The vertical axis is not plumb.
- The vertical angle collimation is out of adjustment.

The trunnion axis is not perpendicular to the vertical axis

When the scope is turning about the trunnion axis, the line of sight should sweep through a vertical plane. If the trunnion axis is not perpendicular to the vertical axis, then this plane will be deflected. On level ground, the error may be very small, but traversing up or down a steep hill will increase the error.

In the formula below, δ is the clockwise horizontal deflection of the line of sight from the scale reading, φ is the true zenith angle, and α is the clockwise deflection of the trunnion axis from the perpendicular. The line of sight must be projected onto the horizontal plane in order to measure the deflection error. Note that δ goes to zero and then changes sign as φ passes 90°.

$$\delta = \sin^{-1}(\cot\varphi\,\tan\alpha)$$

Here is the best reason for reading both sides. When the scope is inverted, the line of sight still travels through an oblique plane, but now it is listing in the opposite direction. On the uphill backsight, the scale reading now misses to the right. On the downhill foresight, it misses to the left. The result of the inverted reading is an angle that is too small, compensating for the error in the direct reading.

The line of sight is not perpendicular to the trunnion axis

Suppose now that the trunnion axis is perpendicular to the vertical axis, but the line of sight is not perpendicular to the trunnion axis. This condition is not actually cause by a poorly mounted telescope. It is more likely a misalignment of the crosshair reticule inside the scope.

This time when the scope turns on the trunnion axis, the line of sight sweeps a cone rather than a plane. While the scope is in the direct position, the deflection is always in the same direction, but variable in magnitude. On steep ground, it even has a tendency to take care of itself, because the backsight and foresight may have close to the same deflection. The worst error occurs when one sight is much steeper than the other.

In this formula, δ is the clockwise horizontal deflection of the line of sight from the scale reading, φ is the true zenith angle, and β is the deflection of the line of sight toward the right end of the trunnion axis in the direct position. The line of sight is again projected onto the level plane.

$$\delta = \sin^{-1}\left(\frac{\sin\beta}{\sin\varphi}\right)$$

Here the deflection is least on level sights, but it is never zero and does not change sign as φ passes the horizon at 90°. Again, inverting the scope provides a reading with compensating error. The conic locus is moved to the opposite side, and in the deflection formula, the sign changes.

The vertical axis is not plumb

Of the three horizontal errors, this one is, perhaps, the least significant and the easiest to correct. It is only a matter of levelling the instrument properly. Unfortunately though, this is one case in which the transiting capability of the theodolite does nothing to correct the error.

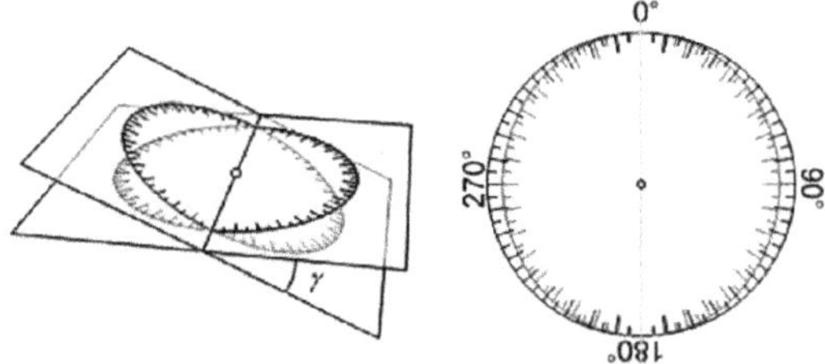

In this image, the black scale is level and shows the true direction, but the tilted blue scale is the one that is actually being read. There is a line of intersection running through the middle of both scales. This line of intersection is arbitrarily given a direction of 0° here, but it has no relationship to the direction in which the instrument is pointed. The error can be observed by projecting the true scale onto the plane of the instrument scale. The (red) projection is elliptical, and the scales coincide only when the line of sight is along or perpendicular to the line of intersection (0°, 90°, 180° and 270°).

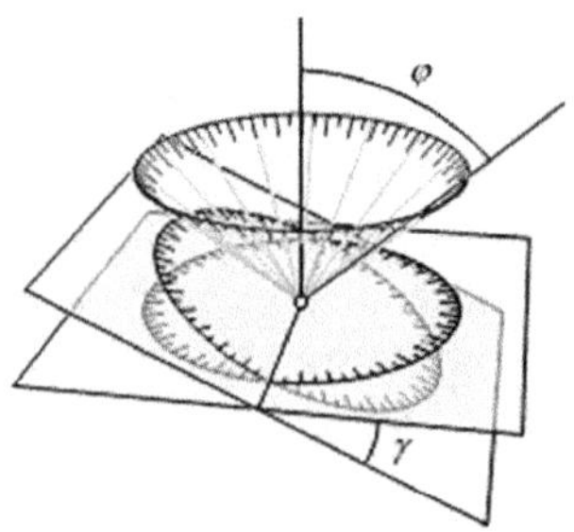

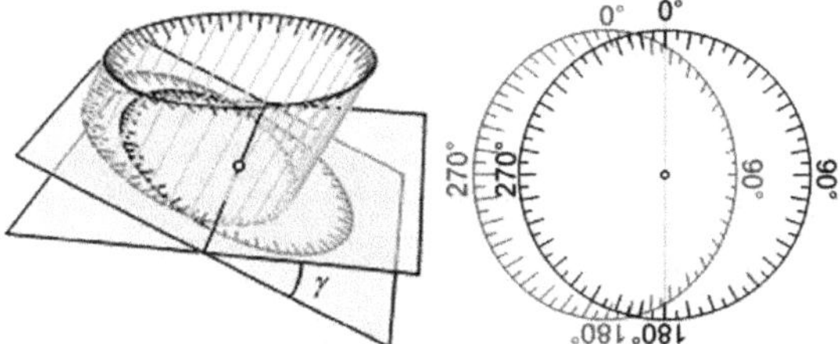

That is not where it ends. That simplified description assumes that the line of sight is level. Suppose that the instrument is pointed upward or downward. As the instrument turns, assuming a constant φ, the locus of the line of sight is a cone with a vertical axis. When the true scale is projected onto this cone, it is still true. This scale in turn is projected onto the plane of the instrument scale. The result is a translation of the elliptical scale above, and it is true only when the line of sight is perpendicular to the line of intersection (90° and 270°).

The geometric transformation of the scale is not really so complicated, but the corresponding analytic formula is. This is no bother since the formula has no practical value anyway. Here δ is again the deflection of the line of sight from the scale reading and φ is the true zenith angle. The variable θ represents the true clockwise horizontal angle from the line of intersection of the two planes. When the instrument is pointed in the direction of the line of intersection, with the "vertical" axis listing to the right, then θ is 0°.

$$\delta = \sin^{-1}\left(\frac{\cos\gamma\,\sin\theta\,\cos\theta - \cot\varphi\,\sin\gamma\,\cos\theta - \sin\theta\,\cos\theta}{\sqrt{(\cos\gamma\,\sin\theta - \cot\varphi\,\sin\gamma)^2 + \cos^2\theta}}\right)$$

The condition described here is an issue of levelling, and transiting the instrument does nothing to compensate for it. Check the level vials frequently.

The vertical angle collimation is out of adjustment

Theodolites measure vertical angles, usually from the zenith direction, sometimes from the horizon, rarely from the nadir. This difference affects nothing but the arithmetic. The vertical axis should point to the zenith, but for greater precision, theodolites have separate collimation systems so that the angle is referenced directly to the gravity vector. This system may use a levelling vial or a pendulum compensator, either of which can go out of adjustment.

If a vertical angle is measured in both direct and inverted positions, then the sum of the observations should be 360°. The collimation error, ε, will either add to both observations or subtract from both, so it will show up in the sum of the two angles. In this picture, two observations are made on the same stationary target. The measured vertical angle is φ_1 in the direct position, and φ_2 in the inverted position. Find ε using the formula below, and subtract it from the direct observation to get the true vertical angle. In the illustration, both measured angles are too small, and ε is negative.

$$\varepsilon = \frac{1}{2}(\varphi_1 + \varphi_2 - 360°)$$

A few seconds, or even minutes, of error here makes no appreciable difference in horizontal distances, but it can play all havoc with elevations. Unlike the horizontal angle errors, this one is constant, which is to say, it is not affected by changes in the direction of the sight. That makes it a fairly simple matter to correct the angle without even adjusting the instrument.

2.(*d*)

$$N = 100$$
$$q_s = 75 \text{ N/mm}^2$$
$$P = 250 \text{ kW} = 250 \times 10^3 \text{ Watts}$$
$$= 250 \times 10^3 \text{ N-m/sec}$$
$$= 250 \times 10^6 \text{ N-mm/sec}$$

From the relation,

$$P = \frac{2\pi NT}{60}$$

$$250 \times 10^6 = \frac{2\pi \times 100T}{60}$$

We get,

$$T = 23.8732 \times 10^6 \text{ N-mm}$$

From torsion formula,

$$T = J\frac{q_s}{R} = \frac{\pi}{32}d^4\frac{q_s}{d/2}$$

$$= \frac{\pi}{16}d^3 q_s$$

$$\therefore \quad 23.8732 \times 10^6 = \frac{\pi}{16}d^3 \times 75$$

or, $\qquad d = 117.473$ mm

Let d_1 be the outer diameter of hollow shaft and d_2 inner diameter.

$$\therefore \qquad d_2 = 0.6d_1$$

$$T = \frac{\pi}{32}\left[d_1^4 - (0.6d_1)^4\right]\frac{q_s}{d_1/2}$$

$$\therefore \ 23.8732 \times 10^6 = \frac{\pi}{16}(1 - 0.6^4)d_1^3 \times 75$$

$$\therefore \qquad\qquad d_1 = 123.036 \text{ mm}$$

$$\therefore \qquad\qquad d_2 = 73.822 \text{ mm}$$

$\therefore$ Cross-sectional area of hollow shaft

$$= \frac{\pi}{4} \times (d_1^2 - d_2^2) = 7609.164 \text{ mm}^2$$

and Cross-sectional area of solid shaft $= \frac{\pi}{4} \times d^2$

$$= 10838.421 \text{ mm}^2$$

% saving in weight

$$= \frac{\begin{array}{c}\text{Weight of solid shaft} -\\ \text{Weight of hollow shaft}\end{array}}{\text{Weight of solid shaft}} \times 100$$

$$= \frac{(10838.421 - 7609.164)\rho L}{10838.421 \times \rho L} \times 100$$

$$= 29.795$$

3. (a) (i) $\qquad$ Pu $= 1.5 \times 1500 = 2250$ kN

$\qquad$ length $= 1 \times 3.5 = 3.5$ m $= 3500$ mm

$$\frac{l_{eff}}{450} = 7.78 \ \Delta^2 \qquad\qquad \text{Short col.}$$

(ii) Min. eccentricity

$$e_{min} = \frac{l_{eff}}{500} + \frac{D}{30} = \frac{3500}{500} + \frac{450}{30} = 22 \text{ mm}$$

or, $\qquad$ 20 mm

22 mm $< .05D$

22 < 22.5 ok

(iii) $\qquad$ Pu $= 1.05 \,(.40\, f_{ck}\, A_c + .67 + f_y\, A_{sc})$

$$2250 \times 10^3 = 1.05 \left(.40 \times 25 \times \frac{\pi}{4}(450^2)\right)$$

$$+ (.67 \times 415 - .4 \times 25 \, A_{sc})$$

$$A_{sc} = 2061 \text{ mm}^2.$$

Use 16 mm ϕ

$$\text{No of bars} = \frac{2061}{\frac{\pi}{4}(16)^2} = 10.25 = 11$$

(iv) Design of helical R/F

(1) $\qquad A_g = \frac{\pi}{4}(450)^2 = 159043 \text{ mm}^2$

(2) $\qquad A_c = \frac{\pi}{4}(450 - 50)^2 = 107521 \text{ mm}^2$

(3) $\qquad V_c = 1000 \times A_c = 107521000$

$$V_n = \frac{1000}{p} \times (\pi \times (370 - 8)) \times \frac{\pi}{4}(8)^2$$

$$= \frac{57164749}{p}$$

$$.36\frac{f_{ck}}{f_y}\left(\frac{A_g}{A_c} - 1\right) \leq \frac{v_h}{v_c}$$

$$.36 \times \frac{25}{415} \times \left(\frac{159043}{107521} - 1\right) \leq \frac{57164749}{p \times 107521000}$$

$$p = 51 \text{ mm}$$

Check $= 1.$ $\quad p \not> 75$ mm

$\qquad\qquad 2.$ $\quad p \not> \dfrac{\phi c}{6} = \dfrac{370}{6} = 61$ mm

$\qquad\qquad 3.$ $\quad p \not< 25$

$\qquad\qquad 4.$ $\quad p \not< (3 \times 8)$

3. (b) $\qquad\qquad P_f = 600$

$$q_u = 200 \text{ kN/m}^2$$

Total load $P = 1.1 p_f$

$$= 1.1 \times 600$$

$$= 660 \text{ kN}$$

Area of footing

$$A_c = \frac{w}{q_u} = \frac{660}{200} = 3.3 \text{ m}^2$$

Assume square footing

$$B^2 = 3.3 \text{ m}^2$$
$$B = 1.81 \text{ m}^2$$

Adopt $\quad$ B = 2 × m

1. Check for one-way shear

$$w_o = \frac{P}{A} = \frac{1.5 \times 600 \times 10^3}{2000 \times 2000}$$
$$= .225 \text{ N/mm}^2.$$

$$\alpha = \frac{B - 300}{2} - d = 850 - d$$

$$\tau_v = \frac{w_o \, \alpha B}{B \times d}, \quad B = 1 \text{ m}$$

$$\tau_v = \frac{.225(850 - d)}{d}$$

$$\tau_v < \tau_c$$

Assume $\qquad$ Pst = .15% $\qquad \because \tau_c = .19$

$$\frac{.225(850 - d)}{d} \le .19$$

$$191.25 - .225d \le .19d$$
$$d > 460.84 \text{ mm}$$
$$d = 470 \text{ mm}$$

2. Check for two way shear

$$x = 300 + d$$
$$y = 300 + d$$

$$\tau_v = \frac{.225 \times \left((2000)^2 - (300 + d)^2\right)}{2(2(300 + d))d}$$

$$\tau_v < k_s \, \tau_c \qquad k_s = 1$$

$$\tau_v < .25\sqrt{25} \quad \tau = .25\sqrt{f_{ck}}$$

$$\tau_v \le 1.25$$

$$.225 \times (2000 - (300 + d)^2)$$
$$\le 1.25 \times 4 \,(300 + d)d$$
$$d \ge 282.64$$

3. Check from BM Consideration

$$\alpha = \frac{2000 - 300}{2} = 850$$

$$BM = \frac{w \circ d^2}{2} = \frac{.225 \times 850^2}{2}$$

$$BM \le .138 \, f_{ck} \, Bd^2$$

$$\frac{.225 \times 850^2}{2} \le .138 \times 25 \times 1000 \times d^2$$

$$d > 23.55$$

$\because$ Take d_{max} from (1), (2) & (3)

$$d = 470 \text{ mm}$$

3. (c) Factors Affecting Field Compaction of Soil: There are many factors which influence the degree of compaction in the field. Some are compactor dependent and some depend on the soil being compacted. The factors which affect the degree of compaction are given below.

1. Type of Soil: Type of soil has a great influence on its compaction characteristics. Normally, heavy clays, clays & silts offer higher resistance to compaction where as sandy soils and coarse grained or gravelly soils are amenable for easy compaction. The coarse grained soils yield higher densities in comparison to clays. A well graded soil can be compacted to higher density.

2. Compactive Effort/Compactive Energy: The term compactive effort or compactive energy simply means type of equipment or machinery used for compaction. Greater the compactive effort, greater will be the compaction. The equipments used for compaction of soil can be broadly classified into the following categories:

1. Kneading type equipment
2. Static type equipment
3. Dynamic or impact type equipment
4. Vibratory type equipment.

Type of compaction equipment to be used is mainly dependent upon the type of soil to be compacted. The following table can be used as a reference to decide type of equipment for different type of soil.

Type of soil	Suggested Equipment/ Machinery
Crushed rock, gravelly sand	Smooth wheel roller
Gravels, sand	Rubber tyred roller
Sands, gravel, silty soil, clayey soils	Pneumatic tyred roller
Silty soil, Clayey soil	Sheepfoot roller
Soils in confined zone	Rammer
Sands	Vibratory roller

3. **Layer Thickness/Thickness of Lift:** Degree of compaction is inversely proportional to the layer thickness, *i.e.* for a given compactive energy, thicker layer will be less compacted as compared to thin layer. The reason is, for thicker soil layer the energy input per unit weight is less. Therefore, it is very important to decide the right thickness of each layer to achieve the desired density. Thickness of layer is dependent upon several other factors such as:

- Type of soil
- Type of roller
- Weight of roller
- Contact pressure of drum
- So on …..

Generally 200 to 300 mm layer thickness is used in the field to achieve homogeneous compaction.

4. **Number of Roller Passes:** It is obvious that density increases as the no. of roller passes increases. But there are two important things we have to remember.

1. After certain number of roller passes, there is no further increase in density.
2. More number of roller passes means more cost of project.

So, it is very crucial to determine the number of roller passes for a given type of equipment, for a given type of soil at optimum moisture content. Therefore, field compaction trial is carried out to economise compaction aspect of earthwork, while achieving desired level of density based on Lab tests (Heavy compaction test, IS:2720-Part-8 and relative density test, IS:2720-Part -14).

5. **Moisture Content:** Proper control of moisture content in soil is necessary for achieving desired density. Maximum density with minimum compacting effort can be achieved by compaction of soil near its OMC (Optimum Moisture Content). In the field the Natural Moisture Content (NMC) of soil is either less than OMC or above OMC. If NMC of the soil is less than OMC, calculated amount of water should be added to soil with sprinkler attached to water tanker and mixed with soil by motor grader for uniform moisture content. When NMC of the soil is more than OMC, it is required to be dried by aeration to reach up to OMC.

6. **Contact Pressure:** Contact pressure depends on the weight of the roller wheel and the contact area. In case of pneumatic roller, the tyre inflation pressure also determines the contact pressure in addition to wheel load. A higher contact pressure increases the dry density and lowers the optimum moisture content.

7. **Speed of Rolling:** Speed of rolling has a very important bearing on the roller output. There are two important things we have to consider:

- First, the greater the speed of rolling, the more length of embankment can be compacted in one day.
- Second, at greater speed there is likely to be insufficient time for the desired deformations to take place and more passes may be required to achieve the required compaction.

So, we need to make a balance between these two things. Generally, the speed of all rollers is limited to about 5 km/hour. In case of vibratory roller speed was found to be significant factor because its number of a vibration per minute is not related to its forward speed. Therefore, the slower the speed of travel, the more vibrations at a given point and lesser number of pass required to attain a given density.

4.(a) Typical classification of solid waste was suggested by Hosetti and Kumar and it is as follows:

1. *Garbage:* Putrecible wastes from food, slaughterhouses, canning and freezing industries.
2. *Rubbish:* Non-putrecible wastes either combustible or non-combustible. These include wood, paper, rubber, leather and garden wastes as combustible wastes whereas the non-combustible wastes include glass, metal, ceramics, stones and soil.
3. *Ashes:* Residues of combustion, solid products after heating and cooking or incineration by the municipal, industrial, hospital and apartments areas.
4. *Large wastes:* Demolition and construction wastes, automobiles, furnitures, refrigerators and other home appliances, trees, fires etc.
5. *Dead animals:* Households pets, birds, rodents, zoo animals, and anatomical and pathological tissues from hospitals.
6. *Sewage sludges:* These include screening wastes, settled solids and sludges.
7. *Industrial wastes:* Chemicals, paints, sand and explosives.
8. *Mining wastes:* Tailings, slug ropes, culm piles at mine areas.
9. *Agricultural wastes:* Farm animal manure, crop residues and others.

Traditionally, these wastes are categorized into the following five types:

1. *Residential:* It refers to wastes generated mainly from dwelling, apartments, and consisted of left over food scrapes, vegetables, peeled material, plastics, wood pieces, clothes and ashes.
2. *Commercial:* This mainly consists of grocery materials, leftover food, glasses, and metals, ashes generated from stores, hotels, markets, shops and medical facilities.
3. *Institutional:* The wastes generated from schools, colleges and offices include, paper, plastics, and glasses.
4. *Municipal:* This includes dust, leaf litter, building debris and treatment plant sediments. These arise from various activities like demolition, construction, street cleaning, land scraping etc.
5. *Agricultural:* This mainly includes spoiled foodgrains, vegetables, grass, litter etc., generated from fields and farms.

Classification Based on Type:

Refuse: This is all putrecible and non-putrecible waste except body wastes. It includes all types of rubbish and garbage.

Rubbish: This refers to that portion of the refuse, which is non-putrecible solid waste such as packaging materials.

Garbage: This refers to that portion of the refuse, which is putrecible component of solid waste. These are produced during cooking and storage of meet, fruits and vegetables.

Bulky wastes: These include household wastes, which cannot be accommodated in the normal storage containers and need a special collection mechanism. These include, household appliances such as refrigerators, washing machine, furniture, vehicle parts, tyres, trees, wood branches etc.

Street wastes: This includes wastes collected from streets, walkways, parks, playgrounds, which include paper, cardboard, plastics, leaves and other vegetable matter in large quantities.

Dead animals: These include dead animals those die naturally or accidentally killed on the road. This category does not include carcasses and animal parts from slaughterhouses, which may be regarded as commercial or industrial components. Many times as in

India, the large animals if died and are not lifted on right time then they may pose a threat to public health through attracting flies and produce bad odour and create an unhygienic scene.

Hazardous wastes: Hazardous wastes are those produced in the industries, institutes, hospitals and laboratories. These are dangerous to the living organisms immediately or in the long run to the environment in which they are disposed. The hazard may be due to their physical, chemical, biological and radioactive characteristics like, ignitibility, corrosivity, reactivity and toxicity. In some cases various chemicals and their mixtures act as hazardous wastes. Those may be pesticides, solvents, acids and bases. Certain hazardous wastes may cause explosions in the incinerators and fires at the landfill sites. Other hazardous waste includes pathological wastes from hospitals and radioactive wastes, which require special handling. A good management practice should ensure that hazardous wastes are stored, collected, transported and disposed separately after suitable treatment.

Sewage Sludge: The sewage treatment plants produce huge amounts of sludge during primary and secondary phase of treatment, these are sticky and rich in pathogens require proper treatment. These are both inorganic and organic. The bulk of dewatered and digested sludge can be used as organic fertilizer or it may be burnt to produce energy.

The six general methods of solid waste disposal are:

1. Open dumps
2. Sanitary landfill
3. Incineration
4. Onsite disposal
5. Feeding of garbage to swine
6. Composting

1. **Open dumps:** Open dumps are by far the oldest and most prevalent method of disposing of solid wastes. In a recent survey, 371 cities out of 1,118 surveyed stated that this method was emphasized within their jurisdictions. In many cases, the dump sites are located indiscriminately wherever land can be obtained for this purpose. Practices at open dumps differ. In some dumps, the refuse is periodically levelled and compacted; in other dumps the refuse is piled as high as equipment will permit. At some sites, the solid wastes are ignited and allowed to burn to reduce volume. In general, though, little effort is expended to prevent the nuisance and health hazards that frequently accompany open dumps.

2. **Sanitary landfill:** Sanitary landfill consists of alternate layers of compacted refuse and soil. Each day the refuse is deposited, compacted, and covered with a layer of soil. Two types of sanitary landfill are common: area landfill on essentially flat land sites, and depression landfill in natural or manmade ravines, gulleys, or pits. Depth of the landfill depends largely on local conditions, types of equipment, availability of land, and other such factors, but it commonly ranges from about 7 feet to as much as 40 feet as practiced by New York City.

3. **Incineration:** Incineration is the process of reducing combustible wastes to inert residue by burning at high temperatures of about $1,700°$ to $1,800°F$. At these temperatures all combustible materials are consumed, leaving a residue of ash and non-combustibles having a volume of 5 to 25 per cent of the original volume.

4. **Onsite disposal:** With the increasing rate of production of solid wastes in the urban environment, there is a growing trend toward handling this waste in the home, apartment and institution. Onsite disposal has become increasingly popular during the past decade as a way of minimizing the waste problem at its source. Most widely used devices for onsite disposal are incinerators and garbage grinders.

5. Swine feed: The feeding of garbage to swine has been an accepted way of disposing of the garbage part of solid wastes from urban areas for quite some time. Even as late as 1960, this method was employed in 110 American cities out of 1,118 cities surveyed on their solid-waste-disposal practices. In addition to the municipal practices of using garbage for swine feed, many cities and municipalities permit private haulers to service restaurants and institutions to collect garbage for swine feed. The feeding of raw garbage led to a wide-spread virus disease in the middle 1950's, which affected more than 400,000 swine.

6. Composting: Composting is the biochemical decomposition of organic materials to a humuslike material. As practiced for solid-waste disposal, it is the rapid but partial decomposition of the moist, solid-organic matter by aerobic organisms under controlled conditions. The end product is useful as a solid conditioner and fertilizer. The process is normally carried out in mechanical digesters.

4.(b) For dynamic similarity Froude number must be the same in the model and prototype. If L_r is the length ratio, then

(i) $$V_r = \frac{V_m}{V_p} = \sqrt{L_r}$$

$$V_p = \frac{V_m}{\sqrt{L_r}} = 2\sqrt{20} = 8.94 \text{ m/s}$$

(ii) Ratio of discharge per unit width

$$= q_r = \frac{(Q/L)_m}{(Q/L)_p}$$

$$q_r = \frac{Q_r}{L_r} = V_r L_r = L_r^{3/2}$$

$$q_p = \frac{q_m}{L_r^{3/2}} = 0.30 \times (20)^{3/2}$$

$$= 26.83 \text{ m}^3/\text{s/m}$$

(*iii*) Pressure ratio

$$p_r = (L_r \rho_r)$$

Assume $\rho_m = \rho_p$, *i.e.* $\rho_r = 1.0$

Hence, $p_r = L_r$

$\therefore$ $p_p = p_m/L_r = 5 \times 20$

$$= 100 \text{ cm of mercury}$$

(*iv*) Power ratio = (Energy loss/second)$_r$

$$= [L_r^{7/2} \rho_r]$$

As $\rho_r = 1.5$ (assumed), $P_r = L_r^{7/2}$

$$P_m = P_p \cdot L_r^{7/2}$$

$$= 1500 \times \left(\frac{1}{20}\right)^{7/2} = 0.042 \text{ W}$$

4.(c) $$D_1 = 35 \text{ cm} = .35 \text{ m}$$

$$N = 1050 \text{ rpm}$$

$$B_1 = .07 \text{ m}$$

$$V_d = 1.5 \text{ m/s}$$

$$V_s = 2.5 \text{ m/sec.}$$

Tangential velocity

$$v_1 = \frac{\pi \times D_1 N}{60}$$

$$= \frac{\pi \times .35 \times 1050}{60}$$

$$= 19.24 \text{ m/s.}$$

Vanes are radial = $V_{w1} = V_1 = 19.24 \text{ m/s}$

$$H_m = \frac{V_{w_1} v_1}{g} \eta_{mano} [V_{w_1-v_1}]$$

$$H_m = \frac{v_1^2}{g} = \frac{(19.24)}{9.81} = 37.735 \text{ m}$$

$$H_m = h_s + h_d + h_f \times d + \frac{vd^2}{2g}$$

$$H_m = H_m \times \left(H_m - \frac{vd^2}{2g}\right)$$

$$= 37.735 - \frac{1.5^2}{2 \times 9.81} = 37.62 \text{ m}$$

$$\text{Power} = \frac{\rho g Q H m}{75 \times 90} \qquad Q = \pi DBV_f$$

$$= \frac{100 \times 9.81 \times (\pi \times .35 \times .07 \times 3) \times 37.735}{75 \times 9.81}$$

$$= 116.177 \text{ Hp}$$

4.(d) The raw materials of cement combine chemically in the kiln to produce cement that has properties completely different from their own. The four important constituents and their properties are summarised in Table.

Types of Cement: The classification of cements is based on their main constituents, for example, Portland–fly ash cement and Portland–pozzolana cement. The European Standard EN 197-1:2000 lists five types of cement that have a wide range of permitted constituents:

- CEM I: Portland cement;
- CEM II: Portland composite cement;
- CEM III: Blast-furnace cement;
- CEM IV: Pozzolanic cement;
- CEM V: Composite cement.

Table: Properties of the Main Constituents of Cement

Name	*Chemical formula*	*% in OPC*	*Properties*
Tricalcium silicate	$3CaO.SiO_2$	45	Short setting time; high early strength
Dicalcium silicate	$2CaO.SiO_2$	28	Long setting time; slow strength development but increases the durability of hardened cement
Tricalcium aluminate	$3CaO.Al_2O_3$	11	Quick setting (delayed by gypsum); attacked by sulphates
Tetracalcium aluminoferrite	$4CaO.Al_2O_3.Fe_2O_3$	9	This constituent has no contribution to setting or strength

Portland Cement CEM I: Formerly known as Ordinary Portland Cement (OPC), CEM I is manufactured to conform to British Standard BS EN 197-1:2000. It is the most commonly used cement in construction work throughout the world. The three strength classes of Portland cement, *i.e.*, 32.5, 42.5 and 52.5, correspond to their lower characteristic strength in MPa (1 MPa = 1 N/mm^2) at 28 days. Where early strength of concrete is required, Portland cement 32.5R or 42.5R or 52.5R can be used. These cements are more finely ground than 32.5 N or 42.5 N or 52.5 N cements to enable faster hydration in the early stages.

CEM I cements are easy to procure, and concretes/mortars made using CEM I are versatile and durable. One major disadvantage is that, due to a high proportion of cement clinker, this is the least sustainable type of cement.

Factory-made Composite Cements: Factory-made cements (CEM II, CEM III, CEM IV and CEM V) have Portland cement clinker varying from 5% to 94% (by mass) and one or more additional constituents. The additional constituents are selected from materials such as fly ash (PFA), blast-furnace slag, limestone and pozzolanic materials to reduce the environmental impact and promote sustainability. Some of these are described here; for more information, refer to BS EN 197-1:2000 and Lafarge Cement's publications.

Portland-Fly Ash Cement: Fly ash (PFA) is produced when coal is burnt in coal-fired power stations and furnaces. Fly ash has high silica and alumina content and is added to Portland cement to produce:

1. CEM II/A-V, which contains 6-20% siliceous fly ash.
2. CEM II/B-V, which contains 21-35% siliceous fly ash.

Calcareous fly ash may also be used to produce CEM II/A-W and CEM II/B-W cements. The use of fly ash in cement increases the strength and durability, improves sulphate resistance and reduces the heat of hydration, the risk of alkali-silica reaction and efflorescence. The use of fly ash has several environmental benefits as well, for example, recycling a waste by-product of coal-fired power stations.

Portland-Slag Cement: Blast-furnance slag is a by-product of iron production. The slag is quenched in water to produce glassy granules that are similar to sand in appearance. Before mixing with Portland cement, the slag is dried and ground to a fineness that is similar to that of cement. There are two types of Portland-slag cement:

1. CEM II/A-S, which contains 6-20% slag.

2. CEM II/B-S, which contains 21-35% slag.

The use of blast-furnace slag in cement improves the sulphate resistance of concrete, workability and resistance to alkali-silica reaction. As with fly ash, the use of blast-furnace slag reduces the environmental impact by recycling the waste by-product of iron production.

5.(a) Ist layer (0 – 3 m)

Cohesion $c' = 0$

$$\varphi = 30$$

Unit wt $\gamma = 18 \text{ kN/m}^2$

2nd layer (3 – 9 m)

$C = 0, \quad \varphi = 35°, \gamma = 20 \text{ kN/m}^3$

$$k_a = \frac{1-\sin\varphi}{1+\sin\varphi} = \frac{1-\sin 30}{1+\sin 30} = 0.33$$

$$k_{a2} = \frac{1-\sin 35}{1+\sin 35} = .271$$

Total earth pressure on wall.

$$P_a = \frac{1}{2} \times k_{a1} \times y_1 \times z_1^2$$

$$(Pa)_{\text{Top}} = \frac{1}{2} \times k_{a1} \times y_1 \times 0 = 0$$

$$(Pa)_{a+3m} = \frac{1}{2} \times k_a \times y_1 \times 3^2$$

$$= 26.73 \text{ kN/m}$$

For layer (3 – 9 m)

$$\sigma_{at}\ 9\ m = \frac{1}{2}k_{az} + y_1 z_1^2 + \frac{1}{z}k_{az}y_2 z_2^2$$

$$= .5 \times .271 \times 18 \times 9 + .5 \times .271 \times 20 \times 36$$

$$= 119.511 \text{ kN/m.}$$

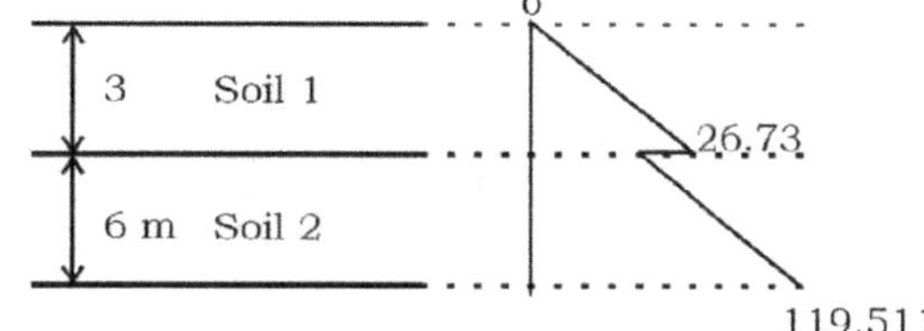

5.(b)

$$(\gamma_b)_{\text{sand}} = \frac{(G+es)\gamma_w}{1+e} \quad \text{let } \gamma_w = 9.81 \text{ kN/m}^3$$

$$= \frac{(2.65+0.6\times 0.4)\times 9.81}{1+0.6}$$

$$= 17.72 \text{ km}$$

$$(\gamma_{\text{sat}})_{\text{sand}} = \frac{(G+e)\gamma_w}{1+e}$$

$$= \frac{(2.65+0.6)\times 9.81}{1+0.6}$$

$$= 19.93 \text{ kN/m}^3$$

$$(\gamma_{\text{sat}})_{\text{clay}} = \frac{(2.7+0.7)\times 9.81}{1.7}$$

$$= 19.62 \text{ kN/m}^3$$

Total stress

$$\sigma_A = 0$$

$$\sigma_B = \gamma_b \times 2 = 17.72 \times 2 = 35.44 \text{ kN/m}^2$$

$$\sigma_C = \gamma_b \times 2 + [\gamma_{\text{sat}}]_{\text{sand}} \times 4$$

$$= 17.72 \times 2 + 19.93 \times 4$$

$$= 115.16 \text{ kN/m}^2$$

$$\sigma_D = \gamma_b \times 2 + (\gamma_{\text{sat}})_{\text{sand}} \times 4$$

$$+ (\gamma_{\text{sat}})_{\text{clay}} \times 4$$

$$= 115.16 + 19.62 \times 4$$

$$= 193.64 \text{ kN/m}^2$$

Neutral Stress

$$u_A = 0$$

$$u_B = 0 \text{ (NOT saturated)}$$

$$u_C = \gamma_w \times 4 = 9.81 \times 4 = 39.24 \text{ kN/m}^2$$

$$u_D = \gamma_w \times 8 = 78.48 \text{ kN/m}^2$$

Effective Stress

$$\overline{\sigma} = \text{Total st.} - \text{Neutral st.}$$

$$\overline{\sigma}_A = 0 - 0 = 0$$

$$\overline{\sigma}_B = 35.44 - 0 = 35.44 \text{ kN/m}^2$$

$$\overline{\sigma}_C = 115.16 - 39.24 = 75.92 \text{ kN/m}^2$$

$$\overline{\sigma}_n = 193.64 - 78.48 = 115.16 \text{ kNm/m}^2$$

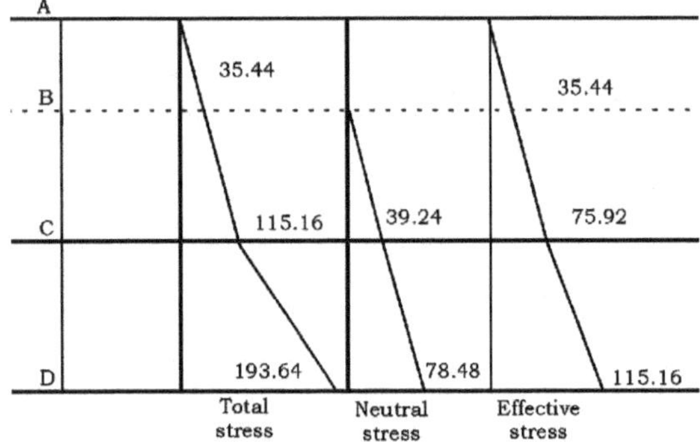

5.(c) Grit chambers are basin to remove the inorganic particles to prevent damage to the pumps, and to prevent their accumulation in sludge digestors.

Horizontal Velocity in Flow Though Grit Chamber: The settling of grit particles in the chamber is assumed as particles settling as individual entities and referred as Type–I settling. The grit chamber is divided in four compartments as inlet zone, outlet zone, settling zone and sludge zone (Figure).

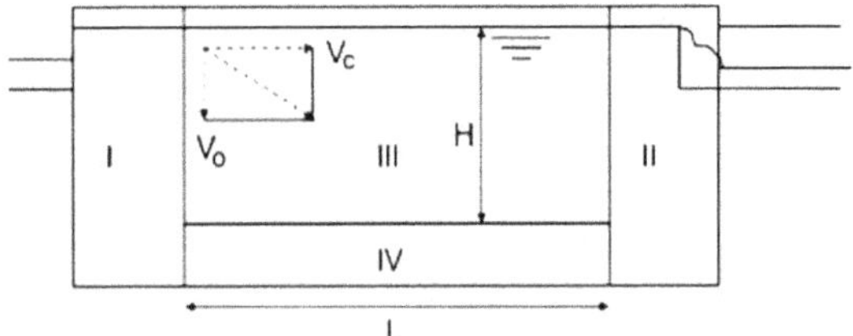

Fig. Compartments of grit chamber

Zone–I: Inlet zone: This zone distributes the incoming wastewater uniformaly to entire cross section of the grit chamber.

Zone–II: Outlet zone: This zone collects the wastewater after grit removal.

Zone–III: Settling zone: In this zone settling of grit material occurs.

Zone–IV: Sludge zone: This is a zone where settled grit accumulates.

L–Length of the settling zone

H–Depth of the settling zone

v–Horizontal velocity of wastewater

V_o–Settling velocity of the smallest particle intended to be removed in grit chamber.

Now, if V_s is the settling velocity of any particle, then

For $V_s \geq V_o$ these particles will be totally removed,

For $V_s < V_o$, these particles will be partially removed,

Where, V_o is settling velocity of the smallest particle intended to be removed. The smallest particle expected to be removed in the grit chamber has size 0.2 mm and sometimes in practice even size of the smallest particle is considered as 0.15 mm. The terminal velocity with which this smallest particle will settle is considered as V_o. This velocity can be expressed as flow or discharge per unit surface area of the tank, and is usually called as 'surface overflow rate' or 'surface settling velocity'. Now for 100 per cent removal of the particles with settling velocity $V_s \geq V_o$, we have

Detention time $= L/v = H/V_o$

Or, $\qquad L/H = v/V_o \qquad\qquad ...(1)$

To prevent scouring of already deposited particles the magnitude of 'v' should not exceed critical horizontal velocity V_c, and the above equation becomes

$$L/H = V_c/V_o$$

The critical velocity, V_c can be given by the following equation:

$$V_c = \sqrt{\left[\frac{8\beta}{f} g(S-1)D\right]} \quad ...(2)$$

Where, $\beta = $ constant

$\qquad = 0.04$ for unigranular sand

$\qquad = 0.06$ for non-uniform sticky material

$f = $ Darcy – Weisbach friction factor

$\qquad = 0.03$ for gritty matter

g = Gravitational acceleration,
S = Specific gravity of the particle to be removed (2.65 for sand), and
D = Diameter of the particle, m

The grit chambers are designed to remove the smallest particle of size 0.2 mm with specific gravity around 2.65. For these particles, using above expression the critical velocity comes out to be V_c = 0.228 m/sec.

Settling Velocity of the Particles: Settling velocity of any discrete particle depends on its individual characteristics and also on the characteristics of the fluid. Assuming particles to be spherical, the settling velocity of any particle, V_s, can be given by the following formula:

$$V_s = \sqrt{\left[\frac{4}{3}\frac{g}{C_D}(S-1)D\right]} \qquad ...(3)$$

Where, C_D = Newton's drag coefficient

$$= \frac{24}{R} + \frac{3}{\sqrt{R}} + 0.34 \text{ for } 0.3 < R < 10^4$$

$$= 24/R, \text{ when } R < 0.3$$

R = Reynold's Number = $V_s.D/v$

v = Kinematic viscosity of the fluid

For the value of $R < 0.3$, C_D = 24/R and the above equation becomes (Stoke's Law)

$$V_s = \frac{g}{18}\left[\frac{S-1}{v}\right]D^2 \qquad ...(4)$$

For the value of $R > 0.3$, the value of V_s should be worked out by trial and error.

Grit removal is the process used to remove sand, silt and grit from water.

Grit (and sand) removal is often found in the headworks of wastewater treatment plants (WWTP). Grit removal can also be used to remove sand from river water intakes prior to processing for potable water, use in industrial applications to remove fine abrasives, as well as being used to remove grit entrained in sludge.

Why Remove Grit?

Sand in treatment plants reduces process capacity and increases maintenance costs.

In WWTPs grit and other solid materials such as sugar sands and silt are a costly component of both process water and wastewater, clogging systems, reducing efficiencies and causing abrasion damage and wear that leads to increased cleaning, maintenance and repair. Conventional assumptions about the nature and behaviour of grit mean that many grit removal systems may only be removing 30-50% of total suspended solids (TSS). That material is passing downstream, abrading critical systems and processes and gradually reducing the overall effectiveness of the facility. In many cases, operators may simply be unaware of how much grit they are missing.

Effective grit removal removes the abrasive solids and sand before they have the chance to enter other processes, erode expensive equipment, and deposit throughout a treatment plant.

6.(a) Designing the splice as a double cover but joint as it will given maximum efficiency

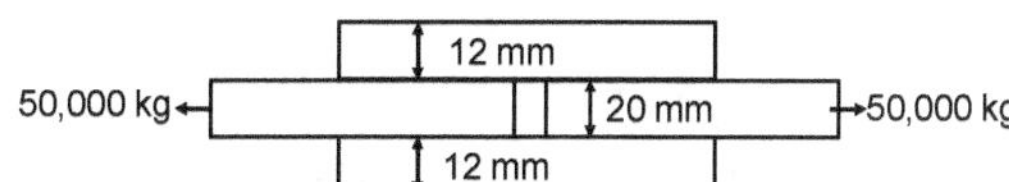

Thickness of cover plate = 12 mm
Thickness of main plate = 20 mm
Width of cover plate = 200 mm
Nominal dia of rivets = 22 mm
Gross dia = 22 + 1.5 = 23.5 mm = 2.35 cm

Calculation of number of rivets required,

Shear strength of rivet in double shear

$$= \left(\frac{\pi}{4} \times d_n^2\right) \times 2 \times \sigma_s$$

$$= (0.7854 \times (2.35)^2 \times 2 \times 1000)$$

$$= 8674.723 \text{ kg}$$

Bearing strength of rivet

$$= d_n \times t \times \sigma_{bt}$$

Where, t = {min (combined thickness of two cover plate, main plate thickness)}

$$t = \{\min (12 + 12, 20)\}$$

$$t = 20 \text{ mm} = 2 \text{ cm}$$

Bearing strength = $(2.35 \times 2 \times 3000)$ N

$$= 14100 \text{ kg}$$

R_v (rivet value) = min {shear strength, bearing strength} = 8674.723 kg

Number of rivet required

$$= \frac{50000}{8674.723} = 5.76 = 6 \text{ rivets}$$

6 numbers of rivets can be arranged in various patterns. However, diamond pattern is generally most economical.

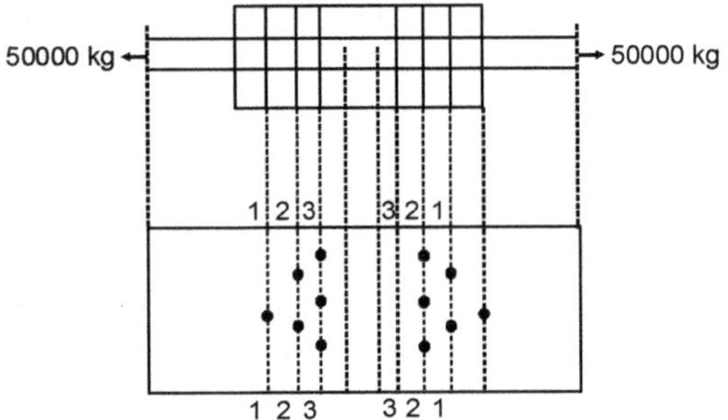

Check for safety of joint in tearing

For main plate:

At see (1) – (1)

$$(B - d_h) \times t \times \sigma_{at} \geq 50000 \text{ kg}$$
$$(20 - 2.35) \times 2 \times 1500 \geq 50000 \text{ kg}$$
$$52950 \geq 50000 \text{ kg}$$

Hence, see (1) – (1) for main plate is safe in tearing.

At see (2) – (2)

$$R + (B - 2d_h) + \sigma_{at} \geq 50000 \text{ kg}$$
$$8674.723 + (20 - 2 \times 2.35) \times 2 \times 1500$$
$$\geq 50000 \text{ kg}$$
$$54574.723 \geq 50000 \text{ kg}$$

Hence, section (2) – (2) for main plate is safe in tearing.

At see (3) – (3)

$$(B - 3d_h)t\, \sigma_{at} + 3R_v \geq 50000 \text{ kg}$$
$$(20 - 3 \times 2.35) \times 2 \times 1500 + 3 \times 8674.923$$
$$\geq 50000 \text{ kg}$$
$$64874.169 \geq 50000 \text{ kg}$$

Section (3) – (3) for main plate is safe in tearing.

For cover plate: For cover plate the most critical section is 3 – 3.

Assuming width for plate to be same as that for main plate.

i.e., $(B - 3d_h) \times t \times \sigma_{at}$ should be > 50000 kg

$$(20 - 3 \times 2.35) \times 2.4 \times 1500 \geq 50000 \text{ kg}$$
$$46620 \text{ kg} \leq 50000 \text{ kg}$$

Hence, cover plate is not safe.

Note that as section (3) – (3) is the 1st line of rivet encountered for cover plate, we do not .... rivet values for tearing strength of cover plate. .... chain rivet

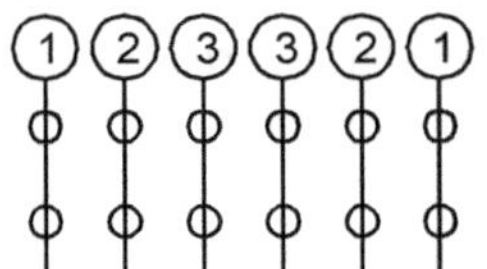

Section (1 – 1) of main plate is checked for the safety

$$(B - 2d_h) \times t \times \sigma_{at} \text{ should be} \geq 50000 \text{ kg}$$
$$(20 - 2 \times 2.35) \times 20 \times 1500 \geq 50000$$
$$45900 \geq 50000$$

Chain riveting is not safe for main plate.

Conclusion: At section 1 – 1 we can apply two rivets

So, the two possible design is as follows.

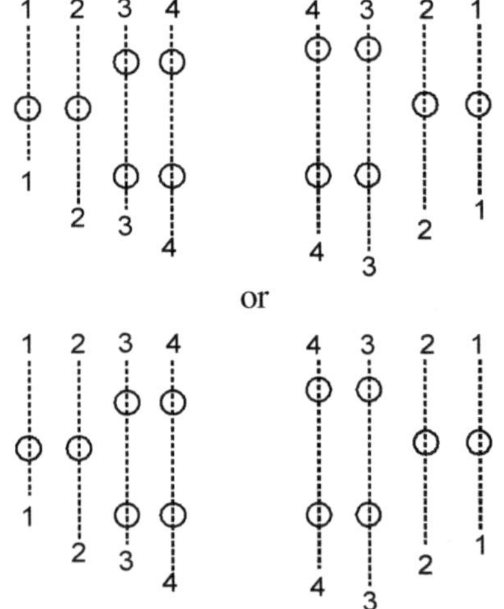

6.(b) Support r_x^n.

$$R_B + R_d = 8 + (2 \times 12) = 32 \text{ m}$$

7 apking moment along B*u* zero

$$\varepsilon\, m_o = 0$$
$$R_B \times 12 = 8 \times 3 + 18 \times 75 + 6 \times 13.5$$

$$R_B = 240/12 = 20 \text{ kN}$$
$$\therefore \qquad R_d = 32.20 = 12 \text{ kN}$$

2. Point of zero S.F.

Let, S.F. is zero at a distance x

From B

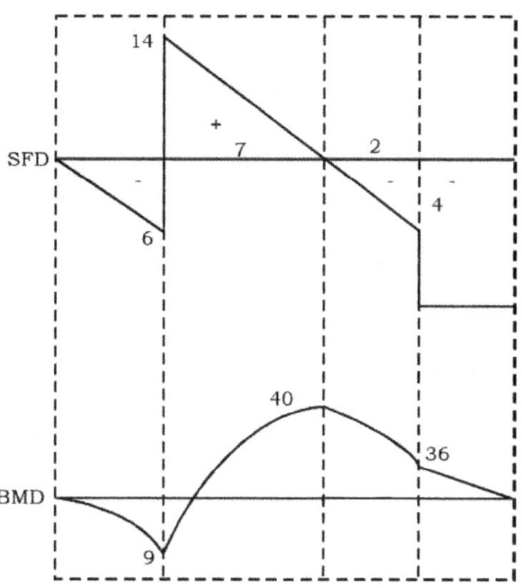

$$\text{SF at B} = 2x$$
$$14 = 2x$$
$$x = 7\text{m}$$

3. SFD

(*i*) From AB

$$V_B = V_A - W_B$$

But, $\qquad V_A = 0$

$$V_B = V_o - 6 = -6 \text{ kN}$$

But due to support x^n, at B

$$V_B \text{ final} = -6 + 20 = 14 \text{ kN}$$

(*ii*) Span *oc*

$$V_C = V_B - W_C$$
$$= .14 - 18 = -4$$
$$V_C \text{ final} = -4 - 8 = -12$$

(*iii*) Span CD

$$V_D = V_C - W_D$$
$$V_D \text{ final} = -12 + 12 = 0$$

BMD

(*i*) Span AB

$$M_B = M_A = -9$$
$$M_B = -9 \text{ kNm}$$

(*ii*) Span BE

$$M_E - M_B = 49$$
$$M_E = 49.9$$
$$= 40 \text{ kNm}$$

(*iii*) Span EC

$$M_C - M_E = -4$$
$$M_C = -4 + 40$$
$$= 36 \text{ kNm}$$

(*iv*) Span CD

$$M_D - M_C = -36$$
$$M_D = -36 + 36$$
$$= 0 \text{ kNm}$$

6.(*c*) Doubly reinforced beams are beams with compressive as well as tensile reinforcement. There is little strength advantage in purposely adding compressive reinforcement to a singly reinforced beam when the concrete can carry the internal compressive force required to balance the tensile force. Most beams would in effect include "incidental compressive reinforcement" in the form of hanger bars required to position stirrups. Such incidental compressive reinforcement would be disregarded when it comes to determining the moment capacity. The additional moment capacity obtained by the inclusion of the hanger bars is too small to warrant the additional effort and cost of the calculations which have now become much more involved. Compressive reinforcement may however be added for the purpose of reducing long-term deflection. If compressive reinforcement is added for the sole purpose of satisfying serviceability, it is disregarded in strength calculations. Doubly reinforced beams are required in circumstances where a singly reinforced beam using the maximum steel ratio cannot carry the design moment and beam size cannot be increased either due to physical restrictions or other conditions beyond the control of the designer.

Compression steel placed in doubly reinforced beams also has to be restrained against local buckling during its action like the compression steel in columns. The same rules regarding restraining of column reinforcements by lateral ties apply to compression reinforcements in beams also. Accordingly, the minimum diameter of the stirrups (ties) should be 5 mm (usually taken as 6 mm) and the pitch should not be more than the least of the following:

1. The least lateral dimension
2. Sixteen times the diameter of the longitudinal steel
3. Forty-eight times the diameter of transverse reinforcement.

A doubly reinforced beam has compression steel A_s' in addition to the tension steel A_s (Figure a). The compression steel could be employed for various purposes: First, to increase the moment capacity of a beam when the cross section is limited. Second, in a continuous beam, ACI code requires that a portion of the bottom positive steel in the center region of a beam must be extended into the supports. These extended bars provide the compression steel for the rectangular support sections that are subjected to negative moment. Third, compression steel could be used to reduce deflections. Fourth, the ductility of a beam could be enhanced by adding compression steel.

The additional compression steel introduces three additional variables, namely, A_s', f_s', and ε_s' for the area, stress, and strain of the compression steel, respectively (Figure a to c). Therefore, the analysis and design of doubly reinforced rectangular concrete beams involve 12 variables, namely, b, d, A_s, A_s', M_u, f_s, f_s', f_c', ε_s, ε_s', ε_u, and c (or a). At the same time, two additional equations are available: one for the compatibility of compression steel and the other for the stress-strain relationship of the compression steel.

The analysis and design of doubly reinforced rectangular sections will be limited to under-reinforced beams using the stress-strain relationships of concrete and steel shown in Fig (f) and (g). In this type of problem the tensile steel will be in the yield range $f_s = f_y$ and the tensile steel strain ε_s is irrelevant to the solution of stress-type variables. Correspondingly, the compatibility equation for the tensile steel and the stress-strain relationship of the tensile steel are not required.

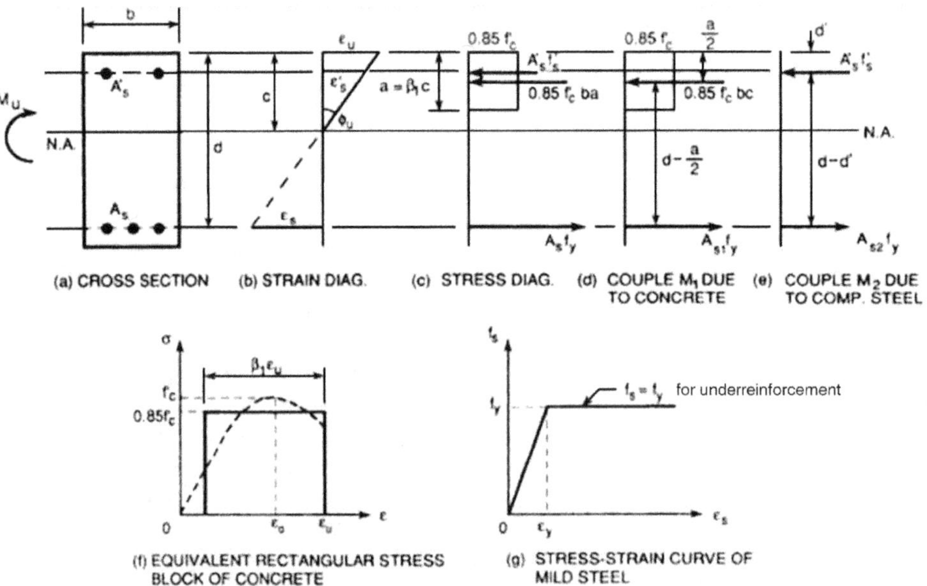

(a) CROSS SECTION (b) STRAIN DIAG. (c) STRESS DIAG. (d) COUPLE M₁ DUE TO CONCRETE (e) COUPLE M₂ DUE TO COMP. STEEL

(f) EQUIVALENT RECTANGULAR STRESS BLOCK OF CONCRETE (g) STRESS-STRAIN CURVE OF MILD STEEL

Fig. Double reinforced rectangular sections at ultimate.

SSC-Junior Engineer (Civil & Structural) Exam, 2015*

PAPER-II (Conventional)

1. (*a*) What are the factors that influence the strength of cement concrete? Briefly discuss the effects of water-cement ratio and workability on the strength of concrete.

(*b*) Explain the purpose of conducting soundness test of cement. Describe the apparatus and method of test with the help of neat sketches.

(*c*) Give a short description of preservation of wood using various wood preservatives.

(*d*) List the four important tests conducted on bricks. Explain the various defects in bricks.

2. (*a*) Write the characteristics of contour lines.

(*b*) The following readings were extracted from a level field book. Some of the entries are missing because of exposure to rain. Insert the missing readings and check your results.

Station	B.S.	I.S.	F.S.	Rise	Fall	RL	Remarks
1	3.250					?	Benchmark
2	1.755		?		0.750	?	Change point
3		1.950				?	
4	?		1.920			?	
5		2.340		1.500		?	
6				1.000		?	
7	1.850		2.185			250.00	Change point
8		1.575				?	
9		?				?	
10	?		1.895		1.650	?	Change point
11			1.350	0.750		?	Last point

(*c*) The soil from a borrow area having an average in-situ unit weight of $15.5\ \text{kN/m}^3$ and water content of 10%, was used for the construction of an embankment (total finished volume 6000 m³). In half of the embankment due to improper rolling, the dry unit weight achieved was slightly lower. If the dry unit weights in the two parts are $16.5\ \text{kN/m}^3$ and $16.0\ \text{kN/m}^3$, find the volume of borrow area soil used in each part and the amount of soil used.

(*d*) A 6.0 m high retaining wall is to support a soil with unit weight 17.4 kN/m^3, ϕ = 26° and c' = 14.36 kN/m^2.

Determine the Rankine active force per unit length of the wall before the tensile crack occurs. Find the critical depth.

3. (*a*) Two pipes of diameters 'D' and '*d*' and equal length 'L' are arranged in parallel. The loss of head for a flow of 'Q' is '*h*'. If the same pipes are arranged in series, the loss of head for the same flow is 'H'. If $d = 0.5$ D, find the percentage of total flow through each pipe when placed in parallel. Also, find the ratio H/h. Neglect minor losses and assume friction factor to be constant.

(*b*) Water flows over the spillway of a dam at a depth of 2.73 m over it. The difference of elevation between spillway crest and downstream bed level is 30 m.

If the discharge coefficient of spillway is 0.75, determine the water depth after the jump and head loss in the jump.

(*c*) Calculate the minimum required sight distance to avoid a head-on collision of two cars approaching from the opposite directions at 90 and 60 kmph. Assume reaction time as 2.5 sec and coefficient of friction of 0.7 and brake efficiency 50% in either case.

(*d*) Differentiate canal design methods by Lacey and Kennedy.

4. (*a*) A cantilever, 3 m long, is loaded with a uniformly distributed load of 15 kN/m over a length of 2 m from the fixed end. Determine the slope and deflection at the free end of the cantilever.

Take E = 2.1 × 10^8 kN/m^2

and I = 0.000095 m^4.

(*b*) Draw the flow sheet showing sequence of a typical water treatment with perennial river as source of water. Explain these treatment units sequentially.

(*c*) What is meant by solid waste management? Describe briefly the principles of design of a sanitary landfill for solid wastes disposal.

5. (*a*) Explain under-reinforced, balanced and over-reinforced section with respect to WSM as well as LSM.

(*b*) Using limit state method (LSM), determine the moment of resistance of the T-Beam as shown in the figure below. Use M 15 concrete and Fe 415 steel.

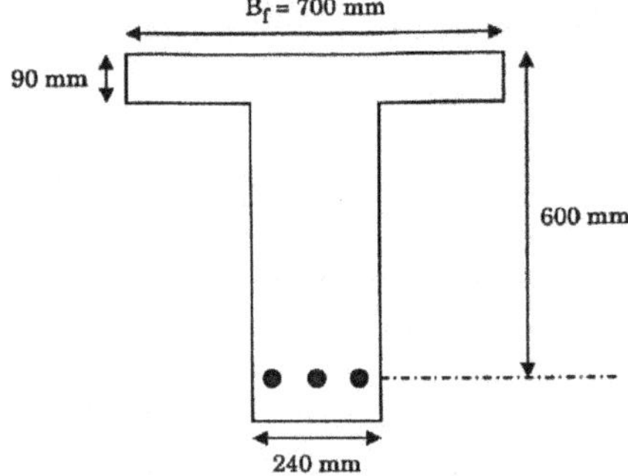

6. (*a*) Explain the following:

(*i*) Elastic curve of mild steel with a suitable diagram showing important points.

(*ii*) Different types of welds with suitable figures and symbols.

(*b*) A single-bolted double cover butt joint is used to connect two plates which are 8 mm thick. Assuming 16 mm diameter bolts of grade 4.6 and cover plates to be 6 mm thick, calculate the strength and efficiency of the joint, if 4 bolts are provided in the bolt line at a pitch of 45 mm as shown in the figure below. Take the end distance of the fastener along bearing direction as 30 mm.

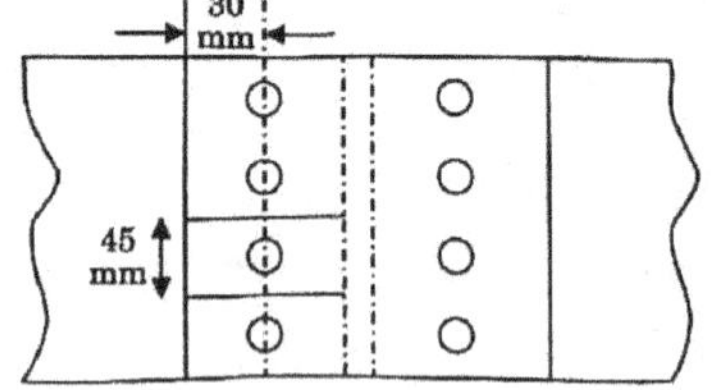

ANSWERS

1. (*a*) Factors Affecting Concrete Strength

Concrete strength is effected by many factors, such as quality of raw materials, water/cement ratio, coarse/fine aggregate ratio, age of concrete, compaction of concrete, temperature, relative humidity and curing of concrete.

(*i*) Quality of Raw Materials:

Cement: Provided the cement conforms with the appropriate standard and it has been stored correctly (*i.e.*, in dry conditions), it should be suitable for use in concrete.

Aggregates: Quality of aggregates, its size, shape, texture, strength etc. determines the strength of concrete. The presence of salts (chlorides and sulphates), silt and clay also reduces the strength of concrete.

Water: Frequently the quality of the water is covered by a clause stating "... the water should be fit for drinking...". This criterion though is not absolute and reference should be made to respective codes for testing of water construction purpose.

(*ii*) Water/Cement Ratio:

The relation between water cement ratio and strength of concrete is shown in the plot as shown below:

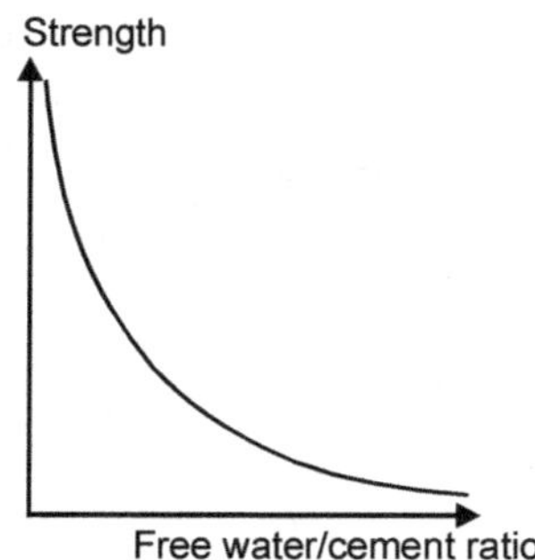

The higher the water/cement ratio, the greater the initial spacing between the cement grains and the greater the volume of residual voids not filled by hydration products.

There is one thing missing on the graph. For a given cement content, the workability of the concrete is reduced if the water/cement ratio is reduced. A lower water cement ratio means less water, or more cement and lower workability.

However, if the workability becomes too low the concrete becomes difficult to compact and the strength reduces. For a given set of materials and environment conditions, the strength at any age depends only on the water-cement ratio, providing full compaction can be achieved.

(*iii*) Coarse/fine Aggregate Ratio:

Following points should be noted for coarse/fine aggregate ratio:

- If the proportion of fines is increased in relation to the coarse aggregate, the overall aggregate surface area will increase.
- If the surface area of the aggregate has increased, the water demand will also increase.
- Assuming the water demand has increased, the water cement ratio will increase.
- Since the water cement ratio has increased, the compressive strength will decrease.

(*iv*) Aggregate/Cement Ratio:

Following points must be noted for aggregate cement ratio:

- If the volume remains the same and the proportion of cement in relation to that of sand is increased the surface area of the solid will increase.
- If the surface area of the solids has increased, the water demand will stay the same for the constant workability.

- Assuming an increase in cement content for no increase in water demand, the water cement ratio will decrease.
- If the water cement ratio reduces, the strength of the concrete will increase.

The influence of cement content on workability and strength is an important one to remember and can be summarized as follows:

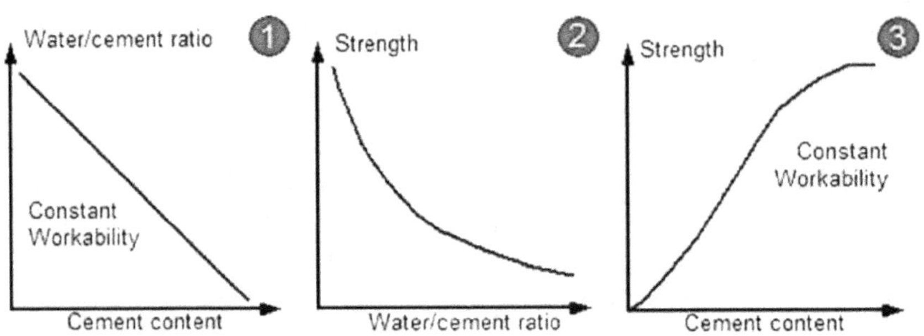

1. For a given workability an increase in the proportion of cement in a mix has little effect on the water demand and results in a reduction in the water/cement ratio.
2. The reduction in water/cement ratio leads to an increase in strength of concrete.
3. Therefore, for a given workability an increase in the cement content results in an increase in strength of concrete.

(v) Age of Concrete:

The degree of hydration is synonymous with the age of concrete provided the concrete has not been allowed to dry out or the temperature is too low.

In theory, provided the concrete is not allowed to dry out, then it will always be increasing albeit at an ever reducing rate. For convenience and for most practical applications, it is generally accepted that the majority of the strength has been achieved by 28 days.

(vi) Compaction of Concrete:

Any entrapped air resulting from inadequate compaction of the plastic concrete will lead to a reduction in strength. If there was 10% trapped air in the concrete, the strength will fall down in the range of 30 to 40%.

(vii) Temperature:

The rate of hydration reaction is temperature dependent. If the temperature increases the reaction also increases. This means that the concrete kept at higher temperature will gain strength more quickly than a similar concrete kept at a lower temperature.

However, the final strength of the concrete kept at the higher temperature will be lower. This is because the physical form of the hardened cement paste is less well structured and more porous when hydration proceeds at faster rate.

This is an important point to remember because temperature has a similar but more pronounced detrimental effect on permeability of the concrete.

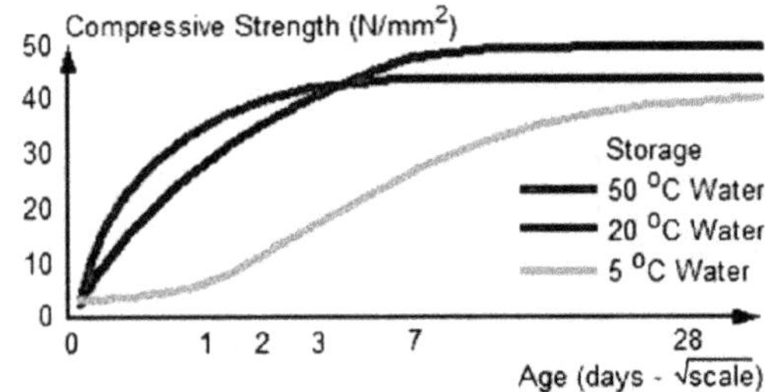

(viii) Relative Humidity:

If the concrete is allowed to dry out, the hydration reaction will stop. The hydration reaction cannot proceed without moisture. The three curves shows the strength development of similar concretes exposed to different conditions.

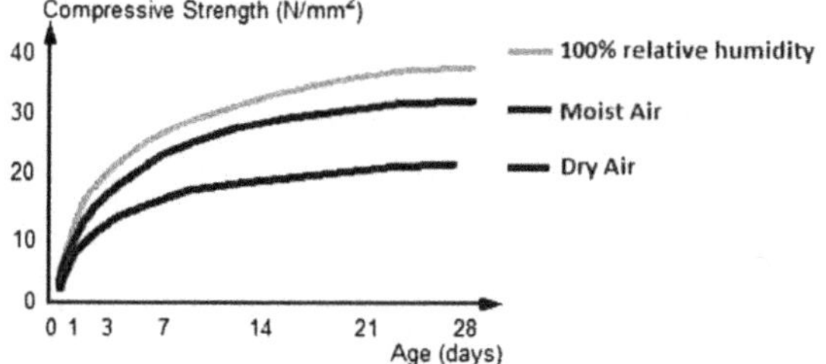

(*ix*) Curing:

It should be clear from what has been said above that the detrimental effects of storage of concrete in a dry environment can be reduced if the concrete is adequately cured to prevent excessive moisture loss.

Water-Cement Ratio: The ratio of water to cement affects the behaviour of concrete in several ways:

1. A minimum amount of water must be added to the cement to ensure that all of it undergoes the hydration reaction. Too little water causes low strength. Normally, however, other factors such as workability place the lower limit on the water-cement ratio.

2. A high water-cement ratio improves the workability of concrete—that is, how easily the concrete slurry can fill all of the space in the form. Air pockets or interconnected porosity caused by poor workability reduce the strength and durability of the concrete structure. Workability can be measured by the slump test. For example, a wet concrete shape 30 cm tall is produced and is permitted to stand under its own weight. After some period of time, the shape deforms. The reduction in height of the form is the slump. A minimum water-cement ratio of about 0.4 (by weight) is usually required for workability. A larger slump, caused by a higher water-cement ratio, indicates greater workability. Slumps of 2.5 to 15 cm are typical: high slumps are needed for pouring narrow or complex forms, while low slumps may be satisfactory for large structures such as dams.

3. Increasing the water-cement ratio beyond the minimum required for workability decreases the compressive strength of the concrete. This strength is usually measured by determining the stress required to crush a concrete cylinder 15 cm in diameter and 30 cm tall.

4. High water-cement ratios increase the shrinkage of concrete during curing, creating a danger of cracking.

1. (*b*) Test for Soundness

The soundness test is an indication of excess of lime caused by inadequate burning of cement or excess of magnesia or sulphates. Excess of these substances is harmful and thus, not allowed in cements, The following two types of tests are used for testing for soundness,

(a) Le Chatelier's test (using Le Chatelier's apparatus)

(b) Autoclave test

Le Chatelier's test: Le Chatelier's test shows unsoundness due to lime only. Unaerated cement paste at normal consistency is first tested for expansion. If the test results does not satisfy requirement of 10 mm expansion, another test shall be made after aeration of the cement by spreading of the sample to a depth of 75 mm at a relative humidity of 50 to 80% for 7 days. The expansion in this aerated cement test should not be more than 5 mm.

The apparatus used is shown in Figure. Cement pastes with normal consistency is filled into the mould. After covering both sides with glass, it is first placed in water of temperature 24 to 35°C for 24 hours. It is taken out and the distance between pointers is measured. The mould is then placed in water and the water is heated to the boiling point in 30 minutes. The boiling of water is continued for one hour. The mould is then removed and after cooling, the distance between the points is again measured.

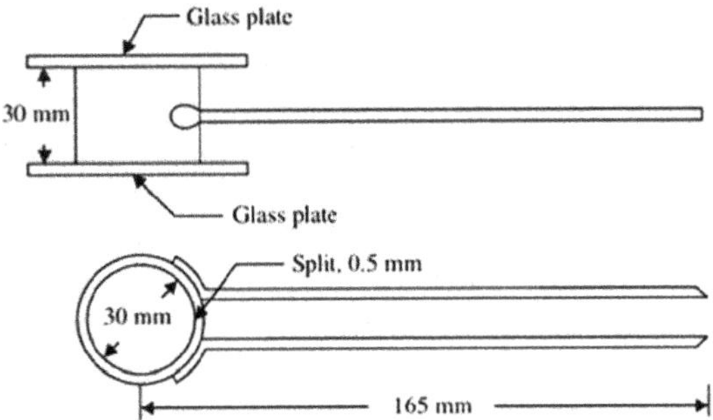

Fig. : Le Chatelier's apparatus

Autoclave test: Autoclave test is another test used for soundness of cement. It is sensitive to both lime and magnesia. All the cement having a magnesia content more than 3 per cent is to be tested for soundness by this test with unaerated cement. The test consists of heating bars made of cement paste with water of normal consistency and measuring its expansion. Effect of unsoundness of cement does not appear in the field for a considerable period of time. Hence, these accelerated tests are needed to determine them. In autoclave test, we use higher pressure and temperature to accelerate the reactions. The autoclave expansion of unaerated cement should not be more than 0.8 per cent and that of aerated cement not more than 0.6 per cent.

1.(c) All measures that are taken to ensure a long life of wood fall under the definition wood preservation (timber treatment). Apart from structural wood preservation measures, there are a number of different (chemical) preservatives and processes that can extend the life of wood, timber, wood structures or engineered wood. These generally increase the durability and resistance from being destroyed by insects or fungus.

Chemical preservatives can be classified into three broad categories: water-borne preservatives, oil-borne preservatives, and light organic solvent preservatives (LOSPs).

Micronized copper technology

Two particulate copper systems, one marketed as MicroPro and the other as Wolmanized using μCA-C formulation, have achieved Environmentally Preferable Product (EPP) certification. The EPP certification was issued by Scientific Certifications Systems (SCS), and is based on a comparative life-cycle impact assessments with an industry standard.

Alkaline copper quaternary

Alkaline copper quaternary (ACQ) is a preservative made of copper, a fungicide, and a quaternary ammonium compound (quat) like didecyl dimethyl ammonium chloride, an insecticide which also augments the fungicidal treatment. ACQ has come into wide use in the US, Europe, Japan and Australia following restrictions on CCA. Its use is governed by national and international standards, which determine the volume of preservative uptake required for a specific timber end use.

Copper azole

Copper azole is similar to ACQ with the difference being that the dissolved copper preservative is augmented by an azole co-biocide like Tebuconazole instead of the quat biocide used in ACQ. The azole co-biocide yields a copper azole product that is effective at lower retentions than required for equivalent ACQ performance.

The copper azole preservative incorporates organic triazoles such as tebuconazole or propiconazole as the co-biocide, which are also used to protect food crops. The general appearance of wood treated with copper azole preservative is similar to CCA with a green colouration.

Chromated copper arsenate (CCA)

In CCA treatment, copper is the primary fungicide, arsenic is a secondary fungicide and an insecticide, and chromium is a fixative which also provides ultraviolet (UV) light resistance. Recognized for the greenish tint it imparts to timber, CCA is a preservative that was extremely common for many decades.

The process can apply varying amounts of preservative at varying levels of pressure to protect the wood against increasing levels of attack. Increasing protection can be applied (in increasing order of attack and treatment) for: exposure to the atmosphere, implantation within soil, or insertion into a marine environment.

Sodium silicate-based preservatives

Sodium silicate is produced by fusing sodium carbonate with sand or heating both ingredients under pressure. It has been in use since the 19th century. It can be a deterrent against insect attack and possesses minor flame-resistant properties; however, it is easily washed out of wood by moisture, forming a flake-like layer on top of the wood.

Oil-borne preservatives

These include pentachlorophenol ("penta") and creosote. They emit a strong petro-chemical odor and are generally not used in consumer products.

Coal-tar creosote

Creosote is one of the oldest wood preservatives, and was originally derived from a wood distillate, but now, virtually all creosote is manufactured from the distillation of coal tar. Creosote is regulated as a pesticide, and is not usually sold to the general public.

Linseed oil

This involves just treating the outer 5 mm of the cross-section of a timber member with preservative (e.g., permethrin 25:75), leaving the core untreated. While not as effective as CCA or LOSP methods, envelope treatments are significantly cheaper, as they use far less preservative. Major preservative manufacturers add a blue (or red) dye to envelope treatments.

Natural Preservatives

Copper plating

Copper plating or Copper sheathing is the practice of covering wood most usually wooden hulls of ships with copper metal. As metallic copper is both repellent and toxic to fungus, insects such as termites, and marine bi-valves this would preserve the wood and also act as an anti-fouling measure to prevent aquatic life from attaching to the ship's hull and reducing a ship's speed and maneuverability.

Naturally rot-resistant woods

These species are resistant to decay in their natural state, due to high levels of organic chemicals called extractives, mainly polyphenols. Extractives are chemicals that are deposited in the heartwood of certain tree species as they convert sapwood to heartwood. Huon pine (*Lagarostrobos franklinii*), merbau (*Intsia bijuga*), ironbark (*Eucalyptus* spp.), tōtara (*Podocarpus totara*), puriri (*Vitex lucens*), kauri (*Agathis australis*), and many cypresses, such as coast redwood (*Sequoia sempervirens*) and western red cedar (*Thuja plicata*), fall in this category. However, many of these species tend to be prohibitively expensive for general construction applications.

Huon pine was used for ship hulls in the 19th century, but over-harvesting and Huon pine's extremely slow growth rate makes this now a speciality timber. Huon pine is so rot resistant, that fallen trees from many years ago are still commercially valuable.

1 (d). To know the quality of bricks following 7 tests can be performed. In these tests some are performed in laboratory and the rest are on field.

1. Compressive strength test
2. Water absorption test
3. Efflorescense test
4. Hardness test

5. Size, shape and colour test
6. Soundness test
7. Structure test

Compressive strength test: This test is done to know the compressive strength of brick. It is also called crushing strength of brick. Generally 5 specimens of bricks are taken to laboratory for testing and tested one by one. In this test a brick specimen is put on crushing machine and applied pressure till it breaks. The ultimate pressure at which brick is crushed is taken into account. All five brick specimens are tested one by one and average result is taken as brick's compressive/crushing strength.

Water Absorption test: In this test bricks are weighed in dry condition and let them immersed in fresh water for 24 hours. After 24 hours of immersion those are taken out from water and wipe out with cloth. Then brick is weighed in wet condition. The difference between weights is the water absorbed by brick. The percentage of water absorption is then calculated.

The less water absorbed by brick the greater its quality. Good quality brick doesn't absorb more than 20% water of its own weight.

Efflorescense test: The presence of alkalis in bricks is harmful and they form a gray or white layer on brick surface by absorbing moisture. To find out the presence of alkalis in bricks this test is performed. In this test a brick is immersed in fresh water for 24 hours and then it's taken out from water and allowed to dry in shade.

If the whitish layer is not visible on surface it proofs that absence of alkalis in brick. If the whitish layer visible about 10% of brick surface then the presence of alkalis is in acceptable range. If that is about 50% of surface then it is moderate. If the alkalis's presence is over 50% then the brick is severely affected by alkalis

Hardness test: In this test a scratch is made on brick surface with a hard thing. If that doesn't left any impression on brick then that is good quality brick.

Size, shape and colour test: In this test randomly collected 20 bricks are staked along lengthwise, widthwise and heightwise and then those are measured to know the variation of sizes as per standard. Bricks are closely viewed to check if its edges are sharp and straight and uniform in shape. A good quality brick should have bright and uniform colour throughout.

Soundness test: In this test two bricks are held by both hands and struck with one another. If the bricks give clear metallic ringing sound and don't break then those are good quality bricks.

Structure test: In this test a brick is broken or a broken brick is collected and closely observed. If there are any flows, cracks or holes present on that broken face then that isn't good quality brick.

Defects in Brick Masonry

Brick masonry may develop the defects due to the following reasons :

(*i*) Sulphate attack

(*ii*) Crystallization of salts from bricks (efflorescence)

(*iii*) Corrosion of embedded fixtures

(*iv*) Drying shrinkage.

(*i*) **Sulphate attack**

This is a common defect, specially at locations where the brick work is either exposed (such as in boundary walls, unplastered external walls etc.) or, where brick work is likely to come in contact with moisture. The sulphate salts present in brick react with hydraulic lime in the case of lime mortar and with alumina of cement in the case of cement mortar. Due to this reaction, the increase in the volume of mortar takes place, resulting in chipping and spalling of bricks. Cracks are formed in joints and rendering.

(*ii*) Crystallization of salts from bricks

If the bricks are manufactured from earth containing excessive soluble salts, entry of moisture, either due to dampness or due to rains etc., dissolves the soluble salts. These salts, after getting dissolved in water, appear in the form of fine whitish crystals on the exposed brick surface. This is known as efflorescence. Such a masonry presents ugly appearance. The situation can be improved by brushing and washing the affected surface from time to time.

(*iii*) Corrosion of embedded fixtures

Iron or steel fixtures, such as the pipes or holdfasts of doors, windows etc., embedded in brick masonry gets corroded with time specially when lime mortar is used. The corrosion results in the increase in the volume, resulting in cracks in brick masonry. Therefore, these fixtures should be well-embedded in cement mortar.

(*iv*) Drying shrinkage

When moisture penetrates the brick work, it swells. On evaporation of moisture during the drying due to atmospheric heat etc., the bricks shrinks, resulting in the development of cracks in the masonry joints. Frequent swelling and shrinkage may cause even the fatigue of masonry.

2. (*a*) Characteristics of Contour Lines

(*i*) All points on a contour line have the same elevation.

(*ii*) Widely separated contour lines indicate flat topography, whereas uniformly spaced contour lines indicate the uniform slope of the ground

(*iii*) The series of closed contour lines represent a hill if the higher values are inside.

(*iv*) Series of contour lines represent depression if one or lower ones are inside.

(*v*) Contour lines cannot end anywhere but close on themselves either within or outside the limit of the map.

(*vi*) Contour lines cannot merge or cross one another except in case of overhanging and vertical cliff and cave.

(*vii*) Contour lines cross ridge or watershed line at right angles. They form U-shaped around the ridge line with concave sides towards the higher ground as shown in Figure (*a*).

(*viii*) Contour lines cut the valley line also at right angles, forming V-shaped curves across the valley line with convex side towards the higher ground is shown in Figure (*b*).

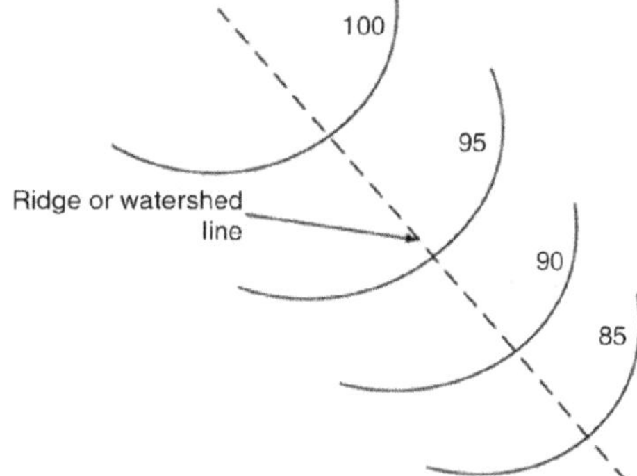

Fig. (a): Contour lines along ridge

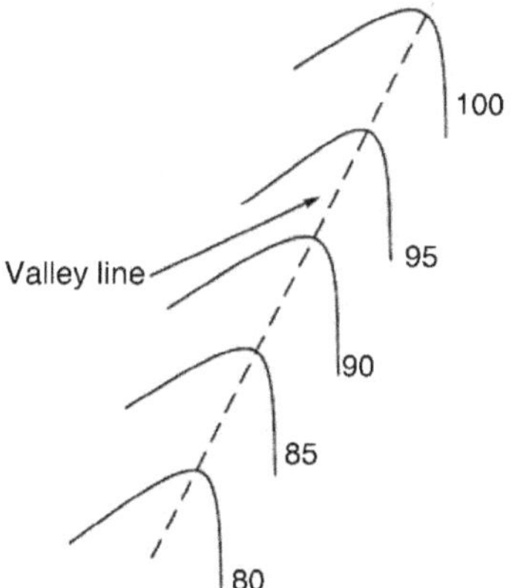

Fig. (b): Contour lines along a valley

(*ix*) Contour lines form four loops in case of a saddle which is junction of two ridges Figure (*c*). In the case of a saddle on two opposite sides, the ground slopes up, whereas on other two sides the ground slopes down.

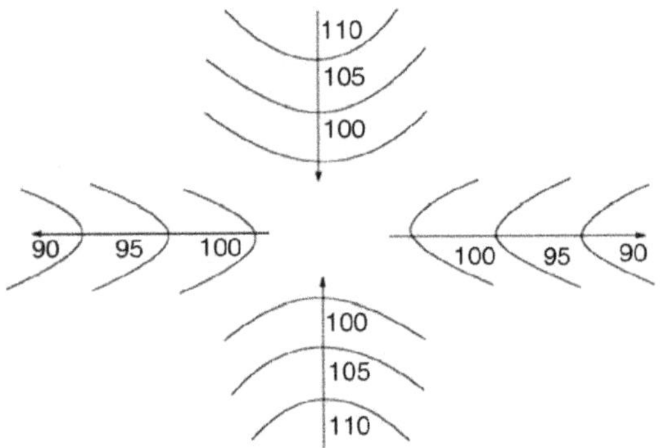

Fig. (c): Contour lines in saddle

2. (c)

Borrow Area	Fill 1	Fill 2
$\gamma_b = 15.5$ kN/m^3	$V_1 = 3000$ m^3	$V_2 = 3000$ m^3
$\omega = 10\%$	$\gamma_{d1} = 16.5$ kN/m^3	$\gamma_{d2} = 16$ kN/m^3
$\gamma_d = 14.09$ kN/m^3	$e_1 = 0.604$	$e_2 = 0.654$
$e = 0.88$	$V_{v1} = 0.604\,V_{s1}$	$V_{v2} = 0.654\,V_{s2}$
$V_v = 0.88\,V_s$	$V_1 = V_{v1} + V_{s1} =$	$V_2 = V_{v2} + V_{s2} =$
	$1.604V_{s1} = 3000$ m^3	$1.654V_{s2} = 3000$ m^3
	$V_{s1} = 1870$ m^3	$V_{s2} = 1814$ m^3

$$G = 2.7$$
$$\gamma_\omega = 9.8 \text{ kN/m}^3$$
$$\gamma_d = \frac{G\gamma_\omega}{1+e}$$
$$V_s = V_{s1} + V_{s2} = 3684 \text{ m}^3$$
$$V_v = 0.88V_s = 3242 \text{ m}^3$$
$$V_{borrow} = V_s + V_v = 6926 \text{ m}^3$$

Amount of soil in fill 1:
$$= \gamma_{d1}\cdot V_1$$
$$= 16.5 \times 3000$$
$$= 49500 \text{ kN}$$

Amount of soil in fill 2:
$$= \gamma_{d2}\cdot V_2$$
$$= 16 \times 3000$$
$$= 48000 \text{ kN.}$$

2. (d) For $\phi = 26°$,

$$K_a = \tan^2\left(45 - \frac{\phi}{2}\right) = \tan^2(45-13)$$
$$= 0.39$$
$$\sqrt{K_a} = 0.625$$

$$\sigma_a = \gamma HK_a - 2c\sqrt{K_a}$$

At $\qquad$ H = 0,
$$\sigma_a = -2c\sqrt{K_a} = -2(14.36)\,(0.625)$$
$$= -17.95 \text{ kN/m}^2$$

At $\qquad$ H = 6 m,
$$\sigma_a = (17.4)(6)(0.39) - 2(14.36)(0.625)$$
$$= 40.72 - 17.95 = 22.77 \text{ kN/m}^2$$

Active force before the occurrence of tensile crack

$$P_a = \frac{1}{2}\left(\gamma H^2\,K_a\right) - 2cH\sqrt{K_a}$$
$$= \frac{1}{2}(6)(40.72) - (6)(17.95)$$
$$= 122.16 - 107.7 = 14.46 \text{ kN/m}$$

The line of action of the resultant can be determined by taking the moment of the area of the pressure diagrams about the bottom of the wall, or

$$P_a\bar{H} = (122.16)\left(\frac{6}{3}\right) - (107.7)\left(\frac{6}{2}\right)$$

or, $\qquad \bar{H} = \dfrac{244.32 - 323.1}{14.46} = -5.45$ m

3. (a) When the two pipes are placed in parallel over an equal length L, the loss of head in each pipe is h and the flow is shared as Q_1 and Q_2, totalling to Q. Hence,

$$h = \frac{f\,LQ_1^2}{12D^5} = \frac{f\,LQ_2^2}{12d^5}$$

which requires

$$\frac{Q_1}{Q_2} = \left(\frac{D}{d}\right)^{5/2} = \left(\frac{D}{0.5D}\right)^{5/2}$$
$$= 2^{5/2} = 5.66$$

Percentages of flow in the pipes are given by 5.66 : 1, *i.e.*, 5.66/6.66 × 100 and 1/6.66 × 100 *i.e.*, 85% and 15%.

When pipes are placed in series, loss of head

$$H = \frac{f\,LQ^2}{12\,D^5} + \frac{f\,LQ^2}{12\,d^5}$$

$$H = \frac{f\,LQ^2}{12}\left(\frac{1}{D^5}+\frac{1}{d^5}\right)$$

If $d = 0.5\,D$,

$$H = \frac{f\,LQ^2}{12\,D^5}\left(1+\frac{1}{(0.5)^5}\right) = 33\frac{f\,LQ^2}{12\,D^5}$$

Also,

$$h = \frac{f\,LQ_1^2}{12\,D^5} = \frac{f\,L(0.85Q)^2}{12\,D^5}$$

$$= 0.722\frac{f\,LQ^2}{12\,D^5}$$

Then,

$$\frac{h}{H} = \frac{0.722}{33} = 0.02$$

i.e., one fiftieth!

3.(c) Given: $V_1 = 90$ Km/hr, $V_2 = 60$ Km/hr, $t = 2.5$ sec. Braking efficiency = 50%, $f = .7$. Stopping distance for one of the cars

$$SD = vt + v^2/2gf$$

Coefficient of friction due to braking efficiency of 50% = 0.5*0.7 = 0.35. Stopping sight distance of first car :

$SD_1 = 153.6$ m

Stopping sight distance of second car :

$SD_2 = 82.2$ m.

Stopping sight distance to avoid head on collision of the two approaching cars :
$SD_1 + SD_2 = 235.8$ m.

3. (d) Steps Required to Canal Design by Kennedy's Theory

The known values are discharge Q, bed slope s_b, CVR m_r and Kutter's n_r. Trial and error method has to be adopted to determine the design values of y and B. Side slope $zH : IV$ is assumed (if not given), *i.e.*, z varies from 0.5 to 2 for hard to loose soil. It is based on angle of repose of earth.

Steps:

(1) Assume a trial value of depth y

(2) Find the velocity by the equation
$$V = 0.55\,m_r\,y^{0.64}$$

(3) Find flow area $A = \dfrac{Q}{V}$

(4) Find B from $A = (B + zy)y$ where A is known from step (3), z is assumed or given, y is assumed in step (1)

(5) Find $P = B + 2y\sqrt{1+z^2}$

(6) Find $R = \dfrac{A}{P}$

(7) Now find velocity V by Kutter's equation.

(8) If the velocity obtained in step (2) and in step (7) are not almost equal, assume second trial values of depth y and repeat steps (1) to (8).

(9) Repeat this process, until velocity in step (2) = velocity in step (7). The value of y at which the two velocities are almost same, is the required depth of flow.

(10) Find B when y is known.

(11) Assume a reasonable free board (FB). Usually 0.6 when $Q < 10$ m³/sec and $FB > 0.75$ when $Q > 10$ m³/sec.

This trial and error method is very tedious and assumption of first trial values of y is very difficult. The design of canal by Kennedy's theory can be designed from Garret's diagram which provide a graphical solution of Kennedy's equation and Ganguillet-Kutter's equation with interpolation.

Steps Required in Design by Lacey's Theory

Data known: Q, sand or sediment size, side slope $zH : 1V$ (if not given assume $\frac{1}{2}H : 1$ or $1H : 1V$)

(*i*) From the known sediment size diameter d in mm, find silt factor $f = 1.76\sqrt{d}$

(*ii*) Find velocity from known Q and f
$$V_c = \left(\frac{Qf^2}{140}\right)^{1/6}$$

(*iii*) From known Q and V_c, find $A = \dfrac{Q}{V_c}$

(*iv*) Find wetted perimeter by
$$P = 4.75\sqrt{Q}$$

(*v*) New area A = (B + *zy*) *y* and P = B + $2y\sqrt{1+z^2}$

(*vi*) In steps (*v*) two equations and two unknowns B and *y*, solve simultaneously

(*vii*) Find bed slope $s_b = \dfrac{f^{5/3}}{3450\,Q^{1/6}}$

It may be mentioned in other books of irrigation constant is written 3340, but correct one is 3450.

(*viii*) Make a check for numerical calculation by

$$V_c = \sqrt{\frac{2}{5}f\,R}$$

∴ $R = \dfrac{5V_c^2}{2f}$, find R from calculation of

B, *y* and *z*

If both the R are same, no mistake in calculations.

(*ix*) Provide a Free Board (FB) based on Q.

Q < 0.75 cumec, FB = 0.45 m

0.75 < Q < 1.50 cumec, FB = 0.60 m

1.5 < Q < 85.00 cumec, FB = 0.75 m

Q > 85.00 cumec, FB = 0.90 to 0.95 m

$\simeq$ 1.0 m

may be provided.

4. (*a*)

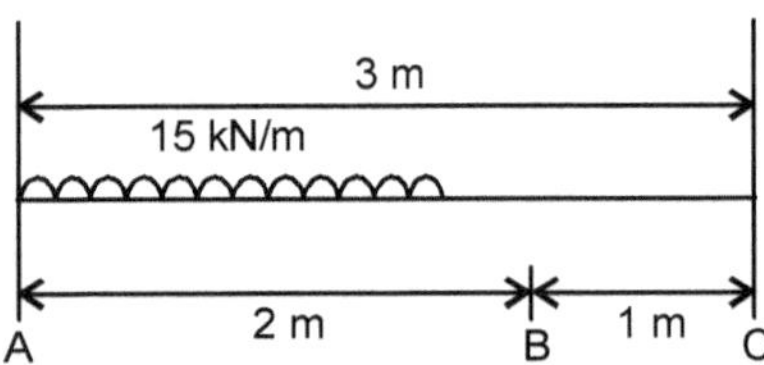

Here, *l* = 3 m = 3000 mm

$u.d.i. = 15$ kN/m $= \dfrac{15 \times 1000}{1000}$ N/mm

= 15 N/mm

Distance AC = *a* = 2 m = 2000 mm

b = 3 m = 3000 mm

I = 0.000095 m⁴ = 9.5 × 10⁷ mm⁴

E = 2.1 × 10⁸ kN/m²

$$= \dfrac{2.1 \times 10^8 \times 10^3}{(1000)^2}\ \text{N/mm}^2$$

= 2.1 × 10⁵ N/mm²

Let θ is the slope at the free end of the cantilever

Then $\theta = \dfrac{w.a^3}{6E \times I}$

$$= \dfrac{15 \times (2000)^3}{6 \times 2.1 \times 10^5 \times 9.5 \times 10^7}$$

= 0.001 rad.

Let *y* is the deflection at the free end due to *u.d.i.*

Deflection at the free end due to uniformly distributed load

$$y = \dfrac{w.a^4}{8E.I.} + \dfrac{w.a^3}{6E.I.}(b-a)$$

$$= \dfrac{15 \times (2000)^4}{8 \times 2.1 \times 10^5 \times 9.5 \times 10^7}$$

$$+ \dfrac{15 \times (2000)^3 \times 1000}{6 \times 2.1 \times 10^5 \times 9.5 \times 10^7}$$

= 1.5 + 1

= 2.5 mm

4. (*b*) Water treatment Plants

The primary purpose of a water treatment system is to bring raw water up to drinking water quality standards. The quality of the source water usually dictates the particular type of treatment process required to meet these standards. In some cases the water source may require only simple disinfection. Surface water will usually need to be filtered and disinfected. Groundwater, on the other hand, will often need to have hardness (calcium and magnesium) removed before disinfection.

A typical water treatment plant for surface water might include the following sequence of steps:

- *screening* to remove relatively large floating and suspended debris
- *mixing* the water with chemicals that encourage suspended solids to coagulate into larger particles of floc

- *flocculation*, which is the process of gently mixing the water and coagulant allowing the formation of large particles of floc

- *sedimentation* in which the flow is slowed enough so that gravity will cause the floc to settle

- *sludge processing* where the mixture of solids and liquids collected from the settling tank are dewatered and disposed of

- *disinfection* of the liquid effluent to ensure that the water is free of harmful pathogens

- *hardness removal:* This process is not usually part of the water treatment process where the source is surface waters. This is the case because surface waters seldom have hardness levels above 200 mg/L as $CaCO_3$. For groundwater, however, hardness levels are often as high as 1,000 + mg/L and must be treated to reduce hardness.

Surface Water Treatment Plant — Flow Diagram

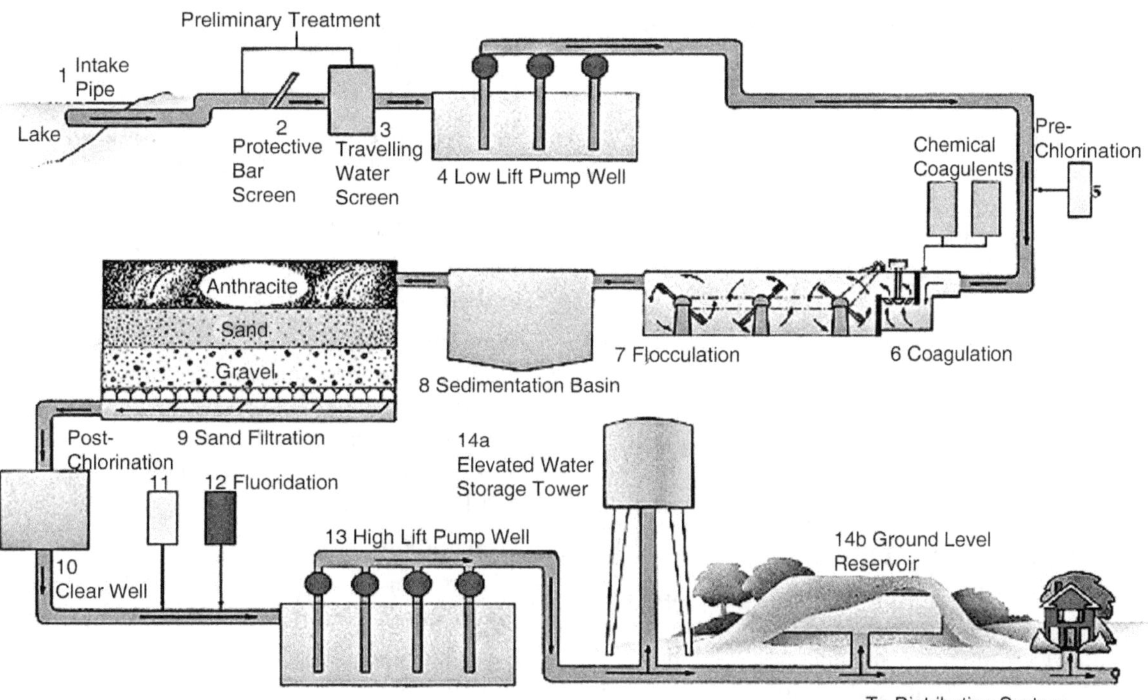

1. Intake Crib

Raw water from a surface water lake or reservoir is drawn into the plant through intake structures. Large debris like logs are prevented from entering and zebra mussel control is performed at the intake.

2. & 3. Screens

Smaller debris like fish, vegetation and garbage are removed from the raw water by protective bar and travelling screens before the water enters the low lift pumps.

4. Low Lift Pump Well

These pumps lift the water to flow through the treatment processes by gravity.

5. Pre-oxidation & Primary Disinfection

Disinfectants or other oxidants are added to disinfect or control tastes and odours. The specific processes used are determined by the chemical and biological raw water characteristics.

6. Coagulation

Coagulants, rapidly add electrochemical charges that attract the small particles in water to clump together as a "floc". This initial charge neutralization process allows the formed floc to agglomerate but remain suspended.

7. Flocculation

By slower mixing, turbulence causes the flocculated water to form larger floc particles that become cohesive and increase in mass. This visible floc is kept in suspension until large enough to settle under the influence of gravity.

8. Sedimentation

Flocculated water is applied to large volume tanks where the flow speed slows down and the dense floc settles. Settled floc is removed and treated as a waste product that is discharged to the sewer system.

9. Media Gravity Filtration

Relatively floc free, settled water flows through a media filter by gravity. Filter media are made from layers of anthracite or granular activated carbon and sand. Gravel or synthetic materials support the media. Physical straining removes the remaining floc. Filters are periodically backwashed to clean off accumulated floc and other trapped impurities.

10. Clear Well

Filtered water in the clear well is used to backwash filters and kept in storage to ensure that disinfectants are in contact with the water long enough to inactivate disease causing organisms.

11. Secondary Disinfection

Supplemental chlorine is added to maintain disinfection concentrations while the water is pumped through the distribution system. The purpose is to ensure minimum residual disinfectant levels at the farthest points of the system.

12. Fluoridation

A process where silicofluoride compounds are added to treated drinking water to artificially raise the fluoride concentration to within a specified range; for example between 0.5 to 0.8 mg/L (ppm). Fluoridation is an optional public health dental policy.

13. High Lift Pump Well

Treat drinking water is pumped through large pressure pumps to other pumping stations, reservoirs or points of supply within the local distribution system.

14a. & 14b. Elevated Water Storage Towers and Ground Level Reservoirs

Water distributed to water towers and storage reservoirs ensures stable water pressure. An adequate supply of water is maintained to meet peak water demands or emergencies such as fires, water main breaks, power outages and pump failures.

Distribution System

Distribution systems are comprised of large pipes known as trunk mains to deliver drinking water. Smaller diameter branch mains feed individual streets. Service connections to branch mains deliver water into residences. Pumping stations are used to increase pressure and to maintain adequate supply flows.

4. (*c*) Waste management is all the activities and actions required to manage waste from its inception to its final disposal. This includes amongst other things, collection, transport, treatment and disposal of waste together with monitoring and regulation. It also encompasses the legal and regulatory framework that relates to waste management encompassing guidance on recycling etc.

The waste hierarchy refers to the "3 R's" reduce, reuse and recycle, which classify waste management strategies according to their desirability in terms of waste minimisation. The waste hierarchy remains the cornerstone of most waste minimisation strategies. The aim of the waste hierarchy is to extract the maximum practical benefits from products and to generate the minimum amount of waste; see: resource recovery. The waste hierarchy is represented as a pyramid because the basic premise is for policy to take action first and prevent the generation of waste. The next step or preferred action is to reduce the generation of waste *i.e.*, by re-use. The next is recycling which would include composting. Following this step is material recovery and waste-to-energy. Energy can be recovered from processes *i.e.*, landfill and combustion, at this level of the hierarchy. The final action is disposal, in landfills or through incineration without energy recovery. This last step is the final resort for waste which has not been prevented, diverted or recovered. The waste hierarchy represents the progression of a product or material through the sequential stages of the pyramid of waste management.

Sanitary Landfilling

Sanitary landfill can be defined as the use of solid wastes for land reclamation. Restoration to original level with solid wastes is a good example for sanitary landfill. This method of waste disposal differs from ordinary dumping in a way that the area is adequately compacted and covered with earth at the end of the day. The disposal of garbage in a well managed land, adopting scientific methods of operation is termed as sanitary landfill. Low lying areas can be used to raise the level so that cultivation or any other activities can be done. Some completed sanitary landfills have been successfully converted into parks, playgrounds and other community land use project. Sanitary landfills are generally more common in advanced countries especially near urban areas where population densities are highest. In order to improve the environment, simple engineering techniques are also used so that landfill does not pose any threat to public health.

The waste must be deposited and levelled in layers. The whole of the surface of each layer of wastes is covered with solid or other suitable materials to a depth of 15-25 cms on the same day as the wastes are delivered to the site. The depth of the layer is limited because of the instability of newly deposited wastes over which vehicles must pass and minimise the fire risks. It is carefully planned and engineered for the facility of solid waste disposal. This means that it is designed, constructed and operated in an environmentally sound manner that does not harm environment and public safety and this also minimise public nuisances. Three key characteristics of a sanitary landfill distinguish it from an open dump.

(A) Solid waste is placed in a suitably selected and prepared landfill site in a carefully prescribed manner.

(B) The waste material is spread out and compacted with appropriate heavy machinery.

(C) The waste is covered each day with a layer of compacted soil.

Perhaps the most salient feature of modern sanitary landfill design is the technology used to prevent ground water pollution. Landfilling method require a proper site which is determined by many factors such as geography of the site, availability of land, density of population and engineering aspects. Adopting this disposal practices environment and esthetic considerations must be taken into account before selecting the dumping sites.

For many urban community it has become increasingly difficult to find suitable landfill sites that are within economically having distance. The public opposition has also become a major consideration. It is believed by many people that it is not possible to build a completely safe and secure solid waste sanitary landfill site. Some of the confined pollutants may eventually escape into the environment in the form of leachate with the potential to harm public health and damage the local ecosystem.

5. (a) Under over and balanced section w.r.t. Working State Method:

For a singly reinforced rectangular beam, having area of reinforcement A_{st}, we have
From Eq.

$$C_u = 0.36\, f_{ck}\, x_u\, b$$

Tensile force in reinforcement,

$$T_u = 0.87\, f_y\, A_{st}$$

For equilibrium of forces, we have

$$C_u = T_u$$

$$\therefore\ 0.36\, f_{ck}\, x_u \cdot b = 0.87\, f_y\, A_{st}$$

or

$$\frac{x_u}{d} = \frac{0.87\, f_y\, A_{st}}{0.36\, f_{ck}\, bd} = 2.417\, \frac{f_y}{f_{ck}} \cdot \frac{A_{st}}{bd}$$

$$= 2.417\, p_t\, \frac{f_y}{f_{ck}} \qquad \dots (i)$$

where $p_t = A_{st}/bd$ = reinforcement ratio.

Thus, for given section, the actual value of x_u/d (*i.e.*, the position of N.A.) can be determined from Eq. (*i*). Three cases may arise:

Case 1 : x_u/d equal to the limiting value, $x_{u,\,max}/d$: Balanced section

Case 2 : x_u/d less the limiting value : under-reinforced section

Case 3 : x_u/d more than limiting value : over-reinforced section

All the above three conditions / positions of N.A. are depicted in Fig.

1. **Balanced section (Fig. *a*)** : In the balanced section, the strain in steel and strain in concrete reach their maximum values simultaneously. Thus, in the balanced section $\varepsilon_u = \varepsilon_{cu}$ and $\varepsilon_s = \varepsilon_{sy}$ (or ε_{su}). The percentage of steel in this

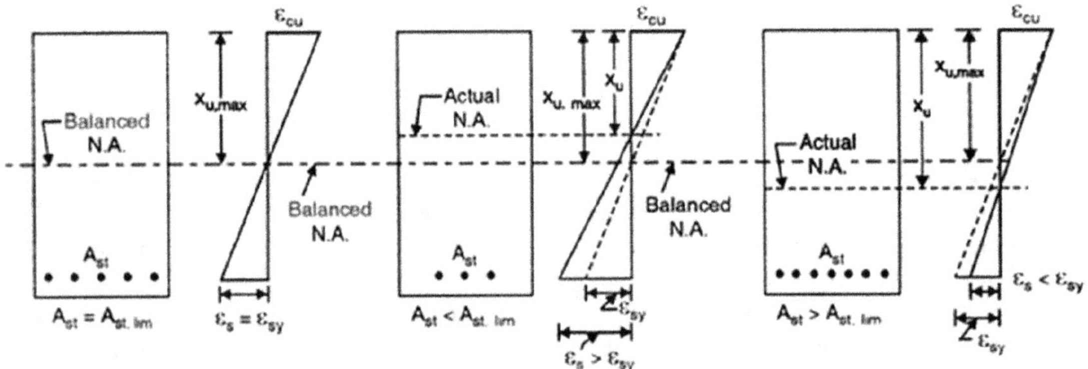

(a) Balanced Section (b) Under-reinforced section (c) Over-reinforced section

Fig.: Types of Sections

section is known as critical or limiting steel percentage $(p_{t,\,lim})$. The depth of N.A. $x_u = x_{u,\,max}$.

2. **Under reinforced section (Fig. *b*)** : An under reinforced section is the one in which steel percentage (p_t) is less than critical or limiting percentage $(p_{t,\,lim})$. Due to this, the actual N.A. is above the balanced N.A. and $x_u < x_{u,max}$.

3. Over reinforced section (Fig. *c*) : In an over-reinforced section, the steel percentage (p_t) is more than limiting percentage $(p_{t,lim})$, due to which N.A. falls below the balanced N.A. and $x_u > x_{u,max}$. Because of higher percentage of steel, yield does not take place in steel and failure occurs when the strain in extreme fibres in concrete reaches its ultimate value. Thus, the failure takes place due to crushing of concrete while strain in steel still remains below the yield strain ε_{su}. It should be noted that compression failure is sudden, and therefore not desirable. The Code recommends that if x_u/d is found to be greater than the limiting value, the beam should be redesigned.

Under, over and balanced section w.r.t Limit state method :

1. **Balanced section or critical section:** When the ratio of steel to concrete in a section is such that the strain in steel and strain in concrete reach their maximum values simultaneously the section is referred to as a balanced or critical section and the percentage of steel in this section is known as critical steel percentage.

2. **Under-reinforced section:** A section having steel percentage less than the critical percentage is known as under-reinforced section. Since steel is insufficient to balance compression in concrete, the tensile strain in steel reaches yield value while the maximum compressive strain in concrete is less than its ultimate crushing value. The section undergoes large rotational deformations from the initial stage of yielding of steel to the final stage of crushing of concrete, giving sufficient warning of impending failure.

3. **Over-reinforced section:** A section having percentage of tension steel greater than the critical percentage is known as over-reinforced section. Since the amount of steel is more than that in balanced section, the neutral axis moves below the balanced neutral axis to satisfy the equilibrium condition resulting in the concrete reaching its ultimate strain while the strain in steel remains less than its yield value. This type of failure is usually avoided in ultimate strength design.

6.(*a*)(*i*)

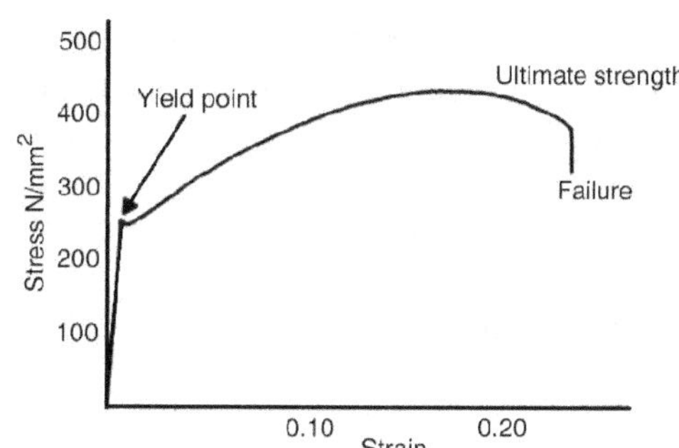

Fig. (a): Stress-strain curve to failure for typical mild steel

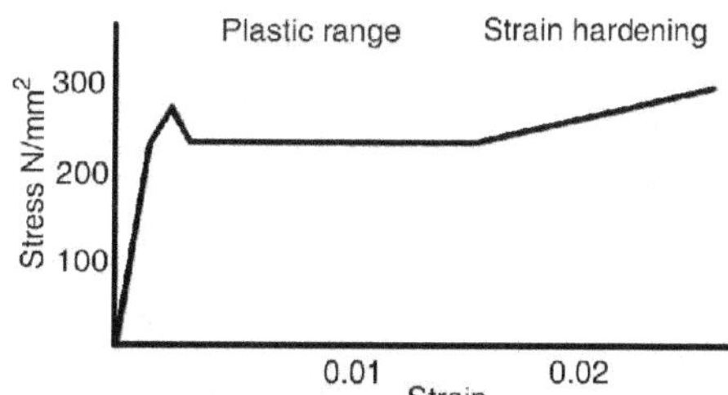

Fig. (b): Part of the stress-strain curve for typical mild steel

Properties of structural steel

To the structural designer, certain properties of steel merit special consideration. As a general introduction to the behaviour of steel under load it is helpful to refer to a tensile stress-strain diagram for an average mild (low carbon) steel. This is shown complete in Figure (*a*) and a portion of it to a larger scale in Figure (*b*). From the diagram the following important characteristics of the material can be deduced:

Elasticity

Up to a well-defined yield point steel behaves as a perfectly elastic material. Removal of stress at levels below the yield stress causes the material to revert to its unstressed dimensions. Elasticity is also exhibited by higher strength steels which do not have a defined yield point (Figure (*c*)). Strictly speaking linear elastic behaviour ceases at a stress level below the yield point known as the proportional limit but this level is difficult to determine and the deviation from straight line behaviour up to yield is very small. The slope of the stress-strain curve in the elastic range defines the modulus of elasticity. For structural steels its value is virtually independent of the steel type and is commonly taken as 205 kN/mm^2.

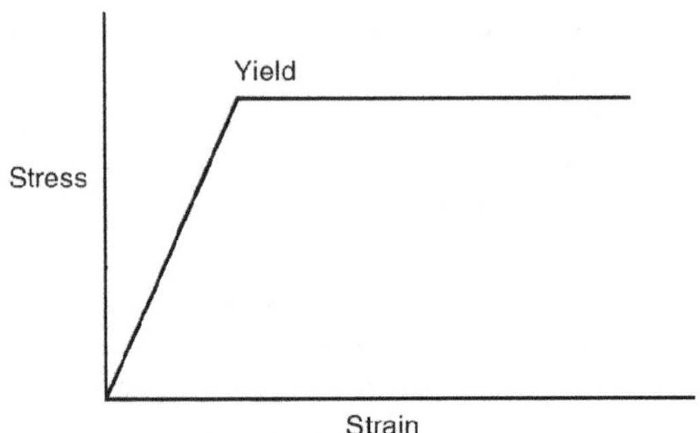

Fig. (d): Elastic-plastic stress strain diagram

Tensile strength

The applied stress to cause failure is considerably greater than the yield stress; in Figure (*a*) for instance the ultimate stress is nearly twice the yield stress.

Ductility

An important property of steel is its ability to undergo large deformations without fracture. The strain to failure may reach 25% in a mild steel, will be less for higher carbon steels and may be drastically curtailed in all steels under circumstances which lead to brittle fracture. From an examination of the stress-strain curve, it will be seen that the elastic strain is a small portion of the total strain possible before fracture occurs.

In order to analyse the behaviour of steel elements which arc stressed beyond the elastic limit (yield point) there is a need to simplify the real stress-strain curve for steel. A suitable simplification is to replace the portion of the curve from yield to failure by a horizontal line representing strain at constant stress. The resulting elastic-plastic stress-strain diagram is illustrated in Figure (*d*). Because it neglects the region of strain hardening the elastic-plastic relationship is a conservative approximation to the real strength of the material.

Apart from the mechanical properties described above an awareness of the susceptibility of steel to certain other effects is essential.

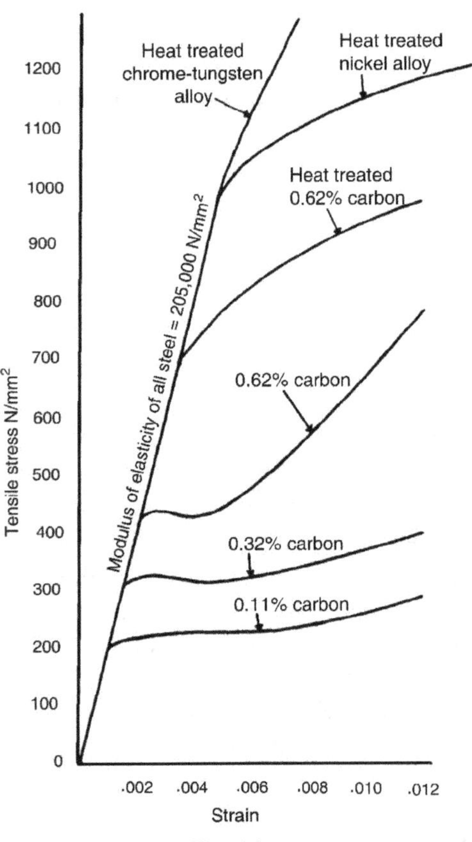

Fig. (c)

6.(*a*)(*ii*)

Form of weld	Sectional representation	Appropriate symbol	Form of weld	Sectional representation	Appropriate symbol
Fillet			Plug of slot		
Square butt			Backing strip		
Single 'V' butt					
Double 'V' butt			Spot		
Single 'U' butt					
Double 'U' butt			Seam		
Single bevel butt			Mashed seam	Before / After	
Double 'J' butt			Stitch		
Single 'J' butt			Mashed stitch	Before / After	
Double 'J' butt			Projection	Before / After	
Stud			Flash	Rod or Bar / Tube	
Bead or edge weld			Butt resistance or pressure (up set)	Rod or Bar / Tube	
Sealing run					

Fig. (a): Types of welds and symbols

S. No.	Particulars	Drawing representation and symbols	
1	Weld all round		O
2	Field or site weld		● A
3	Flash contour		—
4	Convex contour		⌒
5	Concave contour		⌣
6	Grinding finish		G
7	Machining finish		M
8	Chipping finish		C

Fig. (b): Supplementary weld symbols

6. (*b*) For Fe 410 grade of steel:
$$f_u = 410 \text{ MPa}$$
For bolts of grade 4.6:
$$f_{ub} = 400 \text{ MPa}$$
For 16 mm diameter bolt:
$$A_{nb} = 157 \text{ mm}^2 \qquad \text{(Given Table)}$$
γ_{mb} = partial safety factor for material of bolt
$$= 1.25$$
γ_{m1} = partial safety factor for resistance governed by ultimate stress = 1.25

The bolts will be in double shear and bearing. For the calculation of the strength of the bolt in bearing, the thickness to be considered for bearing will be the least of aggregate thickness of cover plates and the minimum thickness of main plates.

Hence, $t = 8$ mm.

The strength of bolt in shear per pitch length,

$$V_{dsb} = 2 \times A_{nb} \times \frac{f_{ub}}{\sqrt{3}\,\gamma_{mb}}$$

$$= 2 \times 157 \times \frac{400}{\sqrt{3} \times 1.25} \times 10^{-3} = 58 \text{ kN}$$

The strength of bolt in bearing per pitch length,

$$V_{dpb} = 2.5\,k_b\,dt\,\frac{f_u}{\gamma_{mb}}$$

Here, k_b is least of

$$\frac{e}{3d_o} = \frac{30}{3 \times 18} = 0.55;$$

$$\frac{p}{3d_o} - 0.25 = \frac{45}{3 \times 18} - 0.25$$

$$= 0.58; \frac{f_{ub}}{f_u} = \frac{400}{410} = 0.975;$$

and 1.0

Hence, $k_b = 0.55$

In the calculation of the value of k_b, the value of bolt hole diameter is referred from (given table). Also, the value of end-distance has been assumed to be for sheared edge.

$$V_{dpb} = 2.5 \times 0.55 \times 16 \times 8 \times \frac{410}{1.25} \times 10^{-3}$$

$$= 57.73 \text{ kN}$$

The net tensile strength of plate per pitch length

$$T_{dn} = 0.9\frac{f_u}{\gamma_{m1}}A_n$$

$$T_{dn} = 0.9\frac{f_u}{\gamma_{m1}}(p - d_h)t$$

(diameter of hole $d_h = 18$ mm, from given table)

$$= 0.9 \times \frac{410}{1.25} \times (45 - 18) \times 8 \times 10^{-3}$$

$$= 63.76 \text{ kN}$$

Strength of the solid plate per pitch length

$$= 0.9\,\frac{f_u}{\gamma_{m1}}\,pt$$

$$= 0.9 \times \frac{410}{1.25} \times 45 \times 8 \times 10^{-3}$$

$$= 106.27 \text{ kN}$$

Hence, the strength of the joint per pitch length will be the least of the strength per pitch length in shear, bearing for bolts and net strength of plate.

Hence, strength of the joint per pitch length $= 57.73$ kN

$$\text{Efficiency of the joint} = \frac{57.73}{106.27} \times 100$$

$$= 54.32\%$$

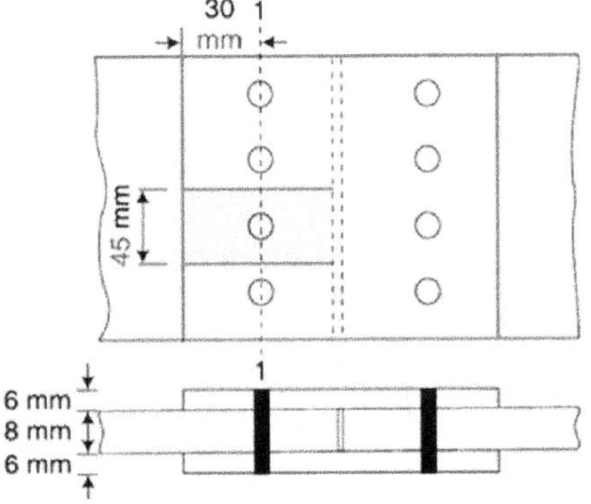

SSC-Junior Engineer (Civil & Structural) Exam 2014*

PAPER-II (Conventional)

1.(*a*) What are the constituents of good brick-earth? What constituents render brick-earth unsuitable for manufacturing bricks?

(*b*) Describe any two tests to be performed in case of burnt clay bricks.

(*c*) State the conditions under which you will recommend the following cements. Give also the reasons.
   (*i*) Rapid hardening cement
   (*ii*) High Alumina cement

(*d*) Briefly explain:
   (*i*) Assessed value
   (*ii*) Sinking fund

(*e*) Determine the number of bags of cement required for a standard brick masonary for a wall of thickness 30 cm for a height of 10 m and length 200 m in 1 : 4 mortar.

2.(*a*) The readings given in the Table below were recorded in a levelling operation from points 1 to 10. Reduce the levels by the height of instrument method and apply appropriate checks. The point 10 is a bench mark having elevation of 66.374 m. Determine the loop closure.

Station	Chainage (m)	B.S.	I.S.	F.S.	Remarks
1	0	0.597			B.M. = 68·233 m
2	20	2.587		3.132	C.P
3	40		1.565		
4	60		1.911		
5	80		0.376		
6	100	2.244		1.522	C.P
7	120		3.771		
8	140	1.334		1.985	C.P
9	160		0.601		
10	180			2.002	

(*b*) A soil sample in its natural state has, when fully saturated, a water content of 32.5%. Determine the void ratio, dry and total unit weights. Calculate the total weight of water required to saturate a soil mass of volume 10 m^3. Assume $G_S = 2.69$.

(*c*) Describe the method of laying Water Bound Macadam (WBM) road.

3.(*a*) Find the discharge through a rectangular orifice 2.0 m wide and 1.5 m deep fitted to a water tank. The water level in the tank is 3.0 m above the top edge of the orifice. Take $c_d = 0.62$.

(*b*) Enumerate the assumptions made in Lacy's theory of canal designs.

(*c*) Write short note on types of impurities in water in the light of domestic supply.

4.(*a*) Draw the shear force and bending moment diagram and label the values of the largest positive and negative shearing forces and bending moments for the beams with overhang as shown in Figure 1.

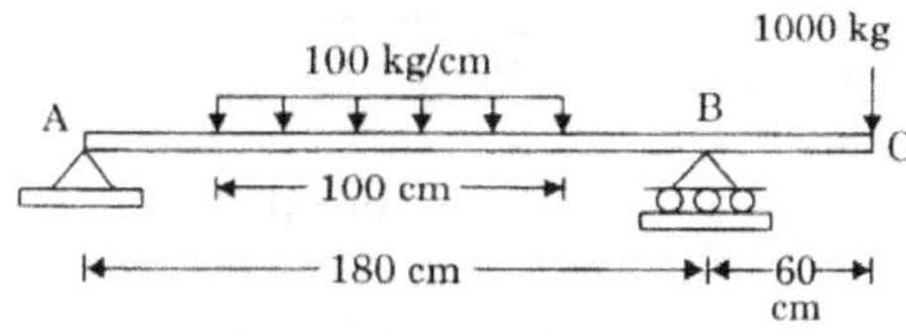

Figure 1

(*b*) Describe the various defects in concrete along with precautions that should be exercised to prevent them.

5.(*a*) Describe briefly creep and shrinkage.

(*b*) A rectangular, singly reinforced beam 300 mm wide and 500 mm effective depth is used as a simply supported beam over an effective span of 6 m. The reinforcement consists of

---

4 bars of 20 mm dia. If the beam carries a load of 12 kN/m (inclusive of self weight), determine the stress developed in concrete and steel. Take $m = 19$.

6.(*a*) Classify welded joints according to type of joints.

   (*b*) A single rivet lap joint is used to connect 12 mm thick plates by providing 20 mm dia rivets at 50 mm pitch. Determine the strength of the joint and joint efficiency. Take working stress in shear in rivets = 80 N/mm^2, working stress in bearing in rivets = 250 N/mm^2 and working stress in axial tension in plates = 156 N/mm^2.

ANSWERS

1.(*a*) **Composition of a Good Brick Earth**

Following are the constituents of a good brick earth:

1. **Alumina (Al$_2$O$_3$):** It is the chief constituent of a good brick earth. A content of about 20% to 30% is necessary to form the brick earth of a good quality. It imparts plasticity to the earth so it helps in the moulding of the brick earth.

   If alumina is present in excess with inadequate quantity of sand then the raw bricks shrink and warp during drying, on burning they become too hard. So, it is important to have an optimum content of alumina.

2. **Silica (SiO$_2$):** It exists in the brick earth either free or combined. As free sand it is mechanically mixed with clay and in combined form it exists in chemical composition with alumina. A good brick earth should contain about 50% to 60% of silica.

   The presence of this constituent prevents the shrinkage, cracking and warping of raw bricks. It, thus, imparts uniform shape to the bricks. The durability of bricks depends upon proper composition of silica in brick earth. The excess of silica destroys the cohesion b/w particles and brick become brittle.

3. **Lime (CaCO$_3$):** A small quantity of lime not more than 5% is desirable in good brick earth. It should be present in very fine state, because even small particles of size of a pin-head can result in the flaking of the brick.

The lime prevents shrinkage of the raw bricks, sand alone is infusible, but it slightly fuses at kiln temperature in presence of lime. Fused sand acts as a hard cementing material for brick particles.

The excess of lime causes brick to melt and, therefore, its shape is lost. The lumps of lime turns into quick lime (CaO) after burning and this free lime can later react with water to form slaked lime. This process is called slaking. It may result in splitting of the brick into pieces.

4. **Oxide of Iron (Fe$_2$O$_3$):** Iron oxide performs two functions, first it helps in fusing of the sand like lime and second it provides the red colour to the bricks. It is kept below 5 to 6% because excess of it may result in the dark blue or black colour of brick.

5. **Magnesia:** A small quantity of magnesia present in the brick earth imparts yellow tinge to the brick and decreases shrinkage. If magnesia is present in excess, it causes brick to decay.

Harmful Constituents of Brick Earth

Following are the ingredients the presence of which render the resulting brick unsuitable for construction.

1. **Pebbles of stone and gravel:** The presence of pebbles does not allow the clay to be mixed uniformly and thoroughly, with the result that weak and porous bricks are obtained. These should be removed from the earth used for moulding the bricks.

2. **Vegetation and organic matter:** The presence of vegetation and organic matter in brick earth helps in it's burning, but if

it is not thoroughly burned, porous bricks will be produced. The porosity so imparted is due to evolution of gases during the burning of the carbonaceous matter present in these ingredients. Hence, thorough burning of such bricks is necessary so that all these gases are removed.

3. **Alkalies:** Alkalies, mainly in the form of soda and potash lower the fusion point of clay. If present in excess, they cause the bricks to fuse, twist and warp during burning and, thus, tend to dis-figure them. Further, alkalies present in bricks affect the brick masonry structure because alkaline salts act like hygroscopic substances, absorbing moisture from the atmosphere in due course of time. Such moisture create damp conditions, and on drying, leave behind grayish white deposits. This is termed as *efflorescence* which spoil the appearance of the building.

4. **Lime stone and Kankar:** Lime should be present in a very finely divided state because even small particles of the size of pin head cause flaking of bricks. A desirable amount of lime present in brick earth acts as a flux upon silica during burning and binds the particles together. However, if present in excess, it melts the brick particles as a result of which the brick looses its shape. Lime should not be present in brick earth in the form of lime stone or kankar, since these get converted to quicklime during burning. The quick lime swells on absorption of moisture and increases in volume two to three times, causing cracking and disintegration of brick.

5. **Iron pyrite:** Iron pyrite if present in brick earth, decomposes, oxidises and finally crystallises in the brick, causing the brick to split to pieces. Hence, it should be carefully removed.

6. **Reh or Kallar:** 'Reh' or 'Kallar', consisting of sodium sulphate with more or less of sodium carbonate and sodium chloride render the clay totally unsuitable for brick making. Its presence prevents bricks from being properly burned. Also, after burning, these salts crystallise and appear as irregular and unsightly white patches on the surface of bricks. This causes the surface of the brick to peel off layer by layer and gradually crumble away. If the brick is plastered, these white patches cause the plaster also to peel off. Presence of reh or kallar in soil could be easily detected by the presence of efflorescence on the side of fresh excavation, if the soil is moist.

7. **Carbonaceous matter:** Carbonaceous matter is harmful ingredient in a brick earth. Presence of carbonaceous matter cause different colours in the interior and exterior of brick. Such bricks do not bear the chipping. Their presence deface the plastering by discolouration.

1. (*b*) Burnt Clay Facing Bricks

These bricks are used in the exposed face of masonry without any further surface protection. Where external plastering or rendering have to be frequently renewed, due to corrosive atmosphere and also for high rise buildings, use of facing bricks is economical. IS specifications as regards burnt clay facing bricks are as follows:

1. Facing bricks are of two classes:
   (*a*) Class I, (*b*) Class II

2. The average compressive strength should not be less than 75 kg/cm^2 for class II and 100 kg/cm^2 for class I.

3. Water absorption requirement for 24 hours immersion should not exceed 15%.

4. Efflorescence requirement should be 'nil' for both classes.

5. The war page for both the classes should not exceed 2.5 mm.

6. These bricks should be free from cracks, flaws and nodules of free lime. The standard size of facing bricks is 19 × 9 × 9 cm and 19 × 9 × 4 cm.

Burnt Clay Hollow Blocks

These blocks are being used in a limited scale for walls and partitions in our country. They are light in weight for masonry construction and also being hollow impart thermal insulation to the building. These blocks should be of uniform colour and should have a fine, compact and uniform texture.

As per IS: 3952–1978.

1. These blocks are of the following three types:

   Type A: Blocks with both faces keyed for plastering or rendering.

   Type B: Blocks with both faces smooth and suitable for use without plastering or rendering on either side.

   Type C: Blocks with one face keyed and one face smooth.

2. The size of burnt clay hollow blocks should be as follows:

Length (cm)	Width (cm)	Height (cm)
19	19	9
29	9	9
29	14	9

3. Thickness of any shell should not be less than 11 mm and that of any web not less than 8 mm.

4. The minimum average crushing strength of the blocks when determined should be 3.5 N/mm^2.

5. The average water absorption of the blocks by mass should not be more than 20%.

1. (c) (i) Rapid Hardening Cement

This cement is similar to ordinary Portland cement. As the name indicates it develops strength rapidly and as such it may be more appropriate to call it as high early strength cement. It is pointed out that rapid hardening cement which develops higher rate of development of strength should not be confused with quick-setting cement which only sets quickly. Rapid hardening cement develops at the age of three days, the same strength as that is expected of ordinary Portland cement at seven days.

The rapid rate of development of strength is attributed to the higher fineness of grinding (specific surface not less than 3250 sq. cm per gram) and higher C_3S and lower C_2S content.

A higher fineness of cement particles expose greater surface area for action of water and also higher proportion of C_3S results in quicker hydration. Consequently, rapid hardening cement gives out much greater heat of hydration during the early period. Therefore, rapid hardening cement should not be used in mass concrete construction.

The use of rapid hardening cement is recommended in the following situations:

(*a*) In pre-fabricated concrete construction.

(*b*) Where framework is required to be removed early for re-use elsewhere.

(*c*) Road repair works.

(*d*) In cold weather concrete where the rapid rate of development of strength reduces the vulnerability of concrete to the frost damage.

(*ii*) High Alumina Cement

High alumina cement has a very rapid rate of development of strength and superior resistance to sea and sulphate waters. It is prepared by heating ferruginous bauxite with limestone at 1500–1600°C.

High alumina cement differs from alumina in a higher content of alumina, Al_2O_3— not less than 72%. It is used as a binder in making refractory mortars or concretes. It is also finding use in the construction of industrial furnaces.

Since concrete made with high-alumina cement gains strength much more quickly than that made with ordinary Portland cement, it is ideally suited in many respects to use in precast concrete work. According to CP114, 'the use of high-alumina cement requires much greater care than the use of Portland type cement' and if it is not correctly treated during its early life or maintained in wet or humid conditions at temperatures above about 27°C conversion is likely to take place of the hydrated cement to a chemically stable, but porous, form.

1. (*d*) (*i*) Assessed Value: For rental properties, method of verifying values is to check property tax bills and the local assessed value. Property tax bills show the property's assessed value, which is the value used to calculate the tax liability. This usually breaks down total value by land and improvements. Assessed value may lag well behind market value. In addition, assessed value is notoriously unreliable because of the time lag. If the local assessor's office is under-staffed, inefficient, or even unqualified, assessments may reflect those problems as well.

With this in mind, checking assessed value for several different properties provides you with a comparison between assessed value and asked price. This is valuable information, since it may reveal inconsistencies or demonstrate an important difference between the realistic market value of properties and the basis used for property taxes. If nothing else, the analysis of assessed values is useful in determining whether those values are reliable from one part of town to another.

Formula: Assessment Ratio

$$\frac{P}{A} = R$$

Where P = asked price

A = assessed value

R = assessment ratio

For example, suppose you check the assessed value for several properties on the market that you are thinking about purchasing. All are in the same city and are located in what you consider to be similar neighbourhoods; the price ranges are similar as well.

(*ii*) Sinking funds: The sinking funds provided for the payment of interest and the extinguishment of the principal of the debts of the state heretofore contracted shall be continued; they shall be separately kept and safely invested, and neither of them shall be appropriated or used in any manner other than for such payment and extinguishment as hereinafter provided.

After any sinking fund shall equal in amount the debt for which it was created no further contribution shall be made thereto except to make good any losses ascertained at the annual appraisals above mentioned, and the income thereof shall be applied to the payment of the interest on such a debt. Any excess in such income not required for the payment of interest may be applied to the general fund of the state.

A sinking fund is a mechanism for systematic retirement of state debt in which revenue is earmarked for a special fund to retire debt created by particular projects. The first paragraph was intended to preserve the inviolability of the sinking funds and had the effect of preventing the state from borrowing from sinking funds for current expenses. By implication, the section provides for the creation of separate sinking funds for each issue. The annual installments are to be computed on the basis of an interest earning at the rate of 3 per cent annually. Any excess in the sinking fund can be used to reduce appropriations to the fund for the payment of interest on the debt for which the fund had been created. Any additional excess can be transferred to the general fund. Because sinking funds are based on the assessed value of state property in the fiscal year, any increase in these values increases the value of the sinking fund, inflating it beyond the projected need and making the tax burden higher than necessary.

2.(a)   **Table**

Station	Chainage (m)	B.S.	I.S.	F.S.	Remarks
1	0	0.597			B.M. = 68·233 m
2	20	2.587		3.132	C.P
3	40		1.565		
4	60		1.911		
5	80		0.376		
6	100	2.244		1.522	C.P
7	120		3.771		
8	140	1.334		1.985	C.P
9	160		0.601		
10	180			2.002	

Reduced levels of the points

$$\text{H.I.}_1 = h_1 + \text{B.S.}_1$$
$$= 68.233 + 0.597 = 68.830 \text{ m}$$
$$h_2 = \text{H.I.}_1 - \text{F.S.}_2$$
$$= 68.830 - 3.132 = 65.698 \text{ m}$$
$$\text{H.I.}_2 = h_2 + \text{B.S.}_2$$
$$= 65.698 + 2.587 = 68.285 \text{ m}$$
$$h_3 = \text{H.I.}_2 - \text{I.S.}_3$$
$$= 68.285 - 1.565 = 66.720 \text{ m}$$
$$h_4 = \text{H.I.}_2 - \text{I.S.}_4$$
$$= 68.285 - 1.911 = 66.374 \text{ m}$$
$$h_5 = \text{H.I.}_2 - \text{I.S.}_5$$
$$= 68.285 - 0.376 = 67.909 \text{ m}$$
$$h_6 = \text{H.I.}_2 - \text{F.S.}_6$$
$$= 68.285 - 1.522 = 66.763 \text{ m}$$
$$\text{H.I.}_6 = h_6 + \text{B.S.}_6$$
$$= 66.763 + 2.244 = 69.007 \text{ m}$$

$$h_7 = \text{H.I.}_6 - \text{I.S.}_7$$
$$= 69.007 - 3.771 = 65.236 \text{ m}$$
$$h_8 = \text{H.I.}_6 - \text{F.S.}_8$$
$$= 69.007 - 1.985 = 67.022 \text{ m}$$
$$\text{H.I.}_8 = h_8 + \text{B.S.}_8$$
$$= 67.022 + 1.334 = 68.356 \text{ m}$$
$$h_9 = \text{H.I.}_8 - \text{I.S.}_9$$
$$= 68.356 - 0.601 = 67.755 \text{ m}$$
$$h_{10} = \text{H.I.}_8 - \text{F.S.}_{10}$$
$$= 68.356 - 2.002 = 66.354 \text{ m}$$

Loop closure and loop adjustment

The error at point 10

$$= \text{computed R.L.} - \text{known R.L.}$$
$$= 66.354 - 66.374 = -0.020 \text{ m}$$

Therefore, correction

$$= +0.020 \text{ m}$$

Since, there are three change points, there will be four instrument positions. Thus, the total number of points at which the corrections are to be applied is four, *i.e.*, three C.P.s and one last F.S. It is reasonable to assume that similar errors have occurred at each station. Therefore, the correction for each instrument setting which has to be applied progressively, is

$$= +\frac{0.020}{4} = 0.005 \text{ m}$$

i.e., the correction at station 1   0.0 m

the correction at station 2   +0.005 m

the correction at station 6   +0.010 m

the correction at station 8   +0.015 m

the correction at station 10   +0.020 m

The corrections for the intermediate sights will be same as the corrections for that instrument stations to which they are related. Therefore,

correction for I.S._3, I.S._4, and I.S._5 = +0.010 m

correction for I.S._7 = +0.015 m

correction for I.S._9 = +0.020 m

Applying the above corrections to the respective reduced levels, the corrected reduced levels are obtained. The results have been presented in Table.

Table

Station	Chainage (m)	B.S.	I.S.	F.S.	H.I.	R.L.	Correction	Corrected R.L.
1	0	0.597			68.830	68.233	-	68.233
2	20	2.587		3.132	68.285	65.698	+0.005	65.703
3	40		1.565			66.720	+0.010	66.730
4	60		1.911			66.374	+0.010	66.384
5.	80		0.376			67.909	+0.010	67.919
6.	100	2.244		1.522	69.007	66.763	+0.010	66.773
7.	120		3.771			65.236	+0.015	65.251
8.	140	1.334		1.985	68.356	67.022	+0.015	67.037
9.	160		0.601			67.755	+0.020	67.775
10.	180			2.002		66.354	+0.020	66.374
Σ		6.762		8.641				

Check: $6.762 - 8.641 = 66.354 - 68.233 = -1.879$ (O.K.)

2.(b) Void ratio: From $S = \dfrac{wG_s}{e}$

$$\therefore \quad e = \frac{wG_s}{S} = \frac{32.5 \times 2.69}{(1) \times 100} = 0.874$$

Total unit weight: From

$$\gamma_t = \frac{G_s \gamma_w (1+w)}{1+e}$$

$$= \frac{2.69(9.81)(1+0.325)}{1+0.874}$$

$$= 18.7 \text{ kN/m}^3$$

Dry unit weight: From

$$\gamma_d = \frac{\gamma_w G_s}{1+e}$$

$$= \frac{2.69 \times 9.81}{1+0.874}$$

$$= 14.08 \text{ kN/m}^3$$

From, $W = \gamma_t V = 18.66 \times 10 = 186.6$ kN

From, $W_s = \gamma_d V = 14.08 \times 10 = 140.8$ kN

Weight of water

$= W - W_s = 186.6 - 140.8 = 45.8$ kN.

2.(c) Water Bound Macadam (WBM) Roads

Water Bound Macadam road is named after a Scot Engineer John Macadam. Water Bound Macadam (WBM) road is of better quality than the ordinary earth, gravel, Kankar and moorum roads. The term macadam nowadays is referred to the crushed stone which is used in the construction of base course of the road. Crushed stone is also referred by the name of road metal. As the name suggests itself, the WBM roads are such roads in which crushed stone is kept bonded by the action of rolling and voids filled with screening and binding materials with the help of water. WBM base course may be laid on a prepared subgrade, subbase, base or existing pavement as the case may be. Binding action in WBM construction is obtained by using stone dust as filler, in the presence of water.

WBM construction are made in layers, each layer not exceeding compacted thickness of about 10–15 cm. The total thickness of WBM construction may vary from 7.5–30 cm, depending upon the traffic and subgrade requirements. WBM constructions as far as possible should not be up to use as the surfacing layer, because in such conditions it will disintegrate immediately under traffic.

Hence, to prevent the disintegration of WBM roads they should be covered either by bituminous surfacing or any other suitable surfacing. A section of WBM road is shown in Fig.

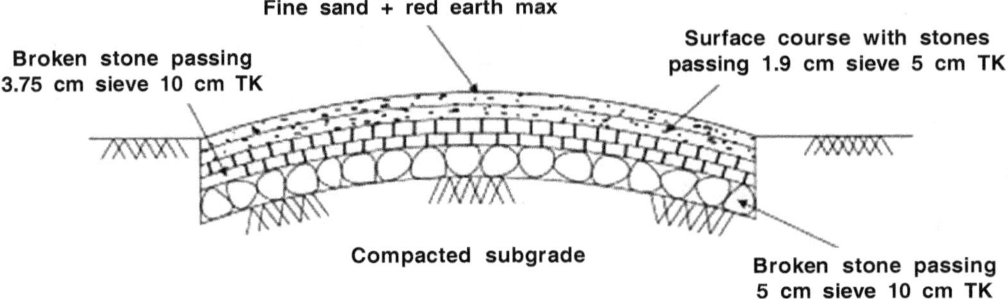

Fig.: *Water bound Macadam road*

3.(a) Given, Width of orifice, $b = 2.0$ m

Depth of orifice, $d = 1.5$ m

Height of water above top edge of the orifice,

$$H_1 = 3 \text{ m}$$

Height of water above bottom edge of the orifice,

$$H_2 = H_1 + d = 3 + 1.5 = 4.5 \text{ m}$$
$$C_d = 0.62$$

Discharge Q is given as

$$Q = \frac{2}{3} C_d \times b \times \sqrt{2g} \left[H_2^{3/2} - H_1^{3/2} \right]$$

$$= \frac{2}{3} \times 0.62 \times 2.0 \times \sqrt{2 + 9.81} [4.5^{1.5} - 3^{1.5}] \text{ m}^3/\text{s}$$

$$= 3.66 [9.545 - 5.196] \text{ m}^3/\text{s} = 15.917 \text{ m}^3/\text{s}.$$

3.(b) Lacey's Regime Theory

Lacey regime theory postulates that dimensions of bed width, depth and slope of canal attain a state of equilibrium with time which is called **regime state.** Lacey defined a regime channel as a stable channel transporting a minimum bed load consistent with fully active bed. According to him, a channel will be in regime if it carries a constant discharge and it flows uniformly in unlimited incoherent alluvium of the same character. Lacey also differentiated regime between the initial and final regime conditions of channel. The initial regime condition is attained shortly after it is put into operation after construction and the channel begins to adjust its bed slope either by silting or scouring although bed width is not altered. The channel then appears to have attained stability, but it is not actually the final state of stability and, hence, it still represents the initial regime condition. Eventually, continuous action of water overcomes the resistance of the banks and sets up a condition such that the channel adjusts its complete section, then final or true regime condition is attained.

According to Lacey, there is only one longitudinal slope at which the channel will carry a particular discharge with a particular silt grade. Natural silt transporting channels have a tendency to assume semi-elliptical section. The coarser the silt, greater the waterway of such channel with narrower depth. The finer the silt, greater is the depth with narrow waterway as shown in Figure.

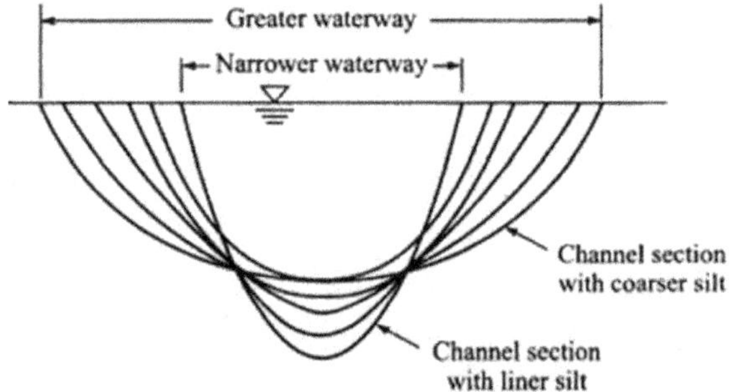

Fig. *Channel section according to Lacey's theory.*

Lacey's Regime Equations: Lacey collected a large number of data of stable channels in Indo-Gangetic plains.

He deduced the relationship between A, V, Q, P, S and 'f' as follows.

1. $f = 1.76\sqrt{m_r}$

2. $Af^2 = 140\,V^5$

3. $V = \left(\dfrac{Qf^2}{140}\right)^{\frac{1}{6}}$

4. $P = 4.75\sqrt{Q}$

5. Regime flow equation
   $V = 10.8\,R^{2/3}\,S^{1/3}$

6. Regime slope equation

   (*a*) $S = \dfrac{f^{3/2}}{4980\,R^{1/3}}$

   (*b*) $S = \dfrac{f^{5/3}}{3340\,Q^{1/6}}$

7. Regime scour depth

   $R = 0.47 \times \left(\dfrac{Q}{f}\right)^{1/3}$

where,

f = silt factor

m_r = mean particle size of silt in mm

A = cross-sectional area in m^2

V = mean velocity in m/sec

Q = discharge in cumec

P = wetted perimeter in m

R = hydraulic mean radius or scour depth

S = bed slope.

Steps Required in Design by Lacey's Theory

Values of discharge Q, sand size d in mm, side slope zH:1V, (if not given, assume $\dfrac{1}{2}$ H:1V

or 1H:1V) or angle of repose of soil to reduce earth pressure are given or known:

1. From the known sediment size d in mm, find silt factor by above equation, *i.e.,*
   $f = 1.76\sqrt{d}$

2. Find the velocity V_c from known Q and f from above equation.

3. Find the area from continuity equation:

   $A = \dfrac{Q}{V_c}$

4. Now, A = (B + zy)y when channel is trapezoidal.

5. $P = 2y\sqrt{1 + z^2} + B = 4.75\sqrt{Q}$ by above equation.

6. In steps 4 and 5, two equations and two unknowns y and B, solve them simultaneously.

7. Find bed slope s_b by above equation. *i.e.,*

   $s_b = \dfrac{f^{5/3}}{3450\,Q^{1/6}}.$

3.(*c*) Water Impurities

Water impurities include dissolved and suspended solids. Calcium bicarbonate is a soluble salt. A solution of calcium bicarbonate is clear, because the calcium and bicarbonate are present as atomic sized ions which are not large enough to reflect light. Some soluble minerals impart a colour to the solution. Soluble iron salts produce pale yellow or green solutions; some copper salts form intensely blue solutions. Although coloured, these solutions are clear. Suspended solids are substances that are not completely soluble in water and are present as particles. These particles usually impart a visible turbidity to the water. Dissolved and suspended solids are present in most surface waters. Seawater is very high in soluble sodium chloride; suspended sand and silt make it slightly cloudy. An extensive list of soluble and suspended impurities found in water is given in Table.

Table: *Common impurities found in fresh water*

Constituent	Chemical Formula	Difficulties Caused	Means of Treatment
Turbidity	non-expressed in analysis as units	imparts unsightly appearance to water; deposits in water lines, process equipment, etc., interferes with most process uses	coagulation, settling and filtration
Hardness	calcium and magnesium salts, expressed as $CaCO_3$	chief source of scale in heat exchange equipment, boilers, pipe lines, etc.; forms curds with soap, interferes with dyeing, etc.	softening; demineralization; internal boiler water treatment; surface active agents
Alkalinity	bicarbonate (HCO_3^-), carbonate (CO_3^{2-}), and hydroxide (OH^-), expressed as $CaCO_3$	foam and carryover of solids with steam; embrittlement of boiler steel; bicarbonate and carbonate produce CO_2 in steam, a source of corrosion in condensate lines	lime and lime-soda softening; acid treatment; hydrogen zeolite softening; demineralization dealkalization by anion exchange
Free Mineral Acid	H_2SO_4, HCl, etc., expressed as $CaCO_3$	corrosion	neutralization with alkalies
Carbon Dioxide	CO_2	corrosion in water lines, particularly steam and condensate lines	aeration, deaeration, neutralization with alkalies
pH	hydrogen ion concentration defined as: $$pH = \log\frac{1}{[H^+]}$$	pH varies according to acidic or alkaline solids in water; most natural waters have a pH of 6.0-8.0	pH can be increased by alkalies and decreased by acids
Sulphate	SO_4^{2-}	adds to solids content of water, but in itself is not usually significant, combines with calcium to form calcium sulphate scale	demineralization, reverse osmosis, electrodialysis, evaporation
Chloride	Cl^-	adds to solids content and increases corrosive character of water	demineralization, reverse osmosis, electrodialysis, evaporation
Nitrate	NO_3^-	adds to solids content, but is not usually significant industrially: high concentrations cause methemo globinemia in infants; useful for control of boiler metal embrittlement	demineralization, reverse osmosis, electrodialysis, evaporation

Constituent	Chemical Formula	Difficulties Caused	Means of Treatment
Fluoride	F^-	cause of mottled enamel in teeth; also used for control of dental decay; not usually significant industrially	adsorption with magnesium hydroxide, calcium phosphate, or bone black; alum coagulation
Sodium	Na^+	adds to solids content of water: when combined with OH^-, causes corrosion in boilers under certain conditions	demineralization, reverse osmosis, electrodialysis, evaporation
Silica	SiO_2	scale in boilers and cooling water systems; insoluble turbine blade deposits due to silica vapourization	hot and warm process removal by magnesium salts; adsorption by highly basic anion exchange resins, in conjunction with demineralization, reverse osmosis, evaporation
Iron	Fe^{2+} (ferrous) Fe^{3+} (ferric)	discolours water on precipitation; source of deposits in water lines, boilers etc; interferes with dyeing, tanning, papermaking, etc.	aeration; coagulation and filtration; lime softening; cation exchange; contact filtration; surface active agents for iron retention
Manganese	Mn^{2+}	same as iron	same as iron
Aluminium	Al^{3+}	usually present as a result of floc carryover from clarifier; can cause deposits in cooling systems and contribute to complex boiler scales	improved clarifier and filter operation
Oxygen	O_2	corrosion of water lines, heat exchange equipment, boilers, return lines, etc.	deaeration; sodium sulphite; corrosion inhibitors
Hydrogen Sulphide	H_2S	cause of 'rotten egg' odour; corrosion	aeration; chlorination; highly basic anion exchange
Ammonia	NH_3	corrosion of copper and zinc alloys by formation of complex soluble ion	cation exchange with hydrogen zeolite; chlorination; deaeration.

5.(*a*) Creep and shrinkage of concrete are two physical properties of concrete. The creep of concrete, which originates from the calcium silicate hydrates (C-S-H) in the hardened Portland cement paste (which is the binder of mineral aggregates), is fundamentally different from the creep of metals and polymers. Unlike the creep of metals, it occurs at all stress levels and, within the service stress range, is linearly dependent on the stress if the pore water content is constant. Unlike the creep of polymers and metals, it exhibits multi-months aging, caused by chemical hardening due to hydration which stiffens the microstructure, and multi-year aging, caused by long-term relaxation of self-equilibrated micro-stresses in the nano-porous microstructure of the C-S-H. If concrete is fully dried, it does not creep, but it is next to impossible to dry concrete fully without severe cracking.

Two major types of volume change of interest to civil engineers are creep and shrinkage. Creep is the increase in strain due to sustained constant load. In most structures above ground, creep is taking place under drying conditions. Drying out of water from the interior of concrete leads to shrinkage. When creep and shrinkage occur simultaneously, it is known as drying creep. Creep without loss of moisture to the exterior is known as basic creep. Drying creep is higher than the sum of basic creep and shrinkage occurring separately. In prestressed concrete, both creep and shrinkage lead to a loss of prestressing force. Allowance for such losses have to be considered in the initial prestress applied.

Another form of shrinkage arises from the consumption of internal moisture due to continuing hydration of cement, drawing water from the capillary pores, without external supply of water (curing). This is known as autogenous shrinkage due to self-desiccation. For mixtures with water/cement ratio above 0.3, the amount of autogenous shrinkage is small compared to drying shrinkage. For low water/cement ratio mixtures, autogenous shrinkage may become the major contribution to total shrinkage.

Carbonation of concrete also induces shrinkage. This is known as carbonation shrinkage, which is accompanied by an increase in mass due to the reaction of carbon dioxide with calcium hydroxide (from hydration of silicates in cement) to form calcium carbonate.

Shrinkage is a three-dimensional change in volume, although it is generally reported as a linear strain. When shrinkage is restrained by boundary conditions, tensile stress is induced. If the magnitude of restrained shrinkage is higher than the ultimate tensile strain capacity of concrete, cracking occurs.

5.(*b*) Let, n = depth of N.A.;

$$A_u = 4 \times \frac{\pi}{4}(20)^2$$

$$= 1256.6 \text{ mm}^2$$

Equating the moments of two areas about N.A., we get

$$b \times n \times \frac{n}{2} = m \, A_{st} \, (d - n)$$

or $\qquad 300 \times \dfrac{n^2}{2} = 19 \times 1256.6 \, (500 - n)$

or $\quad n^2 + 159.2n - 79587 = 0$

From which $n = 213.5$ mm

Lever arm, $\qquad a = d - \dfrac{n}{3}$

$$= 500 - \frac{213.5}{3}$$

$$= 428.8 \text{ mm}$$

$$\text{Maximum B.M.} = \frac{w l^2}{8} = \frac{12(6)^2}{8}$$

$$= 54 \text{ kN-m}$$

$$= 54 \times 10^6 \text{ N-mm}$$

Let, c be the compressive stress in concrete.

$$\therefore \quad M_r = \frac{1}{2} c.n.b \times a$$

$$= \frac{1}{2} c \times 300 \times 213.5 \times 428.8$$

$$= 13.732 \times 10^6 c \text{ N-mm}$$

Equating M_r to the external B.M., we get

$$13.732 \times 10^6 c = 54 \times 10^6$$

or

$$c = \frac{54}{13.732}$$

$$= 3.93 \text{ N/mm}^2$$

If t is the corresponding stress in steel, we get

$$t = \frac{mc}{n}(d-n)$$

$$= \frac{19 \times 3.93}{213.5}(500 - 213.5)$$

$$= 100.2 \text{ N/mm}^2$$

Alternatively, $M_r = A_{st} . ta$

$$= 1256.6 \times t \times 428.8$$

$$\therefore 1256.6 \times 428.8 \ t = 54 \times 10^6$$

or

$$t = \frac{54 \times 10^6}{1256.6 \times 428.8}$$

$$= 100.2 \text{ N/mm}^2.$$

6.(a) Welding is a process of joining two similar or dissimilar pieces of metal by heating to a suitable temperature with or without the application of pressure. Welded joints so formed are permanent joints and they cannot be separated without effecting a fracture.

Types of Welded Joints

Welded joints are classified according to the relative positions of the two parts to be joined. There are five basic types of welded joints.

Butt joint: It is a joint between two plates lying in the same plane. The edges of the plates may be bevelled depending upon their thickness. Generally, a plate of 6 mm thickness is not bevelled and such joints are called *square butt joints*. Plates of thickness from 6-20 mm are bevelled to form a single V shape. However, plates of thickness more than 20 mm are welded from both sides of the plates and such joints are called double V-butt joint. Figure (*i*) shows various types of butt joints.

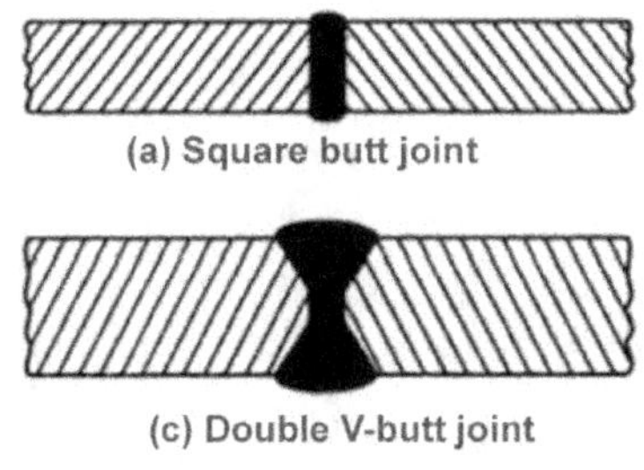

(a) Square butt joint

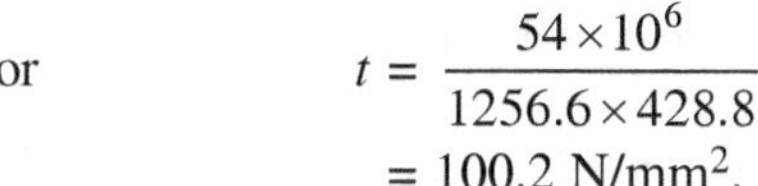

(b) Single V-butt joint

(c) Double V-butt joint

(d) Single U-butt joint

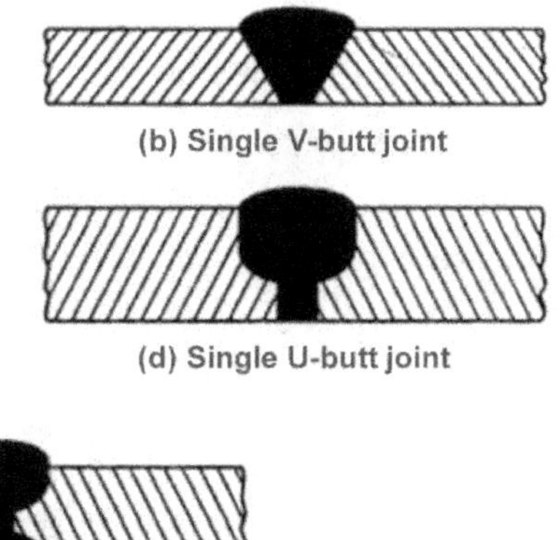

(e) Double U-butt joint

Fig. (*i*) *Various types of Butt joints*

A butt welded joint may be flushed, reinforced on one side or both sides. For fluctuating load conditions, flush butt weld is preferred over to the reinforced one, as the latter type creates discontinuity and gives rise to stress concentration.

Lap joint: In a lap joint, the two plates overlap each other for a certain length and the right angle recess formed between the two plates is filled with the weld metal. Such a weld is also called *fillet weld*. Figure (ii) shows a standard full fillet weld section of a triangle in which the two sides of the right angle are equal to the thickness of the plate.

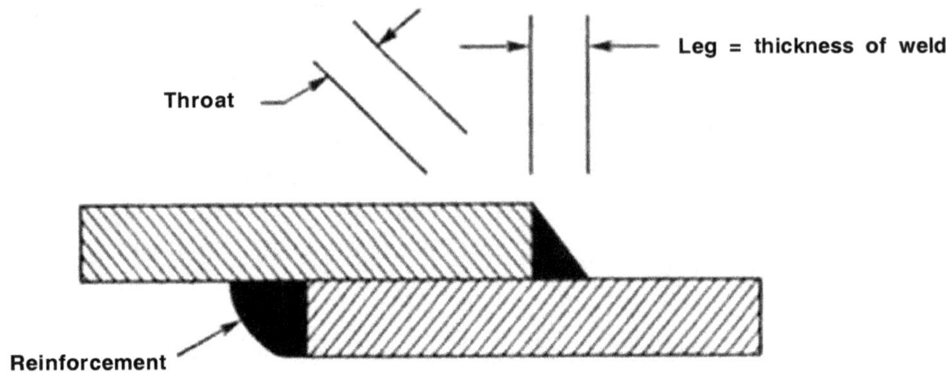

Fig. (*ii*) *Lap joint with fillet Weld*

Edge weld: Four plates of thickness less than 6 mm, the ends of the overlaping plates can be directly welded at the edges, as shown in fig. (*iii*). Such joints are called *edge weld* which can be subjected to light load only.

Corner weld: A corner joint is a joint between two plates which are at right angles to each other in the form of a corner, as shown in fig. (*iv*). In a corner joint, the throat of the weld is of the order of 1.35 times the thickness of the plate.

Tee-weld: It is a joint between two plates located at right angles to each other in such a form of as shown in fig. (*v*). In such joints, the end face of one plate is welded to the sides of the other plate by fillet weld. Generally, both sides of the plate are welded.

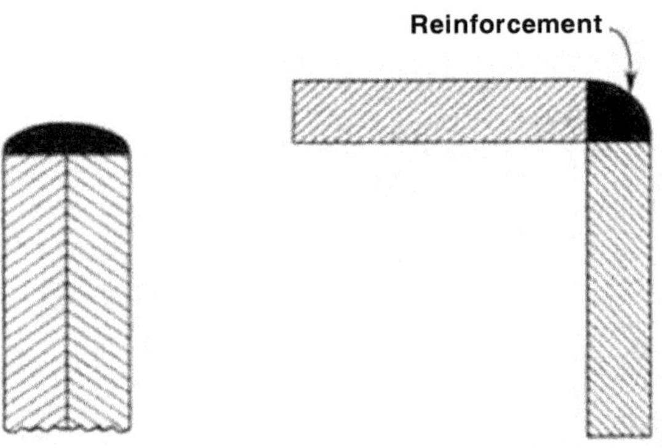

Fig. (*iii*) *Edge weld*   **Fig. (*iv*)** *Corner weld*   **Fig. (*v*)** *Tee-weld*

6.(*b*) Formed diameter of rivets

$$= 20 + 1.5 = 21.5 \text{ mm}$$

Strength of plate in tension, per pitch length;

$$P_t = \sigma_{at}\,(p - d)t$$
$$= 156(50 - 21.5) \times 12$$
$$= 53352 \text{ N}$$

Strength of rivet in single shear:

$$P_s = \tau_{vf} \times \frac{\pi}{4} d^2$$

$$= 80 \times \frac{\pi}{4} (21.5)^2$$

$$= 29044 \text{ N}$$

Strength rivet in bearing:

$$P_b = \sigma_{pf} \times d \times t$$

$$= 250 \times 21.5 \times 12$$

$$= 64500 \text{ N}$$

$\therefore$ Strength of joint

= minimum of the above three values

$$= 29044 \text{ N}$$

Strength of solid plate,

$$P = \sigma_{at}\, pt = 156 \times 50 \times 12$$

$$= 93600 \text{ N}$$

$\therefore$ Joint efficiency

$$= \frac{\text{Least of } P_t, P_s \text{ and } P_b}{P}$$

$$= \frac{29044}{93600} \times 100 = 31.03\%.$$

SSC-Junior Engineer (Civil & Structural) Exam 2013

PAPER-II (Conventional)

1. (a) Write a short note on Night Irrigation.
   (b) Give a brief account of the drawbacks in Kennedy's theory.
   (c) For a Highway project, a straight tunnel is to be run between two points P and Q whose co-ordinates are given below:

Point	Co-ordinates	
	N	*E*
P	0	0
Q	4020	800
R	2110	1900

It is desired to sink a shaft at S, the mid-point of PQ. S is to be fixed from R, the third known point. Calculate

(i) The co-ordinates of S
(ii) The length of RS
(iii) The bearing of RS

(d) Find out the time required for 50% consolidation in a soil having thickness of 800 cm and pervious strata at top and bottom. What will be the value of coefficient of consolidation if coefficient of permeability = 0.0000001 cm/sec?

$$\text{Void ratio} = 1.8 = m_v$$
$$= 0.0008 \text{ cm}^2/\text{gm}$$
$$\text{Time factor } (T_v) = 0.3$$
$$\lambda_w = 1 \text{ gm/cc}$$

2. (a) Calculate the ultimate bearing capacity per unit area of:
   (i) A strip footing 1 m wide
   (ii) A square footing 3 m × 3 m
   (iii) A circular footing of diameter 3 m

   Given:
   Unit weight of the soil 1.8 t/m³, cohesion = 2 t/m² and φ = 20 degree. N_c = 17.5, N_q = 7.5 and N_r = 5.

   (b) Calculate the discharge through a pipe of dia. 200 mm when the difference of pressure head between two ends of a pipe 500 m apart is 4 m of water. Take the value of f = 0.009 in the formula

$$h_f = \frac{4.f.L.V^2}{d.2g}.$$

   (c) Compare and contrast Flexible and Rigid pavements.
   (d) Discuss the impact of Urbanisation and Industrialisation in water resource (in terms of both quantity and quality).

3. (a) The annual sinking fund of a machine costing ₹ 50,000 is ₹ 150 and its salvage value is estimated to be ₹ 5,000. Assuming interest rate as 4%, determine the life of the machine.
   (b) Describe the factors affecting the rate analysis.
   (c) Write a short note on the classification of bricks.
   (d) Discuss the constituent parts of paint and their functions.

4. (a) List the physical tests that are generally used on cement. Describe any three of them.
   (b) Discuss the relation between water/cement ratio and strength.
   (c) Design a cantilever beam which projects beyond the fixed end by 3 m. The superimposed load on it is 10 kN/m. Use M 20 grade (σ_{cbc} = 7 N/mm²) of concrete and Fe 415 steel (σ_{st} = 230 N/mm²). Assume moderate exposure conditions.

5. A simply supported 18 m effective span RCC rectangular beam of 500 mm × 1500 mm (overall depth) section is reinforced throughout with 21 nos. 25 mm diameter bars in three layers of 7 bars each at a clear cover of 37.5 mm on tensile face. The reinforcement on the compression face is 4 – 25 mm + 1 – 20 mm diameter bars in one layer at an effective cover of 50 mm. The clear cover between the different layers on tension face is

25 mm. M 25 grade concrete and Fe 415 grade steel bars are used in the beam throughout. The beam is laterally restrained throughout the span.

(a) What shall be the superimposed uniformly distributed load w, that the beam can carry at working conditions?

(b) Design the shear reinforcement at support if design shear strength of concrete τ_c is given as follows for different values of p = 100 A_s/bd.

P	1.25	1.5	1.75
τ_c (MPa)	0.70	0.74	0.78

(c) Calculate the moment of resistance of the compound steel section shown in the figure. The compound section consists of two steel sections ISMB 200 @ 25.4 kg/m (I_{XX} = 2235.4 cm⁴, A_{XX} = 32.33 cm²) with a single cover plate, 40 cm wide and 16 mm thick connected to the top flange. Assume bending stress = 150 MPa.

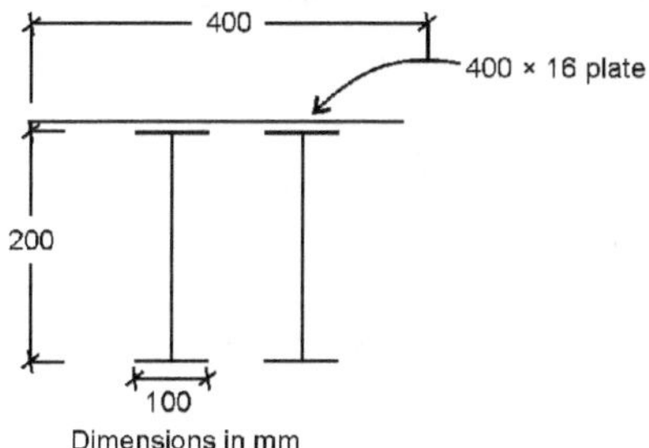

(d) A mild steel T section has the following cross-sectional dimenstions:

Total depth = 200 mm
Width of flange = 120 mm
Thickness of flange = 20 mm
Thickness of web = 20 mm

If the yield stress, σ_y = 250 MPa, determine the plastic moment capacity of the section. Also calculate the shape factor for the section.

6. (a) Analyze the beam shown in figure and determine the end moments. Plot the B.M.D. on the tension side.

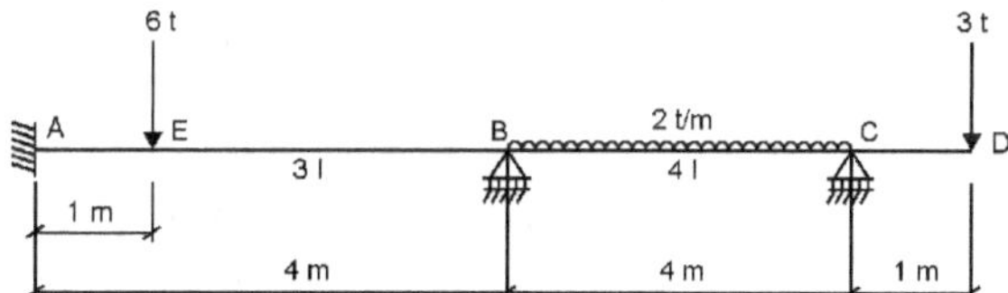

(b) Analyze the portal frame shown in the figure. Also sketch the deflected shape of the frame. The end A is fixed and the end D is hinged. Also, the value of EI is constant throughout.

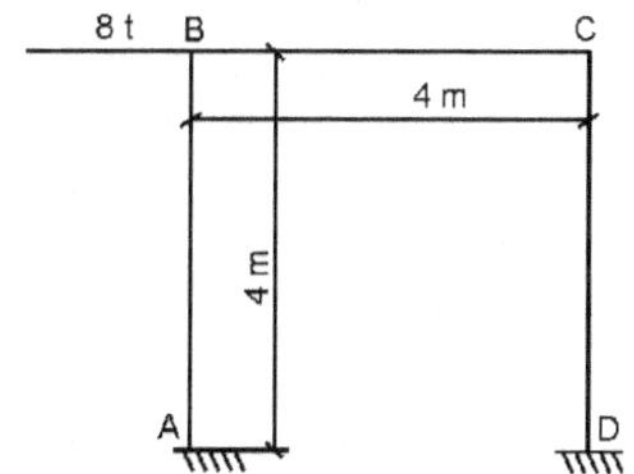

ANSWERS

1. (a) **Night Irrigation in Canal Systems**

Most of the canal irrigation systems in South and Southeast Asia and many other countries continue to flow throughout the day, and much of the night flows are inefficiently used or are wasted, unless effective procedures are adopted for their effective utilization. The importance of efficient utilization of night supplies of canal system has not received the right attention in many of the systems.

Darkness, cold, fear, departure from normal working hours, and desire for sleep deter irrigation staff, farmers and labourers from activities at night. Night irrigation usually requires extra labour and costs. It requires smaller stream flows and well graded fields. Paddy, tree crops and other widely spaced crops are more adaptable to night irrigation, as compared to other crops. Inefficient water application, breaches in channels, and wasted water flowing into drains are common during the night.

Possible measures of combating the problems of managing canal flows during the night are (*i*) reducing irrigation at night—by regulating sluice releases or diversion of flows, providing intermediate storage in canal command areas, diversion of flows for travelling time, redistributing daytime water, and passing water to drains and escapes, and (*ii*) improving irrigation at night—by manageable streamflows, convenient field shaping and water application methods, choice of crops and distribution of flows in distinct zones.

Robert Chambers (1988) has made the flowing observations on the relative advantages of various resources to measure the efficiency of night irrigation: "It is difficult to estimate how much water is currently saved at night through inter-mediate storage in tanks or canals, diversion to 'travelling', or closure of head-works, but it is probably quite a small proportion. A reasonable estimate may be that 40% of the canal irrigation water on medium and major systems is either applied in night irrigation or sent into drains at night ... Night irrigation is often inefficient. Supervision is difficult and minimal ... Night flows are often diverted to crops which tolerate flooding, mainly paddy, or are allowed to flow into drains."

Topography and size of holding: The smaller and more sloping the field is, the more difficult night irrigation becomes. Some large flat fields can be left to flood all night. An extreme case is the Gezire Scheme in Sudan, where impervious soils and flat land permit water to be left to spread unattended. Likewise, some large-scale irrigation schemes in western countries with very large fields could be left unattended at night, and changes made during the day. At the other extreme are the sloping fields with small besins which are difficult to irrigate during the night.

Soil type: The ease, difficulty and efficiency of irrigation at night also depend on the type of soil. Night irrigation is easier on soils which are not sticky, and which make stable bunds. Night irrigation is often difficult in black cotton soils. Hence, the *warabandi,* as followed in northwest India cannot be adopted as such in black soils.

Size of irrigation stream: Handling stream flows is harder at night. The optimal night flow should normally be lower than the day supply, especially on difficult terrain. This requirement is often overlooked in irrigation planning and design.

Crop: The ease and efficiency of water application at night depend on the crop and its stage of growth, as well as the topography and the size of fields. The easiest crops are paddy and trees: paddy can be flooded. Over flows may not raise serious problems. Similarly, trees are tolerant to standing water for some hours. Crops which are widely spaced or in early stages of growth are easier to irrigate at night than those which are tall, dense, or in their later stages of growth.

UTILIZATION OF WASTE FLOW DURING THE NIGHT

When night irrigation is not possible the excess flow can be passed to drains and escapes, instead of canal outlets and then to crop fields. Uncontrolled large flows may cause soil erosion, especially at the tail end of canal minors. Drainage of excess flows at non-erosive velocities will be beneficial, especially when the aim is to avoid water-logging and erosion.

Whether the water is wasted or not will depend on the possible utilization of drainage water which is needed lower down. In regions where there is a cascade or chain of tanks, wastage through night flows in the upper tanks may fill the tanks lower down. Such situations are possible in the plateau region of South India and the Dry Zone of Sri Lanka.

Soil erosion, especially in steep minors and field channels, can occur through large flows at night when extractions upstream cease. Detection and remedial action are difficult in the night. Flooding can also result from uncontrolled flows of water at night. Reducing irrigation at night has many potential advantages, including saving of water, convenience to all concerned, and limiting the damage (flooding, waterlogging, erosion) which night flows can cause.

Following are some of the ways in which irrigation at night can be reduced/improved:

(*i*) *Regulating sluice releases or river diversion flows.* Regulating the sluice gates/diversions on small schemes with command area less than 200 ha where the sluices are desirable. Where canals are long and large, sluice or off-take regulation to reduce night deliveries becomes infeasible.

(*ii*) *Intermediate night storage reservoirs/ offtaking tanks.* Night storage in intermediate reservoirs, diverting part of night flows to tanks is a useful concept. It can reduce night irrigation, save water and introduce flexibility in canal system management. However, design of intermediate storages within the canal network needs careful consideration in relation to silting of canals due to the storage reservoir. Night storage of water can be at the field level as well, if the field conditions and crops permit. It is most feasible with paddy. It is a common practice in Sri Lanka to hold as much water as possible in the upper paddy basin and then release it to the lower fields in the following days.

(*iii*) *Zoning for night flows.* Where a farm or an outlet receives water throughout the day and night, the day flows can be used for the more difficult soils and crops, and the night flows for those which are easier. In South India, on the Sri Ramasagr Project, it is a common practice for an outlet's day flows to be used in a more controlled manner for upland irrigated crops in red soils near the outlet, and the night flows to go in a less controlled manner into low-lying paddy on black soils farther from the outlet.

(*iv*) *On-farm engineering measures.* Night irrigation can be substantially improved by providing appropriate structures in the water distribution network and adopting suitable water application methods.

(*v*) *Choice of crops.* Night irrigation can be improved by selecting crops which are tolerant to flooding and easy to irrigate. Paddy, trees and sugarcane at its early growth stages belong to this category.

Limitations: (*i*) Kennedy did not investigate to find out the correct slope formula applicable directly to the design of canals, and (*ii*) He simply took Kutter's formula and adopted value of N equal to 0.0225 as the average value for all channels. No attempt was made to correlate Kutter's N with CVR, and (*iii*) Kennedy made no correlation between water surface slope of regime channels and the mean velocity or the depth. He relied on Kutter's equation to give slopes for the channels.

1. (*b*) DRAWBACKS IN KENNEDY'S THEORY

Kennedy's theory suffers from the drawbacks (*i*) It does not take cognisance of the width or the shape of the channel which have to be assumed, *i.e.,* importance of bed width and depth ratio is ignored, (*ii*) It involves use of Chezy's formula and Kutter's N for working out mean velocity and as such incorporates limitations of those relations in this theory, (*iii*) Adoption of arbitrary value of N as 0.0225 is not correct, (*iv*) Design of only average regime channel was aimed at, (*v*) Did not specify regime water surface slope relation. His diagrams, however, show that sleeper slopes are required for small channels and flatter ones for large channels, (*vi*) Silt concentration and bed load were not considered, (*vii*) Silt grade and silt charge were not defined, (*viii*) Design of channel involves trial and error as the velocity worked out with assumed depth should give the required discharge for the section and at the same time satisfy Kennedy's equation, and (*ix*) Simply stated that CVR varies according to the silt charge and silt grade but gave no method to measure value of *m* or CVR applicable for channels of different silt grades.

DESIGN OF CANALS BY KENNEDY THEORY

Given: Discharge (Q), water surface slope (S), coefficient of rugosity (N), and critical velocity ratio (m).

Assume reasonable depth (m), and calculate velocity from formula, $V_0 = 0.55 \, m \, D^{0.64}$ m/sec and A = Q/V (m²).

Bed width is calculated from the relation:
$$A = BD + SD^2 = BD + 0.5 \, D^2$$

(with ½ : 1 side slope)

Wetted perimeter P and hydraulic mean depth R are worked out for the calculated cross-section:

$$P = B + \sqrt{5} \, D \text{ (m)}$$

$$\text{and} \quad R = \frac{BD + 0.5D^2}{B + \sqrt{5} \, D},$$

(m) for ½ : 1 side slope

Actual mean velocity is calculated from Kutter's formula by substituting value of R calculated above; if it agrees with that calculated from Kennedy's relation ($V_0 = 0.55 \, m \, D^{0.64}$), the depth, and hence bed width assumed is correct, otherwise trial values of D are adopted till the two values of velocities work out to be approximately the same. The problem is simplified if B/D ratio is assumed or read from Central Water Power Commission curve (Fig. 1).

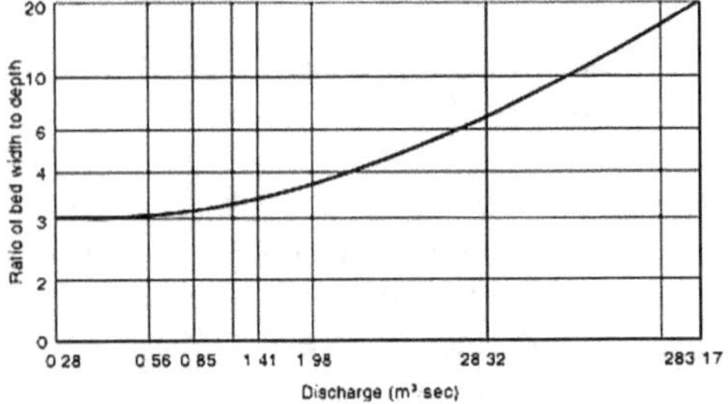

Fig. 1: *Bed width depth ratio*

2. (*c*) **Flexible Pavements**

Flexible pavements are constructed of bituminous and granular materials. The first asphalt roadway in North America was constructed in about 1870.

Conventional flexible pavements are layered systems with better materials on top where the intensity of stress is high and inferior materials at the bottom where the intensity is low. Adherence to this design principle makes possible the use of local materials and usually results in a most economical design. This is particularly true in regions where high quality materials are expensive but local materials of inferior quality and readily available.

Consider the cross-section of a conventional flexible pavement. Starting from the top, the pavement consists of seal coat, surface asphalt course, tack coat, asphalt binder course, prime coat, granular base course, granular subbase course, compacted subgrade, and native subgrade. In some cases the use of various courses is based on either necessity or economy, and some of the courses may be omitted.

According to the Asphalt Institute 1987, full depth asphalt pavements have the following advantages:

(*i*) They have no permeable granular layers to entrap water and impair performance.

(*ii*) Time required for construction is reduced. On widening projects, where adjacent traffic flow must usually be maintained, full depth asphalt can be especially advantageous.

(*iii*) When placed in a thick lift of 100 mm (4 in.) or more, construction seasons may be extended.

(*iv*) They provide and retain uniformity in the pavement structure.

(*v*) They are less affected by moisture or frost.

(*vi*) According to some studies, moisture contents do not build up in subgrades under full depth asphalt pavement structures as they do under pavements with granular bases. Thus, there is little or no reduction in subgrade strength.

RIGID PAVEMENTS

Rigid pavements are constructed of Portland Cement Concrete (PCC) and should be analysed by the plate theory, instead of the layered theory. Plate theory is a simplified version of the layered theory that assumes the concrete slab to be a medium thick plate with a plane before bending which remains a plane after bending. If the wheel load is applied in the interior of a slab, either plate or layered theory can be used and both should yield nearly the same flexural stress or strain. If the wheel load is applied near to the slab edge, say less than 600 mm (2 ft) from the edge, only the plate theory can be used for rigid pavements. The reason that the layered theory is applicable to flexible pavements but not to rigid pavements is that PCC is much stiffer than HMA and distributes the load over a much wider area. Therefore, a distance of 600 mm (2 ft) from the edge is considered to be far in a flexible pavement but not far enough in a rigid pavement. The existence of joints in rigid pavement also makes the layered theory inapplicable.

In contrast to flexible pavements, rigid pavements are placed either directly on the prepared subgrade or on a single layer of granular or stabilized material. Because there is only one layer of material under the concrete and above the subgrade, some call it base course, others a subbase.

2. (*d*) Uncontrolled urbanization and the growing population pressure are essential challenges for the water management in urbanized regions of the emerging—and developing countries. In terms of the environment, the reciprocal impact of urban development and groundwater represents one of the most important aspects of growing cities. The interaction between urban development and groundwater may be explained in the relation with the land use pattern and stage of city evolution on affecting the quantity and quality of groundwater. Quantity and quality changes are caused commonly by the increase of groundwater abstraction and the existing of new sources of recharge.

The main issues are:
— Urbanized area changes groundwater recharge or cycle, with modification to the existing recharge and the introduction of the new sources
— Discharging of new sources of recharge in urbanized area causes extensive but essentially diffuse groundwater contamination.
— Fluctuations in groundwater levels and
— Impact on engineering structure.

It seems that urbanization reduces infiltration to groundwater due to the impermeabilization of the catchment by paved areas, buildings and roads. But recharge beneath cities is usually substantially greater than the pre-urban values. The sources and pathways for groundwater recharge in urban areas are more numerous and complex than in rural environments. The increase of groundwater recharge in urbanized areas is closely related to three main sources: rainwater, wastewater and main leakage from water supply networks. In cities without adequate sewers for waste water transport, as much as 90% of abstracted water may return as groundwater recharge. In these cities, the most important recharge source would be the infiltration of waste water from large numbers of septic tanks, latrines and soakaways as well as inadequate sewers. This is especially relevant for cities that are built atop shallow aquifers and/or for cities being located in a river system. The effect of urban recharge sources will be always significantly larger than precipitation recharge in semi arid and arid regions. But in humid areas, urban recharge may only balance the loss of precipitation recharge caused by the impermeable areas, and the overall effect of urbanization will be small.

Fast growing cities with an inadequate wastewater system have potentially major effect on increasing groundwater recharge than cities with sewerage system. It can be also concluded that almost all urbanization processes can potentially increase the rate of infiltration to groundwater. The effect of urbanization on the quality of recharge is commonly poor, especially if waste water is an important component.

The issue of groundwater contamination of wastewater disposal is a more serious problem in cities of developing countries.

However, it is clear that human activities in urbanized areas threaten the groundwater not only due diffuse contaminant loading from urban recharge system, but also due to many other ways. This means that the different forms of land use such as landfills, urban agriculture, industry and trade as well as diverse residential types with their corresponding wastewater systems influence the emission of pollutants in surface and groundwater, including groundwater recharge.

Also it has to be considered, that the occurrence of contaminants in groundwater does not only depends on the characteristics of contaminant loading as a result of human activity, but also depends on the inherent attenuation capacity of the intervening strata between contaminant source and water table. This inherent attenuation capacity of the intervening strata depends on its geological, hydrological and hydrogeological condition.

3. (c) BRICKS AND BLOCKS

Classification

Brick is defined as a masonry unit with dimensions (mm) not exceeding 337.5 × 225 × 112.5 (L × w × t). Any unit with a dimension that exceeds any one of those specified above is termed a block. Blocks and bricks are made of fired clay, calcium silicate or concrete.

- *Common bricks* are suitable for general building work.
- *Facing bricks* are used for exterior and interior walls and available in a variety of textures and colours.
- *Engineering bricks* are dense and strong with defined limits of absorption and compressive strength as given in Table 2.

Bricks must be free from deep and extensive cracks, from damage to edges and corners and also form expansive particles of lime.

Bricks are also classified according to their resistance to frost and the maximum soluble salt content.

(a) *Designation according to frost resistance*

- *Frost resistant* (F): These bricks are durable in extreme conditions of exposure to water and freezing and thawing. These bricks can be used in all building situations.
- *Moderately frost resistant* (M): These bricks are durable in the normal condition of exposure except in a saturated condition and subjected to repeated freezing and thawing.
- *No frost resistant* (O): These bricks are suitable for internal use. They are liable to be damaged by freezing and thawing unless protected by an impermeable cladding during construction and afterwards.

(b) *Designation according to maximum soluble salt content*

- *Low* (L): These clay bricks must conform to the limit for maximum soluble salt content given in Table 1. All engineering and some facing or common bricks may come under this category.
- *Normal* (N): There is no special requirement or limit for soluble salt content.

Varieties

Bricks may be wire cut, with or without perforations, or pressed with single or double frogs or cellular. Perforated bricks contain holes; the cross-sectional area of any one hold should not exceed 10% and the volume of perforations 25% of the total volume of bricks. Cellular bricks will have cavities or frogs exceeding 20% of the gross volume of the bricks. In bricks having frogs the total volume of depression should be less than or equal to 20%.

Table 1: Maximum salt content of low (L) brick

Soluble radicals	*Maximum content as tasted on 10 brick samples (wt%)*
Sulphate	0.50
Calcium	0.30
Magnesium	0.03
Potassium	0.03
Sodium	0.03

Bricks of shapes other than rectangular prisms are referred to as 'standard special'.
Concrete blocks may be solid, cellular or hollow.
Different varieties of bricks and blocks are shown in Fig. 2.

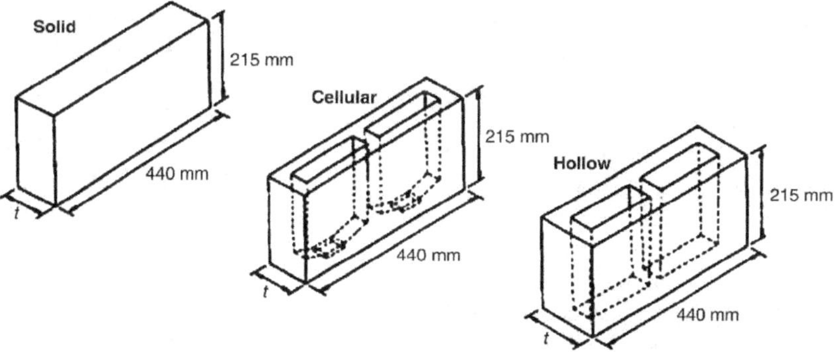

Fig. 2: *Concrete blocks*

Table 2: Classification of clay bricks according to compressive strength and absorption

Designation	*Class*	*Average compressive strength not less than (N/mm^2)*	*Average absorption (5h boiling) not greater than (% by) weight*
Engineering	A	70	4.5
	B	50	7.0
Loadbearing brick		5–100	no specific requirement
Damp-proof course 1		5	4.5
Damp-proof course 2		5	7.0

3. (*d*) GENERAL INDUSTRIAL PAINT COMPONENTS

Industrial paint, as used to protect metal, wood, and a wide range of other materials, possesses a variety of traits that can be manipulated to provide application-specific coverage. Of course, these characteristics depend in a large part upon the ingredients of the paint and the performance specifications of the selected application. Application methods, too, can influence the quality of the paint coverage and determine how well paint adheres to the substrate. Typically, there are four main components in a paint: pigment, binder, liquid, and additives. Application methods depend on the particular paint, but can include spray application, brush methods, and electrostatic spraying.

Pigment

A paint's pigment plays a large role in determining colour and appearance. Some pigments also provide added bulk, helping to thicken a paint when needed. In its unmixed form, a pigment is simply a powder. There are two general categories of pigments: prime and extender.

- **Prime Pigments:** Prime pigments are mainly responsible for colour or whiteness in a paint, as well as the paint's ability to hide undesirable surface flaws. In paints that exhibit a white hue, titanium dioxide is the main ingredient. In paints the express other colours, the pigments are selected to absorb only certain kinds of light, thus yielding a given colour. Organic pigments yield the brightest colours, while inorganic pigments yield less bright but more durable colours.

- **Extender Pigments:** Extender pigments are designed to add bulk, but are not as well-suited to hiding surface flaws as prime pigments. They do, however, influence the paint's overall sheen, colour retention, and abrasion resistance. Silica and silicates, for example, are extender pigments that increase the paint's durability. Zinc oxide helps prevent mildew and corrosion, and is especially useful in outdoor applications.

Binder

In a paint mixture, the binder is responsible for providing adhesion, binding the pigment, and also gives the paint resistance properties which make the final coating tough and durable. The binder itself is clear and glossy, but the presence of pigment interferes with this quality. Depending on the ratio of pigment to binder, or the PVC (pigment volume concentration) the paint can assume varying levels of glossy finish. Paints with the glossiest finish often have a typical PVC of 15 percent, while the most matter paints have a PVC anywhere from 40 to 80 percent. Paints with less gloss have more binder per unit of pigment, and tend to be more durable. There are two specific types of binder: oil-based and latex-based.

- *Oil-Based Binder:* Oil-based paint requires a binder that has similar properties to the paint–in this case, the binder oxidizes or dries when exposed to air, hardening along with the rest of the paint. Once applied, the liquid factor of an oil-based paint evaporates, and the binder then reacts with the air to harden into place with the pigment. However, sometimes this process can result in over-dry, brittle paint, and chipping can occur. Additionally, the oxidation makes the paint prone to yellowing.

- *Latex-Based Binder:* Latex-based paints actually do not possess latex–rather, the binder that is used (plastic–like in nature) creates a film in the paint that resembles natural latex rubber. Almost all water-based paints have a latex-based binder. When the coating is applied, water evaporates from the paint, leaving behind a film of pigment and latex-based binder, which bind together into one continuous coating. The process by which the binder and pigment are fused is called **coalescence**. However, because the binding agent is thermoplastic, it cannot be applied at too low a temperature or the binder will be too hard and difficulty will arise during fusing. Common types of latex-based binder include acrylic and vinyl acrylic.

Liquid

In the most basic sense, the liquid component of a paint is simply responsible for transporting the binder and pigment to the substrate surface. The type of liquid depends upon the other components of the given paint. Oil-based paints, for example, can use a basic paint thinner as the primary liquid. Latex-based paints, on the other hand, tend to use water as their liquid.

Additives

When certain properties need to be manipulated or enhanced, additives are often the solution. Thickeners, for example, are additives that help thicken the paint to make application easier. Surfactants help disperse pigments within the paint, ensuring the coat is even and stays in place. **Co-solvents** help the binder film formation and help prevent paint damage from occurring if the pain is frozen. Co-solvents also make application easier by lengthening the amount of time the paint can be open before beginning to set.

4. (*a*) **Physical Properties**

- Portland cements are commonly characterized by their physical properties for quality control purposes. Their physical properties can be used to classify and compare Portland cements. The challenge in physical property characterization is to develop physical tests that can satisfactorily characterize key parameters.

The physical properties of cement
- Setting Time
- Soundness
- Fineness
- Strength

Setting Time
- Cement paste setting item is affected by a number of items including: cement fineness, water-cement ratio, chemical content (especially gypsum content) and admixtures. Setting tests are used to characterize how a particular cement paste sets.
- For construction purposes, the initial set must not be too soon and the final set must not be too late. Normally, two setting items are defined.
- Initial set. Occurs when the paste begins to stiffen considerably.
- Final set. Occurs when the cement has hardened to the point at which it can sustain some load.

- Setting is mainly caused by C_3A and C_3S and results in temperature rise in the cement paste.
- False set : No heat is evolved in a false set and the concrete can be re-mixed without adding water
- Occures due to the conversion of unhydrous/semihydrous gypsum to hydrous gypsum ($CaSO_4.2H_2O$)
- Flash Set: is due to absence of Gypsum. Specifically used for under water repair.

TESTS:

Consistency
- The consistency is measured by the Vicat apparatus using a 10 mm diameter plunger.
- A trial paste of cement and water is mixed and placed in the mold having an inside diameter of 70 mm at the base and 60 mm at the top, and a height of 40 mm.
- The plunger is then brought into contact with the top surface of the paste and released. Under the action of its weight the plunger will penetrate the paste. The depth depending on the consistency.
- When the plunger penetrates the paste to a point 5 to 7 mm from the bottom of the mold. The paste is considered to be at "normal consistency".
- The water content of the paste is expressed as a percentage by weight of dry cement. The usual range of values being between 26% and 33%.

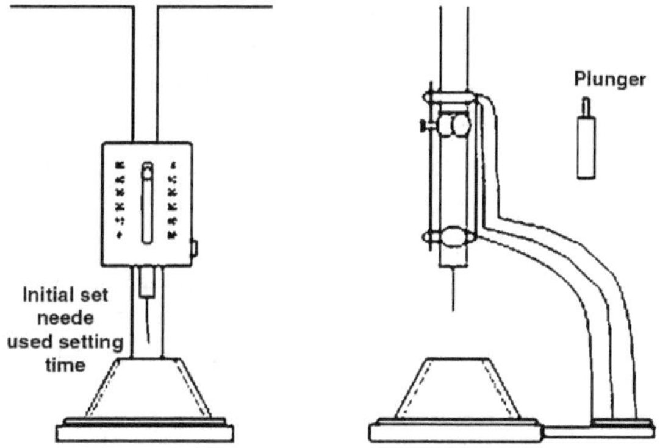

Fig. 3: *Vicat Apparatus: front and side views*

Setting time

- The setting time test is conducted by using the same Vicat apparatus, except that a 1 mm diameter needle is used for penetration.
- The test is started about 15 minutes after placing the cement paste (which has normal consistency) into the mold. Trials for penetration of the needle are made.
- The final setting time is defined as the length of time between the penetration of the paste and the time when the needle (with annular ring) no longer sinks visibly into the paste.
- The initial setting time is defined as the length of time between the penetration of the paste and the time when the needle penetrates 25 mm into the cement paste.

Soundness

- When referring to Portland cement, "soundness" refers to the ability of a hardened cement paste to retain its volume after setting without delayed expansion. This expansion is caused by excessive amounts of free lime (CaO) or magnesia (MgO). Most Portland cement specifications limit magnesia content and expansion.
- The cement paste should not undergo large changes in volume after it has set. However, when excessive amounts of free CaO or MgO are present in the cement, these oxides can slowly hydrate and cause expansion of the hardened cement paste.
- Soundness is defined as the volume stability of the cement paste.

Test for Soundness

- IS prescribe a Soundness Test conducted by using the Le-Chatelier apparatus. The apparatus consists of a small brass cylinder split along its generatrix. Two indicators with pointed ends are attached to the cylinder on either side of the split.
- The cylinder (which is open on both ends) is placed on a glass plate filled with cement paste of normal consistency, and covered with another glass plate.
- The whole assembly is then immersed in water at $20 \pm 1°C$ for 24 hours. At the end of that period the distance between the indicator points is measured. The mold is then immersed in water again and brought to a boil. After boiling for one hour the mold is removed from the water, after cooling, the distance between the indicator points is measured again. This increase represents the expansion of the cement paste for Portland cements, expansion is limited to 10 mm.

Fineness

- Fineness, or particle size of Portland cement affects Hydration rate and thus the rate of strength gain. The smaller the particle size, the greater the surface area-to-volume ratio, and thus, the more area available for water-cement interaction per unit volume. The effects of greater fineness on strength are generally seen during the first seven days.
- When the cement particles are coarser, hydration starts on the surface of the particles. So the coarser particles may not be completely hydrated. This causes low strength and low durability.
- For a rapid development of strength a high fineness is necessary.

Test for Fineness

- There are various methods for determining the fineness of cement particles. The Blaine air-permeability method is the most commonly used method.
- In the Blaine air-permeability method, given volume of air is passed through a prepared sample of definite density. The number and size of the pores in a sample of given density is a function of the particles and their size distribution and determines the rate of air flow through the sample. Calculations are made and the fineness is expressed in terms of cm^2/g or m^2/kg.

4. (*b*) Water/Cement Ratio

Strength of concrete primarily depends upon the strength of cement paste. Strength of cement paste depends upon the dilution of paste or in other words, the strength of paste increases with cement content and decreases with air and water content. In 1918 Abrams presented his classic law in the form:

$$S = \frac{A}{B^x}$$

where x = water/cement ratio by volume and for 28 days results.

The constants A and B are 14,000 lbs/sq. in. and 7 respectively.

Abrams water/cement ratio law states that the strength of concrete is only dependent upon water/cement ratio provided the mix is workable. In the past many theories have been propounded by many research workers. Some of them held valid for some time and then underwent some changes while others did not stand the test of time and hence slowly disappeared. But Abrams water/cement ratio law stood the test of time and is held valid even today as a fundamental truth in concrete-making practices. No doubt some modifications have been suggested but the truth of the statement could not be challenged.

A general rule defining the strength of the concrete paste and concrete in terms of volume fractions of the constituents by the equation:

$$S = K \, (c/c + e + a)^2$$

Where S = strength of concrete

c, e and a = volume of cement, water and air respectively

K = a constant

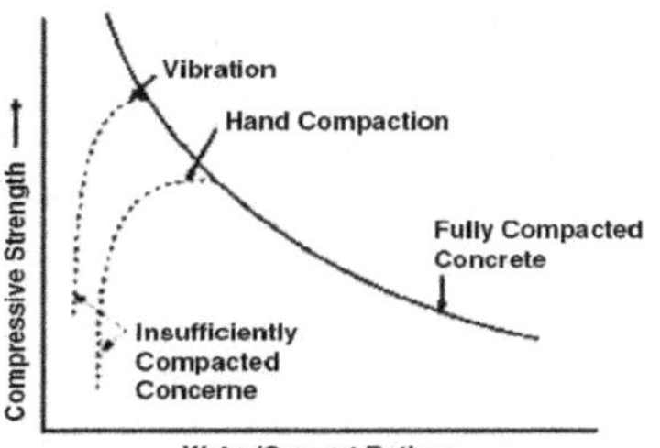

Fig. 4 (*a*): *The relation between strength and water/cement ratio of concrete.*

In this expression the volume of air is also included because it is not only the water/cement ratio but also the degree of compaction, which indirectly means the volume of air filled voids in the concrete is taken into account in estimating the strength of concrete. The relation between the water/cement ratio and strength of concrete is shown in Fig. 4 (*a*). It can be seen that lower water/cement ratio could be used when the concrete is vibrated to achieve higher strength, whereas comparatively higher water/cement ratio is required when concrete is hand compacted. In both cases when the water/cement ratio is below the practical limit the strength of the concrete falls rapidly due to introduction of air voids.

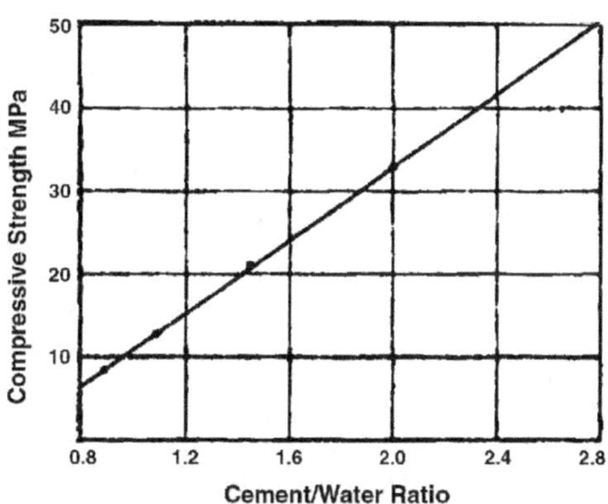

Fig. 4 (*b*): *The relation between strength and water/cement ratio*

The graph showing the relationship between the strength and water/cement ratio is approximately hyperbolic in shape. Sometimes it is difficult to interpolate the intermediate value. From geometry it can be deduced that if the graphs is drawn between the strength and the cement/water ratio an approximately linear relationship will be obtained. This linear relationship is more convenient to use than water/cement ratio curve for interpolation. Fig. 4 (*b*) shows the relationship between compressive strength and cement/water ratio.

SSC-Junior Engineer (Civil & Structural) Exam 2012

PAPER-II (Conventional)

1. (*a*) What are the chief chemical ingredients and their percentage used in the manufacturing of Portland cement? Also briefly explain the Bogue components and their properties in the cement.

(*b*) Explain *any four* of the following thermal insulation:
  (*i*) Slab or block insulation
  (*ii*) Blanket insulation
  (*iii*) Bat insulating materials
  (*iv*) Insulating boards

(*c*) Explain Whole Circle Bearing system. The following bearings were observed with a compass. Calculate the interior angles.

LINE	FORE BEARINGS
AB	60° 30′
BC	122° 00′
CD	46° 00′
DE	205° 30′
EA	300° 00′

2. (*a*) What is super elevation? Derive the relation between super elevation and speed of vehicle on horizontal curve. Design the rate of super elevation for a horizontal curve of a radius 500 m and speed 100 km/hr.

(*b*) Describe the terms-True and Magnetic bearings; local attraction; back bearings and magnetic declination.

(*c*) Explain the term Base period and Crop period. After how many days will you order irrigation in order to ensure healthy growth of crops if:

(*i*) Field capacity of soil = 29%
(*ii*) Permanent wilting point = 11%
(*iii*) Density of soil = 1300 kg/m³
(*iv*) Effective depth of root zone = 700 mm
(*v*) Daily consumptive use of water of the given crop = 12 mm

Consider moisture content must not be less than 25% of the water holding capacity between the field capacity and permanent wilting point.

3. (*a*) What do you mean by "Viscosity"? Velocity distribution of a fluid of dynamic viscosity is 8.63 poise is $U = 2/3y - y^2$ in which U is the velocity in m/sec at a distance y meter above the plate, determine the shear stress at $y = 0$ and $y = 0.15$. Take dynamic viscosity of fluid is 8.63 poise.

(*b*) Define air pollution. Enlist natural and man made air pollution. What are the effects of air pollution on human, plants and materials?

(*c*) Define the term BOD, COD and TDS. The 5 days 30°C BOD of sewage sample is 110 mg/l. Calculate its 5 days 20°C BOD. Assume the deoxygenation constant at 20°C k_{20} as 0.1?

4. (*a*) Two plates 6 mm thick are joined by 14 mm diameter rivets in a triple staggered riveted lap joint as shown in fig 1. In what way will the joint fail if allowable tensile stress for plate = 150 MPa; allowable shear stresses for rivets = 90 MPa and allowable bearing stress for rivets = 270 MPa. Also find the efficiency of the joint.

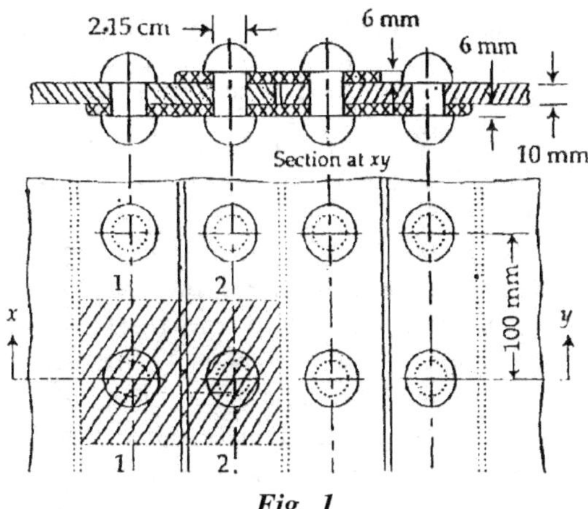

Fig. 1

(*b*) A sand deposit is 10 m thick and overlies a bed of soft clay. The ground water table is 3 m below the surface. If the sand above the ground water table has a degree of saturation of 45%, plot the diagram showing the variation of the total stress, pore water pressure and the effective stress. The void of the sand is 0.70. Take G = 2.65.

(*c*) Draw the shear force and bending moment diagrams for the beam shown in fig. 2.

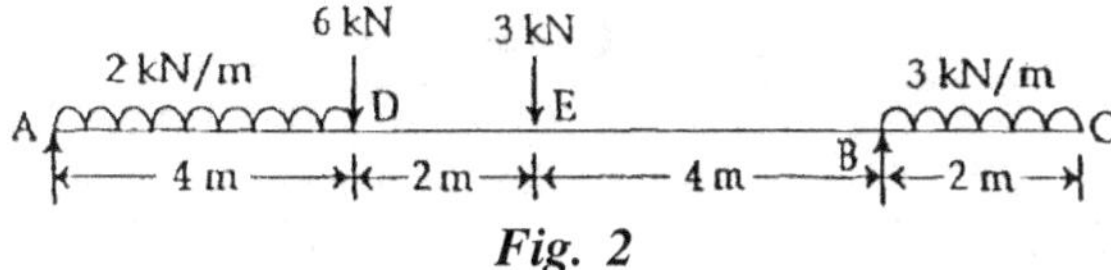

Fig. 2

5. (*a*) The cross-section of a joist is a T-section, 120 mm × 200 mm × 12 mm, with 120 mm side horizontal. Sketch the shear stress distribution and hence find the maximum shear stress if it has to resist a shear force of 200 kN.

(*b*) For the I section shown in fig. 3 determine the position of centroid and moment of inertia about the base flange (I_{KL}).

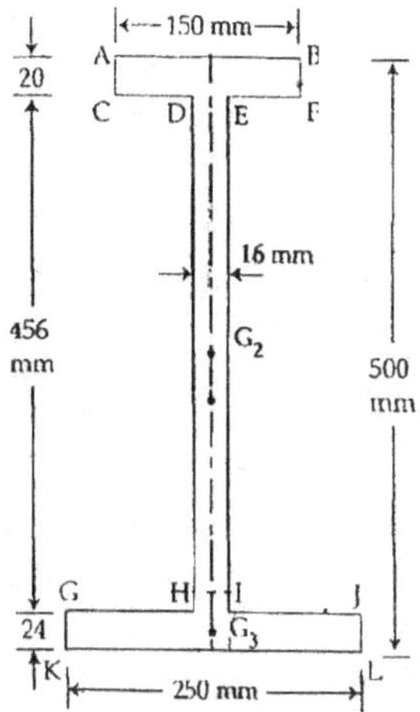

Fig. 3

(*c*) (*i*) What is bond? Explain flexural and anchorage bond.

(*ii*) What is development length? Write its significance in RCC design.

6. (*a*) A singly reinforced beam having a width of 250 mm is reinforced with 3 bars of 16 mm diameter at an effective depth of 400 mm. If M20 grade concrete and Fe415 HYSD bars are used, compute for the section.

(*i*) Working moment of resistance

(*ii*) Ultimate moment of resistance.

(*b*) Design a square column section subjected to concentrated load of 1000 kN at service. Consider concrete grade of M25 and steel grade Fe 415.

(*c*) Design a built-up column composed of two channel sections placed back to back, carrying an axial load of 1345 kN. Effective length of column is 4.95 m. Take f_y = 250 kN/mm^2.

ANSWERS

1. (*a*) Portland cement is the most common type of cement in general use around the world used as a basic ingredient of concrete, mortar, stucco, and most non-speciality grout.

COMPOSITION OF PORTLAND CEMENT

The principle raw materials used in the manufacture of cement are:

(*a*) Argillaceous or silicates of alumina in the form of clays and shales.

(*b*) Calcareous or calcium carbonate, in the form of lime stone, chalk and marl which is a mixture of clay and calcium carbonate.

The ingredients are mixed in the proportion of about two parts of calcareous materials to one part of argillaceous materials and then crushed and ground in ball mills in a dry state or mixed in wet state. The dry powder or the wet slurry is then burnt in a rotary kiln at a temperature between 1400 degree C to 1500 degree C. The clinker obtained from the kiln is first cooled and then passed on to ball mills where gypsum is added and it is ground to the requisite fineness according to the class of product.

The chief chemical constituents of Portland cement are as follows:

Lime (CaO)	60 to 67%
Silica (SiO_2)	17 to 25%
Alumina (Al_2O_3)	3 to 8%
Iron oxide (Fe_2O_3)	0.5 to 6%
Magnesia (MgO)	0.1 to 4%
Sulphur trioxide (SO_3)	1 to 3%
Soda and/or Potash (Na_2O+K_2O)	0.5 to 1.3%

The above constituents forming the raw materials undergo chemical reactions during burning and fusion and combine to form the following compounds called *BOGUE COMPOUNDS*.

Compound	Abbreviated designation
Tricalcium silicate ($3CaO.SiO_2$)	C3S
Dicalcium silicate ($2CaO.SiO_2$)	C2S
Tricalcium aluminate ($3CaO.Al_2O_3$)	C3A
Tetracalcium alumino-ferrite ($4CaO.Al_2O_3.Fe_2O_3$)	C4AF

The proportions of the above four compounds vary in the various Portland cements. Tricalcium silicate and dicalcium silicates contribute most to the eventual strength. Initial setting of Portland cement is due to tricalcium aluminate. Tricalcium silicate hydrates quickly and contributes more to the early strength. The contribution of dicalcium silicate takes place after 7 days and may continue for up to 1 year. Tricalcium aluminate hydrates quickly, generates much heat and makes only a small contribution to the strength within the first 24 hours. Tetracalcium alumino-ferrite is comparatively inactive. All the four compounds generate heat when mixed with water, the aluminate generating the maximum heat and the dicalcium silicate generating the minimum. Due to this, tricalcium aluminate is responsible for the most of the undesirable properties of concrete. Cement having less C3A will have higher ultimate strength, less generation of heat and less cracking. Table below gives the composition and percentage of found compounds for normal and rapid hardening and low heat Portland cement.

Composition and compound content of Portland Cement:

	Normal	Rapid hardening	Low heat
(a) Composition: Percent			
Lime	63.1	64.5	60
Silica	20.6	20.7	22.5
Alumina	6.3	5.2	5.2
Iron Oxide	3.6	2.9	4.6
(b) Compound: Percent			
C3S	40	50	25
C2S	30	21	35
C3A	11	9	6
C3A	12	9	14

1. (*b*) (i) Slab Insulation:

Thermal insulation which is fabricated in rigid or semirigid form; it differs from block or board-type insulation only in physical dimensions. The slab designation usually is applied if the face dimension is much larger than a block but smaller than a board and if the thickness is greater than that of a board.

Benefits of Insulating Slab-on-grade Floors: Slabs lose energy primarily as a result of heat conducted outward and through the perimeter of the slab. In most sections of the country, insulating the exterior edge of the slab can reduce winter heating bills by 10 to 20 percent.

Slab insulation provides a thermal break to the perimeter of slab-on-grade foundations. Slab insulation is important not only to save on energy bills, but also to improve comfort. Cold concrete slabs are one of the most notorious sources of discomfort in a home. Installing slab insulation around the perimeter of the slab will reduce heat loss and make the slab easier to heat. An insulated slab also provides thermal mass to store heat and moderates indoor temperatures.

Slab Insulation Techniques: Slab insulation can be installed following one of two basic techniques: installing rigid insulation directly against the exterior of the slab and footing or building a "contained" or "floating" slab with interior insulation. Whichever design is followed, the keys to an effective slab foundation are:

Moisture control: Using a water-managed foundation system to drain rainwater and groundwater away from the foundation.

Airtight construction: Sealing interfaces between the slab foundation and the exterior wall to reduce infiltration into the house.

Complete insulation coverage: Properly installing the correct insulation levels and making sure the insulation coverage is continuous and complete.

1. (*b*) (*ii*) Blanket insulation

The most common and widely available type of insulation-comes in the form of batts or rolls. It consists of flexible fibers, most commonly fiberglass. You also can find batts and rolls made from mineral (rock and slag) wool, plastic fibers and natural fibers, such as cotton and sheep's wool.

Standard fiberglass blankets and batts have a thermal resistance or R-values between R-2.9 and R-3.8 per inch of thickness. High-performance (medium-density and high-density) fiberglass blankets and batts have R-values between R-3.7 and R-4.3 per inch of thickness. See the table below for an overview of these characteristics.

Table 1. Fiberglass Batt Insulation Characteristics

Thickness (inches)	R-Value Cost	Cost (cents/sq. ft.)
3 1/2	11	12-16
3 5/8	13	15-20
3 1/2 (high density)	15	34-40
6 to 6 1/4	19	27-34
5 1/4 (high density)	21	33-39
8 to 8 1/2	25	37-45
8 (high density)	30	45-49
9 1/2 (standard)	30	39-43
12	38	55-6

* This table is for comparison only.

1. (*b*) (*iii*) Bat Insulating Materials

Unlike rodents, bats will not gnaw their way through wood or building materials. Soft materials such as insulation batting can be easily attached to a building with a heavy duty staple gun.

Effective materials to exclude bats are expansion foam caulking, flashing, screening and insulation. Weatherstripping, stainless steel wool or stainless steel rustproof scouring pads are excellent materials to block long, narrow cracks.

Caulking: Cracks and crevices develop in a structure as it ages and bats will take advantage of these openings. Caulking will seal the openings.

Weatherstripping: When bats crawl under doors, the space between the floor and the door bottom may be sealed with weatherstripping, a draft shield, or a gap stopper to close off the space between the bottom of the door and the door sill or threshold. Weatherstripping is made of a variety of materials including natural fibers, aluminum, fine wire, felt, hard rubber, vinyl and nylon. A nylon strip brush barrier is set in a galvanized steel channel and housed in either aluminum or vinyl. It has several advantages over ordinary weatherstripping. The flexible nylon filaments, which comprise a substantial brush, move easily in any direction permitting the bristles to conform to uneven floor surfaces, including carpet. This seals any gaps, stops drafts and reduces heat loss. It is said to resist rodents and insects.

Screening: Where screening is necessary the mesh must be small enough to prevent the access of bats. Steel hardware cloth should have 0.63 cm (1/4 in.) mesh with three meshes or more to the inch. Insect screening for windows should be 18 × 14 mesh.

Bats can enter ventilators that are not properly screened. Hardware cloth for ventilators should be 8 × 8 mesh. Inlet and outlet ventilators should be properly installed. The type of ventilator used, its location in the building and the direction of prevailing air currents may be important factors because buildings of identical design, but different orientation, vary in their attractiveness to bats. Many ventilators are made with metal louvers and frames, others are custom made of wood to more closely fit the house design.

Bats may use an unused or old chimney because the rough surfaces of chimney walls offer suitable places for bats to hang. Bats will almost never use an active chimney. To prevent bats from entering chimneys, spark arresters or bird screens should be installed. These should be of rust-resistant material and carefully attached. They should completely enclose the flue discharge area and be securely fastened to the top of the chimney. Except when in use, dampers should be closed.

1. (b) (iv) Insulating boards

These are used for interior lining of walls and also for partition walls. Structural insulating board is manufactured by first making a pulp of wood, cane or other materials and then pressing them in form of boards by adding suitable adhesives. They are available in different sizes and thickness.

1. (c) In whole circle bearing (WCB) the bearing of a line at any point is measured with respect to a meridian. Its value varies from zero to 360°, increasing in clockwise direction. Zero is north direction, 90° is east, 180° is south and 270° is west (Ref. Fig.). This type of bearing is used in prismatic compass.

Quadrant in which bearing lies	*Conversion relation*
NE	$\alpha = \theta$
SE	$\alpha = 180° - \theta$
SW	$\alpha = \theta - 180°$
NW	$\alpha = 360° - \theta$

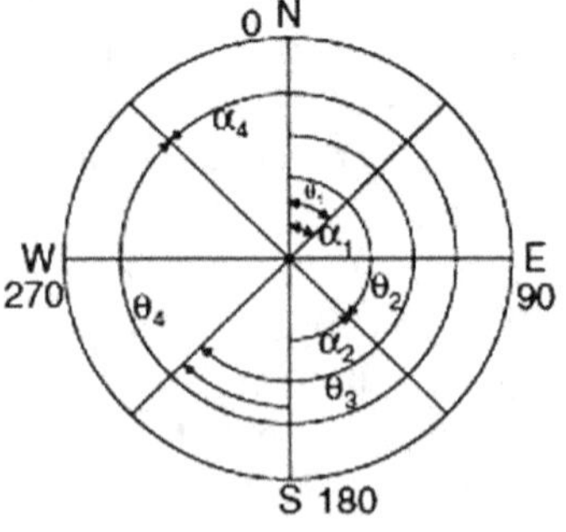

Fig. Whole Circle Bearing

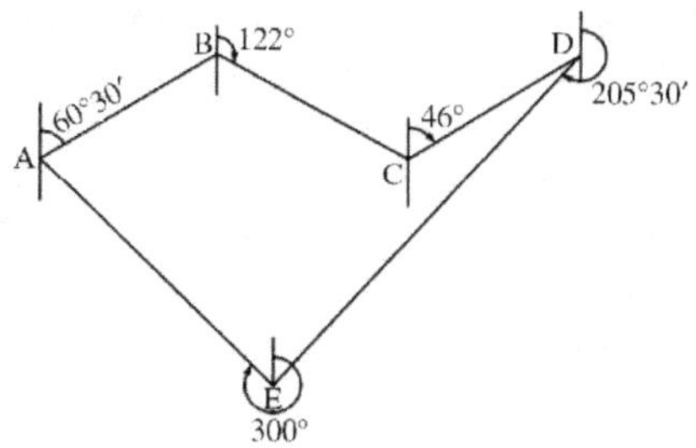

Fig.

(i) Angle A:

Bearing of EA = 300°

∴   Bearing of AE = 300° − 180° = 120°

∴   ∠A = Difference in bearings
of AE and AB
= 120° − 60° 30′
= 59° 30′ **Ans**

(ii) Angle B:

Bearing of BA = 60° 30′ + 180°
= 240° 30′

∴   ∠B = 240° 30′ − 122°
= 118° 30′ **Ans**

(iii) Angle C:

Bearing of CB = 122° + 180° = 302°

∴   ∠C = 302° − 46°
= 256° exterior angle.

(iv) Angle D:

Bearing of DC = 46° + 180° = 226°

∴   ∠D = 226° − 205° 30′
= 20° 30′

(v) Angle E:

Bearing of ED = 205°30′ − 180°
= 25°30′

∴   ∠E = 300° − 25° 30′
= 274°30′ exterior angle
= 85°30′

2. (a) Super elevation: In order to counteract the effect of centrifugal force and to reduce the tendency of the vehicle to overturn or skid, the outer edge of the pavement is raised with respect to the inner edge, thus providing a transverse slope throughout the length of the horizontal curve. The transverse inclination to the pavement surface is known as super elevation/cant/banking.

$$\text{Centrifugal force} = \frac{m\text{V}^2}{\text{R}}$$

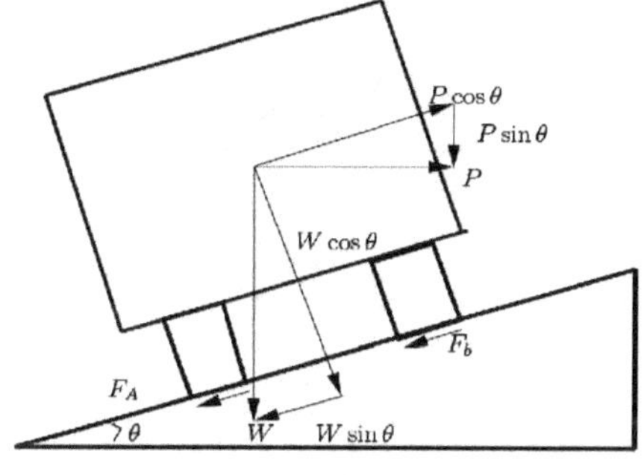

$$W = mg$$

$$F = f\text{R}$$

Equating all forces along road surface

$$mg\sin\theta + f.\text{R} = \frac{m\text{V}^2}{\text{R}} \cdot \cos\theta$$

$$\Rightarrow \quad mg\sin\theta + f.\left(mg\cos\theta + \frac{m\text{V}^2}{\text{R}} \cdot \sin\theta \right)$$

$$= \frac{m\text{V}^2}{\text{R}} \cdot \cos\theta$$

$$\Rightarrow \quad g\sin\theta + f.\left(g\cos\theta + \frac{\text{V}^2}{\text{R}} \cdot \sin\theta \right)$$

$$= \frac{\text{V}^2}{\text{R}} \cdot \cos\theta$$

Put $\tan\theta = e$

Now $\Rightarrow$ $ge + f.g = \dfrac{\text{V}^2}{\text{R}} \cdot 1 + fe$

$$\Rightarrow \quad \frac{g\,e + f}{1 + fe} = \frac{\text{V}^2}{\text{R}}$$

$$\Rightarrow \quad e + f = \frac{\text{V}^2}{g\text{R}}$$

$$ef << 1\ mg$$

Where e = Rate of super elevation = $\tan\theta$

f = design value of lateral friction coefficient
   = 0.15

v = Speed of the vehicle m/sec

R = Radius of horizontal curve in m.

g = Acceleration due to gravity = 9.8 m/sec.

If V in Kmph then v = 0.278V m/sec

Now

$$e + f = \frac{V^2}{gR} = \frac{(0.278\,V)^2}{9.8\,R} = \frac{V^2}{127\,R}$$

$$\Rightarrow \qquad e + f = \frac{V^2}{127\,R}$$

Where, V in Kmph and R in meter

Given R = 500 m and V = 100 Kmph

Assuming coeff. of friction $f = 0$

Now

$$\Rightarrow \qquad e + f = \frac{V^2}{127\,R} = \frac{100^2}{127 \times 500}$$

$$\Rightarrow \qquad e = 0.1575.$$

2. (b) "Bearing" is a term used in navigation to refer, depending on the context, to either (A) the direction of motion, or, (B) the direction of a distant object relative to the current course (or the "change" in course that would be needed to get to that distant object), or (C), the degrees away from North of a distant point relative to the current point .

A true bearing is measured in relation to the fixed horizontal reference plane of true north, that is, using the direction toward the geographic north pole as a reference point, while a magnetic bearing is measured in relation to magnetic north, that is, using the direction toward the magnetic north pole as a reference.

LOCAL ATTRACTION

The magnetic needle does not point to the magnetic north, when it is under the influence of the external attractive forces. In the presence of magnetic materials, such as iron pipes, steel structures, iron lamps, posts, rails, cables, chain, arrows, minerals deposits in the ground, etc., the needle is deflected from its normal position. Hence, local attraction by the magnetic materials is the disturbing influence on the magnetic needle of the compass. The amount of deviation of the magnetic needle is the measure of local attraction.

Detection of Local Attraction: The local attraction at any station is detected by observing the force and back bearings of the line. If the difference between them is 180°, both the end stations are considered to be free from local attraction, provided the compass is devoid of any instrumental errors. If not, the discrepancy may be due to:

1. an error in observation of either fore or back bearing, or both.

2. presence of local attraction at either or both of the stations.

Elimination of Local Attraction: There are two methods by which local attraction can be eliminated.

1. By calculating the local attraction at each station.

2. By included Angles.

Back Bearing: The bearing of a line measured in the backward direction (*i.e.*, opposite to the direction of progress of survey) is known as back bearing. In Figure the back bearing of the line AB is ∠NOA (= 223°). ∠NOA is also called bearing of the line BA. Thus,

Back Bearing = Fore Bearing ± 180°

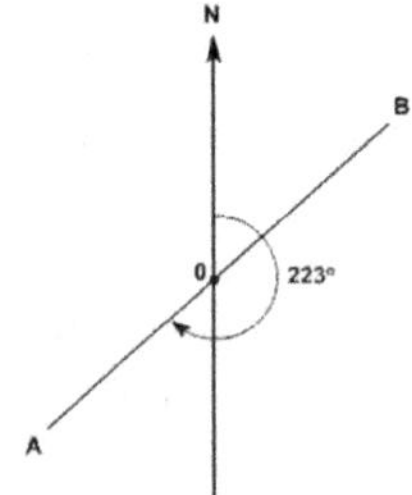

Fig. Back bearing of a line

Magnetic Declination: Over much of the Earth's surface, compass needles point roughly north. However, because of the complex shape of the Earth's magnetic field there are few places where a compass needle will point exactly north. A compass lines up with the horizontal component of the magnetic field in a direction called magnetic north. True north, on the other hand is the direction from a given location to the north geographic pole. The angle between magnetic north and true north is called magnetic declination.

Magnetic declination also undergoes changes that are much more rapid than secular variation and are a result of magnetic activity. These variations can be smooth and cyclic, with amplitudes of several minutes of arc in southern Canada, or, during magnetic storms, large and erratic. Changes in declination become increasingly irregular in both amplitude and frequency as one approaches the North Magnetic Pole, a result of the weak horizontal component of the magnetic field. The number of times per year that a compass user will be affected by changes in declination caused by magnetic storms will depend both on the user's application and location.

2. **(c)** Base period (B), is the time period between the first watering of the crop during its sowing to last watering before its harvesting. It is generally expressed in 'days'.

The another related term is Crop period. For practical purpose Base period and Crop period are taken as same but they have a little difference. Crop period is the time period between sowing of a crop to its harvesting. In this manner, Crop period is slightly greater than the Base period.

1. AM = FC − PWP = 29 − 11 = 18%

2. RAM = 0.25 × 18% = 4.5%

Readily available moisture

$$= 11 + 4.5 = 15.5\%$$

Depth of water stored in the root zone b/n these two limits

$$= \frac{\gamma_d}{\gamma_w}$$

[Field Capacity m.c. − Optimum m.c.]

$$\frac{\gamma_d}{\gamma_w} = \frac{l_d g}{l_w g} = \frac{l_d}{l_w} = \frac{1.3\,gm/cc}{1\,gm/cc} = 1.3$$

Depth of water stored in the root zone
= 1.3 × 0.7 [0.29 − 0.135]
= 1.3 × 0.7 × 0.155 m = 0.14105 m
= 14.105 cm

- Hence, the water available for evapotranspiration = 17.29 cm.
- 12 mm or 1.2 cm of water is utilized by the plant in 1 day

∴ 14.105 cm of water will be utilised by the plant in

$$\text{Irrigation frequency} = \frac{1 \times 14.105}{1.2}\ \text{days}$$

$$= 12\ \text{days}$$

Hence, after 12 days, water should be supplied to the given crop.

3. **(a)** **Viscosity** is an internal property of a fluid that offers resistance to flow. For example, pushing a spoon with a small force moves it easily through a bowl of water, but the same force moves mashed potatoes very slowly.

Viscosity is important in volcanology. The more fluid a magma, the more likely it is to erupt. On the other hand, when more viscous (higher viscosity) lavas do erupt, they usually do so explosively. Viscosity also affects the shapes of lava flows and the mountains they erupt from.

Shear stress in fluids

$$T(y) = \mu \frac{\partial u}{\partial y}$$

where,

μ is the dynamic viscosity of the fluid;

u is the velocity of the fluid along the boundary;

y is the height above the boundary.

Specifically, the wall shear stress is defined as:

$$T_w \equiv T(y = 0) = \mu \left.\frac{\partial u}{\partial y}\right|_{y=0}$$

In case of wind, the shear stress at the boundary is called wind stress.

Shear stress at $y = 0$

$$T_w = \frac{\mu.d\left(\frac{2}{3}y - y^2\right)}{dy}$$

$$= 0.863\left(\frac{2}{3} - 2y\right)$$

$$= 0.863\left(\frac{2}{3} - 2 \times (0)\right)$$

$$= 0.863 \times \frac{2}{3} = 0.575 \text{ N/m}^2$$

Shear stress at $y = 0.15$

$$T = 0.863\left(\frac{2}{3} - 2 \times 0.15\right)$$

$$= 0.316 \text{ N/m}^2.$$

3. (b) Air pollution is the introduction of particulates, biological molecules, or other harmful materials into Earth's atmosphere, causing diseases, death to humans, damage to other living organisms such as animals and food crops, or the natural or built environment. Air pollution may come from anthropogenic or natural sources .

An air pollutant is a substance in the air that can have adverse effects on humans and the ecosystem. The substance can be solid particles, liquid droplets, or gases. A pollutant can be of natural origin or man-made. Pollutants are classified as primary or secondary. Primary pollutants are usually produced from a process, such as ash from a volcanic eruption. Other examples include carbon monoxide gas from motor vehicle exhaust, or the sulphur dioxide released from factories. Secondary pollutants are not emitted directly. Rather, they form in the air when primary pollutants react or interact. Ground level ozone is a prominent example of a secondary pollutant. Some pollutants may be both primary and secondary: they are both emitted directly and formed from other primary pollutants.

Major primary pollutants produced by human activity include:

- Sulphur oxides (SO_x)— particularly sulphur dioxide, a chemical compound with the formula SO_2. SO_2 is produced by volcanoes and in various industrial processes. Coal and petroleum often contain sulphur compounds, and their combustion generates sulphur dioxide. Further oxidation of SO_2, usually in the presence of a catalyst such as NO_2, forms H_2SO_4 and thus acid rain. This is one of the causes for concern over the environmental impact of the use of these fuels as power sources.

- Nitrogen oxides (NO_x)—Nitrogen oxides, particularly nitrogen dioxide are expelled from high temperature combustion and are also produced during thunderstorms by electric discharge. They can be seen as a brown haze dome above or a plume downwind of cities. Nitrogen dioxide is a chemical compound with the formula NO_2. It is one of several nitrogen oxides. One of the most prominent air pollutants, this reddish-brown toxic gas has a characteristic sharp, biting odor.

- Carbon monoxide (CO) — CO is a colourless, odourless, toxic yet non-irritating gas. It is a product by incomplete combustion of fuel such as natural gas, coal or wood. Vehicular exhaust is a major source of carbon monoxide.

- Volatile organic compounds (VOC) — VOCs are a well-known outdoor air pollutant. They are categorized as either methane (CH_4) or non-methane (NMVOCs). Methane is an extremely efficient greenhouse gas which contributes to enhanced global warming.

- Particulates, alternatively referred to as particulate matter (PM), atmospheric particulate matter, or fine particles, are tiny particles of solid or liquid suspended in a gas. In contrast, aerosol refers to combined particles and gas. Some particulates occur naturally, originating from volcanoes, dust storms, forest and grassland fires, living vegetation and sea spray.

- Persistent free radicals connected to airborne fine particles are linked to cardiopulmonary disease.

- Toxic metals, such as lead and mercury, especially their compounds.

- Chlorofluorocarbons (CFCs) — harmful to the ozone layer; emitted from products are currently banned from use. These are gases which are released from air conditioners, refrigerators, aerosol sprays, etc. CFC's on being released into the air rises to stratosphere. Here they come in contact with other gases and damage the ozone layer. This allows harmful ultraviolet rays to reach the earth's surface. This can lead to skin cancer, disease to eye and can even cause damage to plants.

- Ammonia (NH_3) — emitted from agricultural processes. Ammonia is a compound with the formula NH_3. It is normally encountered as a gas with a characteristic pungent odor. Ammonia contributes significantly to the nutritional needs of terrestrial organisms by serving as a precursor to foodstuffs and fertilizers.

- Odours — such as from garbage, sewage and industrial processes

- Radioactive pollutants — produced by nuclear explosions, nuclear events, war explosives, and natural processes such as the radioactive decay of radon.

Secondary pollutants include:

- Particulates created from gaseous primary pollutants and compounds in photochemical smog. Smog is a kind of air pollution. Classic smog results from large amounts of coal burning in an area caused by a mixture of smoke and sulphur dioxide. Modern smog does not usually come from coal but from vehicular and industrial emissions that are acted on in the atmosphere by ultraviolet light from the sun to form secondary pollutants that also combine with the primary emissions to form photochemical smog.

- Ground level ozone (O_3) formed from NO_x and VOCs. Ozone (O_3) is a key constituent of the troposphere. It is also an important constituent of certain regions of the stratosphere commonly known as the Ozone layer. Photochemical and chemical reactions involving it drive many of the chemical processes that occur in the atmosphere by day and by night. At abnormally high concentrations brought about by human activities (largely the combustion of fossil fuel), it is a pollutant and a constituent of smog.

- Peroxyacetyl nitrate (PAN) — Similarly formed from NO_x and VOCs.

Health effects

Air pollution is a significant risk factor for a number of health conditions including respiratory infections, heart disease, COPD, stroke and lung cancer. The health effects caused by air pollution may include difficulty in breathing, wheezing, coughing, asthma and worsening of existing respiratory and cardiac conditions. These effects can result in increased medication use, increased doctor or emergency room visits, more hospital admissions and premature death. The human health effects of poor air quality are far reaching, but principally affect the body's respiratory system and the cardiovascular system.

Agricultural effects: In India in 2014, it was reported that air pollution by black carbon and ground level ozone had cut crop yields in the most affected areas by almost half in 2010 when compared to 1980 levels.

(c) **BOD, biochemical oxygen demand:** The BOD (biological or biochemical oxygen demand) can be considered as the 'mother' of the sum parameters. The BOD indicates the content of oxygen needed to decompose organic compounds in waste water by bacteria. In most cases the special factor BOD_5 is perceived as the BOD, which requires a detailed definition (5 represents the 5 days analysis time). For the determination of BOD_5 there are nitrification inhibitors added to the samples, which suppress the degradation of nitrogen compounds. Consequently, it results in the determination of the decomposition of carbon compounds only.

In the real sense, BOD measurements are respiration measurements. Due to their rapidity, respiration measurements are preferred for online analysis. Provided that the conditions are known, respiration measurements [mg/(1*min)] can be converted into BOD measurements [mg/l].

COD, chemical oxygen demand: The COD value has been developed analogically to the BOD measurement. Since there are many organics which are rather hard or not possible to decompose biologically, a parameter has been defined indicating the amount of oxygen which would be needed when all organic ingredients would be oxidised completely. As, according to the name, the oxidation takes place chemically, the chemical oxygen demand can only be defined indirectly. A chemical oxidant is added to the sample in question, the consumption of which is then determined. The internationally dominant method today is the so-called 'Dichromate' method which is characterized by the acidification of the sample with sulphuric acid and the addition of silver sulphate. To avoid false measurements in chloride-containing samples, the chloride must be masked by mercuric sulphate first. Due to the application of hazardous chemicals and having an analysis time of 2 hours the method is not suitable for online use.

$$K_{D(20°C)} = 0.1/\text{day}$$
$$K_{D(30°C)} = K_{D(20°C)} [1.047]^{(T - 20°)}$$
$$= 0.1 \times (1.047)^{10} = 0.158/\text{day}$$

$$Y_{5(30°C)} = L\left[1 - 10^{-K_{D(30°C)}t}\right]$$
$$\rightarrow \quad L = 110/[1 - 10^{-0.158 \times 5}]$$
$$= 131.3 \text{ mg/l}$$

$$Y_{5(20°C)} = L\left[1 - 10^{-K_{D(20°C)}t}\right]$$
$$= 131.3 \times [1 - 10^{-0.1 \times 5}]$$
$$= 89.8 \text{ mg/l}$$

4. *(a)* Diagram

    Row 1-1

$\Rightarrow$ single shear

$\Rightarrow$ bear against 6 mm plate

Row 2-2

$\Rightarrow$ double shear

$\Rightarrow$ bearing against 10 mm plate

    (Because (6 + 6) > 10)

Gross dia of rivet = 14 + 1.5 = 15.5

(a) Rivet value in sec. 1-1

$$\text{Shearing strength} = \frac{\pi}{4}d^2 f_s$$

$$= \frac{\pi}{4}(15.5)^2 \times 90$$

$$= 16.98 \text{ kN}$$

$$\text{Bearing strength} = d \times t \times f_b$$
$$= 15.5 \times 6 \times 270$$
$$= 25.1 \text{ kN}$$
$$R_{v1} = 16.98 \text{ kN}$$

(b) Rivet value in sec 2-2

$$\text{Shearing strength} = 2 \times \frac{\pi}{4}d^2 f_s$$

$$= 2 \times \frac{\pi}{4}(15.5)^2 \times 90$$
$$= 33.96 \text{ kN}$$

$$\text{Bearing strength} = d \times t \times f_b$$
$$= 15.5 \times 10 \times 270$$
$$= 41.85 \text{ kN}$$
$$R_{v2} = 33.96$$

(*c*) Strength of joint—

Consider one pitch length of the joint we will consider 4 possible chance to failure

(*i*) Failure of rivet at sec 1-1 and 2-2

(*ii*) Failure due to tearing of main plate at 1-1

(*iii*) Failure due to tearing of cover plate at sec 2-2

(*iv*) Failure due to tearing of main plate at 2-2

Now,

(*i*) Strength of joint on the basis of rivet at 1-1 and 2-2

$$\Rightarrow R_{v1} + R_{v2} = 16.98 + 33.96 = 50.94 \text{ kN}$$

(*ii*) St. of main plate at 1-1

$$\Rightarrow \sigma_t(p - d)t$$
$$= 150(100 - 15.5) \times 10 = 126.75 \text{ kN}$$

(*iii*) St. of cover plate at sec 2-2

$$\Rightarrow \sigma_t(p - d)t$$
$$= 150(100 - 15.5)12 = 152.1 \text{ kN}$$

(*iv*) St. of main plate at sec 2-2

$$\sigma_t(p - d)t + R_v$$
$$= 150(100 - 15.5)10 + 16.98$$
$$= 126.77 \text{ kN}$$

$$\Rightarrow \text{St. of joint per pitch length} = \min \text{ of }$$
$$(i), (ii), (iii), (iv)$$
$$= 50.94 \text{ kN}$$

$$\Rightarrow \text{St. of solid plate} = \sigma_t pt$$
$$= 150 \times 100 \times 10$$
$$= 150 \text{ kN}$$

Now, η of joint = st. of joint/ st. of solid plate

$$= \frac{50.94}{150} = 0.3396$$
$$= 33.96\%$$

4. (*b*)

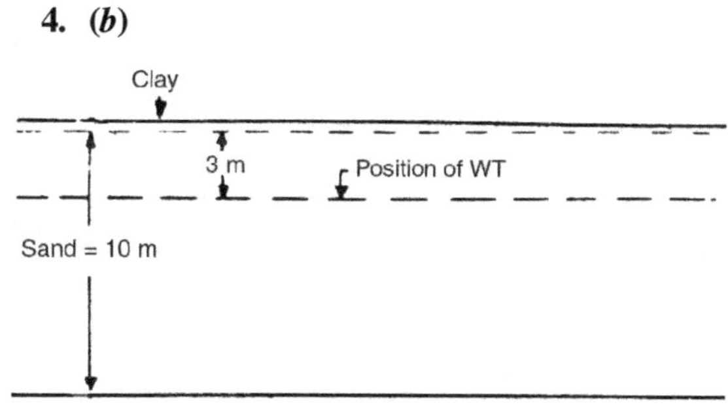

Unit wt. the partially saturated sand above the water table

$$\gamma_{t \text{ sand}} = \frac{G + Se}{1 + e}\gamma_w$$

$$= \frac{2.65 + 0.45 \times 0.7}{1 + 0.7} \times 10$$
$$= 17.44 \text{ kN/m}^3$$

Unit wt. of saturated sand $\gamma_{\text{sat (sand)}}$

$$= \frac{G + Se}{1 + e}\gamma_w$$

$$= \frac{2.65 + 0.7}{1 + 0.7} \times 10$$
$$= 19.71 \text{ kN/m}^3$$

At elevation –3 m

$$\sigma = z\gamma_{tt} = 3 \times 17.44$$
$$= 52.32 \text{ kN/m}^2$$

At elevation –10 m

$$\sigma = 3\gamma_t + 7\gamma_{\text{sat}}$$
$$= 3 \times 17.44 + 7 \times 19.71$$
$$= 190.29 \text{ kN/m}^2$$
$$V = 7 \times \gamma_w = 70 \text{ kN/m}^2$$
$$\sigma = 190.29 - 70$$
$$= 120.29 \text{ kN/m}^2$$

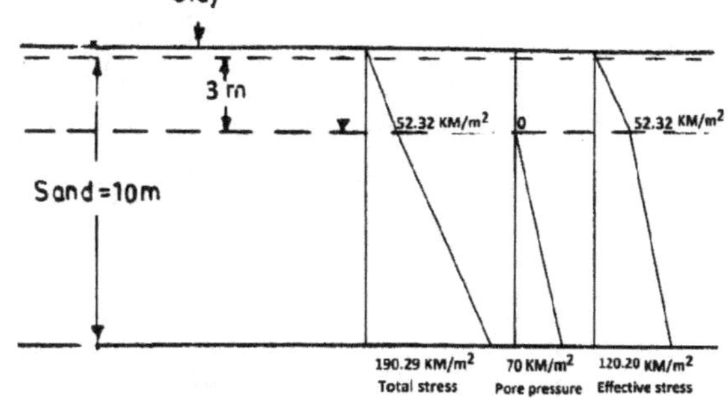

4. (*c*)

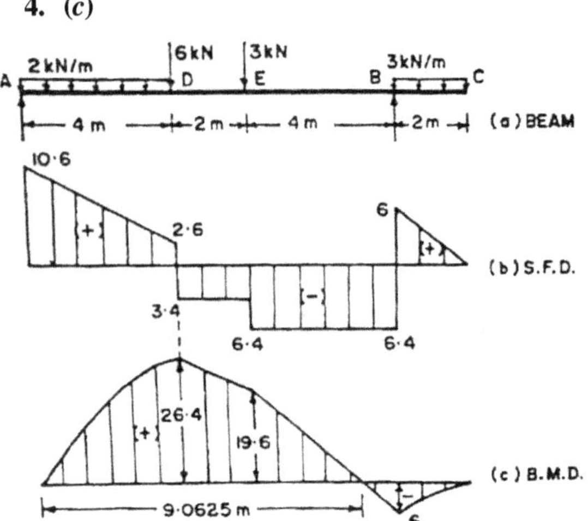

(*a*) Reaction:

$$R_B = \frac{1}{10}(2 \times 4 \times 2 + 6 \times 4 + 3 \times 6 +$$

$$3 \times 2 \times 11) = 12.4 \text{ kN } (\uparrow)$$

$$R_A = (2 \times 4 + 6 + 3 + 3 \times 2) - 12.4$$

$$= 10.6 \text{ kN } (\uparrow)$$

(*b*) S.F.D. for AD,

$$F_x = 10.6 - 2x$$

At $\qquad x = 0$, $F_A = 10.6$ kN;

At $\qquad x = 4$, F_D left $= 2.6$ kN

For DE : $F_x = 10.6 - 8 - 6$

$$= -3.4 \text{ kN (Constant)}$$

$\therefore F_D$ (right) $= -3.4$; F_E (left) $= -3.4$ kN

For EB : $F_x = 10.6 - 8 - 3 - 6$

$$= -6.4 \text{ kN (Constant)}$$

$\therefore F_E$ (right) $= -6.4$ kN; F_B (left)

$$= -6.4 \text{ kN}$$

For BC : $F_x = 10.6 - 8 - 6 - 3 + 12.4 -$

$$3x - 10 = 36 - 3x \text{ kN (linear)}$$

$\therefore F_B$ (right) $= 36 - 3 \times 10 = +6$ kN;

$$F_C = 36 - 36 = 0$$

The complete S.F.D. is shown in fig.

(*c*) B.M.D. for AD,

$$M_x = 10.6x - \frac{2x^2}{2}$$

$$= 10.6x - x^2 \text{ (parabolic)}$$

At $\qquad x = 0$, $M_A = 0$; at $x = 4$ m,

$$M_D = 10.6 \times 4 - (4)^2$$

$$= 26.4 \text{ kN} - \text{m}$$

For $\qquad$ DE $= M_x$

$$= 10.6x - 8(x - 2) - 6(x - 4)$$

$$= 40 - 3.4x \text{ (linear)}$$

At $\qquad x = 4$, $M_D = 26.4$ kN $-$ m

$$\text{(as before)};$$

At $\qquad x = 6$ m, $M_E = 19.6$ kN $-$ m

For EB, $M_x = 10.6x - 8(x - 2) - 6(x - 4)$

$$-3(x - 6)$$

$$= 58 - 6.4x \text{ (linear)}$$

At $\qquad x = 6$ m, $M_E = 19.6$ kN $-$ m

$$\text{(as before)};$$

At $\qquad x = 10$ m, $M_B = -6$ kN $-$ m

Hence, B.M. changes sign in EB, its value

being zero at $x = \dfrac{58}{6.4} = 9.0625$ m from A.

Hence, maximum sagging B.M. is at D
where S.F. changes sign.

For BC; $M_x = 10.6x - 8(x - 2) - 6(x - 4)$

$$- 3(x - 6) + 12.4(x - 10) - \frac{3}{2}x - 10^2$$

$$= 6x - 66 - 1.5x - 10^2,$$

Variation being parabolic, At, $x = 10$ m,
$M_B = -6$ (as before)

While at $x = 12$ m, $M_C = 6 \times -66 - 1.5$
$12 - 10^2 = 0$. The complete B.M.D. is
shown in fig.

5. (*a*)

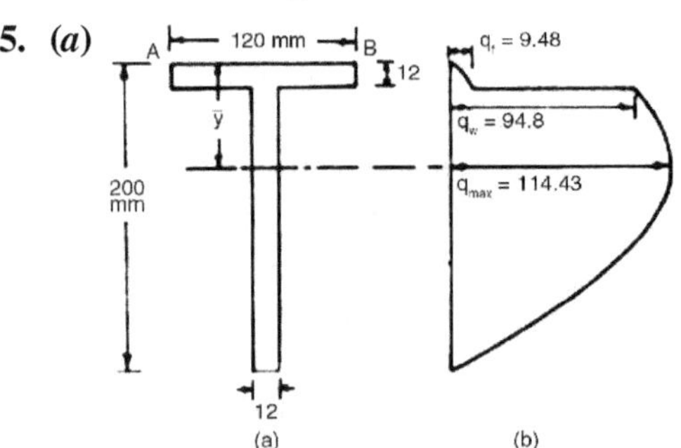

$$\bar{y} = \frac{200 \times 12 \times 100 + 108 \times 12 \times 6}{200 \times 12 + 108 \times 12}$$

$$= \frac{247776}{3696} = 67.04 \text{ mm}$$

$$I_{AB} = \frac{1}{3} \times 12(200)^3 + \frac{1}{3} \times 108(12)^3$$

$$= 3206 \times 10^4 \text{mm}^4$$

$$I_{xx} = 3206 \times 10^4 - 3696 \ (67.04)^2$$

$$= 1545 \times 10^4 \text{ mm}^4$$

q_f (at the junction with the web)

$$= \frac{F}{I \times 20}[120 \times 12(67.04 - 6)]$$

$$= \frac{732.48 \ F}{I} = \frac{732.48 \times 200 \times 10^3}{1545 \times 10^4}$$

$$= 9.48 \text{ N/mm}^2$$

q_w at the junction with flange

$$= 9.48 \times \frac{120}{12} = 94.8 \text{ N/mm}^2$$

$q_{w, \ max}$ at the centroid

$$= \frac{F}{I \times 12}\left[120 \times 12(67.04 - 6) + \frac{12(67.04 - 12)^2}{2}\right]$$

$$= \frac{8840 \ F}{I} = \frac{200 \times 10^3 \times 8840}{1545 \times 10^4}$$

$$= 114.43 \text{ N/mm}^2$$

The variation of shear stress is shown in fig (*b*).

5. (*b*) Let G the centroid of the section distance $\overline{Y}$ from the KL

Area of ABFC = A_1 = 150 × 20

$$= 3000 \text{ mm}^2$$

Distance of its centroid G_1 from KL

$$= Y_1 = 500 - 10$$

$$= 490 \text{ mm}$$

Area of DEIH = A_2 = 456 × 16

$$= 7296 \text{ mm}^2$$

Distance of its centroid G_2 from KL = Y_2

$$= 24 + \frac{1}{2} \times 456$$

$$= 252 \text{ mm}$$

Area of GJLK = A_3 = 250 × 24

$$= 6000 \text{ N/mm}^2$$

Distance of its centroid G_3 from KL

$$= Y_3 = \frac{1}{2} \times 24 = 12 \text{ mm}$$

Total area (A) = $A_1 + A_2 + A_3$

$$= 3000 + 7296 + 6000$$

$$= 16296 \text{ mm}^2$$

Taking moment of the areas about KL, we get

$$16296 = 3000 \times 490 + 7296 \times 252 + 6000 \times 12$$

From which $\overline{Y}$ = 207.4 mm

Moment of inertia:

Here, *y*-axis will be symmetrical

Let *x*-axis be at a distance $\overline{Y}$ above the base KL.

Total A = (150 × 20) + (456 × 16) + (250 × 24) = 16296

$$I_{KL} = \left(\frac{1}{3} \times 20^3 \times 150\right) + \left(\frac{1}{3} \times 456^3 \times 16\right) +$$

$$\left(\frac{1}{3} \times 24^3 \times 250\right) = 507252352$$

$$I_{XX} = 507252352 - 16296 \times 207.4^2.$$

5. (*c*) (*i*) Bond strength results from a combination of several parameters, such as the mutual adhesion between the concrete and steel interfaces and the pressure of the hardened concrete against the steel bar or wire due to the drying shrinkage of the concrete. Additionally, friction interlock between the bar surface deformations or projections and the concrete caused by the micro movements of the tensioned bar results in increased resistance to slippage. The total effect of this is known as *bond*.

Types of Bond: Bond stress along the length of a reinforcing bar may be induced under two loading situations and accordingly bond stresses are of two types:

1. *Flexural bond* or *Local bond*

2. *Anchorage bond* or *development bond*

Flexural bond (τ_{bf}) is one which arises from the change in tensile force carried by the bar, along its length, due to *change in bending moment* along the length of the member. Evidently, flexural bond is critical at points where the shear $\left(V = \dfrac{dM}{dx}\right)$ is significant. Since this occurs at a particular section, flexural bond stress is known as *local bond stress* (Fig. *b*).

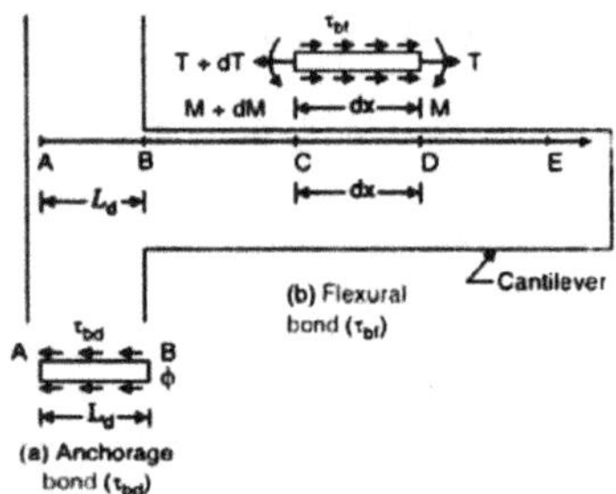

Fig. *Two Types of Bond*

'*Anchorage bond*' (τ_{bd}) is that which arises over the *length of anchorage* provided for a bar. It also arises near the end or cutoff point of a reinforcing bar. The anchorage bond resists the '*pulling out*' of the bar if it is in tension or 'pushing in' of the bar if it is in compression. Fig. (*a*) shows the situation of anchorage bond over a length AB (= L_d). Since bond stresses are *developed* over a specified length L_d, anchorage bond stress is also known as *development bond stress*.

5. (*c*) (*ii*) The development length may be defined as the length of the bar required on either side of the section to develop the required stress in steel at that section.

Let us consider the concept the development. Take your first finger and grab it in the palm of your other hand. Now pull the finger applying as much force as you can. At a certain limit the finder will slip and the contact between the finder and the palm will break. But suppose if my finger is too long or the grip between the finger and the palm is immense such that if you pull your finger then the only way to get your other hand free is breaking up your finger. That is the base concept of development length.

The bond between steel and concrete is somewhat similar. We cannot have a continuous bar of steel throughout the structure. There are always connections, joints and splices. If we do not provide development length, then at the location of these critical areas the structure will fail easily. But if we provide sufficient amount of length to give a continuity to the strength of the structure then the strength will be same everywhere.

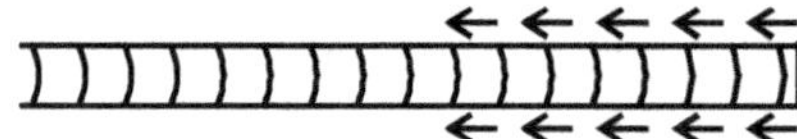

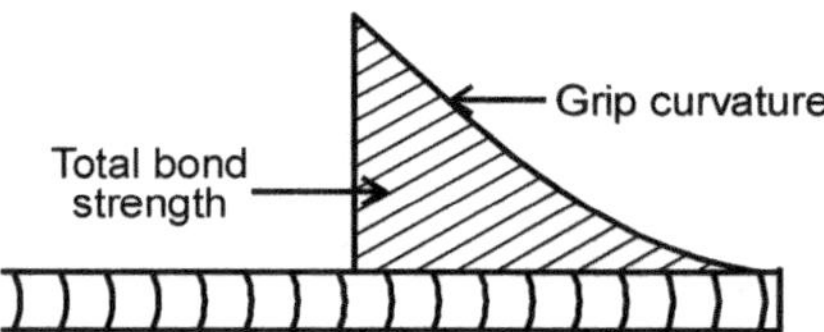

As shown in the picture above, I have chosen an arbitrary size of bar and displayed how the grip between the two surface is gained. Now if you sum up the grip then you can see that the bond strength increases from a zero value to a certain value X. Now we wish to increase the value of X equal to the strength of the steel used in that structure. So whenever the structure is loaded the only possibility of failure is by the rupture of steel and not anything else like failure of bond. So that is why we provide the development length. The minimum amount of length required by the bar to develop the full strength of the bond.

This development length depends on various parameters.
1. Grade of steel
2. Grade of concrete
3. Diameter of steel bar
4. Type of steel bar and so on.

6. (*a*) Diagram

$$A_{st} = 3 \times \frac{\pi}{4} \times 16^2 = 603.2 \text{ mm}^2$$

(*i*) Critical depth of neutral axis

$$x_c = kd = \frac{mc}{t + mc} d$$

$$m = \frac{280}{3\sigma_{cbc}} = \frac{280}{3 \times 7} = 13.33$$

$$x_c = \frac{13.33 \times 7}{230 + 13.33 \times 7} \times 400$$

$$= 115.44 \text{ mm}$$

(*ii*) Actual depth of neutral axis

$$B \times \frac{x_a^2}{2} = m.A_{st}(d - x_a)$$

$$250 \cdot \frac{x_a^2}{2} = 13.33 \times 603.2(400 - x_a)$$

$$\Rightarrow \quad 0.0156\, x_a^2 + x_a = 400$$

$$x_a = 131.25 \text{ mm} > x_c$$

$\Rightarrow$ so it is over reinforced section.

(*iii*) Moment of resistance for over reinforced section

$$x_a > x_c$$
$$c_a = \sigma_{cbc}$$
$$t_a < \sigma_{st}$$

$$MR = B.x_a \frac{c_a}{2} \times \left(d - \frac{x_a}{3} \right)$$

... (in compression side)

$$= 250 \times 131.25 \times \frac{7}{2}\left(400 - \frac{131.25}{2} \right)$$

$$= 38.4 \text{ kN-m}$$

MR for tension side

$$\frac{t_a / m}{d - x_a} = \frac{c_a}{x_a}$$

$$t_a = \frac{d - x_a}{x_a} \times m \times c_a$$

$$= \frac{400 - 131.25}{131.25} \times 13.33 \times 7$$

$$= 191.1$$

$$MR = t_a A_{st}\left(d - \frac{x_a}{3} \right)$$

$$= 191.1 \times 603.2\left(400 - \frac{131.25}{3} \right)$$

$$= 41.1 \text{ kN-m}$$

(*iv*) Balanced and ultimate moment of resistance

$$M.R = QBd^2$$

$$K = \frac{mc}{t + mc} = \frac{13.33 \times 7}{230 + 13.33 \times 7}$$

$$= 0.2886$$

$$j = 1 - \frac{k}{3} = 0.904$$

$$Q = \frac{1}{2}Cjk$$

$$= \frac{1}{2} \times 7 \times 0.904 \times 0.2886$$

$$= 0.913$$

$$MR = 0.913 \times 250 \times 400^2$$

$$= 36.525 \text{ kN-m}$$

$$A_{st}(\text{required}) = \frac{36.525 \times 10^6}{230\left(400 - \frac{131.25}{3} \right)}$$

$$= 445.77 \text{ mm}^2.$$

6. (*b*) By working state method

(1) Size

Min steel = 0.8%

Let us use 1% steel *i.e.* $\Rightarrow$ P = 0.01

σ_{cc} for M25 mix = 6 N/mm^2

For Fe415, σ_{cc} = 190 N/mm^2

Load carrying capacity of a short column (P)

$$P = \sigma_{cc}.A_c + \sigma_{sc}. A_{sc}$$

$$= \sigma_{cc}.(A_g - PA_g) + \sigma_{sc}.PA_g$$

From which, $A_g = \dfrac{P}{\sigma_{cc}(1 - P) + P\sigma_{sc}}$

$$= \frac{1000 \times 10^3}{6(1 - 0.01) + 0.01 \times 190}$$

$$= 127551.0 \text{ mm}^2 \times 1.5$$

Size of square $= \sqrt{127551}$

$$= 357.14 \text{ mm} \approx 358 \text{ mm}$$

However, provided square column of 358×358 mm

(2) Longitudinal reinforcement:

$$A_{sc} = PA = 0.01 \times 127551$$

$$= 1275.51 \text{ mm}^2$$

Using 16 mm ϕ bars,

$$A_\phi = \frac{\pi}{4} \times 16^2 = 201 \text{ mm}^2$$

No of bars required $= \dfrac{1275.51}{201}$

$$= 6.35 \approx 7$$

Assume nominal cover $= 40$ mm

(3) Design of ties:

Dia. of ties = 1/4 dia. of longitudinal reinforcement subjected to a min of 5 mm, however, use 6 mm ϕ bars of ties

c/c spacing of ties should not exceed least of following

(*i*) Least lateral dimension = 400 mm

(*ii*) 16 × dia. of main bar = 16 × 16
$$= 256 \text{ mm}$$

(*iii*) 48 × dia. of ties = 48 × 6 = 288 mm

Hence, provided the ties @ 250 mm c/c

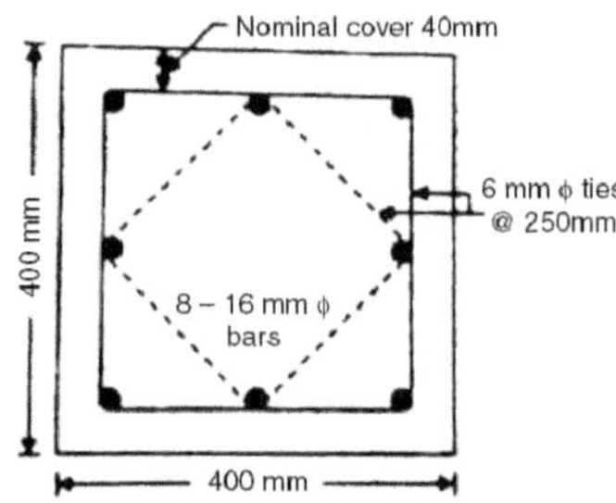

SSC-Junior Engineer (Civil & Structural) Exam 2011

PAPER-II (Conventional)

SECTION-I (Civil)

1. (*a*) Write a short note on Consumptive use of water.

   (*b*) Advantages and disadvantages of concrete sleeper.

2. (*a*) To determine the mean elevation of a station O interpolated in a triangulation system, the following observations were made:

Station	Height of Inst.	Station observed	Distance in m	Height of signal	Vertical angle	Remarks
	1.53	D	3684	5.58	+1° 1′20″	R sin 1° = 30.88 m
O	1.53	E	4698	4.11	−0° 52′50″	m = 0.07
	1.53	F	5028.6	4.9	−0° 34′10″	log sin 1° = 6.685575

   Find the mean elevation of station O, given that the elevations of D, E and F are 293.58, 157.725 and 179.355 respectively.

   (*b*) In a consolidation test on a soil, the void ratio of the sample decreases from 1.24 to 1.12 when the pressure is increased from 20 to 40 tonnes/sq. m. Calculate the co-efficient of consolidation in m^2/year, given that the co-efficient of permeability of the soil during this pressure increment is 8.5×10^{-3} cm/sec.

3. (*a*) In a plate bearing test on pure clayey soil failure occurred at a load of 12.2 tonnes. The size of the plate was 45 cm × 45 cm and the test was done at the depth of 1.0 m below ground level. Find out the ultimate bearing capacity for a 1.5 m wide continuous wall footing with its base at a depth of 2 m below the ground level. The unit weight of clay may be taken as 1.9 gm/cc and N_c = 5.7 and N_q = 1 and N_r = 0.

   (*b*) Write a short note on the significant properties of soil.

4. (*a*) A rectangular channel 2.0 m wide has a discharge of 250 lit/sec which is measured by a right angled V-notch weir. Find the position of the apex of the notch from the bed of the channel if the maximum depth of the water is not to exceed 1.3 m. Take C_d = 0.62.

   (*b*) List down the modes of water penetration into road structure with a neat sketch.

5. (*a*) Measures to control water pollution.

   (*b*) A room 600 cm long and 500 cm wide has a flat roof. There is one T-beam in the centre (cross section below the slab 30 cm × 50 cm) and the slab is 15 cm thick. Estimate the quantity of iron bars required for reinforcement (for the T-beam only) from the data given below:

   Main bars – 8 nos. of 25 mm dia. in 2 rows of 4 each (all 4 in the bottom being straight and others being bent)

   Stirrups – 10 mm dia. and 15 cm centre to centre throughout

   Anchor bars – 2 nos. of 16 mm dia.

6. (*a*) What is analysis of rates? And explain its purpose.

   (*b*) Explain the manufacturing of cement by wet process.

SECTION-II (Structural)

7. (*a*) Discuss the significance of cold weather concreting with special emphasis on problems faced by concrete in freezing conditions.

(*b*) Define workability of concrete and explain briefly the factors affecting workability.

8. Design a cantilever beam with a clear span of 3 m which carries a superimposed load of 15 kN/m. Its depth varies from 500 mm at the fixed end to 150 mm at the free end. Show reinforcement with a neat sketch.

9. A simply supported beam of 4.5 m effective span is carrying a live load of 25 kN/m. The size of the beam has to be restricted to 250 mm × 380 mm depth. Design the beam for bending using limit state method. The design coefficients are K = 0.138; τ = 0.80; K_u = 0.479. Use M20 grade concrete and Fe 415 steel.

10. Design a beam of 6 m span carrying a total load of 14.3 kN/m inclusive of self weight. The beam is laterally supported throughout.

11. (*a*) Compute the allowable compressive load on an axially loaded steel column having a cross section as shown in the figure and an effective length of 3.5 m.

For the purpose of computing the cross sectional area, the moment of inertia and the radius of gyrations, the maximum width of the outstand should be taken out not more than 16 times the thickness of the flange. Also, the maximum depth of web should be taken not more than 50 times its thickness.

Use the following data:

l/r	Allowable stress in axial compression (kg/cm²)
60	1130
70	1075
80	1007
90	928
100	840

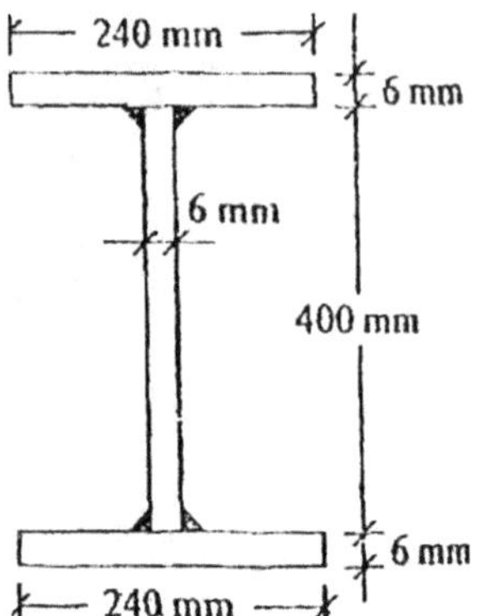

(*b*) Determine the forces in the members of the truss shown in the figure below:

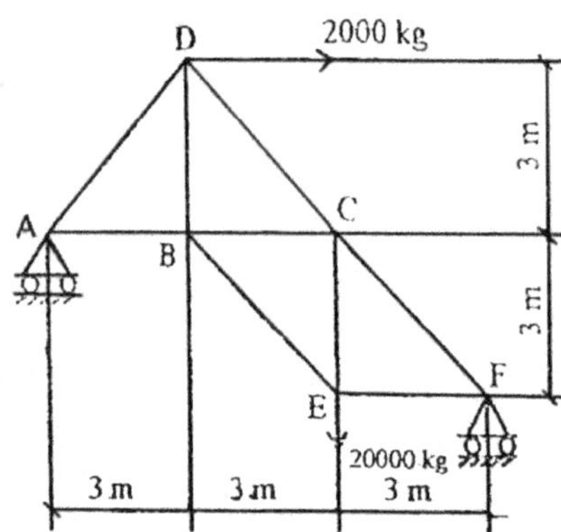

12. A fixed beam of constant section carries a load transferred from a rigid bracket as shown in figure. Find the bending moment and reactions at the fixed ends and plot S.F.D. and B.M.D.

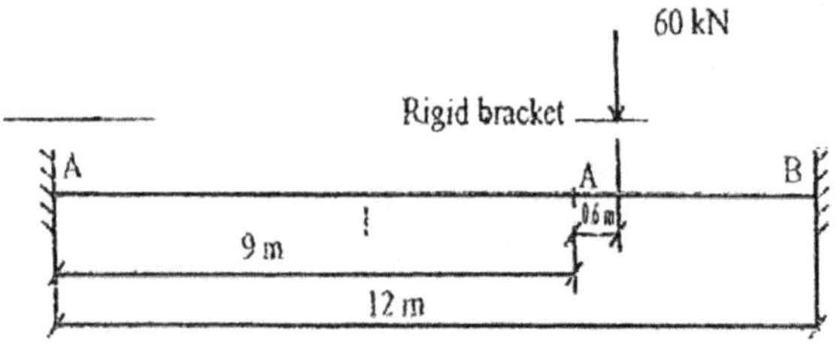

ANSWERS

1. (*a*) Consumptive Use of Water

It is the quantity of water used by the vegetation growth of a given area. It is the amount of water required by a crop for its vegetated growth to evapotranspiration and building of plant tissues plus evaporation from soils and intercepted precipitation. It is expressed in terms of depth of water.

Consumptive use of water by a crop is expressed as the depth of water per unit area for specified period, such as days, months or seasons.

The climatic factors that particularly affect consumptive use are temperature, solar radiation, precipitation, humidity, wind movement, length of growing season, latitude and sunlight.

1. *Precipitation:* The amount and rate of precipitation may have some minor effect on the amount of water consumptively used during any summer. Under certain conditions, precipitation may occur as a series of frequent, light showers during the hot summer. Such showers may add little or nothing to the soil moisture for use by the plants through transpiration but do decrease the withdrawal from the stored moisture. Such precipitation may be lost largely by evaporation directly from the surface of the plant foliage and the land surface.

2. *Temperature:* The rate of consumptive use of water by crops in any particular locality is probably affected more by temperature, which for long-time periods is a good measure of solar radiation, than by any other factor. Abnormally low temperatures retard plant growth and unusually high temperatures may produce dormancy. Consumptive use may vary widely even in years of equal accumulated temperatures because of deviations from the normal seasonal distribution. Transpiration is influenced not only by temperature but also by the area of leaf surface and the physiologic needs of the plant, both of which are related to stage of maturity.

3. *Humidity:* Evaporation and transpiration are accelerated on days of low humidity and slowed during periods of high humidity. During periods of low relative humidity, greater rate of use of water by vegetation may be expected.

4. *Wind Movement:* Evaporation of water from land and plant surfaces takes place more rapidly when there is moving air than under calm air conditions. Hot, dry winds and other unusual wind conditions during the growing period will affect the amount of water consumptively used. However, there is a limit in the amount of water that can be utilized. As soon as the land surface is dry, evaporation practically stops and transpiration is limited by the ability of the plants to extract and convey the soil moisture through the plants.

5. *Growing Season:* The growing season, which is tied rather closely to temperature, has a major effect on the seasonal use of water by plants. It is frequently considered to be the period between killing frosts, but for many annual crops, it is shorter than the frost-free period, as such crops are usually planted after frosts are past and mature before they recur.

Although the frost-free season may be used as a guide for computing consumptive use, actual dates of planting and harvesting of the crops and average annual dates of the first and last irrigation are important in determining the consumptive irrigation requirements of the crops.

6. *Latitude and Sunlight:* Although latitude may hardly be called a climatic factor, it does have considerable influence on the rate of consumptive use of water by various plants. Because of the earth's movement and axial inclination, the hours of daylight during the summer are much greater in the northern latitudes than at the Equator. Since the sun is the source of all energy used in crop growth and evaporation of water, this longer day may allow plant transpiration to continue for a longer period each day and to produce an effect similar to that of lengthening the growing season.

7. *Available Irrigation Water Supply:* All the above-mentioned climatic factors influence the amount of water that potentially can be consumed in a given area. However, there are other factors that also cause important differences in the consumptive use-rates. Naturally, unless water is available from some source (precipitation, natural ground water, or irrigation), there can be no consumptive use. In those areas of the arid and semiarid West where the major source is irrigation, both the quantity and seasonal distribution of the available supply will affect consumptive use. Where water is plentiful and cheap, there is a tendency for farmers to overirrigate. If the soil surface is frequently wet and the resulting evaporation is high, the combined evaporation and transpiration or consumptive use may likewise increase. Also, under more optimum soil moisture conditions, yields of crops such as alfalfa may be higher than average and more water consumed. In irrigating some crops, such as potatoes, water is applied to the field not only for the purpose of supplying the consumptive water needs of the crop but also to help maintain a favourable microclimatic condition.

8. Quality of Water: Some investigations have shown that the quality of the water supply may have an appreciable effect on consumptive use. Whether or not plants actually transpire more or less if water is highly saline may be debatable. However, if it is necessary to apply additional water to the land to leach the salts down through the soil, more water will probably be lost by evaporation from the soil surface and such loss will be chargeable against the consumptive requirement of the cropped area.

9. *Soil Fertility:* If a soil is made more fertile through the application of manure or by some other means, the yields may be expected to increase with an accompanying small increase in use of water. However, an increase in fertility of the soil causes a decrease in the amount of water consumed per unit of crop yield.

10. Plant Pests and Diseases: Where plant pests and diseases seriously affect the natural growth of the plants, it is reasonable to assume that transpiration will likewise decrease. It is recognized that some damage to crops is caused every year by pests and diseases. Ordinarily the losses may not vary greatly from year to year, but in those years when they are unusually severe consumptive use may be lowered materially.

1. (*b*) Concrete Sleepers: Sleepers are reinforced or prestressed. These two types of sleepers are briefly described below:

A. RCC Sleepers: There are one piece through type or Block and tie bar type.

(*i*) *Trough type sleeper. (One type).* The sleeper consists of a number of components of RCC with dimensions similar to wooden sleepers. They are not commonly used since they are likely to crack under vibrations due to loads.

(*ii*) Block and Tie bar type sleeper. (See fig. *a*)

Block and Tie-bar type (Fig. *a*) is also known as composite type sleeper. It contains two block of RCC, one block being placed under each rail. The blocks are joined by a metal tie bar in the form of an inverted T-Section.

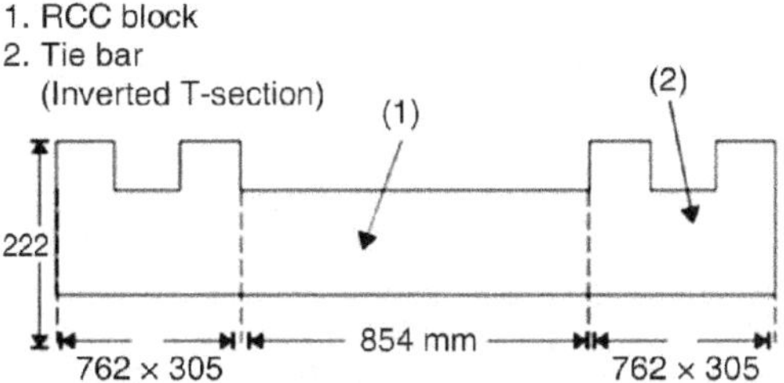

Fig. (a) RCC sleeper (Block and Tie bar)

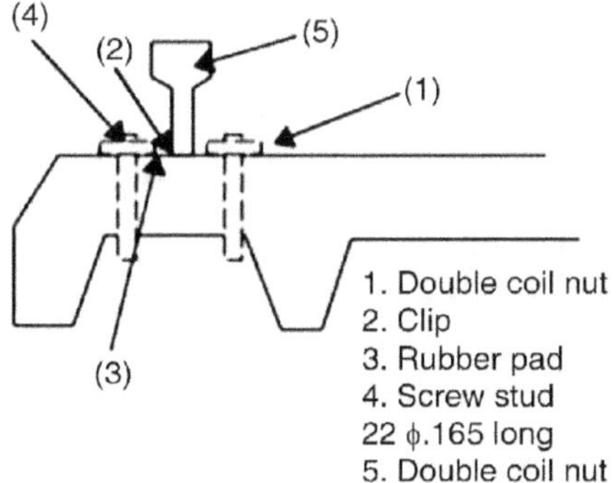

Fig. (b) Prestressed concrete sleeper

B. Prestressed concrete sleeper: These sleepers may be (*a*) Pretensioned, or (*b*) Post-tensioned. The pretensioned type using high tensile steel is tensioned before placing concrete. Reinforcement is kept under tension till concrete hardens. On the wires being released high compressive stresses are developed in the concrete.

In the post tensioned sleepers steel is tensioned after concrete has hardened. Steel tubes are embedded in the concrete sleeper in which high tensile steel bars are passed after hardening of concrete. On completion of tensioning, tubes are foced into cement grout under pressure. Compressive stresses are developed in the concrete after it has hardened. (See. Fig. (*b*))

There are various methods of fixing rails to concrete sleeper. These are:

1. Driving spikes in wooden plugs embedded in concrete sleepers. They have however not been found satisfactory.

2. Fixing coach screws driven through wooden pegs embedded in the sleepers.

3. Inserting bolts and clips in the sleepers. Metal bearing plates are provided to avoid disintegration of concrete sleepers.

Table: Advantages and disadvantages of concrete sleepers

Sl. No.	Items	Particulars
1.	**Advantages**	
	(*i*) Life	Long (50 years)
	(*ii*) Adjustment of gauge	Easy
	(*iii*) Fittings	Less
	(*iv*) Connections between rail and sleeper	Strong
	(*v*) Longitudinal and lateral rigidity	More
	(*vi*) Track circuiting	Possible
	(*vii*) Creep	Less
	(*viii*) Suitability for heavy traffic	Suitable
	(*ix*) Cost of maintenance	Low
2.	**Disadvantages**	
	(*i*) Effect of rough handling	Liable to break
	(*ii*) Suitability for fastening to rail	Suitable only for the gauge for which designed
	(*iii*) Uses over bridges and crossing	Unsuitable
	(*iv*) Renewal	Difficult

2. (*a*)

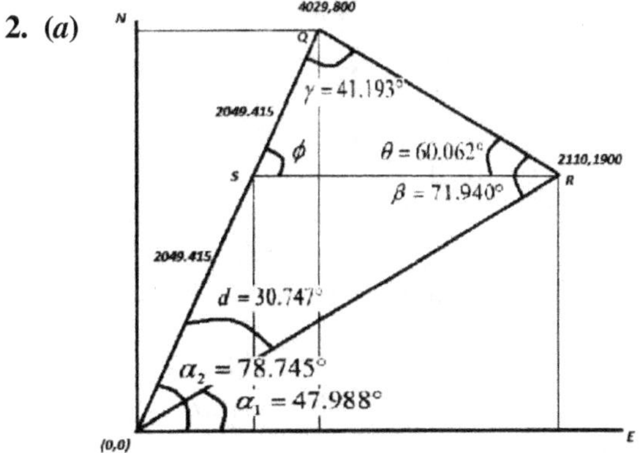

From Pythagoras theorem:

$$PR = \sqrt{2110^2 + 1900^2} = 2839.384 \text{ m}$$

also, $PQ = \sqrt{4020^2 + 800^2} = 4098.829 \text{ m}$

$$QR = \sqrt{(4020 - 2110)^2 + (1900 - 800)^2}$$
$$= 2204.11 \text{ m}$$

$$\tan \alpha_1 = \frac{2110}{1900}$$

$$\alpha_1 = \tan^{-1}\left(\frac{2110}{1900}\right) = 47.998°$$

$$\tan \alpha_2 = \frac{4020}{800}$$

$$\alpha_2 = \tan^{-1}\left(\frac{4020}{800}\right) = 78.745°$$

From Δ PQR:

By sine rule

$$\frac{PQ}{\sin \beta} = \frac{PR}{\sin \gamma} = \frac{QR}{\sin \alpha}$$

$$\frac{4098.829}{\sin \beta} = \frac{2204.11}{\sin 30.747}$$

$$\angle \beta = 72.940°$$

1. Co-ordinates of Rf. 'S'

$$= \frac{N}{2049.415 \times \sin 78.245}$$
$$= 2010.00$$

$$\frac{E}{2049.415 \times \cos 78.245} = 400.00$$

$$\frac{2204.11}{\sin 30.747} = \frac{PR}{\sin \gamma}$$

$$\frac{2204.11}{\sin 30.747} = \frac{2839.384}{\sin \gamma}$$

$$= 41.193°$$

$$\tan \theta = \frac{4020 - 2110}{1900 - 800}$$

$$\theta = \tan^{-1}\left(\frac{1910}{1100}\right)$$

$$\theta = 60.062°$$

From ΔQRS:

$$\angle \phi = 180° - 60.062° - 41.193°$$
$$= 78.745°$$

From ΔQRS:

By using sine rule:

$$\frac{SQ}{\sin 60.062} = \frac{QR}{\sin 78.745} = \frac{SR}{\sin 41.193}$$

$$\frac{2204.11}{\sin 78.745} = \frac{SR}{\sin 41.193}$$

$$SR = 1480.086 \text{ m.}$$

2. (b) Given $\quad \rho_0 = 1.24, \quad \rho_1 = 1.12,$

$$\sigma_1 = 20 \text{ t/m}^2, \quad \sigma_2 = 40 \text{ t/m}^2$$

Coefficient of permeability

$$= 8.5 \times 10^{-3} \text{ cm/sec}$$

$$C_v = \frac{k}{\gamma_w m_v}, \quad m_v = \frac{a_v}{1 + \rho_0}$$

When $\quad m_v$ = coefficient of volume change

a_v = coefficient of compressibility

C_v = ?

$$a_v = \frac{1.24 - 1.12}{40 - 20}$$
$$= 6 \times 10^{-3} \text{ m}^3/\text{tonne}$$

$$m_v = \frac{a_v}{1 + \rho_0} = \frac{6 \times 10^{-3}}{1 + 1.24}$$
$$= 2.68 \times 10^{-3} \text{ m}^3/\text{tonne}$$

$$C_v = \frac{8.5 \times 10^{-3} \text{ cm/sec}}{9.81 \text{ kN/m}^3 \times 2.68 \times 10^{-3} \text{ m}^2/\text{tonne}}$$

$$= \frac{\dfrac{8.5 \times 10^{-3}}{100} \text{ m/year} \times 365 \times 24 \times 60 \times 60}{9.81 \text{ kN/m}^3 \times 2.68 \times 10^{-3} \text{ m}^2 / \left(\dfrac{1000 \times 9.81}{1000}\right) \text{kN}}$$

$$= \frac{8.5 \times 10^{-3} \times 365 \times 24 \times 60 \times 60 \times 9.81}{100 \times 9.81 \times 2.68 \times 10^{-3}}$$

$$C_v = 1000208.95 \text{ m}^2/\text{year}$$

3. (a) Plate bearing capacity of plate

$$Q_{up} = \frac{P}{A_p} = \frac{12.2 \times 9.81}{0.45^2}$$

$$Q_{up} = 591.02 \text{ kN/m}^2$$

In clay $Q_{up} = Q_{uf}$

Hence the ultimate bearing capacity of foundation

$$Q_{uf} = 591.02 \ kN/m^2$$

$$Q_u = cNc + \gamma D_f N_q + \frac{1}{2}\gamma BN_\gamma$$

$$N_\gamma = 0$$

$$591.02 = C \times 5.7 + 1.9 \times 9.81 \times 2 \times 1$$

$$\Rightarrow \quad C = 97.148 \ kN/m^2.$$

(b) SOIL PHYSICAL AND CHEMICAL PROPERTIES

Physical Properties

(a) Horizonation: Soil "horizons" are discrete layers that make up a soil profile. They are typically parallel with the ground surface. In some soils, they show evidence of the actions of the soil forming processes.

(b) Soil Color: In well aerated soils, oxidized or ferric (Fe^{+3}) iron compounds are responsible for the brown, yellow and red colors you see in the soil.

When iron is reduced to the ferrous (Fe^{+2}) form, it becomes mobile and can be removed from certain areas of the soil. When the iron is removed, a gray color remains, or the reduced iron color persists in shades of green or blue.

Soils that are dominantly gray with brown or yellow mottles immediately below the surface horizon are usually hydric.

(c) Soil Texture: Soil texture refers to the proportion of the soil "separates" that make up the mineral component of soil. These separates are called sand, silt and clay. These soil separates have the following size ranges:

- Sand = < 2 to 0.05 mm
- Silt = 0.05 to 0.002 mm
- Clay = <0.002 mm

(d) Soil Structure: The soil separates can become aggregated together into discrete structural units called "peds". These peds are organized into a repeating pattern that is referred to as soil structure. Between the peds are cracks called "pores" through which soil air and water are conducted. Soil structure is most commonly described in terms of the shape of the individual peds that occur within a soil horizon.

(e) Soil Consistence: Soil consistence refers to the ease with which an individual ped can be crushed by the fingers. Soil consistence and its description, depends on soil moisture content.

(f) Bulk Density: Bulk density is the proportion of the weight of a soil relative to its volume. It is expressed as a unit of weight per volume and is commonly measured in units of grams per cubic centimeters (g/cc).

Bulk density is an indicator of the amount of pore space available within individual soil horizons, as it is inversely proportional to pore space:

Pore space = 1 – bulk density/

particle density

Chemical Properties

(a) Cation Exchange Capacity (CEC): Some plant nutrients and metals exist as positively charged ions, or "cations", in the soil environment. Among the more common cations found in soils are hydrogen (H^+), aluminum (Al^{+3}), calcium (Ca^{+2}), magnesium (Mg^{+2}) and potassium (K^+). Most heavy metals also exist as cations in the soil environment. Clay and organic matter particles are predominantly negatively charged (anions) and have the ability to hold cations from being "leached" or washed away. The adsorbed cations are subject to replacement by other cations in a rapid, reversible process called "cation exchange".

Cations leaving the exchange sites enter the soil solution, where they can be taken up by plants, react with other soil constituents, or be carried away with drainage water.

(b) Soil Reaction (pH): By definition, "pH" is a measure of the active hydrogen ion (H^+) concentration. It is an indication of the acidity or alkalinity of a soil and also known as "soil reaction".

The most important effect of pH in the soil is on ion solubility, which in turn affects microbial and plant growth. A pH range of 6.0 to 6.8 is ideal for most crops because it coincides with optimum solubility of the most important plant nutrients. Some minor elements (*e.g.*, iron) and most heavy metals are more soluble at lower pH. This makes pH management important in controlling movement of heavy metals in soil.

4. (b) Modes of water penetration: The process of removing and controlling the access of surface and sub-surface water within the right-of-way of a road is called road drainage.

It also include interception (collection) and diversion of water from the road surface and the subgrade. The process of interception and diversion of surface water through suitable side drains is called surface drainage and the process of interception and removal of sub-soil water through suitable sub-surface drains is called sub-surface drainage.

The main object of road drainage is to keep the road surface and its foundation as dry as possible so as to maintain its stability.

Thus, a good drainage system is essential for efficient highway transportation with minimum maintenance cost.

Modes of water penetration into road structure: The following are the different modes of water penetration into the road structure:

1. Surface water from the top of pavement by percolation through cracks and poor pavement surface.
2. Surface water from sides of the pavement.
3. Sub-soil water from underside of the pavement by capillary rise.
4. Sub-soil water from sides of the pavement.
5. Intercepted water due to overflooding of cross drainage works.

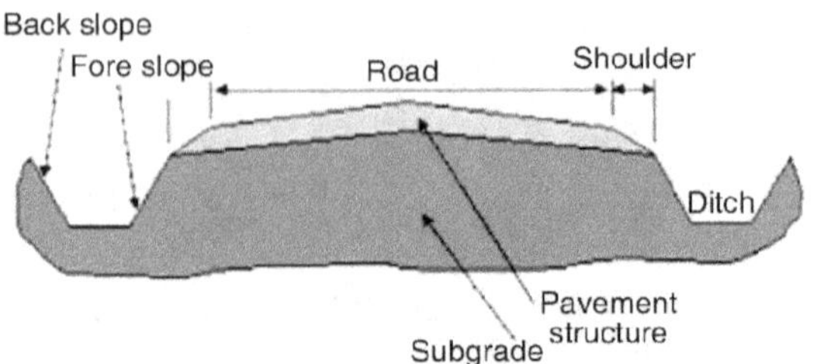

5. (*a*) WATER POLLUTION

Water pollution may be defined as "the alteration in physical, chemical and biological characteristics of water which may cause harmful effects on humans and aquatic life."

Pollutants include:
1. Sewage
2. Industrial effluents and chemicals
3. Oil and other wastes

Chemicals in air dissolve in rain water, fertilizers, pesticides and herbicides leached from land pollute water.

Point and non-point sources of water pollution

Point sources: These are pollutants that are discharged at specific locations through pipes, ditches or sewers into bodies of surface waters.

1. Ex: Factories, sewage treatment plants, abandoned underground mines and oil tankers.

2. **Non point sources:** These pollutants cannot be traced to a single point of discharge. They are large land areas or air-sheds that pollute water by runoff, subsurface flow or deposition from the atmosphere.

   Ex: Acid deposition, runoff of chemicals into surface water from croplands, livestock feedlots, logged forests, urban streets, lawns, golf courses and parking lots.

Control measures of water pollution:

1. Administration of water pollution control should be in the hands of state or central government

2. Scientific techniques should be adopted for environmental control of catchment areas of rivers, ponds or streams

3. Industrial plants should be based on recycling operations as it helps prevent disposal of wastes into natural waters but also extraction of products from waste.

4. Plants, trees and forests control pollution as they act as natural air conditioners.

5. Trees are capable of reducing sulphur dioxide and nitric oxide pollutants and hence more trees should be planted.

6. No type of waste (treated, partially treated or untreated) should be discharged into any natural water body. Industries should develop closed loop water supply schemes and domestic sewage must be used for irrigation.

7. Qualified and experienced people must be consulted from time to time for effective control of water pollution.

8. Public awareness must be initiated regarding adverse effects of water pollution using the media.

9. Laws, standards and practices should be established to prevent water pollution and these laws should be modified from time to time based on current requirements and technological advancements.

10. Basic and applied research in public health engineering should be encouraged.

6. (a) ANALYSIS OF RATES

In order to determine the rate of a particular item, the factors affecting the rate of that item are studied carefully and then finally a rate is decided for that item. This process of determining the rates of an item is termed as analysis of rates or rate analysis.

The rate of particular item of work depends on the following:

1. Specifications of works and material about their quality, proportion and constructional operation method.

2. Quantity of materials and their costs.

3. Cost of labours and their wages.

4. Location of site of work and the distances from source and conveyance charges.

5. Overhead and establishment charges

6. Profit.

Cost of materials at source and at site of construction:

The costs of materials are taken as delivered at site inclusive of the transport local taxes and other charges.

Purpose of Analysis of rates:

Purpose of Analysis of rates:

1. To work out the actual cost of per unit of the items.

2. To work out the economical use of materials and processes in completing the particulars item.

3. To work out the cost of extra items which are not provided in the contract bond, but are to be done as per the directions of the department.

4. To revise the schedule of rates due to increase in the cost of material and labour or due to change in technique.

Cost of labour-types of labour, standard schedule of rates:

The labour can be classified into

1. Skilled – 1st class

2. Skilled – 2nd Class

3. Unskilled

The labour charges can be obtained from the standard schedule of rates 30% of the skilled labour provided in the data may be taken as Ist class, remaining 70% as II class. The rates of materials for Government works are fixed by the superintendent Engineer for his circle every year and approved by the Board of Chief Engineers. These rates are incorporated in the standard schedule of rates.

Lead statement: The distance between the source of availability of material and construction site is known as "Lead" and is expected in Km. The cost of conveyance of material depends on lead.

This statement will give the total cost of materials per unit item. It includes first cost, conveyance loading, unloading stacking, charges etc.

The rate shown in the lead statement are for metalled road and include loading and staking charges. The environment lead on the metalled roads are arrived by multiplying by a factor.

(*a*) For metal tracks – Lead × 1.0
(*b*) For cartze tracks – Lead × 1.1
(*c*) For Sandy tracks – Lead × 1.4

6. (*b*) **Making of cement (wet process technology)**

The manufacture of cement is a very carefully regulated process comprising the following stages:

1. **Quarrying -** a mixture of limestone and clay.

2. **Grinding -** the limestone and clay with water to form a slurry.

3. **Burning -** the slurry to a very high temperature in a kiln, to produce clinker.

4. **Grinding -** the clinker with about 5% gypsum to make cement.

Raw Materials Extraction: The limestone and clay occur together in our quarries at Cape Foulwind. It is necessary to drill and blast these materials before they are loaded in 70t capacity trucks.

The quarry trucks deliver the raw materials to the crusher where the rock is crushed to smaller than 100 mm (4 inches). The raw materials are then stored ready for use.

Raw Materials Preparation: About 80% limestone and 20% clay are ground in ball mills with water, producing very fine, thin, paste called slurry. The chemical composition of the slurry is very carefully controlled by adjusting the relative amount of limestone and clay being used.

The slurry is stored in large basins ready for use.

Clinker Burning: The slurry is fed into the upper end of a rotary kiln, while at the lower end of the kiln, a very intense flame is maintained by blowing in finely ground coal.

The slurry slowly moves down the kiln and is dried and heated until it reaches a temperature of almost 1500 degrees Celsius producing "clinker". This temperature completely changes the limestone and clay to produce new minerals which have the property of reacting with water to form a cementitious binder. The hot clinker is used to preheat the air for burning the coal and the cooled clinker is stored ready for use.

Cement Milling: The clinker is finely ground with about 5% gypsum in another ball mill, producing cement. (The gypsum regulates the early setting characteristic of cement). The finished cement is stored in silos then carted to our wharf or packing plant facilities.

7. (*a*) **COLD WEATHER CONCRETING**

Any concreting operation done at a temperature below 5°C is termed *cold weather concreting*. The concrete in the plastic stage can be damaged if it is exposed to low temperatures which cause ice lenses to form and expansion to occur within the pore structure and subsequent damage may occur due to alternate freezing and thawing when the concrete has hardened. The effects of cold weather concreting may be summarized as follows.

Delayed Setting: At low temperatures, the development of concrete strength is retarded as compared with the strength development at normal temperatures. The setting period necessary before removal of formwork is thus increased. Although the initial strength of concrete is lower, the ultimate strength will not be severely affected provided the concrete has been prevented from freezing during its early life.

Early Freezing of Concrete: When *plastic concrete* is exposed to freezing temperature, it may suffer permanent damage. If the concrete is allowed to freeze before a certain *prehardening period,* it may suffer irreparable loss in its properties so much so that even one cycle of *freezing* and *thawing* during the prehardening period may reduce compressive strength to 50 per cent of what would be expected for normal temperature concrete. The prehardening period depends upon the type of cement and environmental conditions. It may be specified in terms of time required to attain a compressive strength of the order of 3.5 to 7.0 MPa; alternatively it can be specified in terms of period varying from 24 hours to even three days depending upon the degree of saturation and *water-cement ratio.*

Stresses due to Temperature Differential: A large temperature differential within the concrete member may promote cracking and has a harmful effect on *durability.* Such situations are likely to occur in cold weather at the time of removal of formwork.

RECOMMENDED PRACTICE

As per IS: 7861 (Part-11)–1981, the following measures should be taken.

Temperature Control of Ingredients: The temperature at the time of setting of concrete can be raised by heating the ingredients of the concrete mix. It would be easier to heat the *mixing water.* The temperature of the water should not exceed 65°C as the *flash set* of cement will occur when the hot water and cement come in contact in the mixers. Therefore, the heated water should come in direct contact with the aggregate and not the cement, first. The *aggregates* are heated by passing steam through pipes embedded in aggregate storage bins. Another precaution taken along with the heating of ingredients is to construct a temporary shelter around the construction site. The air inside is heated by electric or steam heating or central heating with circulating water. The temperature of ingredients should be so decided that the resulting concrete sets at a temperature of 10 to 20°C.

Use of Insulating Formwork: A fair amount of heat is generated during *hydration* of cement. Such heat can be gainfully conserved by having insulating *formwork* covers capable of maintaining concrete temperature above the desirable limit up to the first 3 days (or even 7 days) even though the ambient temperatures are lower. The formwork covers can be of timber, clean straw, blankets, tarpaulines, plastic sheeting, etc. and are used in conjunction with an air gap as insulation. The efficiency of the covers depends upon the thermal conductivity of the medium as well as ambient temperature conditions. For moderately cold weather, timber formwork alone is sufficient.

Proportioning of Concrete Ingredients: The important factor for cold-weather concreting is the attainment of suitable temperature for fresh concrete. Since the quantity of cement in the mix affects the rate of increase in temperature, an additional quantity of cement may be used. It would be preferable to use high alumina cement for concreting during frost conditions, the main advantage being that a higher heat of hydration is generated during the first 24 hours. During this period, sufficient strength (approximately 10 to 15 MPa) is developed to make the concrete safe against frost action. No accelerator should be used if high alumina cement is used. Alternatively, the rapid hardening Portland cement or accelerating admixtures used with proper precautions can help in getting the required strength in a shorter period. Air-entraining agents are generally recommended for use in cold weather. Air-entrainment increases the resistance of the hardened concrete to *freezing and thawing* and normally, at the same time, improves the *workability* of fresh concrete. The calcium chloride used as accelerating admixture may cause corrosion of reinforcing steel. In any case, calcium chloride should not be used in prestressed concrete construction.

Placement and Curing: Before placing the concrete, all ice, snow and frost should be completely removed. Care should be taken to see that the surface on which the concrete is to be placed and eminent parts are sufficiently warm. During the periods of freezing or in near-freezing conditions, water curing is not applicable.

Delayed Removal of Formwork: Because of slower rate of gain of strength during the cold weather, the formwork and props have to be kept in place for a longer time than in usual concreting practice.

The problem of concreting in cold weather can be minimized by adopting precast construction of structures. Precast members are manufactured in the factories where adequate precautions can be taken and concreting can be done in the controlled conditions.

7. (b) WORKABILITY OF CONCRETE

Workability is often referred to as the ease with which a concrete can be transported, placed and consolidated without excessive bleeding or segregation.

OR

The internal work done required to overcome the frictional forces between concrete ingredients for full compaction. It is obvious that no single test can evaluate all these factors. In fact, most of these cannot be easily assessed even though some standard tests have been established to evaluate them under specific conditions.

In the case of concrete, consistence is sometimes taken to mean the degree of wetness; within limits, wet concretes are more workable than dry concrete, but concrete of same consistence may vary in workability.

Because the strength of concrete is adversely and significantly affected by the presence of voids in the compacted mass, it is vital to achieve a maximum possible density. This requires sufficient workability for virtually full compaction to be possible using a reasonable amount of work under the given conditions. Presence of voids in concrete reduces the density and greatly reduces the strength: 5% of voids can lower the strength by as much as 30%.

Factors affecting concrete workability:

  (*i*) Water-Cement ratio
 (*ii*) Amount and type of Aggregate
(*iii*) Amount and type of Cement
 (*iv*) Weather conditions
    1. Temperature
    2. Wind
  (*v*) Chemical Admixtures
 (*vi*) Sand to Aggregate ratio

(*i*) Water content or Water Cement Ratio: More the water cement ratio more will be workability of concrete. Since by simply adding water the inter particle lubrication is increased. High water content results in a higher fluidity and greater workability but reduces the strength of concrete. Because with increasing w/c ratio the strength decreases as more water will result.

(ii) **Amount and type of Aggregate:** Since larger Aggregate sizes have relatively smaller surface areas (for the cement paste to coat) and since less water means less cement, it is often said that one should use the largest practicable Aggregate size and the stiffest practical mix. Most building elements are constructed with a maximum Aggregate size of 3/4" to 1", larger sizes being prohibited by the closeness of the reinforcing bars.

(iii) **Aggregate Cement ratio:** More ratio, less workability. Since less cement mean less water, so the paste is stiff.

(iv) **Weather Conditions:**

1. Temperature: If temperature is high, evaporation increases, thus workability decreases.

2. Wind: If wind is moving with greater velocity, the rate of evaporation also increase reduces the amount of water and ultimately reducing workability.

(v) **Admixtures:** Chemical admixtures can be used to increase workability.

Use of air entraining agent produces air bubbles which acts as a sort of ball bearing between particles and increases mobility, workability and decreases bleeding, segregation. The use of fine pozzolanic materials also have better lubricating effect and more workability.

(vi) **Sand to Aggregate ratio:** If the amount of sand is more the workability will reduce because sand has more surface area and more contact area causing more resistance.

9. Given, $\qquad l = 4.5$ m

$\qquad$ Live load = 25 kN/m

$\qquad$ (if K, J are given use W.S.M. but if $j = 0.80$ then use only L.S.M.)

$\qquad$ Size of beam = 250 mm $(b) \times 380$ mm (d)

$\qquad$ K = 0.0138, $\tau = J = 0.8$

$\qquad$ $K_u = 0.479$, M 20, Fe 415

Step 1: Calculate bending moment of the section

Self wt. of the beam = $0.25 \times 0.380 \times 125$

$\qquad\qquad = 2.375$ kN/m

Live load (S.I. load) = 25 kN/m

$\qquad$ Total load = 27.375 kN/m

$\qquad$ Factored load w = 41.10 kN/m

$$\text{B.M.} = M = \frac{wl^2}{8} = \frac{41.10 \times 4.5^2}{8}$$

$$= 103.94 \text{ kN-m}$$

Step 2: Assume clear cover = 40 mm

$$M_1 = M_{u_{\lim}} = QBd^2$$

$$= 0.36\, f_{ck} \cdot Bx_{u_{\lim}} (d - 0.42 x_{u_{\lim}})$$

$$= 0.36202500.48340(340 - 0.42 \times 0.48 \times 340)$$

$$= 79.24 \text{ kN-m}$$

$$\text{OR}$$

$$M_1 = 0.138 \times f_{ck} Bd^2$$
$$= 0.138 \times 20 \times 250 \times 340^2 \times 10^{-6}$$
$$= 79.764 \text{ kN-m}$$

B.M. $> M_1$ then we need a doubly reinforcement section

$\qquad$ B.M. = 103.94 kN-m

Step 3: Area of steel

$$(i) \quad A_{st_1} = \frac{M_1}{0.87 f_y (d - 0.42 x_u)}$$

$$= \frac{79.76 \times 10^6}{0.87 \times 415(340 - 0.42 \times 0.48 \times 340)}$$

$$= 814.13 \text{ mm}^2$$

$$(ii) \; A_{st_2} = \frac{M_2}{0.87 f_y (d - d_c)}$$

$$= \frac{(103.94 - 79.76) \times 10^6}{0.87 \times 415(340 - 40)} = 223.24$$

Total A_{st} = 814.13 + 223.24 = 1037.4 mm^2

$$(iii) \quad A_{sc} = \frac{M_2}{(f_{sc} - 0.45 f_{ck})(d - d_c)}$$

$$= \frac{(103.94 - 79.76) \times 10^6}{(350 - 0.45 \times 20)(340 - 40)}$$

$$= 236.364$$

10. Assume M 20 concrete and shear stress in steel as 230 N/mm^2

1. Calculation of Design Constants: For M 20 concrete, $c = \sigma_{cbc} = 7$ N/mm^2 and $m = 13.33$

Also, $\tau = \sigma_n = 230$ N/mm^2

$$\therefore \quad k_c = \frac{mc}{mc+t} = \frac{13.33 \times 7}{13.33 \times 7 + 230}$$

$$= 0.289$$

$$j_c = 1 - k_c/3 = 1 - 0.289/3 = 0.904$$

$$R_c = \frac{1}{2}c \times j_c \times k_c = \frac{1}{2} \times 0.904 \times 0.289$$

$$= 0.914$$

2. Calculation of B.M: Let the effective depth of beam is 1/10 span = 6000/10 = 600 mm
Assume total depth of beam = 600 mm (say), for computation of dead weight of beam
Let the width of the beam = ½d = 300 mm (say)
Given total load per metre run = 14300 N
Effective span = L = I + d = 6 + 0.6 = 6.6 m
(This is smaller than the centre to centre distance of 6.75 m between the supports).

$$M = \frac{wL^2}{8} = \frac{14300 \times 6.6^2}{8}$$

$$= 77870 \text{ N-m} = 77.87 \times 10^6 \text{ N-mm}$$

3. Design of Section:

$$d = \sqrt{\frac{M}{R_c b}} = \sqrt{\frac{77.87 \times 10^6}{0.914 \times 300}}$$

$$= 533 \text{ mm}$$

Let us take $d = 545$ mm
and $\quad\quad\quad$ D = 580 mm
Revised self load of beam

$$= 0.3 \times 0.58 \times 25000$$

$$= 4350 \text{ N/m}$$

$$W = 9800 + 4350$$

$$= 14150 \text{ N/m}$$

Effective span = 6 + 0.545 = 6.545 m

$$M = \frac{14150 \times 6.545^2}{8} = 75770$$

$$\text{N-m} = 75.77 \times 10^6 \text{ N-mm}$$

$$d = \sqrt{\frac{75.77 \times 10^6}{0.914 \times 300}} = 526 \text{ mm}$$

Assuming that 16 mm ϕ bars will be used, with 8 mm dia. Links and a nominal cover of 25 mm, D = 526 + 25 + 8 + 16/2 = 567 mm. Keeping D = 570 mm and providing a nominal cover of 25 mm, and using 8 mm ϕ links, available effective depth = 570 – 25 – 8 – 16/2 = 529. Hence OK.

4. Steel reinforcement:

$$A_{st} = \frac{M}{\sigma_{st} \times j_c \times d}$$

$$= \frac{75.77 \times 10^6}{230 \times 0.904 \times 529} = 688.9 \text{ mm}^2$$

A_ϕ for 16 mm ϕ bars $= \dfrac{\pi}{4}16^2 = 201.06$ mm^2

$\therefore$ No. of bars = 688.9/201.06 = 3.4
Hence provide 4 bars, having $A_{st} = 4 \times 201.06$ = 804.24 mm^2. Keeping 25 mm nominal side cover clear spacing between bars will be
= 1/3(300 – 25 × 2 – 2 × 8 – 4 × 16)
= 56.7 mm.
Which is much more than the diameter of the bar.

Min. reinforcement is given by: $\dfrac{A_{st}}{bd} = \dfrac{0.85}{f_y}$

Taking, $f_y = 415$ N/mm^2,

$$A_{st} = \frac{0.85 \times 300 \times 529}{415} = 325 \text{ mm}^2$$

Since the actual A_{st} provided is much more than this, the design is OK.

5. Check for deflection: I/d = 6600/529 = 12.5 < basic L/d ratio of 20. Hence OK.

Note: since d on the basis of deflection is normally much less than the one provided on the basis of flexure, modification factors have not been applied.

6. Check for shear and design of shear reinforcement: The reaction at the wall supports will be uniformaly distributed over the full width. Hence, the shear force will be maximum at the edge of the support.

$$\text{Max. V} = \frac{wl}{2} = \frac{14150 \times 6}{2} = 42450 \text{ N}$$

$$\text{and } \tau_v = \frac{V}{bd} = \frac{42450}{300 \times 529} = 0.267 \text{ N/mm}^2$$

Assuming that out of 4 bars of main reinforcement, 2 bars will be bent up near the support and, hence, only 2 bars will be available.

$$\therefore \frac{100 \, A_s}{bd} = \frac{100}{300 \times 529} \times 402.12 = 0.25\%$$

From, permissible shear τ_c for M 20 concrete, for 0.25% steel = 0.22 N/mm^2, which is less than the nominal shear stress. Hence, shear reinforcement is required.

$$V_c = \tau_c bd = 0.22 \times 300 \times 529$$
$$= 34914 \text{ N}$$
$$V_s = V - V_c = 42450 - 34914$$
$$= 7536 \text{ N}$$

Using 8 φ 2 lgd stirrups, $A_{sv} = 2\frac{\pi}{4}8^2 = 100.5$

$$\therefore \quad S_v = \frac{\sigma_{sv} A_{sv} d}{V_s}$$

$$= \frac{230 \times 100.5 \times 529}{7536} = 1622 \text{ mm}$$

However, minimum shear reinforcement is governed by the expression:

$$S_v = \frac{2.175 \, A_{sv} f_y}{b}$$

$$= \frac{2.175 \times 100.5 \times 415}{300}$$

$$= 302.4 \text{ mm}$$

Subject to max. of 0.75 d or 300 mm which ever is less. Hence, provide the stirrups @ 300 mm c/c provide 210 mm φ holding bars at top.

7. Check for development length at supports:
The code stipulates that at the simple supports, where the reinforcement is confined by a compressive reaction, the diameter of the

reinforcement be such that $1.3\dfrac{\text{M}_1}{\text{V}} + \text{L}_0 \geq \text{L}_d$

Assuming that 2 bars are bent up and 2 bars are available at the supports,

$$A_{st} = 2\frac{\pi}{4}16^2 = 402.12 \text{ mm}^2$$

M_1 = Moment of resistance of the section, assuming all reinforcement stressed to σ_{st}
$$= 230 \times 402.12 \times 0.904 \times 529$$
$$= 44.23 \times 10^6 \text{ N-mm}$$

V = 42450 N

L_0 = Sum of anchorage value of hooks

Let us provide a support equal to the width of the wall, *i.e.* 600 mm. Let the clear side cover

x' = 40 mm for a 90° bend having anchorage value of 8φ, we have

$$L_0 = \left(\frac{l_s}{2} - x' + 3\varphi\right)$$

$$= \frac{600}{2} - 40 + 3 \times 16 = 308 \text{ mm}$$

$$1.3\frac{\text{M}_1}{\text{V}} + \text{L}_0 = 1.3 \times \frac{44.23 \times 10^6}{42450} + 308$$

$$= 1354 + 308 = 1662 \text{ mm}$$

Development length $L_d = \dfrac{\phi \sigma_{st}}{4\tau_{bd}}$

$$= \frac{16 \times 230}{4 \times 1.6 \times 0.8}$$

$$= 719 \text{ mm}$$

Alternatively, $L_d = 45\phi$
$$= 45 \times 16 = 720 \text{ mm}$$

Thus, $\left(1.3\dfrac{\text{M}_1}{\text{V}} + \text{L}_0\right) > \text{L}_d$

Hence, Code requirements are satisfied.

8. Details of reinforcement
Due the partial fixidity that may be caused at the supports, some reinforcement is always provided at the top of the beam near the ends. Let us bend two bars, one at a distance x_1 from

the support and the other at a distance x_2 from the support.

B.M. at $x_1 = \dfrac{wL}{2}x_1 - \dfrac{wx_1^2}{2}$

This should be $\dfrac{3}{4}$ of the maximum B.M.

$\therefore \dfrac{wL}{2}x_1 - \dfrac{wx_1^2}{2} = \dfrac{3}{4}\dfrac{wL^2}{8}$

This gives $x_1 = 0.25\,L$
$\qquad\qquad = 0.25 \times 6.545 = 1.64$ m

However, bend one bar at a distance of 1.60 m from the support.
Similarly, for the second bar,

$$\dfrac{wLx_2}{2} - \dfrac{wx_2^2}{2} = \dfrac{1}{2}\dfrac{wL^2}{8}$$

This gives $x_2 = 0.14\,L \approx L/7 \approx 0.14 \times 6.545$
$\qquad\qquad = 0.92$ m

However, bend the second bar at a distance of 0.9 m from the face of the support. The remaining 2 bars shall be taken straight into the support. Fig. shows the longitudinal section and the cross-section of the beam

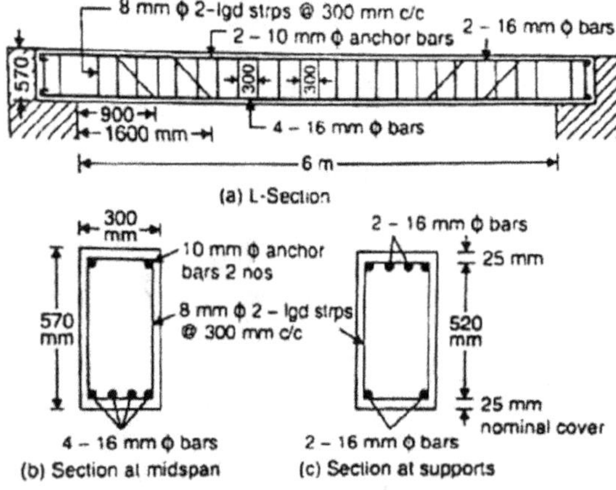

11. (a) $\quad \dfrac{b}{t} = \dfrac{117}{6} = 19.6 > 16$

Any portion beyond $16 \times t\,(16 \times 6)$ will be neglected

$$\dfrac{d'}{t} = \dfrac{400}{6} = 66.67 > 50$$

Any thing beyond $50 \times t\,(50 \times 6)$ will be neglected

Only unshaded area will be taken into account is calculated

Where $A = 2 \times 198 \times 6 + 300 \times 6$
$\qquad\quad = 4176$ mm^2

$\sigma_{ac} \to \lambda = \dfrac{l_{eff}}{r_{min}}$ ...... $(l_{eff} = 3.5$ mm$)$

$I_{xx} = 6 \times \dfrac{(300)^3}{12} + 2\left[198 \times 6 \times (203)^2 + \dfrac{198 \times 6^3}{12}\right]$
$\qquad = 111.41 \times 10^6$ mm^4

$I_{yy} = 2\left[6 \times \dfrac{(198)^3}{12}\right] + \dfrac{300 \times 6^3}{12}$

$\qquad = 7.767 \times 10^6$
$I_{min} = 7.767 \times 10^6$ mm^4

$\gamma_{min} = \sqrt{\dfrac{I_{min}}{A}} = \sqrt{\dfrac{7.767 \times 10^6}{4176}} = 43.14$

$\lambda = \dfrac{3500}{43.14} = 81.12$

$\sigma_{ac} = 99.81$
$P_{max} = 99.81 \times 4176 = 416.82$ kN.

11. (b) $\qquad D_s = D_{si} + D_{se}$
$\qquad\qquad D_{se} = r_e - 3 = 2 - 3 = -1$
$\qquad\qquad D_{si} = m - (2j - 3)$
$\qquad\qquad\qquad = 9 - (12 - 3) = 0$
$\qquad\qquad D_s = -1\text{(unstable structure)}$

Let us consider supported A is hinged
Now, $D_{se} = 3 - 3 = 0$
$\qquad\qquad D_{si} = m - (2j - 3) = 0$
$\qquad\qquad D_s = 0$

Member	Forces	
AB	27996	Compression
AD	42427.2	Tension
DB	13998	Compression
DC	11312.6	Compression
BC	13998	Compression
BE	19799	Tension
CE	6002	Tension
CF	19799	Compression
EF	14000	

61

$\Sigma f_y = 0$

$R_A + R_B = 20000$

$\Sigma f_x = 0$

$H - 2000 = 0$

$\Rightarrow \qquad H = +2000 \text{ kg}$

$\Sigma M_A = 0$

$R_B \times 9 - 20000 \times 6 - 2000 \times 3 = 0$

$R_A = 20000 - 14000 = 6000 \text{ kg}$

At joint F

$\Sigma f_y = 0$

$R_B + P_{cf} \sin 45°$

$14000 + 0.707 P_{cf} = 0$

$P_{cf} = -19799 \qquad ...(c)$

$\Sigma f_x = 0$

$P_{EF} + P_{CF} \cos 45° = 0$

$P_{EF} = 14000 \qquad ...(T)$

At joint E

$\Sigma f_y = 0$

$P_{EC} + P_{EB} \cos 45° = 20000$

$P_{EC} + 0.707 P_{EB} = 20000$

$\Sigma f_x = 0$

$P_{EF} = P_{EB} \sin 45°$

$\Rightarrow \qquad P_{EB} = 19799 \qquad ...(T)$

$\Rightarrow \qquad P_{EC} = 6002 \qquad ...(T)$

At joint C

$\Sigma f_y = 0$

$P_{CD} \sin 45° = P_{CE} + P_{CF} \cos 45°$

$0.707 P_{CD} = 6002 - 14000$

$P_{CD} = -11312.6 \qquad ...(C)$

$\Sigma f_x = 0$

$P_{CB} = -0.707 \times 19799$

$P_{CB} = -13998 \qquad ...(C)$

At point B

$\Sigma f_y = 0$

$P_{BE} \cos 45° + P_{BD} = 0$

$13998 + P_{BD} = 0$

$P_{BD} = -13998 \qquad ...(C)$

$\Sigma f_x = 0$

$P_{BA} + P_{BC} + P_{BE} \sin 45° = 0$

$P_{BA} + 13998 + 19799 \times 0.707 = 0$

$P_{BA} = -27996 \qquad ...(C)$

At joint A

$\Sigma f_x = 0$

$H + P_{AB} = P_{AD} \cos 45°$

$2000 + 27996 = 0.707 P_{AD}$

$P_{AD} = 42427.2 \qquad ...(T)$

SSC-Junior Engineer (Civil & Structural) Exam 2010

PAPER-II (Conventional)

SECTION-I (Civil)

1. (*a*) Describe the classification of rocks.
   (*b*) What are the ingredients of a varnish? Describe the various types of varnishes.
   (*c*) Discuss the manufacture of cement.

2. (*a*) A steel tape is 30 m long at a temperature of 15°C and a pull of 50 N when laid on the flat. The tape weighs 18 N. It is stretched between end supports only allowing it to sag. Find the correct length of the tape at a field temperature of 25°C at a pull of 115 N. If in the above condition a base line is measured and the recorded length of the line is 600 m, find the correct length of the base line.

   Take $\alpha = 12 \times 10^{-6}$ per °C and $E = 2 \times 10^5$ N/mm^2.

   Sectional area of the tape = 7.50 mm^2.

   (*b*) Write brief notes on the following:
   (*i*) Prismatic compass
   (*ii*) Plane table and its accessories

3. (*a*) The following properties of the soil were determined by performing tests on clay sample:

   Natural moisture content = 25%
   Liquid limit = 32%
   Plastic limit = 24%
   Diameter of 60% size = 0.006 mm
   Diameter of 10% size = 0.006 mm

   Calculate the liquidity coefficient, uniformity coefficient and relative consistency.

   (*b*) A sample of soil 10 cm diameter, 15 cm length was tested in a variable head permeameter. The initial head of water in the burette was found to be 45 cm and it was observed to drop to 30 cm in 195 seconds. The diameter of the burette was 1.9 cm. Calculate the coefficients of permeability in metre/day.

4. (*a*) Explain standard penetration test for measuring the penetration resistance of the soil.

   (*b*) An earthen embankment is compacted to a dry density of 1.82 gm/cc at a moisture content of 12%. The bulk density and moisture content are 1.72 gm/cc and 6% at the site from where the soil is borrowed and transported at the site of construction. How much excavation should be carried out in the pit of borrowed area for each cu-m of the embankment.

5. (*a*) An oil of viscosity 1.0 poise and relative density 1.05 is flowing through a circular pipe of diameter 5 cm and of length 200 m. The rate of flow is 3.52 *l*/sec. Find the shear stress at the pipe wall.

   (*b*) Lubricating oil of specific gravity 0.85 and dynamic viscosity 0.01 kgf-s/m^2 is pumped through a 3 cm diameter pipe. If pressure drop per metre length of the pipe is 0.15 kgf/cm^2, determine the mass flow rate in kg/min, the shear stress at the pipe wall, the Reynolds number of flow and the power required per 40 m length of pipe to maintain the flow.

6. (*a*) Discuss in detail the physical and chemical characteristics of sewage.

   (*b*) Design a rapid sand filter system for a water supply of 9 m.l.d. to a township. All the principal components shall be designed. Enumerate your assumptions during the design steps.

SECTION-II (Structural)

7. (*a*) Draw S.F. and B.M. diagrams for the beam shown in Fig. 1.

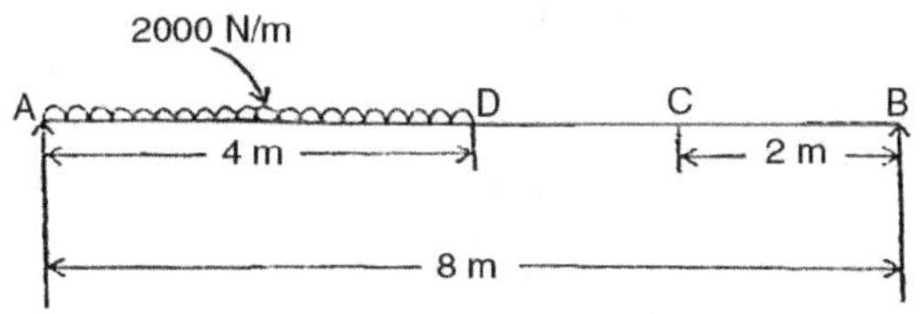

Fig. 1

(*b*) Find the moment of inertia of the triangular section shown in Fig. 2.

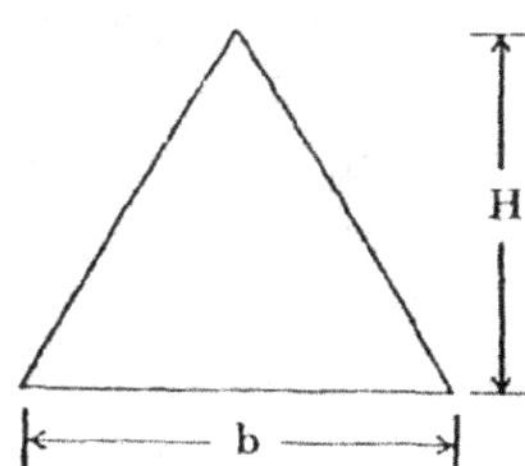

Fig. 2

(*c*) A straight circular bar of steel 1 cm in diameter and 120 cm long is mounted in testing machine and loaded axially in compression till it buckles. Assuming the Euler formula for pinned ends to apply. Estimate the maximum central deflection before the material reaches its yield stress of 350 N/mm². $E = 0.21 \times 10^5$ N/mm².

8. (*a*) For the beam shown in Fig. 3, find deflection at the free end and middle of span.

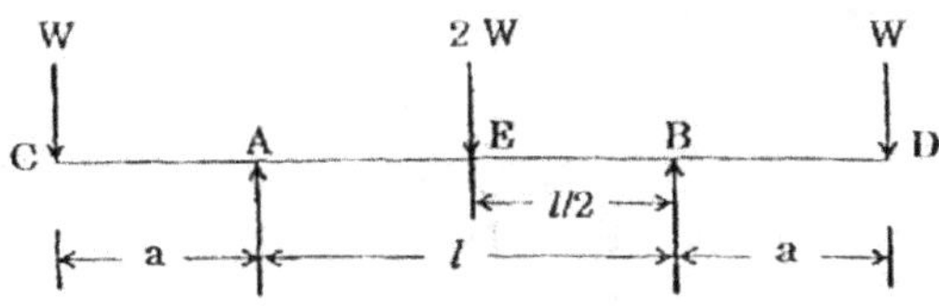

Fig. 3

(*b*) Describe the properties of water which are necessary to be used to get good concrete. What do you understand by the term 'water cement ratio'?

9. (*a*) Describe various methods of mixing concrete.

(*b*) Discuss in the detail the 'underwater concreting'.

10. (*a*) Determine the maximum superimposed distributed load which the beam section 220 mm × 440 mm (effective cover = 40 mm) reinforced with total area of tension steel 1256.64 mm², can carry, if the effective span is 5 m. Use M20 concrete and Fe 415 steel. Take m = 13.33.

(*b*) Design a floor slab simply supported over a clear span of 3.5 m, the roof is to be finished with 18.5 mm thick layer of lime concrete terracing. The superimposed load on the slab is 3000 N/m². Use M20 grade of concrete and high yield strength deformed bars. Take weight of lime concrete as 19.2 kN/m³.

11. Design a square footing of uniform thickness for an axially loaded column of 400 mm × 400 mm is size. The safe bearing capacity of soil is 200 kN/m², load on column = 1000 kN. Use M20 grade of concrete and HYSD bars.

12. (*a*) A 16 mm thick plate is joined by double cover butt joint using a 10 mm thick cover plate. The steel of main and cover plate has permissible tensile strength of 150 MPa. Determine the strength and efficiency of the joint per pitch of 9 cm, if

    (*i*) 20 mm diameter power driven shop rivet is used.

    (*ii*) 20 mm diameter close tolerance and turned bolt are used.

Take σ_p = 300 MPa, T_{vf} = 100 MPa

(*b*) Find the safe load that can be transmitted by fillet welded joint shown in Fig. 4 the size of the Weld is 6 mm. (P_q = 108 MPa)

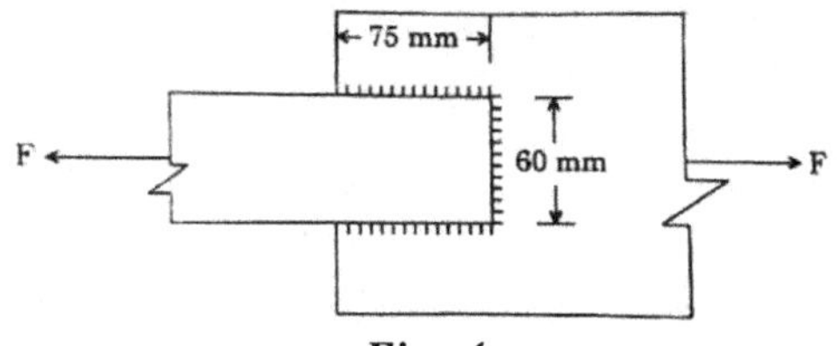

Fig. 4

ANSWERS

1. (*a*) Classification of Common Rocks: Igneous, Sedimentary and Metamorphic

A rock is a naturally occurring aggregate of minerals, and certain non-mineral materials such as fossils and glass. Just as minerals are the building blocks of rocks, rocks in turn are the natural building blocks of the Earth's LITHOSPHERE (crust and mantle down to a depth of about 100 km), ASTHENOSPHERE (although this layer, in the depth range from about 100 to 250 km, is partially molten), MESOSPHERE (mantle in the depth range from about 250 to 2900 km), and even part of the CORE (while the outer core is molten, the inner core is solid). Most rocks now exposed at the surface of the Earth formed in or on continental or oceanic crust. Many such rocks, formed beneath the surface and now exposed at the surface, were delivered to the surface from great depths in the crust and in rare cases from the underlying mantle. There are two general ways that rocks come to be exposed at the surface:

1. Formation at the surface (*e.g.*, crystallization of lava, precipitation of calcite or dolomite from sea water).

2. Formation below the surface, followed by tectonic uplift and removal of the overlying material by erosion.

There are three major classes of rocks, IGNEOUS, SEDIMENTARY, and METAMORPHIC, with the following attributes:

IGNEOUS ROCKS form by crystallization from molten or partially material, called MAGMA. Magma comes mainly from two places where it is formed, (1) in the asthenosphere and (2) in the base of the crust above subducting lithosphere at a convergent plate boundary. There are two subclasses of igneous rock, VOLCANIC (sometimes called EXTRUSIVE), and PLUTONIC (sometimes called INTRUSIVE).

VOLCANIC ROCKS form at the Earth's surface. They cool and crystallized from magma which has spilled out onto the surface at a volcano. At the surface, the magma is more familiarly known as LAVA.

PLUTONIC ROCKS form from magma that cools and crystallizes beneath the Earth's surface. In a sense, this is the portion of the magma that never makes it to the surface. For the plutonic rock to become exposed at the surface, it must be tectonically uplifted and the overlying material must be removed by erosion.

SEDIMENTARY ROCKS form from material that has accumulated on the Earth's surface. The general term for the process of accumulation is DEPOSITION. The material consists of the products of weathering and erosion, and other materials available at the surface of the Earth, such as organic material. The process by which this otherwise unconsolidated material becomes solidified into rock is variously referred to LITHIFICATION (literally turned into rock), DIAGENESIS or CEMENTATION. Like volcanic rocks, some sedimentary rocks are "lithified" right at the surface, for instance by direct precipitation from sea water. Other sedimentary rocks, like plutonic igneous rocks, are "lithified" below the surface, when they are buried under the weight of overlying sediment. And like the plutonic rocks, sedimentary rocks which were lithified below the surface only become exposed at the surface by tectonic uplift and erosion of the overlying material.

METAMORPHIC ROCKS form when a sedimentary or igneous rock is exposed to high pressure, high temperature, or both, deep below the surface of the Earth. The process, METAMORPHISM, produces fundamental changes in the mineralogy and texture of the rock. The original rock, prior to metamorphism, is referred to as the PROTOLITH. The protolith can be either an igneous rock or a sedimentary rock, as just indicated. The protolith could also be a previously metamorphosed rock. Ultimately however, if you go far enough back into the history of a metamorphic rock you would find that the first protolith was either a sedimentary or igneous rock. Because all metamorphic rocks form below the surface, for them to become exposed at the surface, they must undergo tectonic uplift and removal of the overlying material by erosion.

1. (b) Varnish: Varnish is a solution of resin in either oil, turpentine or alcohol. It dries after applying, leaving a hard, transparent and glossy film of resin over the varnished surface.

Varnish is applied (1) to the painted surface to increase its brilliance and to protect it from the atmospheric action and (2) to the unpainted wooden surface with a view to brighten the ornamental appearance of the grains of wood.

Composition of Varnishes:

The ingredients of varnish are:

1. Resins, 2. Solvents, 3. Driers.

1. Resins: Commonly used resins are copal mastic, amber gum and lac. Quantity of varnish depends much upon the quality of resin used. Copal is considered to be the best, toughest, hardest and is very durable for external work.

2. Solvents: These must suit the resins used. Boiled linseed oil us used to dissolve copal or amber, turpentine oil for common resin or mastic, methylated spirit for lac. Wood naphtha, because of its offensive smell is not suited for superior works and is used only for cheap varnish.

3. Driers: These should be added only in small quantities as an excessive injures varnish and impairs its durability. Litharge or lead acetate are the commonly used driers in varnish added to accelerate drying process.

THE QUALITIES OF GOOD VARNISH

1. It should be dry quickly.
2. On drying it should form a hard, tough and durable film.
3. It should have good weathering properties, resist abrasion and wear well.
4. It should be able to retain its colour and shine.
5. It should be uniform and pleasant looking on drying.

Different kinds of Varnishes: Based on the different solvents used, varnishes are classified under the following categories:

Oil Varnish: These are made by dissolving hard resins like amber or copal in oil. They are slow to dry but are hardest and most durable of all varnishes. These are suited for being used on exposed surfaces requiring polishing or frequent cleaning and for superior works.

Turpentine Varnish: These are made from soft resins like mastic, common resin is dissolved in turpentine oil.

Spirit Varnish: Varnishes in which spirit is used as a solvent as known as spirited varnish or French Polish. Shellac is dissolved in spirit and the product is applied in a thin layer. This varnish gives a transparent finish thus showing the grains of the timber. These however, do not weather well and as such are used for polishing wood work not exposed to weather.

Water Varnish: They consists of lac dissolved in hot water with borax, ammonia, potash or soda just enough to dissolve the lac. Varnish so made withstands washing. It is used for painting wall paper and for delicate work.

1. *(c)* Cement is a fine powder which sets after a few hours when mixed with water, and then hardens in a few days into a solid, strong material. Cement is mainly used to bind fine sand and coarse aggregates together in concrete. Cement is a hydraulic binder, *i.e.* it hardens when water is added.

There are 27 types of common cement which can be grouped into 5 general categories and 3 strength classes: ordinary, high and very high. In addition, some special cements exist like sulphate resisting cement, low heat cement and calcium aluminate cement.

The quarry is the starting point: Cement plants are usually located closely either to hot spots in the market or to areas with sufficient quantities of raw materials. The aim is to keep transportation costs low. Basic constituents for cement (limestone and clay) are taken from quarries in these areas.

A two-step process: Basically, cement is produced in two steps: first, clinker is produced from raw materials. In the second step cement is produced from cement clinker. The first step can be a dry, wet, semi-dry or semi-wet process according to the state of the raw material.

Making clinker: The raw materials are delivered in bulk, crushed and homogenised into a mixture which is fed into a rotary kiln. This is an enormous rotating pipe of 60 to 90 m long and up to 6 m in diameter. This huge kiln is heated by a 2000°C flame inside of it. The kiln is slightly inclined to allow for the materials to slowly reach the other end, where it is quickly cooled to 100-200°C.

Four basic oxides in the correct proportions make cement clinker: calcium oxide (65%), silicon oxide (20%), alumina oxide (10%) and iron oxide (5%). These elements mixed homogeneously (called "raw meal" or slurry) will combine when heated by the flame at a temperature of approximately 1450°C. New compounds are formed: silicates, aluminates and ferrites of calcium. Hydraulic hardening of cement is due to the hydration of these compounds.

The final product of this phase is called "clinker". These solid grains are then stored in huge silos. End of phase one.

From clinker to cement: The second phase is handled in a cement grinding mill, which may be located in a different place to the clinker plant. Gypsum (calcium sulphates) and possibly additional cementitious (such as blastfurnace slag, coal fly ash, natural pozzolanas, etc.) or inert materials (limestone) are added to the clinker. All constituents are ground leading to a fine and homogenous powder. End of phase two. The cement is then stored in silos before being dispatched either in bulk or bagged.

2. *(a)* A steel tape was standardised on the flat ground

$$\text{Length of tape} = 30 \text{ m}$$
$$\text{Temperature} = 15°C$$
$$\text{Pull} = 50 \text{ N}$$
$$\text{Wt.} = 18 \text{ N}$$

Length to be measured = 600 m

On field:

$$\text{Temperature} = 25°C$$
$$\text{Pull} = 115 \text{ N}$$
$$\alpha = 12 \times 10^{-6}/°C$$
$$E = 2 \times 10^6 \text{ N/mm}^2$$
$$A = 7.5 \text{ mm}^2$$

1. Correction for temp. (C_t):

$$c_t = \tau\, \alpha\, (T_m - T_s)$$
$$c_t = 600 \times 12 \times 16^{-6}(25 - 15)$$
$$= 0.072 \text{ m.}$$

2. Correction for Pull (C_p):

$$C_P = \frac{P_a - P_s \times L}{AE}$$

$$C_P = \frac{115 - 50 \times 600}{7.5 \times 2 \times 10^6}$$

$$= 2.6 \times 10^{-3} \text{ m.}$$

3. Correction for Sag (C_{sg}):

$$C_{sg} = \frac{hw^2}{24n^2\rho}$$

Where: h = Total length

W = wt. of tape (N)

ρ = pull (N)

N = No. of equal spans of 30 m tape

$$C_{sg} = \frac{30 \times 18^2}{24 \times 20^2 \times 115}$$

$$= 8.804 \times 10^{-3} \text{ m}$$

Correction for 20 No. of spans of 30 m tape = $8.804 \times 10^{-3} \times 20 = 0.176$ m

Correction length of base line

$= 600 + 0.072 + 2.6 \times 10^{-3} - 0.176$

$= 599.899$ m

2. (b) (i) A **prismatic compass** is a navigation and surveying instrument which is extensively used for determining course, waypoints (an endpoint of the leg of a course) and direction, and for calculating bearings of survey lines and included angles between them. Compass surveying is a type of surveying in which the directions of surveying lines are determined with a magnetic compass, and the length of the surveying lines are measured with a tape or chain or laser range finder. The compass is generally used to run a traverse line. The compass calculates bearings of lines with respect to magnetic north. The included angles can then be calculated using suitable formulas in case of clockwise and anti-clockwise traverse respectively. For each survey line in the traverse, surveyors take two bearings that is fore bearing and back bearing which should exactly differ by 180° if local attraction is negligible. The name *Prismatic compass* is given to it because it

essentially consists of a prism which is used for taking observations more accurately.

The essential parts of the prismatic compass are listed below:

- Magnetic needle
- Eye vane
- Eye slit
- Eye hole
- Mirror (adjustable)
- Glass cover
- Graduated ring
- Lifting lever
- Lifting pin
- Metal box (85-100 mm dia)
- Focusing stud
- Object vane
- Sun glasses
- Sliding arrangement for mirror
- Horse hair

Least Count: Least count means the minimum value that an instrument can read which is 15 minutes in case of prismatic compass. It means compass can read only those observations which are multiples of 30 minutes, 5° 25′, 15° 55′, 35° 45′ 30″ (35 degrees 45 minutes 30 seconds) are some examples which cannot be read by prismatic compass. The compass will give approximate values of these angles pertaining to its least count.

Bearings: The compass calculates the bearings in whole circle bearing system which determines the angle which the survey line makes with the magnetic north in the clockwise direction. The included angles can be calculated by the formulas $F - P \pm 180$ in case of anti-clocwise traverse and $P - F \pm 180$ in case of clockwise traverse, where 'F' is the fore bearing of forward line in the direction of survey work and 'P' is the fore bearing of previous line.

2. (b) (ii) In plane table surveying a table top, similar to drawing board fitted on to a tripod is the main instrument. A drawing sheet is fixed on to the table top, the observations are made to the objects, distances are scaled down and the objects are plotted in the field itself. Since the plotting is made in the field itself, there is no chance of omitting any necessary measurement in this surveying. However the accuracy achieved in this type of surveying is less. Hence this type of surveying is used for filling up details between the survey stations previously fixed by other methods.

Features:
- Robust built
- Resistant to corrosion
- Easy to use
- High strength

Plane Table with Accessories

Plane Table Board	600 × 750 × 16 mm	600 × 750 × 22 mm	—	—
Plane Table Stand	Wooden	Teak Wood	Aluminium	—
Plane Table Head	Ordinary	Quality Size	ISI Specification	Johnson Type
Magnetic Compass	150 mm Aluminium	150 mm Brass	—	—
Spirit Level	150 mm Aluminium	150 mm Quality Size	150 mm Brass	—
Alidade/Sight Vane	Brass	Quality Size	ISI Specification	—
Plumbing Fork	Aluminium	Brass	—	—
Plumb Bob	Steel	Quality Size	Brass	—
Canvas Cover	Half	Full	—	—

3. (*a*) Given, Natural moisture content $w = 25\%$

LL or WL = 32, $W_p = 34$,

$D_{60} = 0.006$ mm, $D_{10} = 0.006$ mm

(*i*) Liquid consistency

$$I_L = \frac{w - w_p}{w_L - w_p} \times 100$$

$$I_L = \frac{0.25 - 0.24}{0.32 - 0.24} \times 100$$

$$I_L = 12.5\%$$

(*ii*) Uniformity coefficient (C_u)

$$C_u = \frac{D_{60}}{D_{10}} = \frac{0.006}{0.006} = 1$$

$$C_u = 1$$

(*iii*) Relative consistency (I_c)

$$I_c = \frac{w_L - w}{w_L - w_P} \times 100$$

$$= \frac{0.32 - 0.25}{0.32 - 0.24} \times 100$$

$$= 87.5\%$$

(*b*) Given, D = 10 cm, L = 15 cm,

$$A = \frac{\pi}{4} \times D^2 = \frac{\pi}{4} \times 10^2 = 78.53 \text{ cm}^2$$

Initial head of water in burette $h_1 = 45$ cm

Drop in head is = 30 cm

Final head $h_2 = 45 - 30 = 15$ cm

Time observed to drop is = 195 sec

Dia. of burette = 1.9 cm

Area of burette $A = \frac{\pi}{4} \times 1.9^2 = 2.835 \text{ cm}^2$

So the coefficient of permeability by variable head permeability test is

$$K = \frac{2.303 \log_{10}\left(\frac{45}{15}\right) \times 2.835 \times 15}{78.53 \times 195}$$

$$= 3.05 \times 10^{-3} \text{ cm/sec}$$

$$= \frac{3.05 \times 10^{-3}}{100} \times 24 \times 60 \times 60 \text{ m/day}$$

$$= 2.636 \text{ m/day}.$$

4. (*a*) **Standard Penetration Test (SPT) :** This test method describes the procedure, generally known as the Standard

Penetration Test (SPT), for driving a split-barrel sampler to obtain a representative disturbed soil sample for identification purposes, and measure the resistance of the soil to penetration of the sampler. Another method (Test Method D3550) to drive a split-barrel sampler to obtain a representative soil sample is available but the hammer energy is not standardized. This test is still used because of it's simplicity and low cost. It can provide useful information in very specific types of soil conditions.

For this test, a sample tube, which is thick walled to endure the test environment is placed at the bottom of a borehole. A heavy slide hammer (140 lbs) is dropped repeatedly 30 inches onto the top of the sample tube, driving it into the soil being tested. The operation entails the operator counting the number of hammer strikes it takes to drive the sample tube 6 inches at a time. Each test drives the sample tube up to 18 inches deep. It is then extracted and if desired a sample of the soil is pulled from the tube. The borehole is drilled deeper and the test is repeated. Often soil recovery is poor and counting errors per interval may occur.

The number of hammer strikes it takes for the tube to penetrate the second and third 6 inch depth is called the 'standard penetration resistance', or otherwise called the 'N-value'. The standard penetration resistance offers a gauge of the soil density of soils which are hard to pull up with simply a borehole sampling approach. You can imagine pushing a sample tube into gravel, sand or silt and struggling to recover samples that are useful for analysis. Coupling the standard penetration test with borehole drilling and sampling can be an improvement for understanding certain soil types underground.

The main purpose of the test is to provide an indication of the relative density of granular deposits, such as sands and gravels from which it is virtually impossible to obtain undisturbed samples. The great merit of the test, and the main reason for its widespread use is that it is simple and inexpensive. The soil strength parameters which can be inferred are approximate, but may give a useful guide in ground conditions where it may not be possible to obtain borehole samples of adequate quality like gravels, sands, silts, clay containing sand or gravel and weak rock. In conditions where the quality of the undisturbed sample is suspect, *e.g.*, very silty or very sandy clays, or hard clays, it is often advantageous to alternate the sampling with standard penetration tests to check the strength. If the samples are found to be unacceptably disturbed, it may be necessary to use a different method for measuring strength like the plate test. When the test is carried out in granular soils below groundwater level, the soil may become loosened. In certain circumstances, it can be useful to continue driving the sampler beyond the distance specified, adding further drilling rods as necessary. Although this is not a standard penetration test, and should not be regarded as such, it may at least give an indication as to whether the deposit is really as loose as the standard test may indicate.

The usefulness of SPT results depends on the soil type, with fine-grained sands giving the most useful results, with coarser sands and silty sands giving reasonably useful results, and clays and gravelly soils yielding results which may be very poorly representative of the true soil conditions. Soils in arid areas, such as the Western United States, may exhibit natural cementation. This condition will often increase the standard penetration value.

The SPT is used to provide results for empirical determination of a sand layer's susceptibility to earthquake liquefaction, based on research performed by Harry Seed, T. Leslie Youd, and others.

4. (b) At site from where soil is borrowed

$V_t = 1.72$ gm/cc or 1720 kg/m^3, $m/c = 6\%$

$V_d = 1.82$ gm/cc, $m/c = 12\%$

Volume of embankment soil $= 1$ m^3

Dry density $V_d = \dfrac{W_s}{V}$

Given, $\qquad V_d = 1.82$ gm/cc

$$= \frac{1.82}{1000} \times 10^6 \text{ kg/m}^3$$

$$= 1820 \text{ kg/m}^2$$

Wt. of solids from each cu-m of embankment

$$W_s = 1820 \times 1 = 1820 \text{ kg}$$

As we know, while coring soil from borrow pit to earthen embankment, wt. of solids remain same, hence, wt. of solids at site $= 1820$ kg

Unit wt. of soil at site $V_t = \dfrac{W}{V}$

Also $\qquad W = \dfrac{W_w}{W_s}$

W/C or m/c $= 6\%$ given

$$0.06 = \frac{W_w}{1820}$$

$$\Rightarrow \qquad W_w = 1820 \times \frac{6}{100} = 109.2 \text{ kg}$$

Total wt. of soil at site

$$W = W_w + W_s$$

$$= 109.2 + 1820$$

$$= 1929.2 \text{ kg}$$

$$V_t = 1720 = \frac{1929.2}{V}$$

Volume of soil to be excavated from borrow pit $V = \dfrac{1929.2}{1720} = 1.212$ m^3.

5. (a) Viscosity of oil $= 1.0$ poise $= \dfrac{1}{10}$ kg/m-sec

$$\mu = 0.1 \text{ kg/m-sec}$$

Relative density $= 1.05$

Dia. of circular pipe $= 5$ cm $= 0.05$ m

Length of pipe $= 200$ m

Rate of flow $= 3.52$ l/sec

$$= 3.52 \times 10^{-3} \text{ m}^3/\text{sec}$$

Shear stress at the pipe wall $(\tau_0) = \dfrac{\rho f v^2}{8}$

$\rho = 1.05 \times$ density of water

$$= 1.05 \times 1000 = 1050 \text{ kg/m}^3$$

Reynolds no. $= \dfrac{\rho v D}{\mu} = \dfrac{1050 \times v \times 0.05}{0.1}$

$$Q = A \times V$$

$$\Rightarrow 3.52 \times 10^{-3} = \left(\frac{\pi}{4} \times 0.05\right)^2 \times V$$

$$\Rightarrow \qquad V = 1.79 \text{ m/sec}$$

$$R_e = \frac{1050 \times 1.79 \times 0.05}{0.1}$$

$$= 939.75 < 2000$$

So, the flow is laminar.

Friction factor, $f = \dfrac{64}{R_e}$

For laminar flow $f = \dfrac{64}{939.75} \Rightarrow f = 0.068$

Shear stress $(\tau_0) = \dfrac{\rho f v^2}{8}$

$$= \frac{1050 \times 0.0681 \times 1.79^2}{8}$$

$$(\tau_0) = 28.64 \text{ N/m}^2$$

So, the shear stress is 28.64 N/m^2.

5. (b) $\qquad S = 0.85$

$$\rho = s \times \rho_w$$

$$= 0.85 \times 1000 = 850 \text{ kg/m}^3$$

$$\mu = 0.01 \text{ kg-f-sec/m}^2$$

$$= 0.01 \times 9.81 \text{ N-sec/m}^2$$

$$= 0.0981 \text{ N-sec/m}^2$$

Dia. of pipe $= 3$ cm $= 0.03$ m

Pressure drop/unit length, $\dfrac{P_1 - P_2}{L} = \dfrac{32\mu V}{D^2}$

71

$$\Rightarrow 0.15 \times 9.81 \times 100^2 = \frac{32 \times 0.0981 \times V}{0.03^2}$$

$$\Rightarrow \qquad V = 4.22 \text{ m/sec}$$

$$\text{Discharge } Q = V.A. = 4.22 \times \left(\frac{\pi}{4} \times 0.03^2\right)$$

$$= 178.9 \ l/\text{min}$$

(*i*) Reynolds no. $(R_e) = \dfrac{\rho VD}{\mu}$

$$= \frac{850 \times 4.22 \times 0.03}{0.0981}$$

$$= 1096.94$$

$$\text{Friction factor } (f) = \frac{64}{R_e} = \frac{64}{1096.94}$$

$$= 0.0583$$

(*ii*) Wall shear stress $\tau = \dfrac{\rho f \, V^2}{8}$

$$= \frac{850 \times 0.0583 \times 4.22^2}{8}$$

$$= 110.39 \text{ N/m}^2$$

Power required.

6. (*a*) Physical Characteristics of Sewage

The physical characteristics of wastewater include those items that can be detected using the physical senses. They are temperature, colour, odour, and solids.

Temperature: Temperature of wastewater varies greatly, depending upon the type of operations being conducted at your installation. Temperature of sewage, the sewage is slightly more than that of water, because of the presence of industrial sewage. The temperature changes when sewage becomes septic because of chemical process. The lower temperature indicates the entrance of ground water into the sewage.

Colour: of fresh sewage is yellowish grey to light brown. While that of the septic is black or dark due to oxidation of organic matter.

Odour: smell of the fresh sewage is oily or soapy while the septic sewage develops an objectionable. H_2S is the major source of pollution.

Solids: All matter except the water contained in liquid materials is classed as solid matter. The usual definition of solids, however refers to; "the matter that remain as residual upon evaporation and drying at $103 \pm 20°C$".

Those solids that are not dissolved in wastewater are called suspended solids. When suspended solids float, they are called floatable solids or scum. Those suspended solids that settle are called settleable solids, grit, or sludge.

All solids that burn or evaporate at 500°C to 600°C are called volatile solids. These solids serve as a food source for bacteria and other living forms in a wastewater treatment plant. Most organic solids in municipal waste originate from living plants or animals.

Those solids that do not burn or evaporate at 500°C to 600°C, but remain as a residue, are called fixed solids. Fixed solids are usually inorganic in nature and may be composed of grit, clay, salts and metals.

Turbidity: The term "turbid" is applied to water/wastewater containing suspended matter or in which the visual depth is restricted.

Chemical Characteristics of Sewage (Wastewater)

Sewage contains both organic and inorganic chemicals in addition to various gases like H_2S, CO_2, CH_4 and NH_3 etc that are formed due to the decomposition of sewage. The chemical characteristics of wastewater of special concern are pH, DO (dissolved oxygen), oxygen demand, nutrients and toxic substances.

pH: pH is used to describe the acid or base properties of water solutions. The pH of sewage is initially high and drops when the sewage becomes septic but becomes increases again with the treatment processes.

Dissolved oxygen (DO): Wastewater that has DO is called aerobic or fresh. The solubility of oxygen in fresh water ranges from 14.6 mg/L at 0°C to about 07 mg/L at 35°C at 1.0 atm. pressure.

Oxygen Demand: It is the amount of oxygen used by bacteria and other wastewater organisms as they feed upon the organic solids in the wastewater.

BOD: BOD is defined as the amount of oxygen required by the bacteria while stabilizing decomposable organic matter under aerobic condition. It is written as by BOD or BOD520. "It is the amount of oxygen required by aerobic bacteria to decompose/stabilized the organic matter at a standard temperature of 20°C for a period of 05 days". For domestic sewage 05 days BOD represents approx. 2/3 times of demand for complete decomposition.

COD: By definition the COD is the amount of oxygen required to stabilized the organic matter chemically, *i.e.* the COD is used as a measure of the oxygen equivalent of the organic matter contents of a sample that is susceptible to oxidation by a strong chemical oxidant.

Wastewater characteristics and their sources

Physical		
Colour	Domestic/Industrial wastes, natural decay of organic matter
Odour	Industrial wastes, decomposing wastewater
Solids	Industrial/domestic wastes, soil erosion, inflow etc
Chemical	
Pesticides	Agricultural run-off
Phenols	Industrial wastes
Heavy metals	Industrial wastes
pH	Industrial wastes
Toxic compounds	Industrial wastes
Biological	Open water courses, treatment units etc.

6. (b) Water required per day = 4 ML

Assuming that 45 of filtered water is required for washing of the filter, every day, we have

Total filtered water required per day
$$= 1.04 \times 4 \text{ M.L.} = 4.16 \text{ M.L/day}$$

Now, assuming that 0.5 hour is lost everyday in washing the filter, we have

Filtered water required per hour

$$= \frac{4.16}{23.5} \text{ M.L./hour} = 0.177 \text{ M.L./hr.}$$

Now, assuming the rate of filtration to be 5000 litre/hr/sq m, we have

Thee area of filter required

$$= \frac{0.177 \times 10^6}{5000} \text{ m}^2 = 35.4 \text{ m}^2$$

Now, assuming the length of the filter bed (L) as 1.5 times the width of the filter bed (B), and two beds, the total area provided

$$2 \times \text{L.B.} = 35.4$$
$$\text{or} \quad 2 \times 1.5 \text{ B} \times \text{B} = 35.4$$

$$\Rightarrow \quad \text{B}^2 = \frac{35.4}{3} = 11.8$$

$$\text{or} \quad \text{B} = 3.43 \text{ m}$$
$$\text{L} = 1.5 \text{ B} = 1.5 \times 3.43$$
$$= 5.14 \approx 5.2 \text{ m}$$

or   Use the length of the filter bed as
$$= 5.2 \text{ m,}$$

$$\text{and} \quad \text{B} = \frac{35.4}{2 \times 5.2} = 3.4 \text{ m}$$

Hence, adopt 2 filter units, each of dimensions 5.2 m × 3.4 m.

7. (a)
$$\Sigma F_v = 0$$
$$R_A + R_B = 2000 \times 4 = 8000 \text{ N}$$
$$\Sigma M_A = 0$$

$$R_B \times 8 = 2000 \times 4 \times \left(\frac{4}{2}\right)$$

$$R_B = 2000 \text{ N}$$

$$R_A = 8000 - 2000 = 6000 \text{ N}$$

S.F. at x distance from A

$$S_x = R_A - 2000 \times x$$
$$= 6000 - 2000 \times x$$

At $\quad x = 0$, $\text{S.F.}_A = 6000$ N

At $\quad x = 2$ m

$$\text{S.F.} = 6000 - 2000 \times 2 = 2000 \text{ N}$$

S.F. is Zero at distance of

$$0 = 6000 - 2000 \times x$$

$$x = \frac{6000}{2000} = 3 \text{ m}$$

$$x = 4 \text{ m},$$
$$S_D = 6000 - 2000 \times 4$$
$$= -2000 \text{ N}$$

S_C, x from B, $\quad S_B = -2000$ N
$$S_C = -2000 \text{ N}$$

B.M.

x from A

$$BM_x = 6000x - 2000\frac{x^2}{2}$$

$$BM_A = 0, \ x = 0$$

$$BM_{max} = 6000 - \frac{4000x}{2} = 0$$

$\Rightarrow \qquad x = 3$ m

BM_m at $x = 3$ m,

$$BM = 6000 \times 3 - 2000 \times \frac{(3)^2}{2}$$

$$= 9000 \text{ N-m}$$

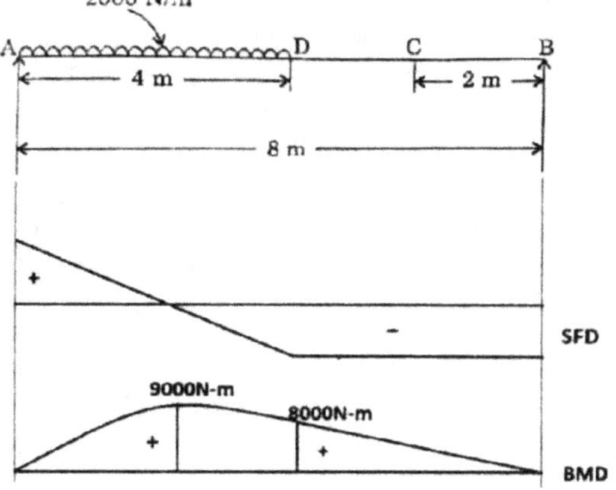

at $x = 4$

$$BM_D = 6000 \times 4 - 2000\frac{4^2}{2}$$

$$= +8000 \text{ N-m}$$

$$BM_{4.5} = 6000 \times 4.5 - 2000\frac{(4.5)^2}{2}$$

$$= 6750 \text{ N-m.}$$

7. (b)

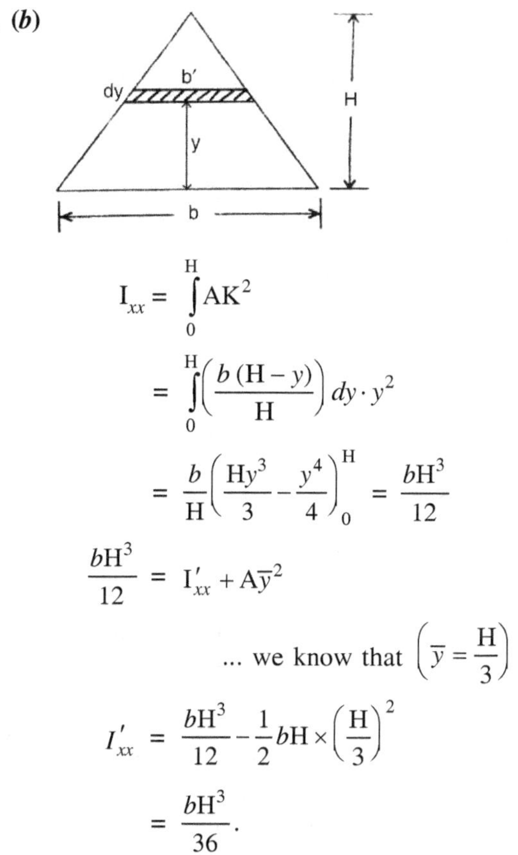

$$I_{xx} = \int_0^H AK^2$$

$$= \int_0^H \left(\frac{b(H-y)}{H}\right) dy \cdot y^2$$

$$= \frac{b}{H}\left(\frac{Hy^3}{3} - \frac{y^4}{4}\right)_0^H = \frac{bH^3}{12}$$

$$\frac{bH^3}{12} = I'_{xx} + A\bar{y}^2$$

$$\ldots \text{ we know that } \left(\bar{y} = \frac{H}{3}\right)$$

$$I'_{xx} = \frac{bH^3}{12} - \frac{1}{2}bH \times \left(\frac{H}{3}\right)^2$$

$$= \frac{bH^3}{36}.$$

8. (a) Free body diagram:

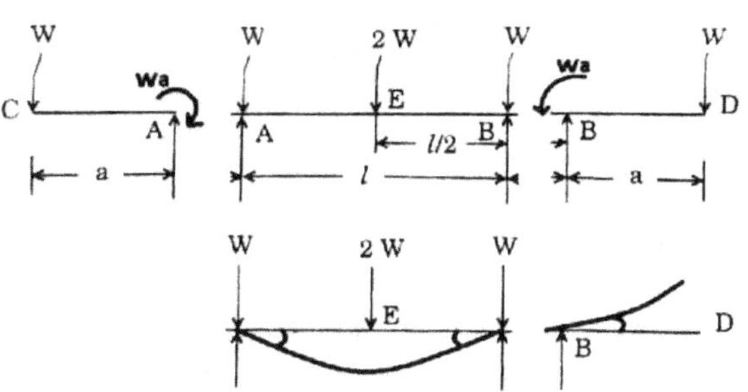

$$\delta_E = \frac{2w\left(\frac{l}{2}\right)^3}{48\,EI} = \frac{2wl^3}{48\,EI \times 8} = \frac{wl^3}{192\,EI}$$

$$\delta_E = \frac{wl^3}{192\,EI}$$

$$\theta_A = \theta_B = \frac{2w\left(\frac{l}{2}\right)^2}{16\,EI} = \frac{wl^2}{32\,EI}$$

Deflection at force end due to $2w$ load $\uparrow$

$$= \theta_{A/B} \times a$$

$$= \frac{wl^2}{32\,EI} \times a$$

Deflection at free end due to (w) load $\downarrow$

$$= \frac{wa^3}{3\,EI}$$

Net deflection $= \dfrac{wl^2 a}{32\,EI} - \dfrac{wa^3}{3\,EI}$

8. (b) The water-cement ratio is the ratio of the weight of water to the weight of cement used in a concrete mix. A lower ratio leads to higher strength and durability, but may make the mix difficult to work with and form.

The Importance of Water/Cement Ratio: Three simple ingredients can be blended and proportioned numerous ways to make concrete: aggregate, cement and water. In concrete, the single most significant influence on most or all of the properties is the amount of water used in the mix.

In concrete mix design, the ratio of the amount of water to the amount of cement used (both by weight) is called the water to cement ratio (w/c). These two ingredients are responsible for binding everything together.

The water to cement ratio, or w/c ratio, largely determines the strength and durability of the concrete when it is cured properly. The w/c ratio refers to the ratio of the weights of water and cement used in the concrete mix. A w/c ratio of 0.4 means that for every 100 lbs of cement used in the concrete, 40 lbs of water is added.

For ordinary concrete (sidewalks and driveways), a w/c ratio of 0.6 to 0.7 is considered normal. A lower w/c ratio of 0.4 is generally specified if a higher quality concrete is desired. The practical range of the w/c ratio is from about 0.3 to over 0.8. A ratio of 0.3 is very stiff (unless superplasticizers are used), and a ratio of 0.8 makes a wet and fairly weak concrete. For reference, a 0.4 w/c ratio is generally expected to make a concrete with a compressive strength (its f'c) of about 5600 psi when it is properly cured. On the other hand, a ratio of 0.8 will make a weak concrete of only about 2000 psi.

The simplest way to think about the w/c ratio is to think that the greater the amount of water in a concrete mix, the more dilute the cement paste will be. This not only affects the compressive strength, it also affects the tensile and flexural strengths, the porosity, the shrinkage and the colour.

The more the w/c ratio is increased (that is, the more water that is added for a fixed amount of cement), the more the strength of the resulting concrete is reduced. This is mostly because adding more water creates a diluted paste that is weaker and more susceptible to cracking and shrinkage. Shrinkage leads to micro-cracks, which are zones of weakness. Once the fresh concrete is placed, excess water is squeezed out of the paste by the weight of the aggregate and the cement paste itself. When there is a large excess of water, that water bleeds out onto the surface. The micro channels and passages that were created inside the concrete to allow that water to flow become weak zones and micro-cracks.

Using a low w/c ratio is the usual way to achieve a high strength and high quality concrete, but it does not guarantee that the resulting concrete is always appropriate for countertops. Unless the aggregate gradation and proportion are balanced with the correct amount of cement paste, excessive shrinkage, cracking and curling can result. Good concrete results from good mix design, and a low w/c ratio is just one part of a good mix design.

Too much water will result in segregation of the sand and aggregate components from the cement paste. Also, water that is not consumed by the hydration reaction may leave concrete as it hardens, resulting in microscopic pores (bleeding) that will reduce final strength of concrete. A mix with too much water will experience more shrinkage as excess water leaves, resulting in internal cracks and visible fractures (particularly around inside corners), which again will reduce the final strength.

9. (a) Methods of Mixing Concrete: The two methods used in mixing concrete are by hand and by machinery. Good concrete may be made by either method. Concrete mixed by either method should be carefully watched by a good foreman. If a large quantity of concrete is required, it is cheaper to mix it by machinery. On small jobs where the cost of erecting the plant, together with the interest and depreciation, divided by the number of cubic yards to be made, constitute a large item, or if frequent moving is required, it is very often cheaper to mix the concrete by hand. The relative cost of the two methods usually depends upon circumstances, and must be worked out in each individual case.

Hand Mixing Concrete: The placing and handling of materials and arranging the plant are varied by different engineers and contractors. In general the mixing of concrete is a simple operation, but should be carefully watched by an inspector. He should see

1. That the exact amount of stone and sand are measured out;
2. That the cement and sand are thoroughly mixed;
3. That the mass is thoroughly mixed;
4. That the proper amount of water is used;
5. That care is taken in dumping the concrete in place;
6. That it is thoroughly rammed.

The mixing platform, which is usually 10 to 20 feet square, is made of 1-inch or 2-inch plank planed on one side and well nailed to stringers, and should be placed as near the work as possible, but so situated that the stone can be dumped on one side of it and the sand on the opposite side. A very convenient way to measure the stone and sand is by the means of bottomless boxes. These boxes are of such a size that they hold the proper proportions of stone or sand to mix a batch of a certain amount. Cement is usually measured by the package, that is by the barrel or bag, as they contain a definite amount of cement.

The method used for mixing the concrete has little effect upon the strength of the concrete, if the mass has been turned a sufficient number of times to thoroughly mix them. One of the following methods is generally used. (Taylor and Thompson's Concrete.)

(a) Cement and sand mixed dry and shoveled on the stone or gravel, leveled off, and wet as the mass is turned.

(b) Cement and sand mixed dry, the stone measured and dumped on top of it, leveled off, and wet, as turned with shovels.

(c) Cement and sand mixed into a mortar, the stone placed on top of it and the mass turned.

(d) Cement and sand mixed with water into a mortar which is shoveled on the gravel or stone and the mass turned with shovels.

(*e*) Stone or gravel, sand and cement spread in successive layers, mixed slightly and shoveled into a mound, water poured into the center, and the mass turned with shovels.

The quantity of water is regulated by the appearance of the concrete. The best method of wetting the concrete is by measuring the water in pails. This insures a more uniform mixture than by spraying the mass with a hose.

Mixing Concrete by Machinery: On large contracts the concrete is generally mixed by machinery. The economy is not only in the mixing itself but in the appliances introduced in handling the raw materials and the mixed concrete. If all materials are delivered to the mixer in wheel-barrows, and if the concrete is conveyed away in wheel-barrows, the cost of making concrete is high, even if machine mixers are used. If the materials are fed from bins by gravity into the mixer, and if the concrete is dumped from the mixer into cars and hauled away, the cost of making the concrete should be very low. On small jobs the cost of maintaining and operating the mixer will usually exceed the saving in hand labour and will render the expense with the machine greater than without it.

Machine Vs. Hand Mixing: It has already been stated that good concrete may be produced by either machine or hand mixing, if it is thoroughly mixed.

Tests made by the U.S. Government engineers at Duluth, Minn., to determine the relative strength of concrete mixed by hand and mixed by machine (a cube mixer), showed that at 7 days, hand-mixed concrete possessed only 53 per cent of the strength of the machine-mixed concrete; at 28 days, 77 per cent; at 6 months, 84 per cent; and at one year, 88 per cent.

It should be noted in this connection, that the variations in strength from highest to lowest were greatest in the hand-mixed samples, and that the strength was more uniform in the machine-mixed.

9. (*b*) Method of underwater concreting— Tremie method: This is a method on how to place concrete underwater, this method place a big role in offshore concreting, since cement looses its strength and fade away under water, Tremie method is to be used. Tremie Concrete is done by using a formwork/pipe which will have one end of the formwork/pipe above water and other bottom end immersed under the water and with the help of gravity.

A tremie is a watertight pipe, generally 250 mm in diameter, having a funnel shape hopper at its upper end and a loose plug at the bottom or discharge end. The valve at the discharge end is used to de-water the tremie and control the distribution of the concrete. The tremie is supported on a working platform above water level, and to facilitate the placing it is built up in 1 to 3.5 m section.

During the concreting, air and water must be exclude from the tremie by keeping the pipe full of concrete all the time; and for this reason the capacity of the hopper should be at least equal to that of the tremie pipe. In charging the tremie a plug formed of paper is first inserted into the pipe as the hopper is filled the pressure of fresh concrete forces the plug down the pipe, and the water in the tremie is displaced by concrete.

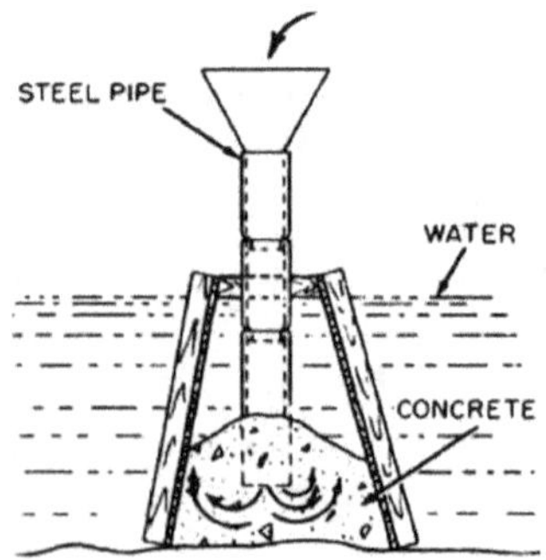

Basic principle behind Method of underwater Concreting — Tremie method

For concreting, the tremie pipe is lowered into position and the discharge end is kept as deeply submerged beneath the surface of freshly placed concrete as the placed concrete as the head of concrete in tremie permits. As concreting proceeds the pipe is raised slightly and the concrete flows outwards. Care should be taken to maintain continuity of concreting without breaking the seal provided by the concrete cover over the discharge end. Should this seal is broken, the tremie should be lift and plugged before concreting is recommended. The tremie should never be moved laterally though freshly placed concrete. It should be lifted vertically above the surface of concrete and shifted to its new position.

When large quantities of concrete are to be placed continuously, it is preferable to place concrete simultaneously and uniformly through a battery of tremies, rather than shift a single tremies from point to point. It has been recommended that the spacing of tremies be between 3.5 and 5 m and that the end tremies should be about 2.5 m from the formwork. The risk of segregation and non-uniform stiffening can be minimized by maintaining the surface of concrete in the forms as level as possible and by providing a continuous and rapid flow of concrete.

For Structural concrete following must be considered:

- Coarse Aggregate: Gravel of 3/4″ (20 mm) max. size. Use 50-55% of the total aggregate by weight.
- Sand, 45-50% of the total aggregate by weight.
- Cement: Type II ASTM (moderate heat of hydration), 600 lbs/yd3
- Pozzolans: ASTM 616 Type N or F, 100 lbs/ yd3
- Water/Cement Ratio: 0.42 (0.45 Maximum).

- Water-Reducing Admixture (preferably it is also plasticizer): Do not use super-plasticizers.
- Air-Entrainment Admixtures: To give 6% total air.
- Retarding Admixture: To increase setting time to 4-24 hours, as required.
- Slump: 6 1/2″ ± 1″
- This mix will develop compressive strength in the range of 5,600–7,000 psi at 28 days.

10. (b) Given, l = 5 m, M-20 concrete, steel Fe-415, n = 13.33

Actual depth of N.A.

$$\frac{Bx_a^2}{2} = mA_{st}(d - x_a)$$

$$\Rightarrow 220 \times \frac{x_a^2}{2} = 13.33 \times 1256.44(400 - x_a)$$

$$x_a = 182.13 \text{ mm}$$

Critical Depth of N.A.

$$x_c = kd = \frac{m\sigma_{cbe} \times d}{m\sigma_{cbe} + \sigma_{st}}$$

$$= \frac{13.33 \times 7}{13.33 \times 7 + 230} \times 400$$

$$= 115.44 \text{ mm}$$

Since the value of $x_a > x_c$, so the section is over reinforcement, concrete reaches its maximum value

$$MR = \frac{1}{2} \times B \times x_a \times C\left(d - \frac{x_a}{3}\right)$$

$$= \frac{1}{2} \times 220 \times 182.13 \times 7\left(400 - \frac{182.13}{3}\right)$$

$$= 47.58 \text{ kN-m}$$

So, this MR is equal to the $(BM)_{max}$

$$BM_{max} = MR = \frac{wl^2}{8}$$

$$\Rightarrow 47.58 = \frac{wl^2}{8} \Rightarrow w = 15.22 \text{ kN/m}$$

So, the U.D.L. is 15.22 kN/m

11. Given, $P = 1000$ kN

Assume wt. of foundation $= 1000 \times 0.10$

$$= 100 \text{ kN}$$

$P_T =$ total load

$$= 1000 + 100 = 1100 \text{ kN}$$

BC of soil $q_0 = 200$ kN/m^2

(*i*) Area of foundation required $A = \dfrac{P_T}{q_0} = \dfrac{1100}{200}$

$$\Rightarrow \qquad A = 5.5 \text{ m}^2$$
$$A = B^2 = 5.5$$
$$\Rightarrow \qquad B = \sqrt{5.5} = 2.34 \text{ m}$$

(*ii*) Design soil pressure $= w_0 = \dfrac{P}{A} = \dfrac{1000}{5.5}$

$$\Rightarrow \qquad w_0 = 181.81 \text{ kN}$$

(*iii*) Check for B.M. $\Rightarrow M = \dfrac{w_0(B-b)^2}{8}$

$$\Rightarrow \qquad M = 181.81 \times \dfrac{(2.34-0.4)^2}{8}$$

$$= 85.53 \text{ kN-m}$$

Depth of foundation $= \sqrt{\dfrac{M}{QB}}$

$$= \sqrt{\dfrac{85.53 \times 10^6}{Q \times 2340}}$$

$$\left[K_c = \dfrac{mc}{mc+t} = 0.289,\ j_c = 1 - \dfrac{K_C}{3} = 0.904, \right.$$

$$\left. Q = 0.914 \right]$$

$$d = \sqrt{\dfrac{85.53 \times 10^6}{0.914 \times 2340}}$$

$$= 199.92 \approx 200 \text{ mm}$$

Check for single shear:

Section is check for single shear at a distance of $d = 200$ mm from the column force, where shear force

$$V = w_0 B\,(B - b) - d$$
$$= 181.81 \times 2.34\,(2.34 - 0.4) - 0.2$$
$$= 306.31 \text{ kN}$$

Shear stress $\tau_V = \dfrac{V}{B \times b} = \dfrac{306.31 \times 10^3}{2340 \times 200}$

$$= 0.523 \text{ N/mm}^2$$

$$A_{st} = \dfrac{M}{\sigma_{st}\, jd}$$

$$= \dfrac{85.53 \times 10^6}{230 \times 0.94 \times 240}$$

$$= 1645.44 \text{ mm}^2$$

$$\% \text{ steel} = \dfrac{A_{st} \times 100}{Bd}$$

$$= \dfrac{1645.44 \times 100}{2340 \times 200} = 0.281\%$$

%P	τ_c
0.25	0.28
0.28	x
0.50	0.36

$$\tau_c = 0.28 + \dfrac{(0.36-0.28)(0.28-0.25)}{0.50-0.25}$$

$$\tau_c = 0.289 \text{ N/mm}^2$$

But here $\tau_v > \tau$, unsafe.

So, for $\tau_c = 0.289$ N/mm^2, depth of foundation

$$0.289 = \dfrac{306.31 \times 10^3}{2340 \times d}$$

$$d = 452.94 \approx 460 \text{ mm}$$

Check for Double Shear

$$\tau_{vp} = \dfrac{\text{Net Punching force}}{\text{C/S area}}$$

$$= \dfrac{F}{4b + d \times d}$$

$$F = p_0[B^2 - b + d^2]$$
$$= 181.81\,[2.34^2 - 0.4 + 0.460^2]$$
$$= 861.05 \text{ kN}$$

$$\tau_{vd} = \dfrac{861.05 \times 1000}{4 \times 400 + 460 \times 460}$$

$$= 0.544 \text{ N/mm}^2$$

$$\tau_{vd} = 0.544 \text{ N/mm}^2 \le k_s \tau_c$$

$$\tau_c = 0.16\sqrt{f_{cx}} = 0.16\sqrt{20}$$

$$= 0.715 \text{ N/mm}^2$$

$$k_s = \left(0.5 + \frac{b}{a}\right) > 1, \ k_s = 1$$

$$k_s\tau_c = 0.715 \times 1 = 0.715 \ \text{N/mm}^2$$

$$\tau_{vd} < k_s\tau_c$$

Steel reinforcement:

$$A_{st} = \frac{M}{\sigma_{st} jd}$$

$$A_{st} = 1645.44 \ \text{mm}^2$$

Provide 12 mm, dia bar.

$$= \frac{1645.44}{\dfrac{\pi}{4}12^2} = 14.54 \approx 15 \ \text{nos.}$$

$$s_v = \frac{\dfrac{\pi}{4} \times 12^2 \times 1000}{1645.44}$$

$$= 68.73 \approx 70 \ \text{mm}$$

Provide 12 mm ϕ bars @ spacing of 70 mm in whole width & length of square footing.

12. (*a*) (*i*) $d = 20$ mm, $d' = 21.5$ mm

Strength of rivet in double shearing

$$= 2 \times \frac{\pi}{4} 21.5^2 \times 100$$

$$= 72.61 \ \text{kN}$$

Strength of rivet in bearing $= d't \ \sigma_p$

$$= 21.5 \times 16 \times 300$$

$$= 103.20 \ \text{kN}$$

(Thickness of cover = 10 mm, so $t = 20$ mm but thickness of main plate = 16 mm, hence, t will be 16 mm)

St. of plate in bearing $(S - d') \times 16 \times 150$

Per pitch length = 164.4 kN

So st. of joint per pitch length is min of these three

St. of joint/pitch length = 72.61 kN

St. of solid plate/pitch length $= \text{St } \sigma_{st}$

$$= 90 \times 16 \times 150 = 216 \ \text{kN}$$

Efficiency of joint $= \dfrac{72.61}{216} \times 100 = 33.61\%.$

12. (*b*) $S = 6$ mm, $P_q = 108$ Mpa

$$P = l \times \frac{S}{\sqrt{2}} \times P_q$$

$$= (75 + 60 + 70) \times \frac{6}{\sqrt{2}} \times 108$$

$$= 93.932 \ \text{kN.}$$

SSC-Junior Engineer (Civil & Structural) Exam 2009

PAPER-II (Conventional)

SECTION-I (Civil)

1. (*a*) Describe briefly the characteristics of good stones.

(*b*) What do you mean by Seasoning of Timber? Describe the methods of seasoning timber.

(*c*) Describe the various ingredients of a paint.

2. (*a*) Discuss in detail the methods of plane table surveying.

(*b*) The true bearing of a tower T as observed from a station A was 357°, the magnetic bearing of the same was 9°. The back bearings of the lines AB, AC and AD were found to be 286°, 337° and 30° respectively when measured with a prismatic compass. Find the true bearings of the lines AB, AC and AD respectively.

3. (*a*) A sample of soil has a porosity of 35 percent and specific gravity of solids is 2.67. Calculate void ratio, dry density and unit weight, if

(*i*) the soil is 50% saturated,

(*ii*) the soil is 100% saturated.

(*b*) A sample of soil is 5 cm high and 8 cm in diameter. It was tested in a constant head permeameter. Water percolates through the soil under a constant head of 45 cm for 8 m. The water was collected and weighed. Its weight was recorded as 500 gm. On oven drying the sample of soil, the weight was recorded as 450 gm. If G is 2.65, calculate

(*i*) coefficient of permeability,

(*ii*) seepage velocity of water when the water was under operation.

4. (*a*) An embankment was compacted at a moisture content of 15%. Its density was determined with the help of a core cutter and the following data was collected.

Empty weight of the cutter = 1200 gm

Weight of cutter when it is full of soil = 3200 gm

Volume of the cutter = 1000 cc

Calculate-bulk density and saturation percentage of the embankment. If the embankment becomes fully saturated due to rains, then, determine its moisture content and saturated density. Take G = 2.70.

(*b*) Explain the factors which affect the bearing capacity of soils.

5. (*a*) The space between two parallel plates 4 mm apart is filled with an oil of specific gravity 0.85. The upper plate of area 800 cm^2 is dragged with constant velocity of 0.75 m/s by applying a force of 0.2 kgf to it. Assume straight line velocity distribution and calculate velocity gradient, dynamic viscosity of oil in poise and kinematic viscosity of oil in stokes.

(*b*) A bend in pipeline conveying water gradually reduces from 60 cm to 30 cm diameter and deflects the flow through an angle of 60°. At the larger end the gauge pressure is 1.75 kg/cm^2. Determine the magnitude and direction of the force exerted on the bend

(*i*) when there is no flow,

(*ii*) when the flow is 876 lit/sec.

6. (*a*) Describe in detail the methods employed to purify water, before supplying to the consumers.

(*b*) Design a septic tank for a small colony of 300 persons with average daily sewage flow of 85 litres per head. Detention period is 30 hours. Clearing interval is 6 months.

SECTION-II (Structural)

7. (*a*) A bar 40 mm in diameter is subjected to a tensile force of 40,000 kg. The extension of bar measured over a gauge length of 200 mm was 0.318 mm. The decrease in diameter was found to be 0.02 mm. Calculate values of Young's modulus of elasticity and modulus of rigidity of the material.

(*b*) Draw S.F. and B.M. diagrams for beam loaded with varying load as shown in Fig.1.

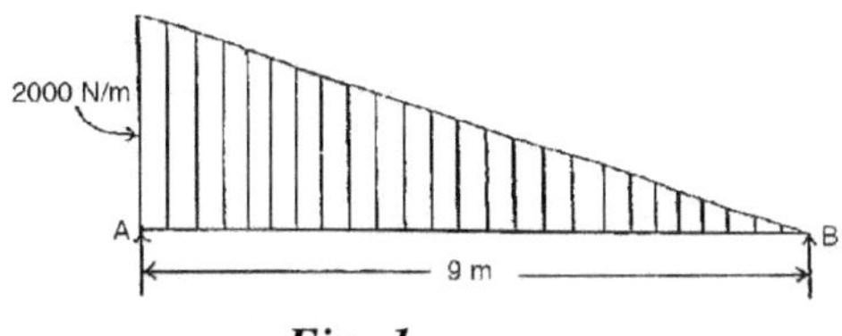

Fig. 1

(*c*) An R.S.J. 55 cm deep and 19 cm wide having flange and web thicknesses of 1.5 cm and 0.99 cm respectively is used as a beam. Calculate the moment of resistance at a section where maximum stress is 100 N/mm².

8. (*a*) A cantilever of length '*l*' and depth '*d*' tapers in plan in such a way that the breadth '*b*' at the fixed end, decreases to zero at the free end. Determine the deflection at the free end due to load 'W' acting at the free end (Fig. 2).

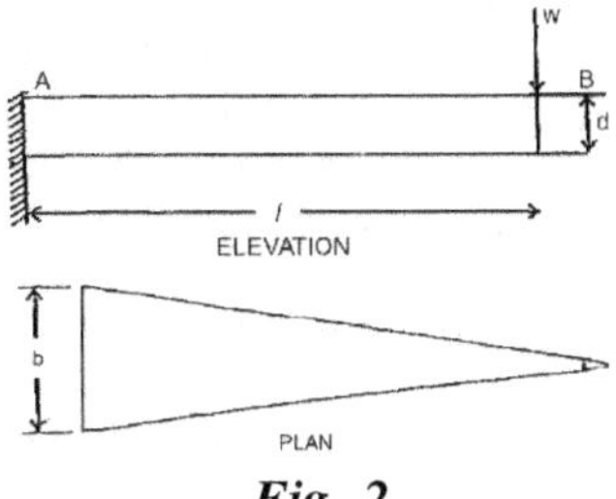

Fig. 2

(*b*) Write short notes on:
(*i*) Workability of concrete
(*ii*) Slump test

9. (*a*) What do you understand by the term 'curing'? Why is it essential to cure concrete? What are the various methods commonly adopted in curing?

(*b*) Discuss in detail "placing of concrete in cold and hot weather".

10. (*a*) A reinforced concrete beam 400 mm × 650 mm (effective) in section is reinforced with 3 bars of 28 mm φ. If the effective span is 5 m, find the concentrated load the beam can support at the centre. Assume M 20 concrete and Fe 250 steel ($n = 13.33$).

(*b*) Design a column to carry a lead of 590 kN. Height of the column is 3.5 m effective, one side of the column is restricted to 250 mm. Use $\sigma_{cc} = 5$ N/mm², $\sigma_{sc} = 190$ N/mm² and 10 mm φ lateral lies.

11. Design a cantilever slab to carry a superimposed load of 4188 N/m². The overhang of the slab is 1.2 m. Adopt M 20 concrete and Fe 415 steel.

12. (*a*) What are the advantages and disadvantages of welded joints?

(*b*) Determine the maximum load in the rivets of the eccentric connection shown in Fig. 3.

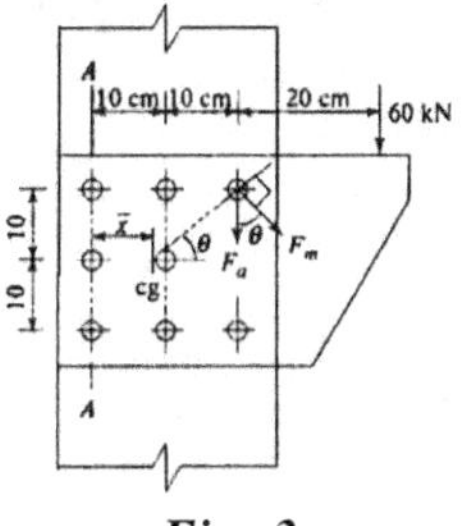

Fig. 3

ANSWERS

1. (*a*) Requirement of good building stones:

- **Compressive Strength:** The compressive strength or the crushing strength of the stone is tested with the help of a crushing strength testing machine and for a good building stone the value should not be less than 100 N/mm².

The various igneous rocks and the metamorphic rocks have the required amount of the strength that is why some of them makes it up to as a building stone.

- **Appearance:** The stones should have a homogeneous color and should be resistant to the weathering agencies. The stone used in the face work should be of decent appearance. The color of the stone chosen should be according to the surrounding environment.

The light colored stones are preferred because they are weathering resistant. A good building stone is of uniform color and do not possess any clay spots or other color spots.

- **Durability:** In general durability is defined as the ability to resist the weathering action of the surroundings. A good building stone should be durable. The various factors contributing to the durability of a stone are its chemical composition, texture, resistance to atmospheric and other influences, location in the structure etc.

The various important environmental agents which affect the durability of a stone are alternate heating and cooling, alternate drying and wetting, chemical agencies such as dissolved gases in the environment, growth of the trees and creepers in the joints between the stone and wind and the high velocity; etc.

For making stone durable some people suggest that the natural bed of the stone should be noted and the stones should be so arranged in a structure such that the natural bed is perpendicular to the direction of the pressure.

- **Work-ability/ Facility of dressing:** The stones should be such that they can be easily carved, molded, cut and dressed. It is important consideration from the economic point of view. However this property of stone is opposed to its strength, durability and hardness. Hence it is to be properly correlated with respect to the situation in which stone is to be used.

- **Fracture:** For a good building stone its fracture should be sharp, even, bright and the grains well cemented together, or as suggested by the several books. A dull, chalky and earthly fracture will indicate an early future decay of the stone.

- **Hardness:** The stone to be used in the building should possess the good hardness. The co-efficient of hardness, as worked out in the hardness test, should be greater than 17 for a stone to be used in road work. If it is between 14 and 17 then the stone is said to be of medium hardness. If the hardness is less than the 14 then the stone is said to be of poor hardness.

- **Porosity/ Percentage water:** The porosity of stone is defined as the ratio of the volume of the air plus water voids present in the stone to the total volume of the stone. If we put the stone in the water for 24 hours it should not absorb the water more than 3% by weight.

The porosity may affect the durability of the stone. The rain water as it descends through atmosphere absorbs some acidic gases forming light acids. Such rain water if absorbed by stone reacts with the constituents of the stone causing them to crumble.

Similarly, in cold regions the low temperature turns the water into ice which has more volume than the water. The absorbed water will further increase the cracks as it needs more volume in the ice form. So, the porous stones should not be used in the places which are subjected to rain, frost or moisture.

- **Resistant to fire:** The minerals composing the stone should be such that the shape of the stone is preserved when a fire occurs. The failure of stone in case of a fire is due to various reasons such as rapid rise in the temperature, sudden cooling, different co-efficient of linear expansion of minerals, etc.

The limestone resists fire up to a temperature of 800 degrees C and then it is split into CaO and CO_2. The sandstone with silicates as binding material can resist a fire in a better way. The argillaceous stones are weak in strength but they can resist fire quite well.

- **Seasoning:** The stones should be well seasoned before putting into use. The stone obtained fresh from the quarry contain some moisture which is known as the quarry sap. The presence of this moisture makes the stone soft.

Hence, the stones quarried freshly are easy to work. It is advised to dress them when the stone contain the quarry sap. The stones should be dried or seasoned before they are used in the structural use. A period of about 6 to 12 month is advised for the proper seasoning.

- **Specific Gravity:** For a good building stone its specific gravity should be greater than 2.7 or so. The heavy stones are compact and dense, thus less porous and they can be used for various civil engineering applications such as dams, weirs, retaining walls, docks, harbors etc. On the other hand if the stones are to be used for domes, roof coverings, etc. the lighter varieties of the stones are preferred.

1. (b) Seasoning timber causes many changes in its properties and in practically every case the change is an improvement. There is only one principal disadvantage in drying timber, namely, the loss in volume due to shrinkage. However, by a correct understanding of the shrinkage of timber this effect can be minimized and timber can then be confidently used without fear of adverse behaviour subsequently in service.

Shrinkage of timber

All timber shrinks to some extent as it dries, resulting in a direct loss in volume. It should be noted that shrinkage is a direct cause of the cracks that occur on the surface or ends of sawn timber and is also the primary cause of the warping which sometimes occurs.

Seasoning aims at drying a set quantity of timber uniformly to the equilibrium moisture content required with a minimum of degrade in the shortest possible time. There are many ways of seasoning or drying timber, but only two methods have been found satisfactory, principally for economic reasons. They are air drying and kiln drying.

SEASONING OF WOOD

The process of removal of moisture content from wood so as to make it useful for construction and other uses is called drying of wood or seasoning of wood. This reduces the chances of decay, improves load bearing properties, reduces weight and exhibits more favourable properties like thermal & electrical insulation, glue adhesive capacity & easy preservative treatment etc .

Natural or air seasoning

The traditional method of seasoning timber was to stack it in air and let the heat of the atmosphere and the natural air movement around the stacked timber remove the moisture. The process has undergone a number of refinements over the years that have made it more efficient and reduced the quantity of wood that was damaged by drying too quickly near the ends in air seasoning.

The basic principle is to stack the timber so that plenty of air can circulate around each piece. The timber is stacked with wide spaces between each piece horizontally and with strips of wood between each layer ensuring that there is a vertical separation too.

Air-drying is necessarily a slow process, particularly for hardwoods, typically taking 6 to 9 months to reach moisture content in the range 20% to 25%. Air seasoning is the method used with the timber stacked in the open air.

Artificial (kiln) seasoning

Kiln drying of lumber is perhaps the most effective and economical method available. Drying rates in a kiln can be carefully controlled and defect losses reduced to a minimum. Length of drying time is also greatly reduced and is predictable so that dry lumber inventories can often be reduced. Where staining is a problem, kiln drying is often the only reasonable method that can be used unless chemical dips are employed.

1. (*c*) Basic Paint Ingredients and Additives

For most of the paints the basic ingredients are:

1. Solvent
2. Binder
3. Pigment
4. Additives

1. Solvent / Diluent

It is a volatile liquid used to obtain desired viscosity and flow of the paint. It keeps the solid components of paint in suspension and also influences the adhesion properties of the surface. It is an optional component of paint *i.e.* some paints may not have solvent. The solvent after application of paint evaporates to leave a solid dry film on the surface. The most common solvents used in architectural paints are water and mineral spirits. Water is used in acrylic paints (both interior and exterior) while mineral spirits are used in oil based paints.

2. Binder / Vehicle / Resin

It is one of the most important and necessary components of paint. The purpose of binder in paint is to impart adhesion to the layer as well as cohesion to the pigment particles. It binds the pigment particles together to form a cohesive layer after the evaporation of the solvent. It strongly influences other properties such as gloss, toughness, flexibility and durability. Linseed oil and poppy seed oil are two of the most common oils used as binders in paint. In solvent based paints the binder is usually an alkyd resin while in water based paints the binder is usually an acrylic emulsion but some vinyl emulsions are also used. The binder, or resin component is either dissolved in liquid solvent or dispersed in non-solvent. Paints that contain solid binder dissolved in a solvent and dry due to the evaporation of solvent are known as lacquers.

3. Pigments and Fillers

Pigments are granular solids which impart paint its most important properties of colour and opacity. The pigments used in paint are normally present as fine solid particles that are dispersed, but not soluble, in the binder and solvent. Majority of white paints use Titanium Dioxide as a pigment. Sometimes dyes are used instead of pigments or in combination with pigments to impart colour to the paint. **Fillers** are a special type of pigment that is used to thicken the film, support its structure and increase the volume of the paint. Fillers are usually cheap and used to reduce the cost of paint. They are inert materials, such as clay, lime, talc etc.

Differences between Pigment & Dye

A pigment is a colouring material, usually in the form of an insoluble powder that is mixed with oil, water, etc. to make paint. While **dye** is soluble in water and is used to colour cloth and other porous materials.

4. Additives:

Additives are the special components of paint and are used in small quantities to impart additional characteristics to the paint. The purpose of using additives is to;

- Improve the production and storing properties
- Reduce the drag of the paint
- Make the paint flow on a surface
- Add texture to the paint
- Enhance the adhesive characteristics for special surfaces
- Give pleasant odour in case of interior painting
- Provide water proofing characteristics

2. (*a*) In plane table surveying a table top, similar to drawing board fitted on to a tripod is the main instrument. A drawing sheet is fixed on to the table top, the observations are made to the objects, distances are scaled down and the objects are plotted in the field itself. Since the plotting is made in the field itself, there is no chance of omitting any necessary measurement in this surveying. However, the accuracy achieved in this type of surveying is less. Hence, this type of surveying is used for filling up details between the survey stations previously fixed by other methods.

The following accessories are required to carry out plane table survey:

1. Alidade
2. Plumbing fork with plumb bob
3. Spirit level
4. Trough compass
5. Drawing sheets and accessories for drawing.

1. Alidade

It is a straight edge ruler having some form of sighting device. One edge of the ruler is bevelled and is graduated. Always this edge is used for drawing line of sight. Depending on the type of line of sight there are two types of alidade:

(a) Plain alidade

(b) Telescopic alidade

2. Plumbing Fork and Plumb Bob

Plumbing fork is a U-shaped metal frame with a upper horizontal arm and a lower inclined arm. The upper arm is provided with a pointer at the end while the lower arm is provided with a hook to suspend plumb bob. When the plumbing fork is kept on the plane table the vertical line (line of plumb bob) passes through the pointed edge of upper arm. The plumb bob helps in transferring the ground point to the drawing sheet and vice versa also.

3. Spirit Level

A flat based spirit level is used to level the plane table during surveying. To get perfect level, spirit level should show central position for bubble tube when checked with its positions in any two mutually perpendicular directions.

4. Trough Compass

It consists of a 80 to 150 mm long and 30 mm wide box carrying a freely suspended needle at its centre. At the ends of the needle graduations are marked on the box to indicate zero to five degrees on either side of the centre. The box is provided with glass top to prevent oscillation of the needle by wind. When needle is centred (reading 0-0), the line of needle is parallel to the edge of the box. Hence, marking on the edges in this state indicates magnetic north-south direction.

5. Drawing Sheet and Accessories for Drawing

A good quality, seasoned drawing sheet should be used for plane table surveying. The drawing sheet may be rolled when not in use, but should never is folded. For important works fibre glass sheets or paper backed with thin aluminium sheets are used.

Clips clamps, adhesive tapes may be used for fixing drawing sheet to the plane table. Sharp hard pencil, good quality eraser, pencil cutter and sand paper to keep pencil point sharp are other accessories required for the drawing work. If necessary, plastic sheet should be carried to cover the drawing sheet from rain and dust.

2. (b)

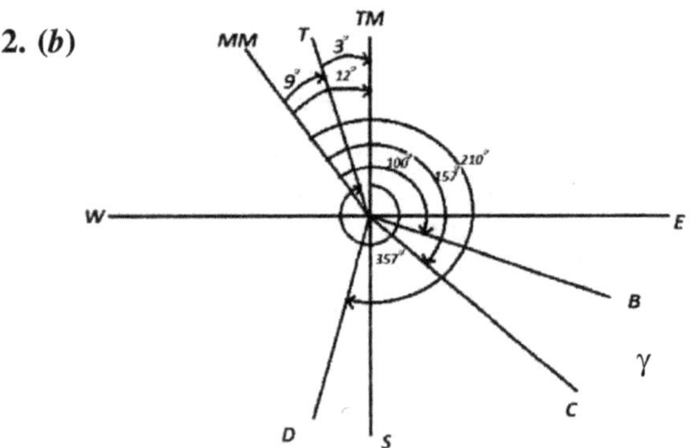

Magnetic declination (ref. fig.) = 9° + 3°
= 12°W

Line	BB	FB	TB
AB	286°	286°–180° = 106°	106°–12° = 94°
AC	337°	337°–180° = 157°	157°–12° = 145°
AD	30°	30°+180° = 210°	210°–12° = 198°

3. (a) Given,

$n = 0.35$, $G = 2.67$, $e = ?$, $\rho_d = ?$, $\gamma = ?$,
$w = 0.5$

$$\gamma = \left(\frac{G+Se}{1+e}\right)\gamma_w = \left(\frac{2.67+0.5\times2.67}{1+0.2593}\right)\times1$$

$$\gamma = 3.18$$

void ratio $e = \dfrac{n}{1-n} = \dfrac{0.35}{1-0.35} = 0.54$

dry density $\rho_d = \left(\dfrac{G\rho}{1+e}\right) = \dfrac{2.67\times9.8}{1+0.54}$
$$= 17 \text{ kN/m}^3$$

1. if the soil is 50% saturated
$S_r = 50\% = 0.50$

$$e = \frac{wG}{S_r} \Rightarrow w = \frac{es_r}{G}$$

$$= \frac{0.54\times0.5}{2.67} = 0.101$$

$\gamma = \gamma_d(1+w) = 17\times(1+0.101)$
$$= 18.72$$

2. if the soil is 100% saturated = 1

$$\gamma = \left(\frac{G+Se}{1+e}\right)\gamma_w = \left(\frac{(2.67+0.54\times1.0)\times9.81}{1+0.54}\right)$$

$$= 20.45 \text{ KN/m}^3$$

3. (b) Given,

Height of soil sample L = 5 cm, dia D = 8 cm

then, $\quad A = \dfrac{\pi}{4}\times8^2 = 50.26$ cm^2

head of water, $h = 45$ cm, volume of soil
sample = A × L = 50.26 × L
$$= 50.26\times5 = 251.33 \text{ cm}^3$$
Wt. of water recorded = 500 gm.

Vol. of water = wt. of water/unit wt. of water

$$= \frac{500}{9.81} = 50.968 \text{ m}^3$$

Permeability of soil by constant head
permeability method

$$K = \frac{QL}{Ath} = \frac{qL}{Ah} = \frac{50.968\times5}{50.26\times45}$$

$$= 0.11 \text{ cm/sec} \dots \left(\frac{Q}{t} = 50.968 \text{ m}^3\right)$$

Seepage velocity $(v_s) = k_p i$

i = head of water/length of soil sample

$$= \frac{45}{5} = 9$$

$$k_p = \frac{k}{n}$$

Dry unit weight = dry wt. of soil sample/
vol. of soil sample

$$= \frac{450}{251.33 \text{ cm}^3} = 1.79 \text{ gm/cc}$$

$$y_d = \frac{G\gamma_w}{1+e} = \frac{2.65\times1}{1+e}$$

$$e = 0.48$$

$$n = \frac{e}{1+e} = \frac{0.48}{1.48} = 0.32$$

$$k_p = \frac{k}{n} = \frac{0.11}{0.32} = 0.34$$

$$v_s = k_p\times i = 0.34\times9 = 3.05 \text{ m/sec}$$

4. (a) Given,

Mass of soil in cutter
$$3200 - 1200 = 2000 \text{ g}$$
Bulk density ρ = M/V
$$= 2000/1000 = 2 \text{ g/cm}^3$$

Bulk unit weight $\gamma = 9.81 \times \rho$

$$= 9.81 \times 2$$
$$= 19.62 \ \text{kN/m}^3$$

$$\gamma_d = \frac{\gamma}{1+w} = \frac{19.62}{1+0.15}$$
$$= 17.06 \ \text{kN/m}^3$$

$$e = \frac{G\gamma_w}{\gamma_d} - 1$$

$$= \frac{2.7 \times 9.81}{17.06} - 1$$

$$= 0.553$$

$$Sr = \frac{w.G}{e} = \frac{0.15 \times 2.7}{0.553}$$

$$= 0.732 = 73.2\%$$

At saturation:

Since the volume remains the same, the voids ratio also remains unchanged.

$$e = w_{sat.} G$$
$$w_{sat.} = e/G = 0.553/2.7$$
$$= 0.2048 = 20.48\%$$

$$\gamma_{sat} = \frac{(G+e)\gamma_w}{1+e}$$

$$= \frac{(2.7+0.553)9.81}{1+0.553}$$

$$= 20.55 \ \text{kN/m}^3.$$

4. (*b*) All civil engineering structures whether they are buildings, dams, bridges etc. are built on soils. A foundation is required to transmit the load of the structure on a large area of soil. The foundation of the structure should be so designed that the soil below does not fail in shear nor there is excessive settlement of the structure. The conventional method of foundation design is based on the concept of bearing capacity.

The bearing capacity of foundation is the maximum load per unit area which the soil can support without failure. It depends upon the shear strength of soil as well as shape, size, depth and type of foundation.

Factors Affecting Bearing Capacity of Soils

The following factors affect the bearing capacity of soils:

(*i*) Type of soil

(*ii*) Physical characteristics of foundation

(*iii*) Soil properties

(*iv*) Type of foundation

(*v*) Water table

(*vi*) Amount of settlement

(*vii*) Eccentricity of loading.

(*i*) Type of soil:
The bearing capacity of soils depends upon the type of soil. Depending upon the type of soil, the bearing capacity of soil is different which is clear from Terzaghi bearing capacity equation.

$$q_u = CN_C + 0.5 \ yBN_y + qN_q$$

For purely cohesion less soil

$$q_u = 5.7C + q$$

(*ii*) Physical characteristics of foundation:
Physical characteristics like width, shape and depth of foundation affect the bearing capacity of soils. The bearing capacity of soils depends upon the width B and depth D of foundation. So, any change in the value of B and D of foundation will affect the bearing capacity.

The shape of foundation also affects the bearing capacity which is as follows:

For square footings:

$$q_u = 1.2 \ CN_C + 0.4 \ yBN_y + yDN_q$$

For circular footings:

$$q_u = 1.2 \ CN_C + 0.3 \ yBN_y + yDN_q$$

where, B is the diameter of circular footing.

(*iii*) Soil properties:
Soil properties like shear strength, density, permeability etc., affect the bearing capacity of soil. Dense sand will have more bearing capacity than loose

sand as unit weight of dense sand is more than loose sand.

(*iv*) Type of Foundation:

The type of foundation selected also affects the bearing capacity of soils. Raft or mat foundation adopted supports the load of structure safely by spreading the load to a wider area, even if the soil is having low bearing capacity.

(*v*) Water Table:

When the water is above the base of the footing, the submerged unit weight of soil is used to calculate the overburden pressure and the bearing capacity of the soil reduces by 50%.

(*vi*) Amount of Settlement:

The amount of settlement of the structure also affects the bearing capacity of soil. If the settlement exceeds the possible settlement, the bearing capacity of soil is reduced.

(*vii*) Eccentricity of Loading:

If the load acts eccentrically in a footing the width 'B' and length 'L' should be reduced as under

$B' = B - 2e$

$L' = L - 2e$ and

$A' = B' \times L'$

The ultimate bearing capacity (q_u) of such footings are determined by using B' and L' instead of 8 and L. Hence, q_u is less than that corresponds to actual size of footing.

5. (*a*) Space between the parallel plates,

$$Y = 4 \text{ mm} = 0.4 \text{ cm} = 0.004 \text{ m}$$

Sp. Gravity of the soil = 0.85

Upper plate area = 800 cm²

$$\text{Area A} = \frac{800}{100^2} \text{ cm}^2 = 0.08 \text{ m}^2$$

Velocity of dragged = 0.75 m/sec

Shear force = 0.2 kgf = 0.2 × 9.81 N

$$= 1.962 \text{ N}$$

(*i*) Dynamic viscosity

Shear force $F = \dfrac{\mu v A}{Y}$,

$$\Rightarrow 1.96 = \frac{\mu \times 0.75 \text{ m/sec} \times 0.08 \text{ m}^2}{0.004 \text{ m}}$$

$$\Rightarrow \mu = \frac{1.96 \times 0.004}{0.75 \times 0.08} = 1.306 \text{ poise}$$

(*ii*) Velocity gradient,

$$\tau = \mu \frac{du}{dy}$$

Shear force/area of plate $= \mu \dfrac{du}{dy}$

$$\frac{1.96}{0.08} = \mu \frac{du}{dy} \Rightarrow \frac{du}{dy} = \frac{1.96}{0.08 \times \mu}$$

$$= \frac{1.96}{0.08 \times 1.306}$$

$$\Rightarrow \frac{du}{dy} = 18.75 / \text{sec}$$

(*iii*) Kinematic viscosity,

$$K = \frac{\mu}{\rho} = \frac{1.306 \text{ kg/m} - \text{sec}}{0.85 \times 1000 \text{ kg/m}^3}$$

$$\Rightarrow K = 1.536 \times 100^2 \text{ cm}^2/\text{sec}$$

$$\Rightarrow K = 15.36 \text{ stokes}$$

5. (*b*)

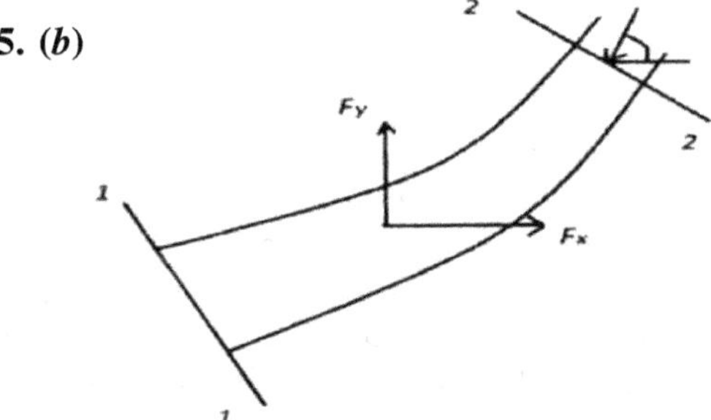

Given,

$$D_1 = 0.6 \text{ m} \dots \text{ at sec (1) (1)}$$

$$A_1 = \frac{\pi}{4} \times D_1^2 = 0.283 \text{ m}^2$$

and $D_2 = 0.3$ m .... at sec (2) (2)

$$A_2 = \frac{\pi}{4} \times (0.3)^2 = 0.0706 \text{ m}^2$$

Moment equation X-direction

$P_1A_1 + F_x - P_2A_2 \cos 60° = \rho Q(V_2 \cos 60° - V_1)$

Pressure at 60 cm section is given

$P_1 = 1.75 \text{ kg/cm}^2 = 1.78 \times 9.81 \times (100)^2$

$P_1 = 174618 \text{ N/m}^2$

Let us assume the water is freely discharging at section 2 into atmosphere.

Hence, $P_2 = 0$,

$P_1A_1 + F_x = \rho Q(V_2 \cos 60° - V_1)$ is X-direction

Moment equation in Y-direction

$F_y - P_2A_2 \sin 60° = \rho Q(v_2 \sin 60°)$

(*i*) When there is no flow

$$\theta = 0$$

$P_1A_1 + F_x = 0$

$$F_x = -174618 \times 0.283$$

$$= -49416.89 \text{ N}$$

....(act in the negative 'X' direction)

$$F_y - P_2A_2 \sin 60 = 0$$

$$\Rightarrow F_y = 0 \text{ N}$$

(*ii*) When the flow is 876 lit/sec

$$Q = 876 \text{ lit/sec} = \frac{876}{1000} \text{ m}^3/\text{sec}$$

$$= 0.876 \text{ m}^3/\text{sec}$$

$$V_1 = \frac{Q}{A_1} = \frac{0.876}{0.283} = 3.095 \text{ m/sec}$$

$$V_2 = \frac{Q}{A_2} = \frac{0.876}{0.0706} = 12.407 \text{ m/sec}$$

(*a*) $F_x + P_1A_1 - P_2A_2 \cos \theta = \rho Q(V_2 \cos \theta - V_1)$

$P_2 = 0$, then $F_x + P_1A_1 = \rho Q(V_2 \cos \theta - V_1)$

$\Rightarrow F_x + 174618 \times 0.283 = 1000 \times 0.876$
$\times (12.407 \cos 60° - 3.095)$

$\Rightarrow F_x = -46693.898 \text{ N}$

(*b*) $F_y - P_2A_2 \sin \theta = \rho Q(V_2 \sin \theta)$,

put $P_2 = 0$, then $F_y = 9412.42$

6. (*a*) Drinking water sources are subject to contamination and require appropriate treatment to remove disease-causing agents. Public drinking water systems use various methods of water treatment to provide safe drinking water for their communities. Today, the most common steps in water treatment used by community water systems include:

- **Coagulation and Flocculation**

  Coagulation and flocculation are often the first steps in water treatment. Chemicals with a positive charge are added to the water. The positive charge of these chemicals neutralizes the negative charge of dirt and other dissolved particles in the water. When this occurs, the particles bind with the chemicals and form larger particles, called floc.

- **Sedimentation**

  During sedimentation, floc settles to the bottom of the water supply, due to its weight. This settling process is called sedimentation.

- **Filtration**

  Once the floc has settled to the bottom of the water supply, the clear water on top will pass through filters of varying compositions (sand, gravel and charcoal) and pore sizes, in order to remove dissolved particles, such as dust, parasites, bacteria, viruses and chemicals.

- **Disinfection**

  After the water has been filtered, a disinfectant (for example, chlorine, chloramine) may be added in order to kill any remaining parasites, bacteria and viruses and to protect the water from germs when it is piped to homes and businesses.

Household Water Treatment

Even though EPA regulates and sets standards for public drinking water, many Americans use a home water treatment unit to:

- Remove specific contaminants

- Take extra precautions because a household member has a compromised immune system

- Improve the taste of drinking water

Household water treatment systems are composed of two categories: point-of-use and point-of-entry (NSF). Point-of-entry systems are typically installed after the water meter and treat most of the water entering a residence. Point-of-use systems are systems that treat water in batches and deliver water to a tap, such as a kitchen or bathroom sink or an auxiliary faucet mounted next to a tap.

The most common types of household water treatment systems consist of:

- **Filtration Systems**

  A water filter is a device which removes impurities from water by means of a physical barrier, chemical and/or biological process.

- **Water Softeners**

  A water softener is a device that reduces the hardness of the water. A water softener typically uses sodium or potassium ions to replace calcium and magnesium ions, the ions that create "hardness."

- **Distillation Systems**

  Distillation is a process in which impure water is boiled and the steam is collected and condensed in a separate container, leaving many of the solid contaminants behind.

6. (b) The quantity of water supplied = per capita rate population

$$= 85 \times 300 \ l/\text{day}$$
$$= 25500 \ l/\text{day}$$

Assuming 80% of water supplied become sewage

Quantity of sewage produce $= 25500 \times 0.8$
$$= 20400 \ l/\text{day}$$

Detention period = 30 hour (given)

Quantity of sewage produced during detention

time $= 20400 \times \dfrac{30}{24} = 25500 \ $ litre

Assuming rate of deposition sludge

$$= 30 \ \text{litre/c/year}$$

And given that period of cleaning = 6 month

Now, volume of sludge deposited

$$= 30 \times 300 \times 0.5 = 4500 \ \text{litre}$$

Total required capacity of tank = capacity for sewage + capacity for sludge

$$= 25500 + 4500$$
$$= 30000 \ \text{litre} = 30 \ \text{cu-m}$$

Assuming 1.5 m as the depth of the tank, we have

The surface area of the tank $= \dfrac{30 \ \text{m}^3}{1.5 \ \text{m}} = 20 \ \text{m}^2$

Assuming length to width ratio 3:1

$$3 \ B^2 = 20$$

$$B = \sqrt{\dfrac{20}{3}} = 2.582 \ \text{m} \approx 2.6 \ \text{m}$$

Provide width = 2.6 m and length = 7.8 m

Area of cross section provided $= 7.8 \times 2.6$
$$= 20.2 \ \text{m}^2$$

Dimension of septic tank will be:

7.8 m × 2.6 m × (1.5 + 0.3) m
$$= 7.8 \ \text{m} \times 2.6 \ \text{m} \times 1.8 \ \text{m}$$

7. (a) $\quad \mu = \dfrac{\text{lat. strain}}{\text{log. strain}} = \dfrac{\dfrac{\delta d}{d}}{\dfrac{\delta l}{l}} = \dfrac{0.02}{40} \times \dfrac{200}{0.318}$

$$= 0.314$$

$$\delta l = \dfrac{PL}{AE} \Rightarrow 0.318 = \dfrac{40000 \times 200}{\dfrac{\pi}{4} 40^2 \times E}$$

$$\Rightarrow \quad E = 20029.64 \ \text{Kg/mm}^2$$

$$G = \dfrac{E}{2(1+\mu)} = \dfrac{20029.64}{2(1+0.314)}$$

$$= 7621.6 \ \text{kg/mm}^2$$

7. (b) $\quad \Sigma F_v = 0$

$$R_A + R_B = \dfrac{1}{2} \times 9 \times 2000$$

$$\Rightarrow R_A + R_B = 9000 \ \text{N} \qquad \qquad ...(1)$$

$$\Sigma M_B = 0$$

$$R_A \times 9 = \dfrac{1}{2} \times \dfrac{2000x}{9} \times x \times \dfrac{2x}{3}$$

$$\Rightarrow \quad R_A = \dfrac{2000x^3}{27 \times 9}$$

$$\Rightarrow \quad R_A = 6000 \ \text{N}$$

$$\Rightarrow \quad R_B = 3000 \ \text{N}$$

S.F. at x distance from B

$$\Rightarrow \quad R_B - \dfrac{1}{2} \times x \times \dfrac{2000x}{9} = 3000 - \dfrac{1000x^2}{9}$$

S.F. is zero at distance of

$$0 = 3000 - \frac{1000x^2}{9} \Rightarrow \frac{x^2}{9} = \frac{3000}{1000}$$

$\Rightarrow \quad x = \sqrt{27} = 5.196 \text{ m}$

At $\quad x = 0$, S.F.$_B = 3000$ N

At $\quad x = 4.5$ m, S.F. $= 3000 - \dfrac{1000 \times 4.5^2}{9}$

$\qquad = 3000 - 2250 = 750$ N

At $\quad x = 9$ m, S.F. $= -6000$ N

B.M.

$$M = R_B \times x - \frac{1}{2} \times x \times \left(\frac{2000x}{9}\right) \times \frac{1}{3} x$$

$$= 3000x - \frac{1000 \times x^3}{27}$$

B.M. is maximum at distance $\dfrac{dm}{dx} = 0$

$$3000 - \frac{3000 \times x^2}{27} = 0 \Rightarrow x = \sqrt{27} = 5.196 \text{ m}$$

$$\text{B.M}_{max} = 3000 \times 5.196 - \frac{1000 \times 5.196^3}{27}$$

$$= 10392.3 \text{ N}$$

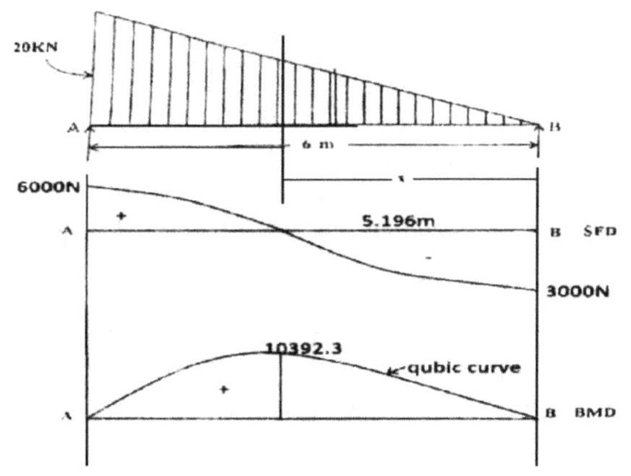

8. (a)

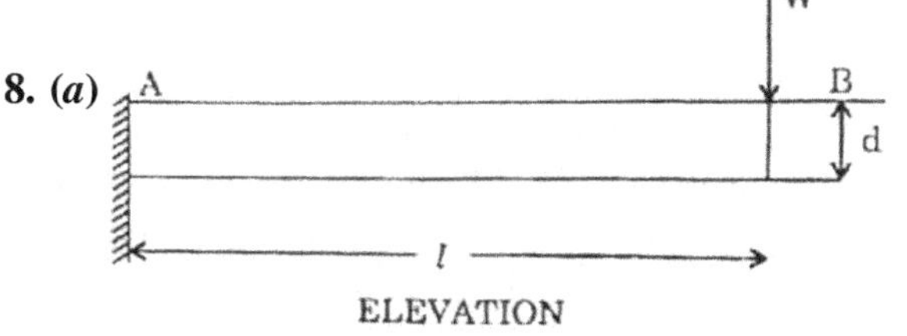

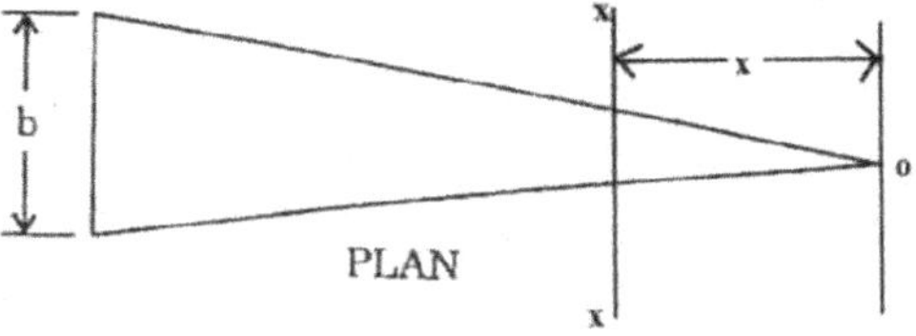

$$M_x = EI_{xx} \frac{d^2 y}{dx^2} = wx$$

$$\Rightarrow \quad E \times \frac{b}{l} \times \frac{d^3}{12} \times \frac{d^2 y}{dx^2} = wx$$

$$\frac{dy}{dx} = \frac{12lw}{Ebd^3} x + c_1$$

$$x = l, \frac{dy}{dx} = 0$$

$$c_1 = 0$$

$$y = \frac{12lw}{Ebd^3}\left[\frac{x^2}{2}\right]_0^l = 6\frac{wl^3}{Ebd^3}$$

8. (b) (i) Workability of Concrete

Workability is one of the physical parameters of concrete which affects the strength and durability as well as the cost of labour and appearance of the finished product. Concrete is said to be workable when it is easily placed and compacted homogeneously *i.e.* without bleeding or Segregation. Unworkable concrete needs more work or effort to be compacted in place, also honeycombs and/or pockets may also be visible in finished concrete.

Definition of Workability

The property of fresh concrete which is indicated by the amount of useful internal work required to fully compact the concrete without bleeding or segregation in the finished product.

Factors affecting workability:

1. Water content in the concrete mix
2. Amount of cement & its Properties
3. Aggregate Grading (Size Distribution)
4. Nature of Aggregate Particles (Shape, Surface Texture, Porosity etc.)
5. Temperature of the concrete mix

6. Humidity of the environment
7. Mode of compaction
8. Method of placement of concrete
9. Method of transmission of concrete

Methods to improve the workability of concrete

1. Increase water/cement ratio
2. Increase size of aggregate
3. Use well-rounded and smooth aggregate instead of irregular shape
4. Increase the mixing time
5. Increase the mixing temperature
6. Use non-porous and saturated aggregate
7. With addition of air-entraining mixtures

(*ii*) A slump test is a method used to determine the consistency of concrete. The consistency, or stiffness, indicates how much water has been used in the mix. The stiffness of the concrete mix should be matched to the requirements for the finished product quality.

Concrete Slump Test

The concrete slump test is used for the measurement of a property of fresh concrete. The test is an empirical test that measures the workability of fresh concrete. More specifically, it measures consistency between batches. The test is popular due to the simplicity of apparatus used and simple procedure.

Principle

The slump test result is a measure of the behaviour of a compacted inverted cone of concrete under the action of gravity. It measures the consistency or the wetness of concrete.

Procedure of Concrete Slump Test:

1. The mold for the slump test is a frustum of a cone, 300 mm (12 in) of height. The base is 200 mm (8 in) in diameter and it has a smaller opening at the top of 100 mm (4 in).
2. The base is placed on a smooth surface and the container is filled with concrete in three layers, whose workability is to be tested.
3. Each layer is temped 25 times with a standard 16 mm (5/8 in) diameter steel rod, rounded at the end.
4. When the mold is completely filled with concrete, the top surface is struck off (leveled with mould top opening) by means of screening and rolling motion of the temping rod.
5. The mould must be firmly held against its base during the entire operation so that it could not move due to the pouring of concrete and this can be done by means of handles or foot - rests brazed to the mould.
6. Immediately after filling is completed and the concrete is leveled, the cone is slowly and carefully lifted vertically, an unsupported concrete will now slump.
7. The decrease in the height of the center of the slumped concrete is called slump.
8. The slump is measured by placing the cone just besides the slump concrete and the temping rod is placed over the cone so that it should also come over the area of slumped concrete.
9. The decrease in height of concrete to that of mould is noted with scale. (Usually measured to the nearest 5 mm (1/4 in).

Types of Slump

The slumped concrete takes various shapes and according to the profile of slumped concrete, the slump is termed as;

1. Collapse Slump
2. Shear Slump
3. True Slump

Applications of Slump Test

1. The slump test is used to ensure uniformity for different batches of similar concrete under field conditions and to ascertain the effects of plasticizers on their introduction.

2. This test is very useful on site as a check on the day-to-day or hour-to-hour variation in the materials being fed into the mixer. An increase in slump may mean, for instance, that the moisture content of aggregate has unexpectedly increases.

3. Other cause would be a change in the grading of the aggregate, such as a deficiency of sand.

4. Too high or too low a slump gives immediate warning and enables the mixer operator to remedy the situation.

5. This application of slump test as well as its simplicity, is responsible for its widespread use.

9. (*a*) Curing is the process in which the concrete is protected from loss of moisture and kept within a reasonable temperature range. This process results in concrete with increased strength and decreased permeability. Curing is also a key player in mitigating cracks, which can severely affect durability.

Reasons to Cure Concrete

There are several important reasons why one should cure concrete:

Concrete strength gain : Concrete strength increase with age as moisture and a favorable temperature is present for hydration of cement. An experimental investigation was conducted by "Cement, Concrete & Aggregates Australia" (CCAA) and the same was published in their data sheet on "Curing of Concrete," which has been included in this article for reference. Figure-1 illustrates a comparison of the strength of concrete at 180 days of moist curing with various periods of moist curing (0, 3, 7, 14 & 28 days) and then allowing it to dry out. From the graph below, it can be observed that concrete allowed to dry out immediately, achieves only 40% of the strength of the same concrete water cured for the full period of 180 days.

- **Improved durability of concrete :** The durability of concrete is affected by a number of factors including its permeability, porosity and absorptivity. Well cured concrete can minimize thermal, plastic & drying shrinkage cracks, making concrete more water tight, thus preventing moisture and water borne chemicals from entering into the concrete and thereby increasing its durability.

- **Enhanced serviceability :** Concrete that is allowed to dry out quickly undergoes considerable early age shrinkage. Inadequate curing contributes to weak and dusty surfaces having a poor abrasion resistance.

- **Improved microstructure :** Material properties are directly related to their microstructure. Curing assists the cement hydration reaction to progress steadily and develops calcium silicate hydrate gel, which binds the aggregates leading to a rock solid mass, makes the concrete denser, decreases the porosity and enhances the physical and mechanical properties of concrete.

$$2(CaO)_3(SiO_2) + 6H_2 \rightarrow$$
$$(CaO)_3(SiO_2)3(H_2O) + 3\,Ca(OH)_2$$
$$\text{C-S-H gel}$$

$$2(CaO)_2(SiO_2) + 4H_2O \rightarrow$$
$$(CaO)_3(SiO_2)_2 3(H_2O) + Ca(OH)_2$$
$$\text{C-S-H gel}$$

Methods commonly adopted in curing:
- Shading concrete work
- Covering concrete surfaces with hessian or gunny bags
- Sprinkling of water
- Ponding method
- Membrane curing
- Steam curing

1. SHADING OF CONCRETE WORK

The object of shading concrete work is to prevent the evaporation of water from the surface even before setting. This is adopted mainly in case of large concrete surfaces such as road slabs. This is essential in dry weather to protect the concrete from heat, direct sun rays and wind. It also protects the surface from rain. In cold weather, shading helps in preserving the heat of hydration of cement, thereby, preventing freezing of concrete under mild frost conditions. Shading may be achieved by using canvas stretched on frames. This method has a limited application only.

2. COVERING CONCRETE SURFACES WITH HESSIAN OR GUNNY BAGS

This is a widely used method of curing, particularly for structural concrete. Thus, exposed surface of concrete is prevented from drying out by covering it with hessian, canvas or empty cement bags. The covering over vertical and sloping surfaces should be secured properly. These are periodically wetted. The interval of wetting will depend upon the rate of evaporation of water. It should be ensured that the surface of concrete is not allowed to dry even for a short time during the curing period. Special arrangements for keeping the surface wet must be made at nights and on holidays.

3. SPRINKLING OF WATER

Sprinkling of water continuously on the concrete surface provides an efficient curing. It is mostly used for curing floor slabs. The concrete should be allowed to set sufficiently before sprinkling is started. The spray can be obtained from a perforated plastic box. On small jobs sprinkling of water may be done by hand. Vertical and sloping surfaces can be kept continuously wet by sprinkling water on top surfaces and allowing it to run down between the forms and the concrete. For this method of curing the water requirement is higher.

4. PONDING METHOD

This is the best method of curing. It is suitable for curing horizontal surfaces such as floors, roof slabs, road and air field pavements. The horizontal top surfaces of beams can also be ponded. After placing the concrete, its exposed surface is first covered with moist hessian or canvas. After 24 hours, these covers are removed and small ponds of clay or sand are built across and along the pavements. The area is thus divided into a number of rectangles. The water is filled between the ponds. The filling of water in these ponds is done twice or thrice a day, depending upon the atmospheric conditions. Though this method is very efficient, the water requirement is very heavy. Ponds easily break and water flows out. After curing it is difficult to clean the clay.

5. MEMBRANE CURING

The method of curing described above come under the category of moist curing. Another method of curing is to cover the wetted concrete surface by a layer of water proof material, which is kept in contact with the concrete surface of seven days. This method of curing is termed as membrane curing. A membrane will prevent the evaporation of water from the concrete. The membrane can be either in solid or liquid form. They are also known as sealing compounds. Bituminised water proof papers, wax emulsions, bitumen emulsions and plastic films are the common types of membrane used.

Whenever bitumen is applied over the surface for curing, it should be done only after 24 hours curing with gunny bags. The surface is allowed to dry out so that loose water is not visible and then the liquid asphalt sprayed throughout. The moisture in the concrete is thus preserved. It is quite enough for curing.

This method of curing does not need constant supervision. It is adopted with advantage at places where water is not available in sufficient quantity for wet curing. This method of curing is not efficient as compared with wet curing because rate of hydration is less.

Moreover the strength of concrete cured by any membrane is less than the concrete which is moist cured. When membrane is damaged the curing is badly affected.

6. STEAM CURING

Steam curing and hot water curing is sometimes adopted. With these methods of curing, the strength development of concrete is very rapid.

These methods can best be used in pre cast concrete work. In steam curing the temperature of steam should be restricted to a maximum of 75°C as in the absence of proper humidity (about 90%) the concrete may dry too soon. In case of hot water curing, temperature may be raised to any limit, say 100°C.

At this temperature, the development of strength is about 70% of 28 days strength after 4 to 5 hours. In both cases, the temperature should be fully controlled to avoid non-uniformity. The concrete should be prevented from rapid drying and cooling which would form cracks.

9. (b) Hot and Cold Weather Concreting

It is generally well recognised that when concrete has to be mixed and placed in either very hot or very cold weather, it is necessary to take precautions to ensure that the concrete is not damaged or adversely affected by the ambient weather conditions. At temperatures below freezing, for example, freshly placed concrete may be damaged by the formation of ice within its pore structure. In very hot weather the concrete may stiffen prematurely, preventing it from being compacted and finished properly, or the temperature of the concrete may rise to the point where thermal cracking occurs as it cools. It is perhaps not so well recognised, however, that even at moderate air temperatures, strong dry winds can cause concrete to dry out prematurely and to crack.

There are a few fixed rules on what constitutes hot or cold weather in respect of concreting operations. NZS 3109 Concrete Construction discusses the range 5°C to 30°C and AS 1379. The Specification and Manufacture of Concrete to be within the range of 5°C to 35°C at the point of delivery. Precautions will always be necessary when ambient air temperatures lie outside this range.

Concreting in Hot Weather

The effects of high temperatures can be summarised as follows:

- Shorter setting times and early stiffening
- Increased rates of hardening
- Possible 28 day strength loss
- Increased tendency for plastic shrinkage
- Difficulties in placing and finishing
- Danger of cold joints - a cold joint is formed when plastic concrete is placed against concrete that has set and commenced hardening.

They may well be necessary, however, at air temperatures within this range, at less than 10°C or more than 30°C, say. At the lower temperatures, the concrete, whilst in no danger of freezing, may take an excessively long time to gain its specified strength. At the higher temperatures, particularly if accompanied by hot dry winds, plastic cracking and premature stiffening of the concrete may take place.

Precautions for hot-weather concreting should be initiated when the ambient temperature is expected to exceed 30 to 35°C. These precautions may consist of one or more of the following practices:

- Dampening forms, reinforcement and subbase
- Erecting wind breaks and sunshades to protect exposed concrete surfaces
- Cooling concrete ingredients
- (During transport of wet concrete) cooling containers, pipelines, chutes, etc
- Completing the transporting, placing and finishing of concrete as rapidly as is practicable

- Informed usage of set-retarding admixtures (to counter premature stiffening of the fresh mix)
- Immediately following the initial finishing operation, spraying a fine film of aliphatic alcohol over the exposed concrete
- Surface - to limit evaporation and help control plastic shrinkage cracking (this should be repeated as necessary during
- Any subsequent operations up to final finishing
- Immediate curing after final finishing is complete
- Moist curing to control concrete temperature
- Restricting placing to night time when ambient temperatures are generally lower.

Concreting in Cold Weather

The prime effects of low temperature on freshly placed concrete are:

- A decrease in the rate at which the concrete sets and gains strength, with a resultant increase in the time taken to finish the concrete;
- (at temperatures below freezing) physical damage to the concrete in the form of surface scaling or bursting and the cessation of hydration.

Precautions which may be taken to protect the concrete in cold weather may consist of one or more of the following practices:

- Providing heaters, insulating materials and enclosures if sub-zero temperatures are expected
- Using high-early-strength cement
- Heating the raw materials (the temperature of the concrete when it is placed in the forms should be above 5°C)
- Not placing concrete on frozen ground
- Ensuring means of maintaining suitable curing temperatures (when using Type GP (general purpose portland) cement

- The temperature of the concrete should be maintained at 20°C or above for 3 days
- Insulating the concrete (a thick insulating blanket is often sufficient protection for pavements)

10. (*a*) Effective span (l) = 5 m

$$A_{st} = 3 \times \frac{\pi}{4} 28^2 = 1847.256 \text{ mm}^2$$

Modular Ration = 13.33

M20 conc. & Fe 250 steel

For,

M20 $\Rightarrow \sigma_{cbc} = 7.0$ N/mm²

Fe250 $\Rightarrow f_{st} = 130$ N/mm²

Position of critical N.A. X_c

$$\frac{m\sigma_{cbc}}{f_{st}} = \frac{x_c}{d - x_c}$$

$$\Rightarrow \frac{13.33 \times 7}{130} = \frac{x_c}{650 - x_c}$$

$$\Rightarrow \quad x_c = 271.626 \text{ mm}$$

Position of actual N.A.-(x)

$$\frac{bx^2}{2} = mA_{st} (d - x)$$

$$400 \times \frac{x^2}{2} = 13.33 \times 1847.256 (650 - x)$$

$$x^2 = 123.12 \times 650 - 123.12x$$

$$x^2 + 123.12x - 123.12 \times 650 = 0$$

$$x = 227.953 \text{ mm}$$

As $x < x_c$

(Hence, section is under reinforce section)

Here, steel reaches to its strength prior to cone.

i.e., $\quad f_{st} = \sigma_{st} = 130$ N/mm².

12.(*a*)**Welding Joints:** A welding joint is a point or edge where two or more pieces of metal or plastic are joined together. They are formed by welding two or more workpieces (metal or plastic) according to a particular geometry. Five types of joints referred to by the American Welding Society: butt, corner, edge, lap and tee.

Advantages of Welding Joints

1. As no hole is required for welding, hence no reduction of area. So, structural members are more effective in taking the load.
2. In welding filler plates, gusseted plates, connecting angles etc, are not used, which leads to reduced overall weight of the structure.
3. Welded joints are more economical as less labour and less material is required.
4. The efficiency of welded joint is more than that of the riveted joint.
5. The welded joints look better than the bulky riveted/butted joints.
6. The speed of fabrication is faster in comparison with the riveted joints.
7. Complete rigid joints can be provided with welding process.
8. The alternation and addition to the existing structure is easy.
9. No noise is produced during the welding process as in the case of riveting.
10. The welding process requires less work space in comparison to riveting.
11. Any space of joint can be made with ease.

Disadvantages of Welding Joints

1. Welded joints are more brittle and therefore their fatigue strength is less than the members joined.
2. Due to uneven heating & cooling of the members during the welding, the members may distort resulting in additional stresses.
3. Skilled labour and electricity are required for welding.
4. No provision for expansion and contraction is kept in welded connection, and therefore, there is possibility of racks.

5. The inspection of welding work is more difficult and costlier than the riveting work.
6. Defects like internal air pocket, slag inclusion and incomplete penetration are difficult to detect.

12.(*b*) Direct force carried by each Rivet

$$f_1 = \frac{60}{9} = 6.67 \text{ kN}$$

Here joint is subjected to torsion due to torsion Moment of P_e which cause Torsional shear force in the Rivet

i.e.
$$f_2 = \frac{T}{J} \times r = \frac{P_e \times .r}{\Sigma A r^2}$$

Here all the rivets are of same dia. Hence torsional shear induced is

$$f_2 = \frac{P_e A r}{A \Sigma r^2} = \frac{P_e r}{\Sigma r^2}$$

Torsional shear force in i^{th} rivet

$$f_{2\,i} = \frac{P_e r_i}{\Sigma r^2}$$

Note: When Rivet are subjected to torsional shear force and direct force then critical rivet is the one which is farthest from the C.G of rivet group and in which Angle between Direct for f_1 & Torsion shear force f_2 in minimum. Here Rivet (1) & (3) are critical rivets. Torsional Shear force in 1st Rivet

$$f_2 = \frac{60 \times 30 \times 14.14}{\Sigma\left[14.14^2 \times 4 + 4 \times 10^2\right]}$$

$$f_2 = \frac{60 \times 30 \times 14.14}{1199.7584}$$

$$f_2 = 21.214 \text{ kN}$$

Resultant force

$$f_r = \sqrt{6.67^2 + 21.214^2 + 2 \times 6.67 \times 21.214 \cos 45°}$$
$$f_r = 26.356 \text{ kN}$$

SSC-Junior Engineer (Civil & Structural) Exam 2008

PAPER-II (Conventional)

SECTION-I (Civil)

1. (*a*) Discuss the operations involved in the manufacture of bricks.

   (*b*) Describe the following tests to be performed in case of burnt clay bricks:

   (*i*) Compressive strength test

   (*ii*) Water absorption test

   (*c*) Write a brief note on the characteristics of good timber.

2. (*a*) A chain line CDE crosses a river, D and E being on the near and distant banks respectively. A perpendicular DF 54.865 m long is set out at D on the left of the chain line. The respective bearings of E and C taken at F are 67° 30′ and 157° 30′. Find the chainage of E, given that CD is 27.630 m and the chainage of D is 382.52 m.

   (*b*) Define and explain contour, contour interval, necessity of contour plotting. Discuss factors affecting the choice of contour interval.

3. (*a*) A sample of dry soil having specific gravity of 2.74 and having a mass of 133.7 gm is uniformly dispersed in water to form 1000 cc of suspension.

   (*i*) Determine the density of suspension immediately after it is prepared.

   (*ii*) A 10 cc of the suspension was removed from the depth of 21 cm beneath the top surface after the suspension was allowed to stand for 2 min 30 sec. The dry mass of the soil in the sample drawn was found to be 0.406 gm. Determine one point on the grain-size distribution curve corresponding to this observation.

Temperature of suspension = 20°C

Viscosity of water at 20°C = 0.0102 poise

   (*b*) 60 cm diameter well is being pumped at a rate of 1360 litres/minute. Measurements in a nearby test well were made at the same time as follows. At a distance of 60 m from the well being pumped, the drawdown was 6 m and at 15 m the drawdown was 1.5 m. The bottom of the well is 90 m below the ground water table.

   (*i*) Find out the coefficient of permeability.

   (*ii*) If all the observed points were on the Dupuit curve, what was the drawdown in the well during pumping?

   (*iii*) What is the specific capacity of the well?

   (*iv*) What is the rate at which water can be drawn from this well?

4. (*a*) A direct shear box test performed on a remoulded sand sample yielded the following observations at the time of failure:

   Normal load = 0.36 kN

   Shear load = 0.18 kN

   The sample area was 36 cm^2.

   Determine:

   (*i*) the angle of internal friction,

   (*ii*) the magnitude and direction of the principal stresses in the zone of failure and

   (*iii*) the magnitude of maximum deviator stress if a sample of the same sand with the same void ratio were tested in a triaxial test with an all-round pressure of 60 kN/m^2. Assume $c = 0$.

(*b*) A 2.2 m square footing is located at a depth of 4.4 m in a stiff clay of saturated unit weight 21 kN/m³. The undrained strength of clay at a depth of 4.4 m is given by parameter w = 120 kN/m² and φ_u = 0. For a factor of safety 3, with respect to shear failure, compute

    (*i*) the net value of bearing capacity and

    (*ii*) the value of maximum load that could be carried by the footing.

5. (*a*) The space between two square flat parallel plates is filled with oil. Each side of the plate is 60 cm. The thickness of the oil film is 12.5 mm. The upper plate, which moves at 2.5 m per sec requires a force of 98.1 N to maintain the speed. Determine:

    (*i*) the dynamic viscosity of the oil, in poise and

    (*ii*) the kinematic viscosity of the oil, in stokes, if the specific gravity of the oil is 0.95.

(*b*) A pelton wheel is to be designed for the following specifications:

    Shaft power = 11,772 kW; Head = 380 m; Speed = 750 r.p.m.; Overall efficiency = 86%,

    Diameter is not to exceed one-sixth of the wheel diameter.

Determine:

    (*i*) the wheel diameter,

    (*ii*) the number of jets required and

    (*iii*) diameter of the jet.

Take coefficient of velocity = 0.985 and speed ratio = 0.45.

6. (*a*) Write short notes on the following:

    (*i*) Sewer

    (*ii*) Sewage

    (*iii*) Sewerage system

    (*iv*) Drain and trench drain

(*b*) Design a 15×10^6 l.p.d. water treatment plant with rapid gravity sand filter. Assume suitable design parameters.

SECTION-II (Structural)

7. (*a*) When a bar of certain material 40 cm square is subjected to an axial pull of 1,60,000 N the extension on a gauge length of 200 mm is 0.1 mm and the decrease in each side of the square is 0.005 mm. Calculate Young's modulus, Poisson's ratio, shear modulus and bulk modulus for this material.

(*b*) Draw S.F. and B.M. diagrams for the beam having overhangs on both sides and loaded as shown in Fig. 1.

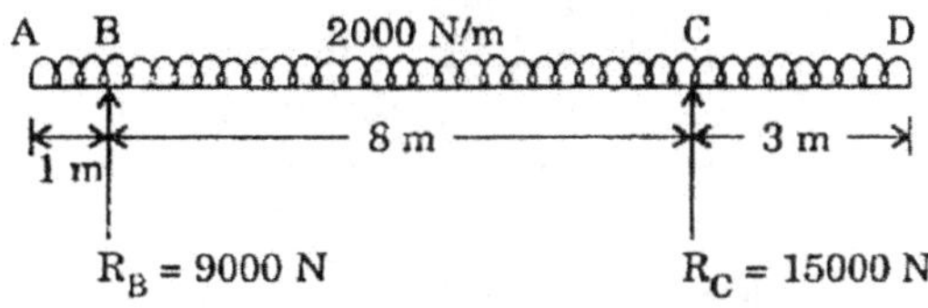

Fig. 1

8. (*a*) Find the deflections at points D and C of the beam loaded as shown in Fig. 2.

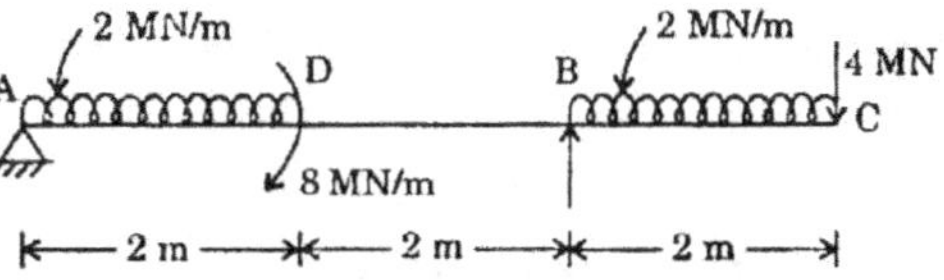

Fig. 2

(*b*) A solid steel column and a hollow steel column, both have the same length and same cross-section area and are fixed at the ends. If the internal diameter of hollow column is 2/3 of its external diameter, find the ratio of buckling strengths of solid steel column to that of hollow steel column.

9. (*a*) Explain the important properties of cement concrete both in plastic and hardened stage.

(*b*) Describe the sequence of concreting operations.

10. (*a*) A particular sand sample of 250 grams, when sieved successively through the following sieves, left retentions on the sieves as follows:

IS sieve	10 mm	480	240	120	60	30	15
Retention grams	NIL	10	15	50	50	75	50

What is its fineness modulus? What sand is it – fine, medium or coarse?

(*b*) Design a simply supported R.C.C. slab for an office floor having clear dimensions of 4 m by 10 m with 230 mm walls all-around. Adopt M-20 grade concrete and Fe-415 grade HYSD bars.

11. Design a cantilever retaining wall to retain an earth embankment 4 m high above ground level. The density of earth is 18 kN/m^3 and its angle of repose is 30°. The embankment is horizontal at top. The safe bearing capacity of the soil may be taken as 200 kN/m^2 and the coefficient of friction between soil and concrete is 0.5. Adopt M-20 grade concrete and Fe-415 HYSD bars.

12. (*a*) Find the suitable pitch for single riveted lap joint for plates 1 cm thick, if
σ_t = 150 N/mm^2, σ_s = 100 N/mm^2 and σ_b = 300 N/mm^2.

(*b*) Calculate the maximum load that the bracket shown in Fig. 3 can carry if the size of the weld on flange is 8 mm and that on the web is 5 mm. The allowable shear stress is 102.5 N/mm^2.

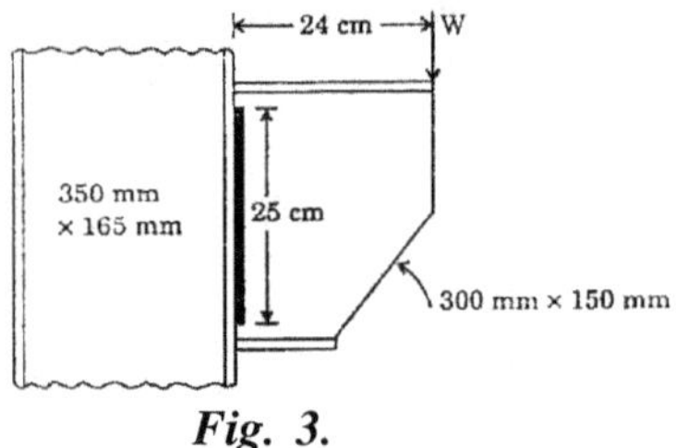

Fig. 3.

ANSWERS

1. (*a*) The manufacture of bricks involves the following operation:

1. Preparation of brick earth
2. Moulding of bricks
3. Drying of moulded bricks
4. Burning of dried bricks.

Selection of site for brick making: The site selected for the manufacture of the bricks should be such that sufficient quantity of suitable brick making earth is available in near vicinity. Also, the site should be such that sufficient quantity of water is available. The site should be such that transportation facilities are available for (*i*) transportation of suitable earth in the nearby area, (*ii*) transportation of fuel required for the burning of bricks and (*iii*) transportation of manufactured bricks. Also, the site should be such that man power, involved in the manufacturing process is available cheaply. The site should be slightly away from the populated area so that people are not affected by the pollution caused due to burning of bricks.

1. Preparation of Brick-Earth: In this step the soil is excavated in steps and then laid on leveled ground. Then the soil is cleaned of impurities such as vegetation matter, stones or pebbles etc. After removing impurities it is exposed to weather for few months. This is called the process of weathering. After completion of weathering process the soil is blended with other material to prepare good brick earth. Then the mixed soil is tempered by being thoroughly broken up, watered and kneaded. The tempering is usually done in pug mill.

Following are well defined operations involved in preparing earth to be used for the manufacture of bricks.

1. Unsoiling   2. Digging

3. Cleaning   4. Weathering

5. Blending   6. Tempering or pugging

2. **Moulding of Bricks:** Bricks are moulded in many ways depending on the quality of the product to be made. Generally the moulding is done in the following two ways

- Hand moulding
- Machine moulding

For hand moulding the tempered clay is forced in the mould in such a way that it fills all the corners of the mould. Extra clay is removed either by wooden strike or frame with wire. Mould is then lifted up and raw brick is left on ground.

Machine moulding is used where large numbers of bricks are to be made. Machines used for moulding is generally of two types:

- Plastic clay machines
- Dry clay machines

In plastic clay machine the clay in plastic state is forced to rectangular openings of a size equal to the length and breadth of the bricks and are then cut into strips of thickness of the brick with wires in frames.

In dry clay machines, dry clay is reduced to powder, filled dry into mould by the machine and then are subjected to high pressure to form hard and well shaped bricks.

3. **Drying of Bricks:** Drying is usually done by placing the bricks in sheds with open sides so as to ensure free circulation of air and protection from bad weather and rains. The bricks are allowed to dry till they are left with 5 to 7 per cent moisture content. The drying period usually varies from 7 to 14 days. The moulded bricks are dried because of the following reasons.

- If damp bricks or green bricks are directly taken to burning then, they are likely to be cracked and distorted.

- To remove maximum moisture from the brick so as to save time and fuel during burning
- To increase the strength of raw bricks so that they can be handled and stacked in greater heights in the kiln for burning without damage.

Methods of drying: Drying of bricks may be done in two ways: (*a*) Natural drying and (*b*) Artificial drying.

4. **Burning of Bricks:** Burning of air dried bricks is a very important and essential operation because it imparts (*i*) strength, (*ii*) hardness, (*iii*) durability, (*iv*) denseness, (*v*) pleasing red colour and (*vi*) imperviousness. Most of the free or un-combined moisture gets evaporated during the process of air-drying, but the water of crystallisation is removed on burning. At a temperature of 650°C, called the temperature of dull red heat, the organic matter contained in the bricks is oxidised and also the water of crystallisation is driven away. If the heating of bricks is stopped at this temperature of 650°C, the bricks, on cooling will absorb moisture from air and get rehydrated. At higher temperature, different constituents of the brick react chemically and the properties of the brick are completely changed. The bricks become hard and strong and absorb very small amount of water. As the temperature further increases, say at 1100°C, particles of alumina and sand, the two major constituents of brick earth, bind themselves together, resulting in increase in strength and density of bricks. Also, a small amount of fusible glass is formed which binds the particles of clay together. Further heating to obtain temperatures higher than 1100°C, is not desirable, because fusible glass will be formed in a large quantity causing distortion of brick due to vitrification of the brick. Beyond a certain limit, vitrification results in the general softening of the clay and the brick begins to loose its shape. Burning of

brick is achieved by following two ways: 1. Clamp burning and 2. Kiln burning

The clamps are temporary structures and are used for manufacture of bricks on a small scale to meet local demand. The kilns are permanent structures used for manufacture of bricks on a large scale.

1. (*b*) (*i*) Testing of Bricks: According to IS: 3495-1976, clay bricks are to be tested for

- Compressive strength
- Water absorption
- Efflorescence
- Warpage

Test for Compressive Strength: The specimen brick is immersed in water for 24 hours. The frog of the brick is filled flush with 1:3 mortar and the brick is stored under damp jute bags for 24 hours followed by immersion in clean water for three days. The specimen is then placed between the plates of the compression testing machine. Load is applied axially at a uniform rate of 14 N/mm^2 (140 kgf/cm^2) and the maximum load at which the specimen fails is noted for determination of compressive strength of brick given by

$$\text{Compressive strength} = \frac{\text{Max. load at failure}}{\text{Loaded Area of brick}}$$

(Average of five results shall be reported)

1. (*b*) (*ii*) Test for Water Absorption: The absorption of bricks is not related directly to the porosity. Some of the absorption may be through the pores, which permit air to escape in absorption tests but others are cue-de-sac or even completely sealed and inaccessible to water under ordinary conditions. For these reasons it is seldom possible to fill more than about 75% of the pores by simple immersion in cold water and boiling method is adopted for measuring complete absorption. In both cold water test and boiling water test, the specimen is dried in a ventilated oven at 110°C to 115°C till it attains a substantially constant mass.

In cold water test the specimen is then immersed in clean water at 27°C for 24 hours. It is weighed again to determine the weight of water absorbed and water absorption percentage is given by

$$\text{Water absorption percentage by weight} = \frac{\text{Weight of water absorbed}}{\text{Weight of dried specimen}} \times 100$$

In the boiling water test after the dried specimen is immersed in a tank such that water can circulate freely on all sides of the specimen. Water is heated to boiling in one hour and boiled continuously for five hours. The water is allowed to cool to 27°C by natural loss of heat for 16 to 19 hours. The specimen is again weighed and the water absorption percentage is given by

$$\text{Water absorption percentage by weight} = \frac{\text{Weight of water absorbed during boiling}}{\text{Weight of dried specimen}} \times 100$$

(Average of five results shall be reported)

1. (*c*) Timber is the wood suitable for building or engineering purposes and it is applied to trees measuring not less than 0.6 m in girth.

Characteristics of Good Timber

Following are the characteristics of good timber:

1. It should have a uniform colour.
2. A freshly cut surface should give a sweet smell.
3. It should have regular annular rings.
4. It should be sonorous when struck.
5. It should have straight and close fibres.
6. It should be heavy in weight.
7. It should be free from shakes, flaws, dead knots or blemishes of any kind.
8. There should be firm adhesion of fibres and compact medullary rays.
9. The cellular tissue of the medullary rays should be hard and compact.
10. When planed, its surface should present a firm bright appearance with a silky lustre.
11. Its fibrous tissues should adhere firmly together and should not clog the teeth of the saw and freshly-cut surface should not show wooliness.

12. A good timber should be durable. It should be capable of resisting the actions of fungi, insects, chemicals, physical agencies and mechanical agencies.

13. A good timber should possess the property of elasticity. The timber is elastic when it regains its original shape and size when the load is removed. This property of timber would be essential when it is to be used for bows, sports goods, carriage shafts etc.

14. It should be fire-resistant. Wood having dense texture offers great resistance to fire. It should not contain resins and other inflammable oils which accelerate the action of fire.

15. A good timber should be hard (*i.e.*, it should offer resistance when it is being penetrated by another body). The chemicals present in heartwood and density of wood impart hardness to the timber.

16. A good timber should be strong for working as structural member such as joint, beam, rafter etc. It should be capable of taking loads slowly or suddenly.

Note. The heavier and dark coloured timber is usually strong.

2. (*a*)

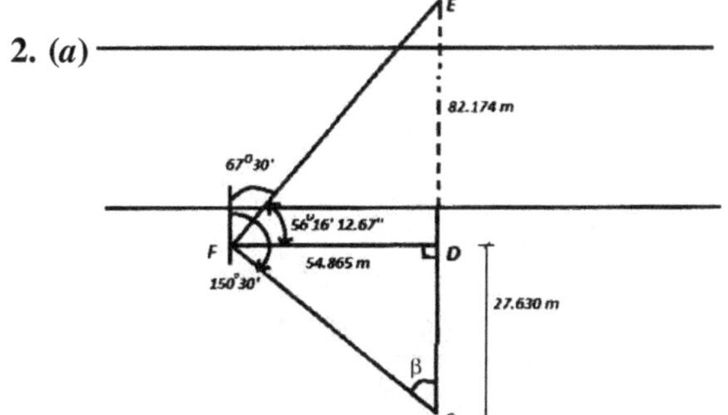

Chainage of 'D' = 382.52 m

Length of 'CD' = 27.630 m

From Δ FDC:

$$\tan \beta = \frac{54.865}{27.630}$$

$$\beta = \tan^{-1}\left(\frac{54.865}{27.630}\right) = 63°16'12.67''$$

$$\angle DFC = 180° - 90° - 63°16'12.67''$$
$$= 26°43'47.33''$$

From Δ FED:

$$\angle EFD = 150°30' - 67°30' - 26°43'47.33''$$
$$= 56°16'12.67''$$

Length of 'ED'

$$\frac{ED}{FD} = \tan 56°16'12.67''$$

$$ED = 54.865 \times \tan 56°16'12.67''$$
$$= 82.174 \text{ m}$$

Chainage of 'E' = Chainage of 'D' + 82.174 m
$$= 382.52 + 82.174 = 464.694 \text{ m}$$

2. (*b*) Contour: An imaginary line on the ground surface joining the points of equal elevation is known as contour.

In other words, contour is a line in which the ground surface is intersected by a level surface obtained by joining points of equal elevation. This line on the map represents a contour and is called contour line.

Contour Map

A map showing contour lines is known as Contour map.

A contour map gives an idea of the altitudes of the surface features as well as their relative positions in plane serves the purpose of both, a plane and a section.

Contouring

The process of tracing contour lines on the surface of the earth is called Contouring.

Purpose of Contouring

Contour survey is carried out at the starting of any engineering project such as a road, a railway, a canal, a dam, a building etc.

(*i*) For preparing contour maps in order to select the most economical or suitable site.

(*ii*) To locate the alignment of a canal so that it should follow a ridge line.

(*iii*) To mark the alignment of roads and railways so that the quantity of earthwork both in cutting and filling should be minimum.

(*iv*) For getting information about the ground whether it is flat, undulating or mountainous.

(*v*) To find the capacity of a reservoir and volume of earthwork especially in a mountainous region.

(*vi*) To trace out the given grade of a particular route.

(*vii*) To locate the physical features of the ground such as a pond depression, hill, steep or small slopes.

Contour Interval

The constant vertical distance between two consecutive contours is called the contour interval.

Horizontal Equivalent

The horizontal distance between any two adjacent contours is called as horizontal equivalent.

The contour interval is constant between the consecutive contours while the horizontal equivalent is variable and depends upon the slope of the ground.

Factors on Which Contour-interval Depends

The contour-interval depends upon the following factors:

(*i*) The nature of the ground in flat and uniformly sloping country, the contour interval is small, but in broken and mountainous region the contour interval should be large otherwise the contours will come too close to each other.

(*ii*) The purpose and extent of the survey. Contour interval is small if the area to be surveyed is small and the maps are required to be used for the design work or for determining the quantities of earth work etc., while wider interval shall have to be kept for large areas and comparatively less important works.

(*iii*) The scale of the map. The contour interval should be in the inverse ratio to the scale of the map i.e. the smaller the scale, the greater is the contour interval.

(*iv*) Time and expense of field and office work. The smaller the interval, the greater is the amount of field-work and plotting work.

Common Values of the Contour-interval

The following are the common values of the contour interval adopted for various purposes:-

(*i*) For large scale maps of flat country, for building sites, for detailed design work and for calculation of quantities of earth work; 0.2 to 0.5 m.

(*ii*) For reservoirs and town planning schemes; 0.5 to 2 m.

(*iii*) For location surveys 2 to 3 m.

(*iv*) For small scale maps of broken country and general topographic work; 3 m, 5 m, 10 m, or 25 m.

3. (*a*)

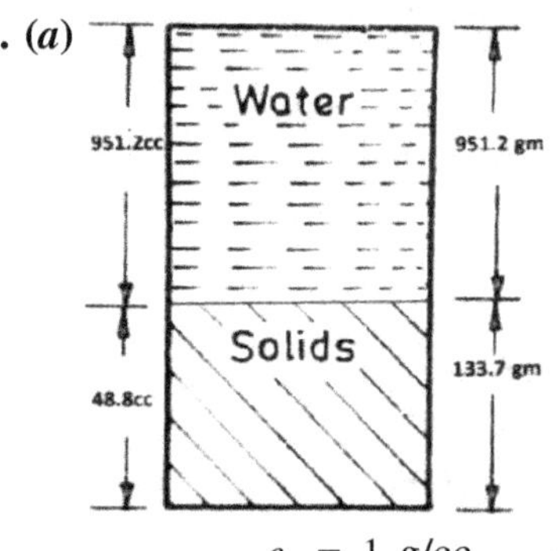

$$e_w = 1 \text{ g/cc}$$

$$V_t = \frac{951.2 + 133.7}{1000}$$

(*i*) $\qquad V_t = 1.0849$ g/cc

(*ii*) Setting velocity acc. to Stroke's law

$$V_s = \frac{(V_s - V_w)D^2}{18\mu} = \frac{g(\rho_s - \rho_w)D^2}{18\mu}$$

$$= \frac{g\,\rho_w(G_s - 1)D^2}{18\mu}$$

$$V_s = \frac{g(G_s - 1)D^2}{18\upsilon} \qquad \left[\because \frac{\mu}{\rho_w} = \upsilon\right]$$

Also, $V_s = \dfrac{He}{t} = \dfrac{10}{120 + 30} = \dfrac{10}{150}$ cm/sec

(As std. ht. of sample collection is 10 cm in Apette)

$$\frac{10}{150} = \frac{9.81 \times 100(2.74 - 1)D^2}{18 \times 0.0102}$$

$$D = 0.00268 \text{ cm} = 0.0268 \text{ mm}$$

$$\% \text{ finer} = \frac{(0.406/10)}{(133.7/1000)} = 0.3036 \text{ or}$$

30.36%

3. (b) According to Thiem's formula for unconfined aquifers.

$$Q = \frac{\pi K\left[h_2^2 - h_1^2\right]}{2.3 \log_{10} \dfrac{r_2}{r_1}}$$

Here, $r_1 = 6$ m $\quad r_2 = 15$ m

$s_1 = 6$ m $\quad s_2 = 1.5$

$d = 90$ m

$Q = 1360$ litres/minute

$\quad = 1.36$ m³/min

$h_1 = 90 - 6 = 84$ m

$h_2 = 90 - 1.5$

$\quad = 88.5$ m

(a) $\quad 1.36 = \dfrac{\pi K\left[88.5^2 - 84^2\right]}{2.3 \log_{10} \dfrac{15}{6}}$

or $\quad \pi K = \dfrac{1.36 \times 2.3 \times 0.398}{172.5 \times 4.5}$

or $\quad \pi K = 1.603 \times 10^{-3}$

and $\quad K = 0.51 \times 10^{-3}$ m/min.

(b) Now $r_w = 0.3$ m, $\quad r_2 = 15$ m

or $\quad h_2 = 88.5$ m, $h_w = ?$

Using $\quad Q = \dfrac{\pi K.\left[h_2^2 - h_w^2\right]}{2.3 \log_{10} \dfrac{r_2}{r_w}}$

We get, $\quad Q = \dfrac{\pi K\left[88.5^2 - h_w^2\right]}{2.3 \log_{10} \dfrac{15}{0.3}}$

But $\quad Q = 1.36$ m³/min

and $\quad \pi K = 1.603 \times 10^{-3}$

$\therefore \quad 1.36 = \dfrac{1.603 \times 10^{-3}\left[88.5^2 - h_w^2\right]}{2.3 \log_{10} 50}$

or $\dfrac{1.36 \times 2.3 \times 1.69}{1.603 \times 10^{-3}} = 88.5^2 - h_w^2$

or $\quad 3290 = 7820 - h_w^2$

or $\quad h_w^2 = 7820 - 3290 = 4530$

or $\quad h_w = 67.4$ m

$\therefore$ Drawdown in the pumped well

$\quad = 90 - 67.4 = 22.6$ m

(c) Specific capacity of the well. It is the discharge for a unit (i.e. 1 m) drawdown in the pumped well.

Let us first find out the value of R

Use Dupuit's equation for unconfined aquifers, i.e. eq. as

$$Q = \frac{\pi K\left[d^2 - h_w^2\right]}{2.3 \log_{10} R/r_w}$$

$\therefore \quad 1.36 = \dfrac{\pi K\left[90^2 - 67.4^2\right]}{2.3 \log_{10} R/0.3}$

or $\quad 1.36 = \dfrac{1.603 \times 10^{-3} \times 157.4 \times 22.6}{2.3 \log_{10} R/0.3}$

$\log_{10} R/0.3 = \dfrac{1.603 \times 157.4 \times 22.6}{2.3 \times 1360}$

Taking antilog, we get $\dfrac{R}{0.3} = 66.7$

R = 20.01; say R = 20 m.

Now, specific capacity = $Q_{\text{unit drawdown}}$

$$= \frac{\pi K\left[90^2 - 89^2\right]}{2.3 \log_{10} 20/0.3}$$

$$= \frac{1.603 \times 10^{-3} \times 179 \times 1}{2.3 \times 1.824}$$

$$= 68.3 \times 10^{-3} \text{ m}^3/\text{min}$$

Hence, the specific capacity

$\quad = 68.3$ liters/minute.

(*d*) Maximum discharge will occur when
$$h_w = 0$$

$$\therefore \quad Q_{max} = \frac{\pi K\left[90^2 - 0^2\right]}{2.3\log_{10} 20/0.3}$$

$$= \frac{1.603 \times 10^{-3} \times 8100}{2.3 \times 1.824}$$

$$= 3.09 \text{ m/min.}$$

Hence, the maximum rate of discharge
$$= 3090 \text{ l/m.}$$

4. (*a*) Direct shear box results

Normal load = 0.36 kN

$\therefore$ Normal stress at failure

$$\sigma = \frac{0.36}{36 \times 10^{-4}} = 100 \text{ kN/m}^2$$

Similarly, $\quad \tau = \dfrac{0.18}{36 \times 10^{-4}} = 50 \text{ kN/m}^2$

(*i*) Using Coulomb's equation
$$\tau = \sigma.\tan\phi$$

$$\tan\phi = \frac{\tau}{\sigma} = \frac{50}{100} = 0.50$$

$$\phi = \tan^{-1} 0.50 = 26.6°$$

But, τ is also equal to $\sigma \tan\beta_m$
$$\beta_m = \phi = 26.6°$$

(*ii*) Also using equation, we have

$$\sigma_1 = \frac{\sigma_{at\ failure}}{1-\sin\beta_m}$$

$$\sigma_1 = \frac{100}{1-\sin 26.6°} = \frac{100}{1-0.448}$$

$$= 181 \text{ kN/m}^2$$

Similarly, $\sigma_3 = \dfrac{\sigma_{at\ failure}}{1+\sin\beta_m} = \dfrac{100}{1+0.448}$

$$= 69 \text{ kN/m}^2$$

The angle made by the failure plane with the major principal plane is given as;

$$\alpha = 45° + \frac{\beta_m}{2} = 45° + 13.3°$$

$$= 58.3°$$

That means the failure plane makes an angle of 58.3° with the major principal plane. Also

the failure plane is horizontal (as is there in a direct shear box test). Hence, the major principal plane makes an angle of 58.3° with the horizontal and the minor principal plane makes 90° with the major principal plane, *i.e.* 90° − 58.3° = 31.7° with the horizontal.

These values and positions etc. can also be worked out graphically by Mohr circle.

(*iii*) In a triaxial testing,
$$\sigma_3 = 60 \text{ kN/m}^2, \ \sigma_d = ?, \ \beta_m = 26.6°$$

To find σ_d we must find σ_1

So, using relation between σ_1 and σ_3, *i.e.* equation we have

$$\frac{\sigma_1}{\sigma_3} = \frac{1+\sin\beta_m}{1-\sin\beta_m} = \frac{1+\sin\phi}{1-\sin\phi}$$

$$\sigma_1 = \frac{\sigma_3(1+\sin 26.6°)}{1-\sin 26.6°}$$

$$= \frac{60 \times (1+0.448)}{1-0.448} \text{ kN/m}^2$$

$$= \frac{60 \times 1.448}{0.552} = 157.4 \text{ kN/m}^2$$

Now, $\quad \sigma_1 = \sigma_d + \sigma_3$
$$\sigma_d = \sigma_1 - \sigma_3 = 157.4 - 60$$
$$= 97.4 \text{ kN/m}^2$$

4. (*b*) $\qquad D_f = 4.4 \text{ m}; \ B = 2.2 \text{ m}$

$$\frac{D_f}{B} = \frac{4.4}{2.2} = 2$$

Since, it is a deep footing, we shall use Skempton's equations

$$q_f = c_u.N_c' + y.D_f \text{ for } \phi_\mu = 0$$

where, $\quad c_u = 120 \text{ kN/m}^2; \ y_{sat} = 21 \text{ kN/m}^2$

Value of N_c' for a square footing with

$$\frac{D_f}{B} = \frac{4.4}{2.2} = 2$$

$$N_c' = 5\left(1+0.2\frac{D_f}{B}\right) \text{ for strip footing}$$

$$N_{c(s)}' = N_c' \times 1.2$$
$$\text{for square and circular footing}$$

$$= 5\left(1 + 0.2\frac{D_f}{B}\right) \times 1.2$$

$$= 6(1 + 0.2 \times 2) = 8.4$$

(To be limited to $1.2 \times 7.5 = 9$)

$$q_f = 120 \times 8.4 + 21 \times 4.4$$

$$= 1100.4 \text{ kN/m}^2$$

Now, net ultimate bearing capacity q_{nf}

= ultimate bearing capacity $q_{nf} - \gamma D$

$$= 1100.4 - 21 \times 4.4 = 1008 \text{ kN/m}^2$$

(*ii*) Now $\quad F = \left(\dfrac{q_f - \gamma D_f}{q - \gamma D_f}\right)$

or $\qquad 3 = \dfrac{1100.4 - 92.4}{q - 92.4}$

or $\quad q - 92.4 = \dfrac{1008}{3} = 336$

$$q = 336 + 92.4 = 428.4 \text{ kN/m}^2$$

Hence, the total load that can taken by the footing of area 2.2 m × 2.2 m

$$= 428.4 \times 2.2 \times 2.2$$

$$= 2073.5 \text{ kN}$$

5. (*b*) Assume $\quad K_v = 0.98$, speed ratio $K_u = 0.46$

$$v = K_v \sqrt{2gH} = 0.98\sqrt{2 \times 9.81 \times 380}$$

$$= 84.62 \text{ m/s}$$

$$u = K_u \sqrt{2gH} = 0.46\sqrt{2 \times 9.81 \times 380}$$

$$= 39.72 \text{ m/s}$$

$$\eta_0 = \frac{P}{w\text{QH}}$$

$\Rightarrow \qquad 0.86 = \dfrac{11772 \times 10^3}{9810 \times Q \times 380}$

$\Rightarrow \qquad Q = 3.672 \text{ m}^3\text{/s}$

$$u = \frac{\pi DN}{60}$$

$\Rightarrow \qquad 39.72 = \dfrac{\pi \times D \times 750}{60}$

$\Rightarrow \qquad D = 1.012 \text{ m}$

Since, $\quad \dfrac{d}{D} = \dfrac{1}{6}$

$\Rightarrow \qquad d = \dfrac{1.012}{6} = 0.169 \text{ m} = 169 \text{ mm}$

Area of jet $a = \dfrac{\pi}{4} \times 0.169^2 \text{ m}^2 = 0.0223 \text{ m}^2$

Total jet area required $= \dfrac{Q}{v} = \dfrac{3.672}{84.62}$

$$= 0.0434 \text{ m}^2$$

$\therefore$ No of jets required $= \dfrac{0.0434}{0.0223}$

$$= 1.95 \approx 2 \text{ Nos.}$$

Thus, two jets are required each having a diameter

$$d = \left(\frac{0.0434}{2\dfrac{\pi}{4}}\right)^{\frac{1}{2}} = 0.166 \text{ m} = 166 \text{ mm}$$

$$\frac{d}{D} = \frac{0.166}{1.012} = \frac{1}{6.096}$$

Which are close to the given value.

6. (*a*) (*i*) A **sanitary sewer** or "foul sewer" is an underground carriage system specifically for transporting sewage from houses and commercial buildings through pipes to treatment or disposal. Sanitary sewers are part of an overall system called sewerage or sewage system.

Separate sanitary sewer systems are designed to transport sewage alone. In municipalities served by sanitary sewers, separate storm drains may be constructed to convey surface runoff directly to surface waters. Sanitary sewers are distinguished from combined sewers, which combine sewage with storm water runoff in the same pipe. Sanitary sewer systems are considered beneficial because they avoid combined sewer overflows.

Types:

Conventional gravity sewers; Force mains; Effluent sewer; Simplified sewer; Vacuum sewer

(*ii*) **Sewage** is a water-carried waste, in solution or suspension, that is intended to be removed from a community. Also known as domestic or municipal wastewater, it is characterized by volume or rate of flow, physical condition, chemical and toxic constituents and its bacteriologic status. It consists mostly of greywater (from sinks, tubs, showers, dishwashers and clothes washers), blackwater (the water used to flush toilets, combined with the human waste that it flushes away); soaps and detergents; and toilet paper (less so in regions where bidets are widely used instead of paper). Whether it also contains surface runoff depends on the design of sewer system.

Types:

- The wastewater from residences and institutions, carrying body wastes (primarily feces and urine), washing water, food preparation wastes, laundry wastes and other waste products of normal living, are classed as domestic or sanitary sewage.

- Liquid-carried wastes from stores and service establishments serving the immediate community, termed commercial wastes, are included in the sanitary or domestic sewage category if their characteristics are similar to household flows. Wastes that result from an industrial processes such as the production or manufacture of goods are classed as industrial wastewater, not as sewage.

- Surface runoff, also known as storm flow or overland flow, is that portion of precipitation that runs rapidly over the ground surface to a defined channel. Precipitation absorbs gases and particulates from the atmosphere, dissolves and leaches materials from vegetation and soil, suspends matter from the land, washes spills and debris from urban streets and highways and carries all these pollutants as wastes in its flow to a collection point.

(iii) Sewerage system: Network of pipes, pumps and force mains for the collection of wastewater, or sewage, from a community.

Modern sewerage systems fall under two categories: domestic and industrial sewers and storm sewers. Sometimes a combined system provides only one network of pipes, mains and outfall sewers for all types of sewage and runoff. The preferred system, however, provides one network of sewers for domestic and industrial waste, which is generally treated before discharge and a separate network for storm runoff, which may be diverted to temporary detention basins or piped directly to a point of disposal in a stream or river.

Municipal sewerage systems (either in new developments or as system replacements) will more than likely be a choice between:

- Septic Tanks
- Gravity Sewers
- Low Pressure Pumping Systems
- Vacuum Sewer Systems

(iv) Drainage is the natural or artificial removal of surface and sub-surface water from an area. Many agricultural soils need drainage to improve production or to manage water supplies.

The civil engineer is responsible for drainage in construction projects. They set out from the plans all the roads, street gutters, drainage, culverts and sewers involved in construction operations. During the construction process he/she will set out all the necessary levels for each of the previously mentioned factors..

Drainage options for the construction industry include:

- Point drainage, which intercepts water at gullies (points). Gullies connect to drainage pipes beneath the ground surface and deep excavation is required to facilitate this system. Support for deep trenches is required in the shape of planking, strutting or shoring.

- Channel drainage, which intercepts water along the entire run of the channel. Channel drainage is typically manufactured from concrete, steel, polymer or composites. The interception rate of channel drainage is greater than point drainage and the excavation required is usually much less deep.

A trench drain (also channel drain, line drain, slot drain, linear drain or strip drain) is a specific type of floor drain containing a dominant trough - or channel-shaped body. It is used for the rapid evacuation of surface water or for the containment of utility lines or chemical spills. Employing a solid cover or grating that is flush with the adjoining surface, this drain is commonly made of concrete in-situ and may utilize polymer- or metal-based liners or a channel former to aid in channel crafting and slope formation. Characterized by its long length and narrow width, the cross-section of the drain is a function of the maximum flow volume anticipated from the surrounding surface. Channels can range from 1 inch (25 mm) to 2 feet in width, with depths that can reach 4 feet (120 cm).

Types

There are four common types of trench drains which are based on forming or installation method. These are cast-in-place, pre-cast concrete, liner systems and former systems. Newer Stainless steel drains are available for residential and commercial shower installs and more commonly called "Channel Drains".

6. (b) Water required per day = 4 ml

Assuming that 45 of filtered water is required for washing of the filter, every day, we have

Total filtered water required per day

$$= 1.04 \times 4 \text{ ml} = 4.16 \text{ ml/day}$$

Now, assuming that 0.5 hour is lost everyday in washing the filter, we have

Filtered water required per hour

$$= \frac{4.16}{23.5} \text{ml/hour} = 0.177 \text{ ml/hr}$$

Now, assuming the rate of filtration to be 5000 litre/hr/sq. m, we have

The area of filter required

$$= \frac{0.177 \times 10^6}{5000} \text{ m}^2 = 35.4 \text{ m}^2$$

Now, assuming the length of the filter bed (L) as 1.5 times the width of the filter bed (B), and two beds, the total area provided

$$2 \times \text{L.B.} = 35.4$$

or $2 \times 1.5\text{B} \times \text{B} = 35.4$

or $$\text{B}^2 = \frac{35.4}{3} = 11.8 \text{ or B} = 3.43 \text{ m}$$

$$\text{L} = 1.5 \text{ B} = 1.5 \times 3.43$$
$$= 5.14 \text{ say } 5.2 \text{ m}$$

or Use the length of the filter bed as = 5.2 m,

and $$\text{B} = \frac{35.4}{2 \times 5.2} = 3.4 \text{ m}$$

Hence, adopt 2 filter units, each of dimensions 5.2 m × 3.4 m.

9. (a) Cement is actually an ingredient of concrete. It is the fine powder that, when mixed with water, sand, and gravel or crushed stone (fine and coarse aggregate), forms the rock-like mass known as concrete.

Concrete properties are greatly influenced by aggregate characteristics given as under:

- Size and grading of aggregate
- Shape and surface texture
- Strength
- Specific gravity and bulk density
- Water absorption and surface moisture
- Bulking of sand
- Soundness and durability including alkali-aggregate reactivity
- Deleterious substances.

The size, shape, surface texture, surface moisture and grading directly influence the water requirement for the desired workability during plastic stage. Other characteristics have influence on the strength and durability during the hardened stage and proportions of concrete. The aggregate should satisfy the requirements laid in IS: 383-1976 in regard to its properties.

Cement Concrete Properties

To obtain quality concrete, its properties in plastic as well as hardened stage play important roles. The properties in plastic stage include:

- Workability
- Segregation
- Bleeding
- Harshness

The properties on the hardened stage include:

- Strength
- Durability
- Impermeability
- Dimensional changes

From research and practical experience it is observed that denser the concrete, greater is its strength. To obtain the optimum density, it is essential to compact concrete fully to drive away all entrapped air. For good compaction of fresh concrete, it should be of such plasticity that all particles can easily move with the available external effort to the remotest corner of the mould.

9. (*b*) Concreting

Process of making concrete.

1. Collection of Ingredient

Collect all the ingredient that is required for making concrete.

Where we should store the ingredient?

No moisture will be contact with the ingredient.

2. Batching of Ingredient

Measuring of ingredient that is required for making concrete.

(*i*) Volume batching

(*ii*) Weight batching

3. Mixing of Ingredient

The aim of mixing of concrete is to produce homogenous, consistent and uniform coloured concrete. Methods are:

(*i*) Hand mixing

(*ii*) Machine mixing

4. Transporting the Concrete

Transfer the concrete from the place where it is mixed to the formwork.

(*i*) Pan

(*ii*) Wheel barrow

(*iii*) Truck mixer

(*iv*) Belt conveyor

(*v*) Pumps

5. Placing of Concrete

Process of fill the formwork with the concrete.

6. Compaction of Concrete

Reducing the air voids that is present in freshly mixed concrete at the time of placing & make the concrete dense.

(*i*) Tamping rod

(*ii*) Vibrator

7. Finishing of Concrete

Process of levelling, smoothing, compacting of freshly and recently placed concrete to provide desired appearance.

Method of finishing of concrete.

(*i*) Screeding

(*ii*) Trowelling

8. Curing of Concrete

The operation of maintaining the temp. of freshly placed concrete for some definite period after placing the concrete for sufficient hydration.

Objective of Curing

(*i*) Improve weather resisting quality

(*ii*) Durability

(*iii*) Impermeability

(*iv*) Reduce shrinkage

Method of Curing

(*i*) Sprinkle of water

(*ii*) Ponding method

(*iii*) Steam method

(*iv*) Covering concrete surface with wet sack.

10.(*a*) Sieve Size	Wt. of Retention	Cumulative wt. of retained sand	Cumulated %age of wt. Retained
10 mm	Nil	–	0
4.80 mm	10 gm	10	3.448
240 μ	15 gm	25	8.621
120 μ	50	75	25.862
60 μ	50	125	43.103
30 μ	75	200	68.966
15 μ	90	290	100
	290 gm		250

Fineness modulus

$$= \frac{\Sigma \text{ cumulative \%age of wt. retained}}{100}$$

$$FM = \frac{250}{100} = 2.50$$

Now if F.M = 2.3 – 2.6 (Fine sand)

F.M = 2.6 – 2.9 (Medium sand)

F.M = 2.9 – 3.2 (Course sand)

Here, as FM is 2.50. Hence, sand is classified as fine sand.

12. (a) 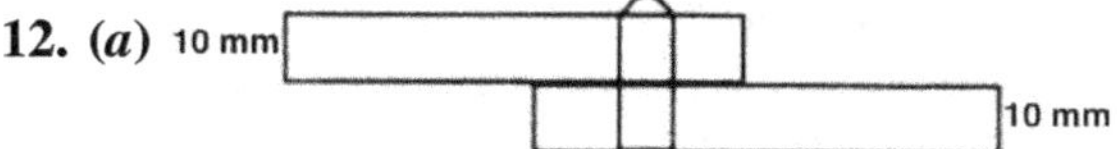

Permissible stress in tearing = 150 MPa

Permissible stress in Rivets in bearing

$$= 300 \text{ MPa or } 300 \text{ N/mm}^2$$

Permissible stress in Rivets in shearing

$$= 100 \text{ MPa or } 100 \text{ N/mm}^2$$

Dia. of Rivet is given by : (Unwin's formula)

i.e. $\quad d = 6.06\sqrt{10} = 19.163 \cong 20$ mm

Nominal dia. of Rivet = 20 mm

Gross dia. of Rivet = 20 + 1.5 = 21.5 mm

Shearing strength of Rivet

$$= h' \times wf \times \frac{\pi}{4} \times d^2$$

$h' = 1.$

($\because$ as single riveted lap it is formed)

$$P_s = L \times 100 \times \frac{\pi}{4} \times 21.5^2$$

$$= 36305.03$$

Bearing strength of Rivet

$$P_B = \sigma_{br} \times d' \times t$$

$$= 300 \times 21.5 \times 10 = 64500 \text{ N}$$

Rivet value = least value of P_S P_B

Rivet value = 36305.03 N

Strength of plates in tearing

$$= 6_{at} \times (p - d') \times t$$

$$= 150 \times (P\text{-}21.5) \times 10$$

For economical design of joint

Strength of plate in tearing

$$= \text{Strength of Rivet or Rivet value}$$

$$150 \times (P\text{-}21.5) \times 10 = 36305.03$$

$$P = 45.703 \text{ mm}$$

Min. pitch between the Rivets

$$= 2.5 \times 20 = 50 \text{ mm} > 45.703 \text{ mm}$$

Adopt P = 50 mm

12. (b)

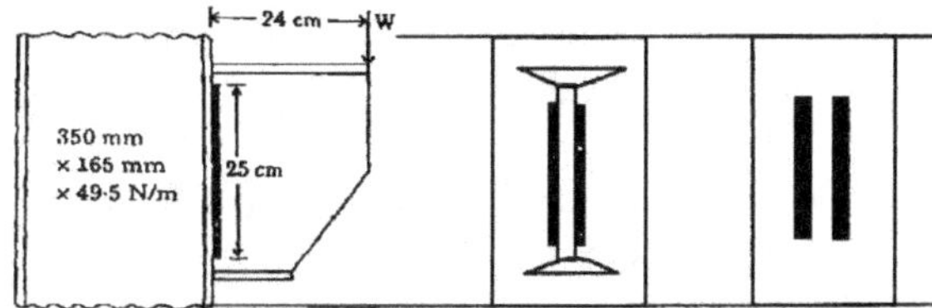

Allowable shear stress = 102.5 N/mm²

Throat thickness = 0.7 × 8 = 5.6 mm

In their case weld is subject to shear and bending.

F_d = Direct shear stress

$$= \frac{w}{2 \times 5.6 \times 250} = 0.000352 \ w$$

F_b = Bending stress

$$= \frac{w \times e}{I_{XX}} \times y = \frac{w \times 240}{I_{XX}} \times \left(\frac{250}{2}\right)$$

$$I_{XX} = 2 \times \left(\frac{5.6 \times 250^3}{12}\right)$$

$$= 14583333.33 \text{ mm}^4$$

$$F_b = \frac{w \times 240}{14583333.33} \times 125 = 0.0021 \ w$$

F_r = Resultant stress = $\sqrt{F_b^2 + F_d^2}$

$$= \sqrt{0.0021 \ w^2 + 0.000357 \ w^2}$$

$$= 2.1301 \times 10^{-3} \ w$$

$$\Rightarrow \quad w \leq 48.119 \text{ kN}$$

SSC-Junior Engineer (Civil & Structural) Exam 2007

PAPER-II (Conventional)

SECTION-I (Civil)

1. Differentiate between the following materials, giving specific uses in the building industry:
   (a) Igneous, sedimentary and metamorphic rocks
   (b) Bitumen, coal tar and asphalt
   (c) Common burnt clay bricks, firebricks and flyash bricks
   (d) Paints and varnish

2. (a) A river is flowing from West to East. For determining the width of the river, two points A and B are selected on the Southern bank such that the distance AB = 75 m. Point A is Westward. The bearings of a tree C on the Northern bank are observed to be 38° and 338°, respectively, from A and B. Calculate the width of the river.

   (b) What are contour gradients? Explain their importance in the location of a hill road.

3. (a) A 12 m thick bed of sand is underlain by a layer of clay 6 m thick. The water table that was originally at ground level is lowered by drainage to a depth 4 m, whereupon the degree of saturation above lowered water table reduces to 20%. Determine the increase in the effective pressure at mid of clay layer due to water table lowering. Given saturated densities of sand and clay as 2.05 g/cm³ and 1.85 g/cm³, and the dry density of sand = 1.76 g/cm³.

   Note: [g/cm³ = 10³ kg/m³ × 9.8 m/s² = 9.81 kN/m²]

   (b) An earth embankment is compacted at water content of 17% to a bulk density of 1.9 g/cc. If the specific gravity of soil grains is 2.65, calculate the void ratio of the compacted embankment.

4. (a) The space between two parallel horizontal plates is kept 5 mm apart. This is filled with crude oil of dynamic viscosity 2.5 kg/m.s. If the lower plate is stationary and the upper plate is pulled with velocity of 1.75 m/s, determine the shear stress on the lower plate.

   (b) An open tank 5 m long, 2 m deep and 3 m wide contains oil of relative density 0.9 to a depth of 0.9 m. If the tank is accelerated along its length on a horizontal track at a constant value of 3 m/s², determine the new position of oil surface.

5. (a) Calculate the diameter and discharge of a circular sewer laid at a slope of 1 in 400, running half-full and with velocity 1.9 m/s. ($n = 0.012$)

   (b) The 5-day BOD of a waste is 280 mg/l. The ultimate BOD is reported to be 410 mg/l. At what rate the waste is being oxidised?

6. (a) What are the various methods of doing theodolite traversing? Describe the deflection angle method in detail.

   (b) What soil investigations are required for constructing (i) an embankment and (ii) a building? Give details.

   (c) Write a note on flow measurement methods employed for pipe flow and open channels (with specific reference to drains).

SECTION-II (Structural)

7. (*a*) Draw SF and BM diagram for the beam with applied moment as shown in Fig. 1.

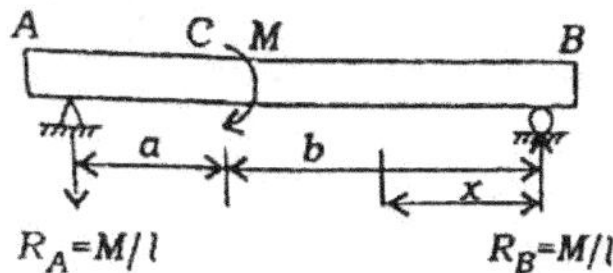

Fig. 1

(*b*) A bar of 40 mm in diameter is subjected to a tensile force of 40000 kg. The extension of bar measured over a gauge length of 200 mm was 0.318 mm. The decrease in diameter was found to be 0.02 mm. Calculate the values of Young's modulus of elasticity and modulus of rigidity of the material.

8. (*a*) Find the slope and deflection at the free end of a cantilever shown in Fig. 2. Moment of inertia of AC is twice the moment of inertia of BC.

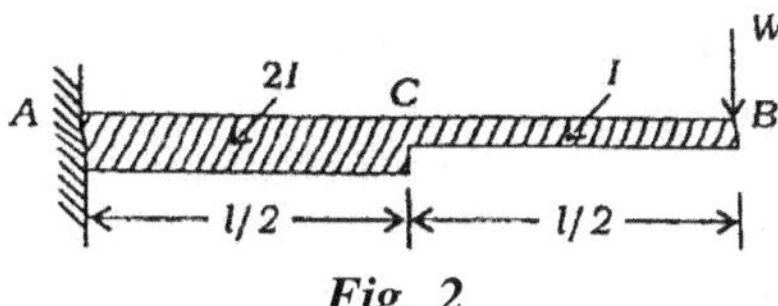

Fig. 2

(*b*) The I-beam shown in Fig. 3 is simply supported at its ends over a 4 m span and carries central load of 50000 N which acts through the centroid, the line of action being as shown in Fig. 3. Calculate the maximum stress.

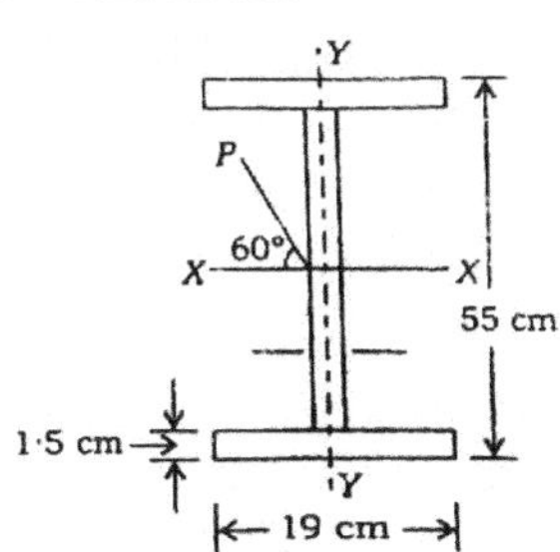

Fig. 3

9. (*a*) Explain briefly the importance of different concretes in construction.

(*b*) List the properties of cement concrete in plastic and hardened stage.

(*c*) Explain briefly the terms batching, mixing, transporting, compacting and curing.

10. (*a*) A reinforced concrete beam 30 cm × 60 cm in section is reinforced with 4 bars 16 ϕ at top and 5 bars 22 ϕ at bottom with an effective cover of 4 cm. Assume safe compressive strength of concrete = 50 kg/cm^2; σ_{sc} = 1400 kg/cm^2; m = 19. Find moment of resistance. (WSM)

(*b*) Design a reinforced concrete beam with balanced section for flexure by working stress method for the data given below: (WSM)

Effective span (simply supported) = 8 m

Live load = 12 kN/m

Breadth of the beam = 300 mm

Concrete grade = M 20

Reinforcement steel grade = Fe 415

11. Design a circular tank of 13.75 m diameter and 3.0 m height of wall. Free board = 0.3 m. The tank rests on a firm ground. The walls are fixed at base and free at top. (LSM)

12. (*a*) The bracket shown in Fig. 4 consists of pair of mild steel plates riveted to the flanges of 305 mm × 152 mm I-column. If the resultant force on the critical rivet is limited to 45 kN, determine the load P, the bracket can support.

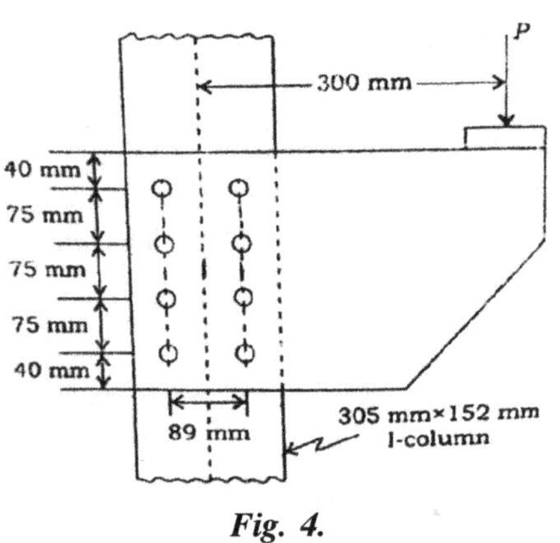

Fig. 4.

(b) Calculate the size of the weld required for the welded bracket loaded as shown in Fig. 5.

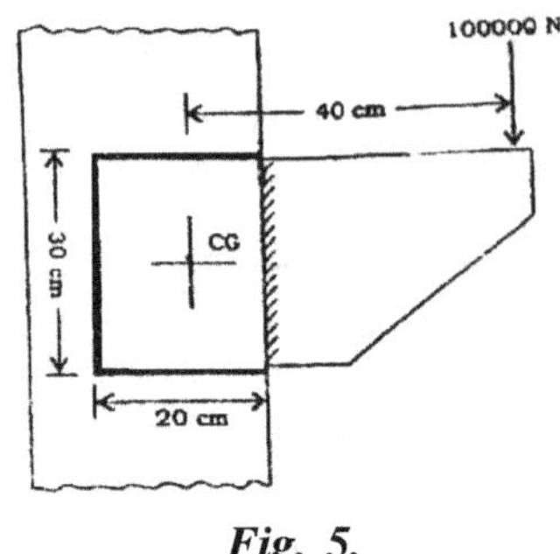

Fig. 5.

ANSWERS

1. (a) What are the 3 basic types of rocks?

Just as any person can be put into one of two main categories of human being, all rocks can be put into one of three fundamentally different types of rocks. They are as follows:

Igneous Rocks

Igneous rocks are crystalline solids which form directly from the cooling of magma. This is an exothermic process and involves a phase change from the liquid to the solid state. The earth is made of igneous rock — at least at the surface where our planet is exposed to the coldness of space. Igneous rocks are given names based upon two things: composition (what they are made of) and texture.

Sedimentary Rocks

In most places on the surface, the igneous rocks which make up the majority of the crust are covered by a thin veneer of loose sediment, and the rock which is made as layers of this debris get compacted and cemented together. Sedimentary rocks are called secondary, because they are often the result of the accumulation of small pieces broken off of pre-existing rocks. There are three main types of sedimentary rocks:

Clastic: Your basic sedimentary rock. Clastic sedimentary rocks are accumulations of clasts: little pieces of broken up rock which have piled up and been "lithified" by compaction and cementation.

Chemical: Many of these form when standing water evaporates, leaving dissolved minerals behind. These are very common in arid lands, where seasonal "play a lakes" occur in closed depressions. Thick deposits of salt and gypsum can form due to repeated flooding and evaporation over long periods of time.

Organic: Any accumulation of sedimentary debris caused by organic processes. Many animals use calcium for shells, bones, and teeth. These bits of calcium can pile up on the seafloor and accumulate into a thick enough layer to form an "organic" sedimentary rock.

Metamorphic Rocks

The metamorphics get their name from "meta" (change) and "morph" (form). Any rock can become a metamorphic rock. All that is required is for the rock to be moved into an environment in which the minerals which make up the rock become unstable and out of equilibrium with the new environmental conditions. In most cases, this involves burial which leads to a rise in temperature and pressure. The metamorphic changes in the minerals always move in a direction designed to restore equilibrium. Common metamorphic rocks include slate, schist, gneiss, and marble.

1. (*b*) Bitumen: Bitumen is an unsung hero of our modern world. A crucial component of the asphalt we use to build roads, bitumen holds our city streets together and connects cities and countries across vast distances. It provides a backbone for personal and business travel, tourism and logistics.

But it's not just roads — bitumen is vital to all kinds of construction and infrastructure projects, large and small. Without bitumen our world would be a very different place; Our cities and our houses would be very different; our lives would be less mobile and less connected. This valuable material has countless uses and applications, and more are being discovered every year, thanks to research and development within the bitumen industry.

Bitumen is not only flexible and multi-functional, it has a number of other benefits, too; It is fast to install and safe to use, as well as being durable and hard-wearing. It is easy to maintain and 100% recyclable, making it the perfect choice for forward-thinking construction and infrastructure projects.

Coal Tar: Coal tar is a by-product derived from coal during the manufacture of domestic town gas. It was commonly used in the UK as a binding agent for aggregate in the construction of highways, car parks and paving until the 1980's when North Sea gas was introduced and town gas works closed. Bitumen was then adopted as the binding agent for macadam and top dressings.

Coal tar can have a high concentration of carcinogenic material such as benzo(a)pyrene and many other polynuclear aromatic hydrocarbines (PAH's). This means it is potentially hazardous to human health (a potential cause of cancer) particularly when mixed with other materials such as asphalt waste.

Asphalt: Asphalt is a mixture of aggregates, binder and filler, used for constructing and maintaining all kind of roads, parking areas but also play and sport areas. Aggregates used for asphalt mixtures could be crushed rock, sand, gravel or slags. In order to bind the aggregates into a cohesive mixture a binder is used. Most commonly, bitumen is used as a binder. An average asphalt pavement consists of the road structure above the formation level which includes unbound and bituminous-bound materials. This gives the pavement the ability to distribute the loads of the traffic before it arrives at the formation level.

Although asphalt is mainly used for paving roads, it can also be used for various other purposes. The versatility of asphalt makes it such a widely used material. Among others, it can be found in the following sectors:

- Transportation (e.g. roads, railway beds or airport runways, taxiways, etc.)
- Recreation (playgrounds, bicycle paths, running tracks, tennis courts...)
- Agriculture (barn floors, greenhouse floors...)
- Industrial (ports, landfill caps, work sites...)
- Building construction (floorings...)

1. (*c*) Various Types of Bricks

There are various types of bricks used in masonry.

1. Common Burnt Clay Bricks
2. Sand Lime Bricks (Calcium Silicate Bricks)
3. Concrete Bricks
4. Fly ash Clay Bricks
5. Fire Clay Bricks

Common Burnt Clay Bricks

Clay bricks are fired bricks. These are formed by pressing in moulds or by an extrusion and wire cutting process. Then, these bricks are dried and fired in a kiln.

Fly ash Clay Bricks

Fly ash is used along with clay in these bricks. Fly ash is obtained from boilers of thermal power stations.

Fire Clay Bricks

Fire clay exists at much depth below the surface and is usually mined. Generally, Fire clays contain metallic oxides less than surface clays and have more uniform chemical and physical properties.

1. (*d*) Paints and Varnish

A wide variety of raw materials are used in the manufacture of paints but they can be grouped according to their function.

Medium, vehicle or binder are terms used to refer to the oils or resins or combinations of the two that form the basis of all paints. Linseed oil is an example of a vegetable oil used as a binder. In all cases it must have the ability to change from a low viscosity liquid into a hard plastic film at the same time binding together the fine particles of pigment. The actual properties of the binder may be modified to a large extent by the pigment. Three main properties are required of the solid film:

(*a*) It must have the correct gloss: All binders are glossy but have considerable variations.

(*b*) It must adhere to the substrate (the surface being painted).

(*c*) It needs the correct mechanical properties, this refers to the qualities of the combined film and substrate and include bending, scratching ad impact.

Varnish

Varnish is a solution of resin in either oil, turpentine or alcohol. It dries after applying, leaving a hard, transparent and glossy film of resin over the varnished surface.

Varnish is applied (1) to the painted surface to increase its brilliance and to protect it from the atmospheric action and (2) to the unpainted wooden surface with a view to brighten the ornamental appearance of the grains of wood.

Composition of Varnishes

The ingredients of varnish are:

1. Resins
2. Solvents
3. Driers

The Qualities of Good Varnish

1. It should be dry quickly.
2. On drying it should form a hard, tough and durable film.
3. It should have good weathering properties, resist abrasion and wear well.
4. It should be able to retain its colour and shine.
5. It should be uniform and pleasant looking on drying.

Different kinds of Varnishes

Based on the different solvents used, varnishes are classified under the following categories:

Oil Varnish

These are made by dissolving hard resins like amber or copal in oil. They are slow to dry but are hardest and most durable of all varnishes. There are suited for being used on exposed surfaces requiring polishing or frequent cleaning and for superior works.

Turpentine Varnish

These are made from soft resins like mastic, common resin is dissolved in turpentine oil.

Spirit Varnish

Varnishes in which spirit is used as a solvent is known as spirited varnish or French Polish.

Shellac is dissolved in spirit and the product is applied in a thin layer. This varnish gives a transparent finish, thus, showing the grains of the timber. These, however, do not weather well and as such are used for polishing wood work not exposed to weather.

Water Varnish

They consist of lac dissolved in hot water with borax, ammonia, potash or soda just enough to dissolve the lac. Varnish so made withstands washing. It is used for painting wall paper and for delicate work.

2. (a)

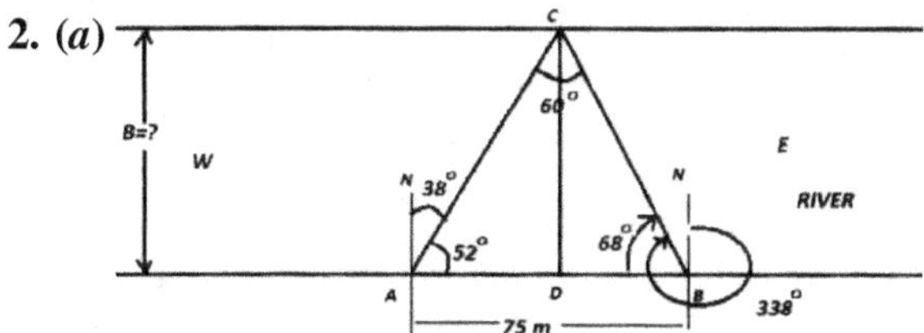

Applying sin rule:

$$\frac{AB}{\sin 60°} = \frac{AC}{\sin 68°} = \frac{BC}{\sin 52°}$$

(Given AB = 75 m)

$$\frac{75}{\sin 60°} = \frac{AC}{\sin 68°} \Rightarrow AC = 80.3 \text{ m}$$

In ΔACD

$$\sin \theta = \frac{CD}{AC}$$

$\Rightarrow$ CD = AC sin θ = AC × sin 52°

$\Rightarrow$ CD = 80.3 × sin 52° = 63.43 m

Hence, width of the river CD = 63.43 m

2. (b) An imaginary line on the surface of the earth having a constant inclination with the horizontal (slope) is called contour gradient. The inclination of a contour gradient is generally given either as rising gradient or falling gradient, and is expressed as ratio of the vertical height to a specified horizontal distance. If the inclination of a contour gradient is 1 in 50, it means that for every 50 m horizontal distance, there is a rise (or fall) of 1 m.

When the inclination of a contour gradient is given its direction from a point may be easily located either on the map or on the ground by the methods discussed below.

Locating Contour Gradient on a Map

With the aid of contour plan, it is easy to trace a contour gradient of desired inclination on a paper, and even transfer it later to the ground.

To locate a rising gradient of 1 in 100 from a point say P situated on 200 m contour on the map having contour interval 5 m at a scale of 1 : 5000, draw an arc of radius

$$= \frac{100 \times 5 \times 100}{5000} = 10 \text{ cm}$$

with radius at P. The arc cuts the 205 m contour at Q. Locate R and S on 210 m and 215 m contours taking arcs of radius of 10 mm with centres at R and S, respectively. Join P, Q, R and S. The line P to S represents the contour gradient on the ground having constant slope of 1 in 100.

To locate a rising gradient of 1 in 100 from the station P, a level is set up at a commanding position and back sight is taken at P. Let, the back sight reading be 1.255 m. The staff reading at any point X on the contour gradient can be calculated from its distance from P. For the distance XP of 20 m, the required staff reading would be

$$1.255 - \frac{20}{100} = 1.055 \text{ m}$$

To locate the point X on the ground, the staff man holds the 20 m-mark of the tape, keeping the zero-mark at P, and moves till the staff reading of 1.055 m is obtained. Likewise, the staff readings for other points at known distance from P, are calculated, and the points are located. If the point Q is on the contour of 105 m, its distance from P would be 500 m in this case. The instruments such as Indian clinometer, theodolite and Ghat tracer may also be used for tracing the contour gradient on the ground.

Contour map provides useful information for locating a route at a given gradient such as highway, canal, sewer line etc.

Let it be required to locate a route from P to Q at an upward gradient of 1 in 100. The contour map of the area is available at a contour interval of 5 meter at a scale of 1:10000. The horizontal equivalent will therefore be equal to 100 meter. Then with centre at P with a radius of 2 cm draw an arc to cut the next higher contour, say at q. With q as centre, mark the next higher contour by an arc of radius 2 cm say at r. Similarly, other points such as s, t, u…. etc are obtained and joining the points provides the location of route.

When the intervisibility between two points can not be ascertained by inspection of the area, it can be determined using contour map.

3. (a) Case-1. When the water-table is a ground level.

The effective pressure at datum A-A (*i.e.* middle of clay layer) w.r. to Fig. is given as:

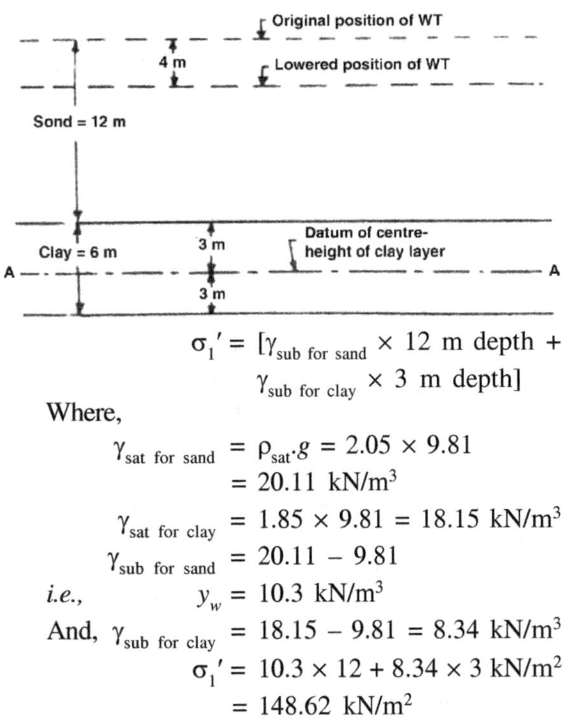

$$\sigma_1' = [\gamma_{sub\ for\ sand} \times 12\ m\ depth + \gamma_{sub\ for\ clay} \times 3\ m\ depth]$$

Where,

$$\gamma_{sat\ for\ sand} = \rho_{sat}\cdot g = 2.05 \times 9.81$$
$$= 20.11\ kN/m^3$$
$$\gamma_{sat\ for\ clay} = 1.85 \times 9.81 = 18.15\ kN/m^3$$
$$\gamma_{sub\ for\ sand} = 20.11 - 9.81$$

i.e., $y_w = 10.3\ kN/m^3$

And, $\gamma_{sub\ for\ clay} = 18.15 - 9.81 = 8.34\ kN/m^3$

$$\sigma_1' = 10.3 \times 12 + 8.34 \times 3\ kN/m^2$$
$$= 148.62\ kN/m^2$$

Case-2. When the water-table gets lowered by 4 m; then the effective stress at A-A would be given as;

$$\sigma_2' = \gamma_{sand} \times 4\ m\ depth + \gamma_{sub\ for\ sand} \times 8\ m\ depth + \gamma_{sub\ for\ clay} \times 3\ m\ depth \qquad ...(i)$$

Now, γ_{sand} for top 4 m layer is to be determined, where the water content is reduced to such an extent that the degree of saturation reduces to 20% of the original.

$\therefore \qquad S = 0.2$

$$\rho_{dry} = 1.76\ given$$
$$\gamma_{dry} = 1.76 \times 9.81\ kN/m^3$$
$$= 17.27\ kN/m^3$$
$$\gamma_{sat} = 20.11\ kN/m^3$$
$$\gamma = ?$$

γ for sand can be determined by using.

$$\gamma = \gamma_{dry} + S(\gamma_{sat} - \gamma_{dry})$$
$$= 17.27 + 0.2\ (20.11 - 17.27)$$
$$= 17.84\ kN/m^3$$

Substituting this value of γ_{sand} in (i), we get

$$\sigma_2' = 17.84 \times 4 + 10.3 \times 8 + 8.34 \times 3$$
$$= 178.78\ kN/m^3$$

$\therefore$ Increase in effective pressure

$$\sigma_2' - \sigma_1' = 178.78 - 148.62$$
$$= 30.16\ kN/m^2$$

Note: Lowering of water-table increases the effective stress.

3. (b) Given $\qquad w = 17\% = 0.17$
$$\rho = 1.9\ g/cc$$
$$G = 2.65,\ e = ?$$

$$\rho = \left(\frac{(G+Se)}{1+e}\right)\rho_w$$

$$1.9 = \left(\frac{2.65 + 0.17 \times 2.65}{1+e}\right) \times 1$$

$$1 + e = 1.6318$$
$$e = 0.6318$$

So that the void ratio of the compacted embankment is

$$e = 0.63.$$

4. (a)

Given the discharge between plates is zero, it mean fluid is static and only upper is moving.
Velocity of upper plate v = 1.75 m/s

Viscosity = 0.025 Ns/m²

Shear stress on the lower plate

$$\tau = \mu \frac{du}{dy} = \mu \frac{(v-0)}{y}$$

$$= \frac{0.025 \times 1.75}{5 \times 10^{-3}} = 8.75 \text{ N/m}^2$$

5. (a) Using Manning's eqn.

$$v = \frac{1}{n} R^{2/3} S^{1/2}$$

$$R = \frac{D}{4} \text{ for circular}$$

$$1.9 = \frac{1}{0.012} \left(\frac{D}{4}\right)^{2/3} \left(\frac{1}{400}\right)^{1/2}$$

$$\Rightarrow \qquad D = 1.23 \text{ m}$$

We know, $Q = aV$

Where,

For half running full,

$$\frac{d}{D} = 0.5$$

$$0.5 = \frac{1}{2}\left(1 - \cos\frac{\alpha}{2}\right)$$

$$\Rightarrow \qquad \alpha = 180°$$

$$\frac{a}{A} = \left(\frac{\alpha}{360°} - \frac{\sin\alpha}{2\pi}\right)$$

$$\Rightarrow \qquad a = \frac{\pi}{4} D^2 \left(\frac{1}{2} - 0\right) \Rightarrow a = \frac{\pi}{8} D^2$$

Now, $\quad Q = \dfrac{\pi}{8} D^2 \times 1.9 = \dfrac{\pi}{8} \times 1.23^2 \times 1.9$

$$= 1.128 \text{ m}^3/\text{sec}$$

5. (b)

$$BOD_5 = 280 \text{ mg/l}$$
$$BOD_0 = 410 \text{ mg/l}$$
$$K_D = 0.434 \text{ K}$$
$$280 = 410 \left(1 - e^{-k \times 5}\right)$$
$$0.638 = \left(1 - e^{-k \times 5}\right)$$
$$e^{-5k} = 0.3171 \quad \Rightarrow 5k = 0.499$$
$$\Rightarrow \qquad k = 0.0998$$

Now, $\quad K_D = 0.434 \text{ k} = 0.0433132$

6. (a) Traverse Surveying is a popular method of surveying. This article includes definition of traverse surveying along with its classification, errors in traversing, checks, the completed method of traversing and plotting of traverse survey.

Traversing is that type of survey in which a number of connected survey lines form the framework and the directions and lengths of the survey lines are measured with the help of an angle measuring instrument and a tape or chain respectively.

Methods of Traversing

There are several methods of traversing, depending on the instruments used in determining the relative directions of the traverse lines. The following are the principal methods:

1. Chain traversing
2. Chain and compass traversing
3. Transit type traversing (a) By fast needle method (b) By measurement of angles between the lines
4. Plane table traversing

1. **Chain Traversing:** The method in which the whole work is done with chain and tape is called chain traversing. No angle measurement is used and the directions of the lines are fixed entirely by linear measurements. Angles fixed by linear or tie measurements are known as chain angles. The method is unsuitable for accurate work and is generally used if an angle measuring instrument such as a compass, sextant or theodolite is available.

2. Chain and Compass Traversing: In chain and compass traversing, the magnetic bearings of the survey lines are measured by a compass and the lengths of the lines are measured either with a chain or with a tape. The direction of magnetic meridian is established at each traverse station independently. The method is also known as tree or loose needle method.

3. Traversing by Fast Needle Method: The method in which the magnetic bearings of traverse lines are measured by a theodolite fitted with compass is called traversing by fast needle method. The direction of the magnetic meridian is not established at each station but instead, the magnetic bearings of the lines are measured with reference so that direction of the magnetic meridian established at the first station. There are three methods of observing the bearings of lines by fast needle method.

1. Direct method with transiting
2. Direct method without transiting
3. Back bearing method

Traversing by Direct Observation of Angles

In this method, the angles between the lines are directly measured by a theodolite and the magnetic bearing of other lines can be calculated in this method. The angles measured at different stations may be either

1. Included angles or
2. Deflection angles

Traversing by Included Angle

An included angle at a station is either of the two angles formed n\by two survey lines meeting there and these angles should be measured clockwise. The method consists simply in measuring each angle directly from a back sight on the preceding station. The angles may also be measured by repetition. The angles measured from back station may be interior or exterior depending on the direction of progress.

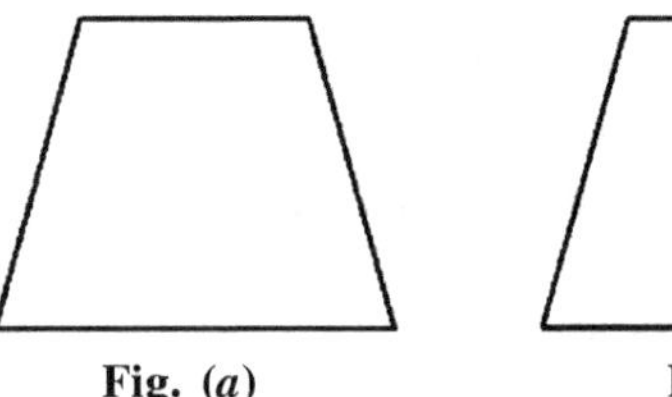

Fig. (a)   Fig. (b)

In the Fig. (*a*) the direction of progress is counter-clockwise and so the angles measured clockwise are interior angle. In the Fig. (*b*) the direction of progress is clockwise and so the angles measured clockwise are exterior angle.

Traverse by Deflection Angles

A deflection angle is the angle which a survey line makes with the prolongation of the preceding line. It is designated as right (R) or left (L) according to as it is measured clockwise or anti-clockwise from the prolongation of the previous line. This type of traversing is more suitable for survey of roads, railways, pipe-lines etc where the survey lines make small deflection angles.

Errors in Traversing

The errors involved in closed traversing are two kinds:

1. linear and
2. angular

The most satisfactory method of checking the linear measurements consists in chaining each survey line a second time, preferably in the reverse direction on different dates and by different parties. The following are checks for the angular work:

1. Traverse by included angles:
- The sum of measured interior angles should be equal to (2N-4), where N = number of sides of the traverse.

- If the exterior angles are measured, their sum should be equal to (2N = 4)p/2

2. Traverse by definition angles: The algebraic sum of the deflection angles should be equal to 360°, taking the right hand and deflection angles as a positive and left hand angles as negative.

3. Traversing by direct observation of bearings: The force bearing of the last line should be equal to its back bearing ±180° measured from the initial station.

6. (b) Soil investigations involve the following steps:

1. Planning the details and sequence of operations
2. Collection of soil samples from the field
3. Conducting all field tests for determining the strength and compressibility characteristics of the soil
4. Study of ground water level conditions and collection of water samples for chemical analysis
5. Geophysical exploration if necessary
6. Testing in the laboratory of all samples of soil, rock, and water
7. Preparation of drawings and charts
8. Analysis of the results of the tests
9. Preparation of report

Methods of Soil Investigations

The normal methods of soil investigations are:

- Inspection
- Test pits
- Probing
- Boring.

Inspection

The first step in this connection is the inspection of the site and its vicinity to get a preliminary idea of the site conditions. This includes the study of the existing buildings in the neighbourhood and if possible the type of their foundations. The cuts made in the nearby areas should also be looked into. The subject can be discussed with those persons who were associated in constructing buildings in the surroundings with regard to their experiences and difficulties encountered by them.

Test Pits

Test pits are dug by hand or by excavating machines. The size of the pit should be such that a person can easily enter the pit and have a visual inspection. Both disturbed and undisturbed soil samples are collected from the pit for detailed analysis.

Probing

This will give a rough idea of the underlying soil. In this, a steel bar of 25 to 40 mm (1 inch to 1.5 inch) in diameter is driven into the ground until a hard stratum is met with. The bar is driven by a hammer. The bar is then drawn out at intervals and the soil sticking to the bar is examined to get an idea of the type of the soil. An experienced workman can assess the nature of the soil by observing the way the rod is penetrated into the soil.

6. (c) Pipeline Flow Measurement Basics

Miner's Inches

- Flow through an orifice with an area of one square inch under a head of six inches
- Uncommon measurement except in AG (Anion Gap)
- Varies state to state
- 1 cfs = 40 miner's inch
- 1 miner's inch = 11¼ gallons per minute.

Example = District measures 5 cfs

Then, 5 cfs * 40 miner's inches/cfs

$$= 200 \text{ miner's inches}$$

Pipeline Flow Measurement Devices

- Open pipe Discharge
- Propeller Flow Meter
- Electromagnetic Meters
- Ultrasonic Pipe Meters
- Venturi Meters
- Collins Flow Gauge.

Pipeline Flow Measurement: Propeller Flow Meter

Flow measurement based on measuring the velocity of water by turning a propeller in the water. A readout of a flow meter gives both instantaneous flow rate (needle gauge) and volume (totalizer).

Pipeline Flow Measurement: Open Pipe Discharge

Flow measurement is based on measuring the trajectory (path) of the water as it discharges from a pipe and into the air.

Pipeline Flow Measurement : Pitot Tube Meters (Collins Flow Gauge)

Flow measurement is based on obtaining a pitot tube measurement of the velocity head ($H = V^2/2g$) in pipeline. The Collins Flow gauge consists of two mains parts: a hollow impact tube (inserted in pipe) and a water-air manometer connected to the two ends of the tube by hoses.

Pipeline Flow Measurement: Venturi Meters

Flow measurement is used to measure the flow of water in pipes under pressure. It utilizes the Venturi principle: flow passing through a constricted section of pipe is accelerated and the head is lowered. With cross sectional areas of pipe know, the flow can be determined.

Pipeline Flow Measurement: Portable Ultrasonic Pipe Meters

Ultrasonic pulses are transmitted through a moving liquid. The pulses that travel in the same direction as the fluid flow (downstream) travel faster than the pulses that travel against the flow (upstream).

Pipeline Flow Measurement: Electro-magnetic Flow Meters

Fluid passes through pipe and a voltage proportional to flow rate is generated. The voltage is measured by electrodes. The reading is converted to give a rate of flow.

Methods of Measuring Flows in Open Channels

As man's need to use and measure water has increased, a number of different and varied methods have been developed to measure the flow of water in open channels. Open channels are those natural and man-made structures through which water flows with a free surface. Examples of such structures include streams, rivers, irrigation ditches, canals, partially full pipes, and water conveyance flumes.

Some of the more common methods currently in use to measure open channel flows are:

- Timed Gravimetric
- Tracer-Dilution
- Area-Velocity
- Manning's Equation / (Gauckler-Manning-Strickler Formula)
- Hydraulic Structures.

Timed Gravimetric : The complete flow stream is collected in a container for a fixed length of time. The contents of the container are then weighed to determine the volume of water. This in turn allow for the direct calculation of the flow rate for the period observed.

Tracer-Dilution : The tracer-dilution method consists of adding a known amount of concentrated tracer at a constant rate to the flow stream. Chemical analysis is used to determine the dilution of the uniformly mixed concentrate at some downstream point. It is important that the tracer be added at a known and constant discharge rate.

Area-Velocity Method : Measurement of the mean flow velocity (commonly by doppler or electromagnetic field) over a determined cross-sectional area (the depth of which is determined by pressure transducer or ultrasonic sensor) yields the stream flow rate.

Manning's Equation (Gauckler-Manning-Strickler Formula) : Manning's Equation, as it is commonly referred to in the United

States, is an empirically derived formula for estimating the average velocity of a liquid flowing in an open channel. The formula utilizes the cross-sectional average velocity, hydraulic radius, roughness coefficient, and the slope of the channel.

Hydraulic Structures : In general, a hydraulic structure is anything that can be used to divert, dam, restrict, or otherwise manage the flow of open channel waters. For flow measurement purposed, a hydraulic structure is a fixed geometry device that is placed into the flow so that all of the flow is directed through or over the device.

7. (a)

- On pt 'A' there is downward reaction of
$$\frac{M}{l}$$

- Acc. to sign convention of SF $\downarrow|\uparrow$, there is downward SF of $\dfrac{M}{l}$

- There is no force on beam b/w 'A' & 'B' & SFD is constant and there is upward reaction at 'B' of $\dfrac{M}{l}$

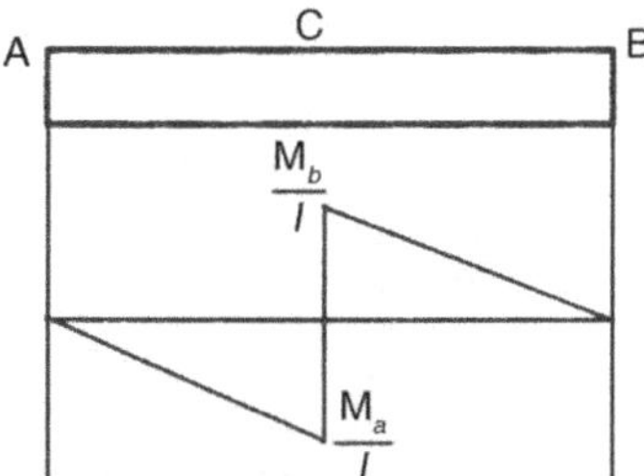

- $BM_{@A} = 0$

- $BM_C = -\dfrac{M}{l} \times a$ (as hogging moment is taken as $-v$)

- As there is a clockwise moment of μ at 'C' hence BM at 'C' changes to
$$-\frac{M_a}{l} + M = \frac{M_b}{l}$$

- $BM_{(B)} = 0$

7. (b)

$$D = 40 \text{ mm} = 0.04 \text{ m}$$
$$P = 40000 \text{ kg} = 40 \text{ kN}$$
$$\Delta l = 0.318, \; l = 200 \text{ mm}$$
$$\Delta d = 0.02$$
$$E = ?$$
$$G = ?$$

$$\sigma = P/A = \frac{40}{\frac{\pi}{4}(0.04)^2} = 31821.8$$

$$\varepsilon = \frac{\Delta l}{l} = \frac{0.318}{200} = 0.00159$$

$$\sigma = \frac{40}{1.26 \times 10^{-3}} = 31746$$

$$\sigma = 3.18 \times 10^4 \text{ kN/m}^2$$

$$E = \frac{\sigma}{\varepsilon} = \frac{3.18 \times 10^4}{0.00159}$$
$$= 2 \times 10^7 \text{ kN/m}^2$$

$$G = \frac{\tau}{\phi} = \frac{\text{shear stress}}{\text{shear strain}}$$

We know that,
$$E = 2G (1 + \mu),$$
$$\mu = \text{lateral strain/longitudinal strain}$$
$$= \left(\frac{\Delta d}{D} \times \frac{l}{\Delta l}\right) = \left[\frac{0.02}{40} \times \frac{200}{0.318}\right]$$
$$= 0.3145$$
$$E = 2G (1 + \mu), \text{ then}$$
$$2 \times 10^7 = 2G(1 + 0.3145)$$
$$G = 0.761 \times 10^7 \text{ kN/m}^3$$

Alternate method:
$$\mu = 0.3145$$

Change in length $\Delta l = \dfrac{pl}{AE}$

$$0.318 = \frac{40000 \times 200}{\frac{\pi}{4}40^2 \times E}$$

$$E = 20019.48 \text{ kg/mm}^2$$
$$= 2.002 \times 10^7 \text{ kN/m}^2$$

8. (*a*)

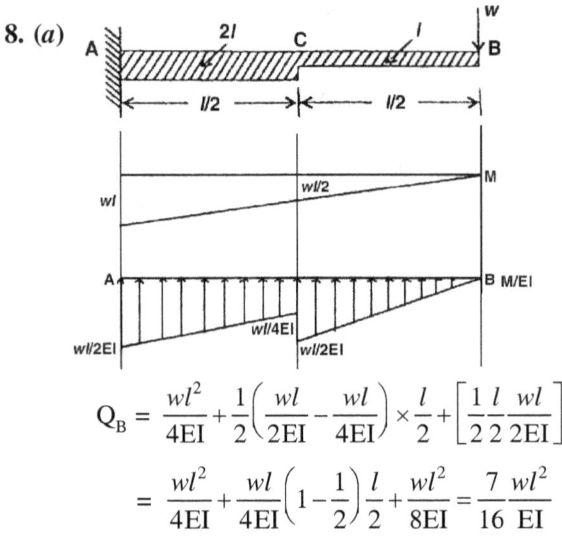

$$Q_B = \frac{wl^2}{4EI} + \frac{1}{2}\left(\frac{wl}{2EI} - \frac{wl}{4EI}\right) \times \frac{l}{2} + \left[\frac{1}{2}\frac{l}{2}\frac{wl}{2EI}\right]$$

$$= \frac{wl^2}{4EI} + \frac{wl}{4EI}\left(1 - \frac{1}{2}\right)\frac{l}{2} + \frac{wl^2}{8EI} = \frac{7}{16}\frac{wl^2}{EI}$$

$$\Delta = \frac{wl^2}{4EI}\left(\frac{l}{2} + \frac{l}{4}\right) + \frac{l}{4}\left[\frac{wl}{2EI} - \frac{wl}{4EI}\right]$$

$$\times\left[\left(\frac{2}{3} \times \frac{2}{2}\right)l + \frac{l}{2}\right] + \left[\frac{wl^2}{8EI} \times \frac{2}{3} \times \frac{l}{2}\right]$$

$$= \frac{wl^2}{4EI} \times \frac{3l}{4} + \frac{wl^2}{16EI} \times \frac{5l}{6} + \frac{wl^3}{24EI}$$

$$= \frac{9}{32}\frac{wl^3}{EI}$$

9.A. Types of concrete with applications for different structural components like beams, columns, slabs, foundations are explained here. Special concrete with uses.

Table: Type of Cement in Relation to Type of Concrete

Portland cement	Type of concrete	Major use
Type I, Normal	Normal standard-type concrete	For general construction purposes
Type IA, air-entraining	Standard with air entraining, more workability, and resistance to freezing and thawing	For general construction purposes
Portland blast-furnace slag IS	Standard-type concrete	For general construction purposes
Portland blast-furnace slag, air-entraining IS-A	Standard-type concrete with more workability and resistance to freezing and thawing	For general construction purposes
Type II, Moderate	Slower setting, lower heat generation, and smaller volume change than Type I and I-A; develops strength in 28 days	For general construction purposes and where exposed to moderate sulfate action
Type IIA, air-entraining	Same as concrete using Type-II moderate cement, but with more workability and resistance to freezing and thawing	For general constructions purposes and where exposed to moderate sulfate action
Type III, High-Early-Strength	Rapid setting, higher heat generation (which helps offset freezing), some volume change, develops strength in 7 days	For construction where rapid development of strength is essential
Type IIIA, air-entraining	Same as concrete using Type III high-early-strength, but with more workability and resistance to freezing and thawing	For construction where rapid development of strength is essential

Type IV, Low Heat of Hydration	Slow setting, low heat generation, small volume change, good strength with age	For massive concrete constructions
Type V, Sulfate-Resisting	High resistance to sulfate attack, fairly low heat generation, high strength with age	Where there is ground water or soil that has sulfates
Portland-pozzolan P and PIP	A hydraulic concrete	For large hydraulic structures
Portland-pozzolan, air-entraining P-A and IP-A	A hydraulic concrete with air entraining	For large hydraulic structures

9. (b) The basic ingredients for manufacturing cement concrete are: cement as binding material, aggregate (fine and coarse) as inert material, and water for chemical reaction (i.e., hydration). Sometimes to modify or improve certain properties of concrete, a small proportion of admixture (also called additive) may also be used.

Cement Concrete Properties

To obtain quality concrete, its properties in plastic as well as hardened stage play important roles. The properties in plastic stage include:

- Workability
- Segregation
- Bleeding
- Harshness.

The properties in the *hardened* stage include:

- Strength
- Durability
- Impermeability
- Dimensional changes.

From research and practical experience, it is observed that denser the concrete, greater is its strength. To obtain the optimum density, it is essential to compact concrete fully to drive away all entrapped air. For good compaction of fresh concrete, it should be of such plasticity that all particles can easily move with the available external effort to the remotest corner of the mould.

9. (c) Concreting Operations

To obtain good quality concrete, not only materials and their proportions are important but the concreting operations also play a very critical role. Concreting operations include storage of materials, proportioning and batching, mixing, transporting, placing, compacting, finishing, jointing and curing. The concreting operations influence the strength and other properties of concrete. By using suitable controls on various concreting operations, the desired strength and other properties can be achieved as per requirements.

Batching

Materials should be measured properly by volume or by mass to satisfy the required mix proportions of the desired concrete grade. For volumetric measurements standard boxes in various sizes of 25 to 50 litres are available. For mass measurements platform weighing or swing weigh batchers may be used. Each batch is prepared as per convenience of handling. While using volumetric batching care should be taken to compensate for bulking of sand. For important and large size jobs weigh batching should be used for better control on quality of concrete.

Mixing

Mixing of various ingredients is essential for obtaining uniformity and homogeneity of the concrete mix. It brings intimate contact of cement and water for chemical reaction and covers aggregate particles with cement mortar for proper bondage of ingredients. Mixing of ingredients can be done by hand or by a mixer.

Hand mixing is carried on a water-tight platform about 2 m × 3.5 m or in a mixing trough of about 1.80 m × 2.70 and 0.30 m deep made of 2-3 mm thick steel or iron sheets. First sand and cement are spread and mixed uniformly. Then coarse aggregate is spread over the uniformly distributed dry mix of sand-cement and mixed thoroughly. This dry mix is then spread with a depression in the middle into which about three quarters of the total quantity of water required is poured and mixed with shovels. The remaining quantity of water is then added and mixed thoroughly, ensuring that no water is lost.

Machine mixing can be done by various types of mixers available in different capacities. The ingredients are fed in the mixer drum which rotates and turns the ingredients with inside blades provided in the drum. The material is discharged after about 20 revolutions. There are mainly two type of mixers: tilting and non-tilting. These mixers have the following capacities of yield of concrete:

Tilting (T) 100, 140 and 200 litres

Non-tilting (NT) 140, 200, 280, 400 and 800 litres.

According to the mix proportions and quantity of concrete, appropriate size of the mixer is chosen. One complete cycle of mixing operation takes about 2½ to 3 minutes. The mixer should be maintained properly by washing the drum, cleaning and oiling the movable parts for its efficient use.

Transporting

The mixed concrete should be transported to the place of deposition without loss of much time (before initial setting time) and without causing segregation and bleeding. The concrete can be transported manually by pans, wheel barrows, chutes, belt conveyors, lorries, truck mixers, buckets, cranes and concrete pumps according to quantity, site conditions and requirements.

Compacting

After the concrete is deposited in its final position, it is compacted for achieving the maximum density. The process of compacting concrete comprises of the elimination of entrapped air resulting in denser concrete. The strength of concrete is highly influenced by the presence of entrapped air.

Compaction can be carried out manually by "tamping" (moving rammer up and down) or by mechanical vibrators of different types. Compaction by vibrators is more effective and can be used for stiffer concrete mixes having low W/C ratios. Mechanical vibration leads to quicker compaction with lesser labour than hand compaction. Depending on the nature, size and quantity of reinforcement in the concrete member, a suitable type of vibrator is used. Internal (immersion or needle) vibrator compacts concrete by direct contact. A form vibrator attached to a formwork transfers vibrations to concrete through the formwork. Surface vibrators such as screed board vibrators, are placed on the top of the concrete and are suitable for thin layers of concrete. Generally, these vibrators have frequencies of 6000 to 9000 vibrations per minute.

Curing

After laying and finishing cement concrete, curing is necessary for promotion of hydration of cement. Curing is defined as maintaining of controlled moisture and temperature conditions for freshly placed concrete for some definite period for proper hardening of concrete. Curing should ensure preservation of internal water content and uniform favourable temperature, protection of structural elements from mechanical disturbances and adequate period of hydration. Generally, uninterrupted moist curing at normal temperatures should be carried out for at least 14 days.

Curing may be carried out by retaining the formwork, shading concrete, covering concrete surfaces with moist hessian or cotton mats, sprinkling water, ponding, chemical membrane, or passing steam according to the type of concrete element and facilities available.

10. (*a*) Given, $\delta = 5$ N/mm^2, $\delta_{st} = 140$ N/mm^2, $m = 19$,

$$A_{st} = 5 \times \frac{\pi}{4} \times 22^2 = 1900.66 \text{ mm}^2$$

$$A_{SC} = 4 \times \frac{\pi}{4} \times 16804.24 \text{ mm}^2$$

$$d_c = 40 \text{ mm}$$

$$K = \frac{m\delta_c}{m\delta_c + \delta_{st}} = \frac{19 \times 5}{19 \times 5 + 140} = 0.404$$

$$j = 1 - \frac{k}{3} = 0.865,$$

$$Q = \frac{1}{2} \times Ckj = \frac{1}{2} \times 5 \times 0.404 \times 0.865$$

$$= 0.873$$

x_c = critical depth of NA

$$= Kd = 0.404 \times 560$$

$$= 226.24 \text{ mm}$$

Actual depth of NA, $\dfrac{Bx_a^2}{2} + (1.5 \text{ m} - 1)$

$$A_{SC}(x_a - d_c) = mA_{st}(d - x_a)$$

$$\Rightarrow 300 \times \frac{x_a^2}{2} + (1.5 \times 19 - 1) \times 804.24(x_a - 40)$$

$$= 19 \times 1900.66 \ (560 - x_a)$$

$$\Rightarrow \qquad x_a = 228.26 \text{ mm}$$

$x_a > x_c$ over reinforced section, so that stress in concrete reached its maximum volume.

$$\text{M.R.} = \frac{1}{2} \times B \times x_a \times c \times \left(d - \frac{x_a}{3}\right)$$

$$+ (1.5 \text{ m} - 1) \ A_{sc} C' \ (d - d_c)$$

Stress at the level of compressive steel.

$$\frac{x_a}{x_a - d_c} = \frac{5}{C'}$$

$$\Rightarrow \qquad C' = \frac{5 \times 228.26 - 40}{228.26} = 4.12 \text{ B/mm}^2$$

$$\mu R = \frac{1}{2} \times 300 \times 5 \times 228.26 \left(560 - \frac{228.26}{3}\right)$$

$$+ (1.5 \times 19 - 1) \times 804.24 \times$$

$$4.12 \times (560 - 40)$$

$$= 141.63 \times 10^6 \text{ N-mm}$$

$$= 141.63 \text{ kN-m}$$

10. (*b*) Given affective span $l = 8$ m

Live load = 12 kN/ m

Width of beam = 300 mm

Let the depth of beam

$$= \frac{\text{span}}{10} = \frac{8000}{10} = 800 \text{ kN/m}$$

Live load = 12 kN/m

Total load $w = 18$ kN/m

$$\text{Maximum B.M.} = \frac{wl^2}{8} = \frac{18 \times 8^2}{8} = 144 \text{ kN-m}$$

Depth of beam $d = \sqrt{\dfrac{M}{Q_b}} = \sqrt{\dfrac{B.M.}{Q_b}}$

$$m = \frac{280}{3\delta \, cbc} \times \frac{280}{3 \times 7} = 13.33$$

$$k = \frac{mc}{mc + t} = 0.288,$$

$$j = 1 - \frac{k}{3} = 0.904, \ Q = 0.911$$

$$d = \sqrt{\frac{144 \times 10^6}{0.911 \times 300}} = 725.87 \text{ mm}$$

$$\approx 726 \text{ mm} < 800 \text{ mm OK}$$

Total depth $d = 730 + 40$ mm = 770 mm

$$A_{st} = \frac{M}{jd\delta_{st}} = \frac{144 \times 10^6}{0.904 \times 730 \times 230}$$

$$= 948.73 \text{ mm}^2$$

Let us provide 16 mm ϕ bars.

No. of bars $= \dfrac{948.73}{\dfrac{\pi}{4} \times 16^2} = 4.71 \approx 5$ Nos.

12.(a)

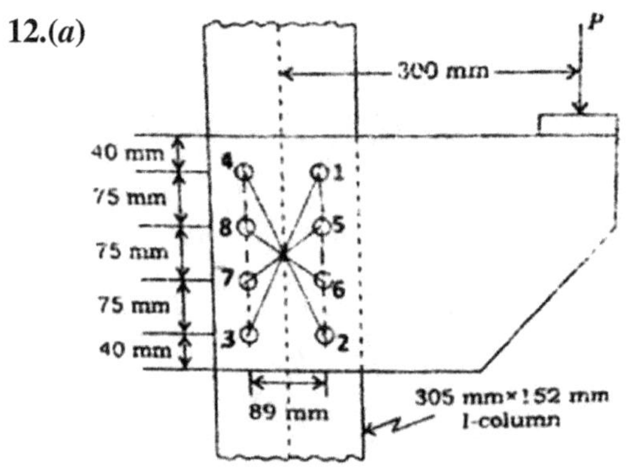

$$F_{Di} = P/8 = 0.125 \text{ P Newton}$$

$$F_{Ti} = \dfrac{Per_i A_i}{\sum\limits_{i=1}^{4} A_i r_i^2}$$

$$e = 300 \text{ mm}$$

$$r_{1,2,3,4} = \sqrt{44.5^2 + 112.5^2} = 120.98 \text{ mm}$$

$$r_{5,6,7,8} = \sqrt{44.5^2 + 37.5^2} = 58.19 \text{ mm}$$

$$F_{Ti} = \dfrac{P \times 300 \times 120.98}{4(120.98)^2 + 4(58.19)^2} = 0.503P \text{ N}$$

$$F_r = \sqrt{0.125P^2 + 0.503P^2 + 2\,0.125P \times 0.503P \cos\theta}$$

$$\tan\theta = \dfrac{112.5}{44.5} \Rightarrow \theta = 68.14$$

Now, $F_r = 0.561P = R_v$ (rivet value)

$$F_r = 0.561P = 45 \text{ kN}$$

$$P = 80.214 \text{ kN}$$

12. (b) Let the size of the weld is S mm, then

$$t = \dfrac{S}{\sqrt{2}} \quad \text{(throat thickness)}$$

$$\overline{X} = \dfrac{2\,X_1 A_1 + X_2 A_2}{A_1 + A_2 + A_3}$$

$$= \dfrac{2(200 \times t \times 100) + (0 \times 300 \times t)}{(300 + 200 + 200)t}$$

$$= 57.14 \text{ mm}$$

$$\overline{Y} = \dfrac{300}{2} = 150 \text{ mm}$$

$$r = \sqrt{150^2 + (100 - 57.14)^2} = 207.14 \text{ mm}$$

$$F_D = \dfrac{100000}{(400 + 300)t} = \dfrac{142.85}{t} \text{N/mm}^2$$

$$F_T = \dfrac{Tr}{J}$$

When, $T = P.e = 100000 \times 400$

$$= 4 \times 10^7 \text{ N-mm}$$

$$J = I_{xx} + I_{yy}$$

Where,

$$I_{xx} = 6750000t \text{ mm}^4$$

$$I_{yy} = 3047619.05t \text{ mm}^4$$

Now, $J = I_{xx} + I_{yy} = 9797619.05t \text{ mm}^4$

$$F_T = \dfrac{4 \times 10^7 \times 207.14}{9797619.05} = \dfrac{845.67}{t} \text{ N/mm}^2$$

$$F_t = \sqrt{\left(\dfrac{142.85}{t}\right)^2 + \left(\dfrac{845.67}{t}\right)^2 + 2 \times \dfrac{142.85}{t} \times \dfrac{845.67}{t} \cos 46.39}$$

$$= \dfrac{949.83}{t} \leq 110 \text{ N/mm}^2$$

(allowable stress in weld)

$$\Rightarrow \quad t \geq 8.63 \Rightarrow \dfrac{S}{\sqrt{2}} \geq 8.63$$

$$\Rightarrow \quad S \geq 12.21 \text{ mm}$$

Here,

$$\tan\theta = \dfrac{150}{142.86}$$

Then, $\theta = 46.39$.

9 789350 128213